Indians and English

WITHDRAWN

Indians and English

Facing Off in Early America

Karen Ordahl Kupperman

CORNELL UNIVERSITY PRESS

ITHACA AND LONDON

First published 2000 by Cornell University Press
First printing, Cornell Paperbacks, 2000

Printed in the United States of America

Library of Congress Cataloging-in-Publication Data

Kupperman, Karen Ordahl
    Indians and English : facing off in early America / Karen Ordahl Kupperman.
        p.   cm.
    Includes bibliographical references and index.
    ISBN 0-8014-3178-6 (cloth) — ISBN 0-8014-8282-8 (paper)
        1. Indians of North America—First contact with Europeans. 2. Indians of North
    America—Public opinion. 3. Indians of North America—History—Colonial period,
    ca. 1600–1775. 4. America—Discovery and exploration—English. 5. America—
    Foreign public opinion, British. 6. United States—History—Colonial period, ca.
    1600–1775. I. Title.

    E59.F53 K86   2000
    973.2—dc21   99-052767

Cornell University Press strives to use environmentally responsible suppliers and
materials to the fullest extent possible in the publishing of its books. Such materials
include vegetable-based, low-VOC inks and acid-free papers that are recycled, totally
chlorine-free, or partly composed of nonwood fibers. Books that bear the logo of the
FSC (Forest Stewardship Council) use paper taken from forests that have been in-
spected and certified as meeting the highest standards for environmental and social
responsibility. For further information, visit our website at www.cornellpress
.cornell.edu.

Cloth printing   10 9 8 7 6 5 4 3 2 1
Paperback printing   10 9 8 7 6 5 4 3 2 1

FSC FSC Trademark © 1996 Forest Stewardship Council A.C.
     SW-COC-098

Contents

List of Illustrations   vii
Preface   ix

Introduction   1

1 Mirror Images   16

2 Reading Indian Bodies   41

3 Indian Polities   77

4 The Names of God   110

5 Village Life   142

6 Incorporating the Other   174

7 Resisting the Other   212

Notes   241
Index   291

Illustrations

New England Indians trade with Bartholomew Gosnold's party,
  1602   8

Ole Worm's Cabinet of Curiosities   21

Pages from the Tradescant collection catalogue   24

Powhatan's mantle   26

Pomeiooc mother and daughter, painted by John White and engraved
  by Theodore de Bry   44

Wingina's wife   57

Ancient British man and Pictish woman   60

Sir Walter Ralegh and his son Wat   65

Roanoke Indian leader   66

Wingina   67

Secoton woman   68

Southern Algonquian man and identifying marks   70

Captain John Smith's Map of Ould Virginia   99

Samuel de Champlain's Map of Port Fortuné, Cape Cod   101

Kiwasa, statue of Algonquian deity   123

Algonquian priest   126

The Flyer, Algonquian shaman   127

Carolina Algonquian mortuary   136

The village of Secoton   145

The village of Pomeiooc   146

Algonquian man and woman eating   163

Cooking in a pot over a fire   165

Canoe manufacture   167

Southern Algonquian fishing scene with weirs   169

Ralph Hamor's embassy to Powhatan   198

Pocahontas   201

Eiakintomino in London   202

Pocahontas being persuaded to board the English ship
  before her capture   209

Engraving of the great attack of 1622 in Virginia   225

Engraving of the English attack on the Pequot fort at Mystic,
  1637   231

Preface

This is a propitious moment to consider the confrontation between American and European peoples at the time when North America was being colonized. Scholarly work in many fields has produced new awareness of how Europeans and Indians thought about their own societies and about human nature, as well as understanding of the structures of authority in those cultures. Scholars of early modern England have led us to see the veil of historical lore through which venturers viewed the world and how modes of self-presentation shaped relationships. Archaeologists, particularly in very recent decades, have made possible a more profound understanding of American life on the eve of colonization, and have given us the basis for new comprehension of the early English documents. And native people's maintenance of their own oral tradition enhances our ability to interpret those documents. The discussions surrounding the 500th anniversary of Columbus's first voyage brought scholars from a wide variety of disciplines together and spurred continuing exchange.

Indians and English: Facing Off in Early America, which began from the same set of preoccupations as my first book, *Settling With the Indians: The Meeting of English and Indian Cultures in America, 1580–1640* (1980), takes up issues and approaches of which I was unaware twenty years ago. We now know a great deal more about the assumptions of both Europeans and Americans, and specialists have shown us how to understand topics ranging from how to read the posture in a portrait to the spectrum of meanings in a label such as "subtle" or "politique." Not only does *Indians and English: Facing Off in Early America* draw on the wealth of new scholarship on encounters, diasporas, and new and transformed early modern societies, it also attempts to understand more fully the Indians' response to the new elements in their lives and the changed circumstances within which they maneuvered. The Americans' own knowledge is embedded in the early English texts, especially those written by English observers who formed close relationships with their neighbors, and over the intervening centuries many Indian people have recorded their oral traditions about the early period.

The key to understanding this early tentative period is, as far as possible, to sweep away our knowledge of the eventual outcome of the train of events set in motion during it. *Indians and English: Facing Off in Early America* seeks to recover the uncertainty and fear in which all sides lived, as well as the genuine curiosity and sense of unimagined possibilities with which groups of people approached each other. This book, like its predecessor, is based on a firm commitment to intensive reading of the early documents, and to recognizing the reality of the human beings who created this history. Too often modern writers "prove" their arguments with telling quotes, and often the best quotes come from writers with little or no direct experience of Indian life. Those who stayed home could be much more definite in their judgments than the confused and self-contradictory writings of those who struggled to make some sense of their manifold observations and experiences. English who actually spent time with Americans and tried to understand what American associates told them about their history, religious beliefs, and cultural practices exhibited a range of responses—within a single brief book writers could be contemptuous and admiring, hostile and friendly, self-confident and terrified—and it is the scope and complexity of these reactions that this book seeks to elucidate. Achieving such comprehension requires seeking to understand English culture of the sixteenth and early seventeenth centuries as well as the cultures of the eastern Algonquians. Both are foreign to us, and we cannot understand the true import of the words the writers used to describe themselves and the Americans without immersing ourselves in recent work in English history.

One goal of *Settling With the Indians* was to demonstrate the broad agreement among eyewitness English writers about the essential humanity and high level of organization among the Indians at the time of colonization. Therefore that book provides massive documentation of English writing on the coastal North American Algonquians at the time when colonization began. Each claim the book makes about English views is documented by reference to every instance of the appearance of that view. Readers who find their curiosity piqued by *Indians and English: Facing Off in Early America* and who therefore seek documentation on that scale will find it amply in the earlier book.

The bulk of this book was written while I held the Times Mirror Foundation chair at the Huntington Library. The wonderfully supportive staff at the Huntington led by Roy Ritchie and the tremendously lively sharing of ideas and knowledge among the Huntington community enriched my writing and the thinking and reading that went into it. Its great strength lies in part in its inclusion of historians, literary scholars, and art historians among its scholars. New York University gave me a period of leave to complete the manuscript.

My argument has been sharpened by the responses I have received when I have presented portions of the work to seminars in many venues. I particularly benefited from the seminar held at the Omohundro Institute of Early American History and Culture in which all the participants in the special issue of the *William and Mary Quarterly* on "Constructing Race" (1997) came together to discuss the issues raised by our work and to critique one another's papers. The article I published in that number, "Presentment of Civility: English Response to American Self-Presentation, 1580–1640," is incorporated into *Indians and English: Facing Off in Early America*.

Many friends and colleagues have helped me in shaping this project. Peter Mancall read the manuscript for the Press and gave me extremely valuable suggestions for improvement. Janet and James Robertson encouraged me in composing the original proposal and offered criticisms of several versions until I got it right. Donald R. Kelley and Bonnie G. Smith have answered numerous queries and discussed a great many topics spanning history from Tacitus to the present, and their insights have always been valuable to me. I have also benefited from discussions with David Harris Sacks, Cynthia Van Zandt, and Walter W. Woodward. As always, my greatest debt is to Joel Kupperman, who reads everything.

KAREN ORDAHL KUPPERMAN

New York, New York

Indians and English

Introduction

Indians and English: Facing Off in Early America looks at the meeting between American Indians and English people in the first decades of contact and colonization, and especially at their attempts to understand and place each other's ways within their own familiar schemes of how human society is supposed to function. It is not about *the* Indians and *the* English, but about individual people caught up in novel situations and trying to operate by timeworn methods. They did not come to these confrontations with set, preconceived categories for describing others; both the native Americans and the English were evolving definitions of themselves as groups in this period, so the processes of defining self and other went forward together and were mutually reinforcing.

The first response on all sides was curiosity; the Americans and the English were drawn to early meetings because they wanted to understand something about the different people they met. Both naturally sought to incorporate these new people into their own systems, but even doing that necessarily involved trying to figure out the nature of the others. Early encounters provoked a complex and varied series of reactions, and these were recorded in a mountain of sources, which tell the careful reader much about the reactions of everyone involved in these confrontations.

All but a handful of eyewitness reports represented a collaboration between native hosts and their English visitors; most of the information they contain was contributed by the Indians as they told inquiring travelers about their history and society. The early sources were written down by English people. Most were exclusively in the English language, although many of these scribes tried to record something of the Indians' languages and some included extensive lists of natives' words and sentences with their meaning.

Partly because those who wrote about their own experiences necessarily became pupils of their Indian collaborators, there was no doubt on the part of any English person who actually went to America that the Indians were fully human. More important, those who had some firsthand understanding of Indian societies and wrote about that experience all found those societies admirably complex and sophisticated. This is not to say that English reporters, or some of them, were "soft" in their thoughts or actions toward Indian societies. Many of these writers were hostile much of the time; all were hostile some of the time. But in their hostility they were communicating very clearly the true quality of the societies they faced. Had those cultures been negligible, or so primitive as not worthy of the name society, the colonists would not have been so scared and their backers would not have been so interested in sustaining the ventures in which they were involved. Colonists, English men and women who actually tried to make a go of establishing themselves in America, could not simply dismiss the American natives as negligible or as cultureless savages—and none did.[1]

Early modern Europeans believed in a close correspondence between environment and human societies. The science of the time taught that the quality of the environment was reflected in the population's level of development. Colonists clearly understood that if they presented the Americans as irredeemably savage—primitive and uninteresting—that would imply a devastating comment on the American environment and its capability of sustaining complex cultures. Investment in American colonies would have been far less attractive in that case. The human-land relationship had other dimensions for Europeans. Human beings, beginning with Adam in the book of Genesis, were charged with taming and developing the environment. If left to their own devices, the land and the species of plants and animals on it would degenerate. When English commentators praised the abundance of America, and the goodness of its plants and animals, they were also implicitly or explicitly crediting the Americans. In transmitting a portrait of Indians as simple yet admirable people, who were intelligent and developed enough to be interested in European civility, they were enhancing the value of their own work. To have done otherwise would have been suicidal. The American natives in these early works were ready to be taught, and ripe for study.

The complexity and sophistication of American cultures, then, made them formidable opponents but also important prospective trading partners. For one thing, as all the early writers made clear, the Indians lived comfortably and well in an environment that baffled the newcomers to the point that the early colonists were utterly dependent on them for their food supply and had to be taught in patient detail by native instructors how to live there. Native oral traditions remembered this early relationship. During King Philip's War, Metacom reminded English leaders that in the early days of settlement his father Massasoit had been "as a great man and the English as a litell Child." Not only did he protect the Pilgrims, but he "gave them Coren and shewed them how to plant."[2] Nor did any of the English try to disguise the facts of their dependence. They wanted their readers at home to understand that life in America was hard for English migrants; investors could not expect them to sail in, get established, and begin sending home valuable products right away. They also wanted their readers to know that, partly because Indian cultures were so highly developed, eventually the colonists would be able to send home those "merchantable commodities" their backers looked for.

The literature created in the first wave of English colonization of America was massive, and ranged from letters home by nearly illiterate servants to the official propaganda of colonizing companies. And this literature, regardless of its source, shares several characteristics: it sought to tell people at home about America and why it was important for England to be involved there; and it tried desperately to make readers in England understand how difficult it was to establish thriving settlements. The American natives were central to both themes. In English colonization, unlike that sponsored by other European powers, the government contributed nothing but official patents and encouragement; every venture had to be backed by a joint-stock company created for the purpose. With the opening of greater trade to the Levant, Muscovy, and the East Indies, investors had many good opportunities, and therefore a strong case had to be made for America.[3] The letters, sermons, pamphlets, and treatises surrounding American colonization all contained the same subtext: "Do not abandon us." They had to make America attractive and interesting, and they had to make believable claims that backers would soon see a return on their investment. This mission was especially important for the early colonies with their record of failure, low productivity, and high death rates. Their descriptions of competent Indian societies provided hope for the future; not only could the land support European settlement, but good commodities for export to repay investors would surely be found or developed soon. Learning about

Indian technology would be a source of such commodities. Even reports that portrayed the Indians as formidable enemies were positive, as they implicitly endorsed the idea that the land was capable of producing highly developed societies. The Indians were potentially both powerful foes and valuable partners, whom the English colonists could neither ignore nor sweep away.

Beyond the practical reasons for their interest in Indian cultures, the English were just plain curious. They were looking at a world that God had kept hidden for thousands of years and had now revealed to Europe. Migrants and their readers at home wanted to know about this other world, and those who wrote answered a great jumble of questions. What were their family arrangements like? Did they have laws? What gods did they worship, and how? How did they define virtue and vice? What did they look like, and how did they manipulate their self-presentation? One of the most pressing questions that received the fullest answers was, surprisingly, how did they wear their hair? The English public had an insatiable thirst for knowledge about these hitherto hidden peoples, and this thirst made for a rich and varied collection of documents.

As colonists and native peoples observed each other, they also thought in novel ways about their own identities. Because of the fundamental changes native societies faced, they were altering the way they thought about themselves, and sometimes glimpses of that rethinking emerge from these accounts. Many were coming to think of themselves in terms of new tribal entities, and even the most basic category had to be created. Narragansett friends told Roger Williams that before the coming of the Europeans Indians had words for the human race as a category and names for particular tribes but did not have "any Names to difference themselves from strangers, for they knew none." Now, they had adopted the term "Indians" for themselves "in opposition to English, &c."[4] English migrants, too, used unexpected categories to describe themselves, as when Anthony Parkhurst, who was in Newfoundland in 1578 at the very beginning of English interest in colonization, said he was from "Kent and Christendome."[5] "Englishman" was not the first classification that came to mind; in fact "English" and "European" are rarely seen in this literature. Local roots and the large, culturally determined notion of Christendom furnished the labels migrants applied to themselves. They, like the American natives, were engaged in finding the appropriate self-definitions. By the middle of the seventeenth century that engagement had progressed to more recognizably modern self-definitions. This book is an examination of how all parties tried to make sense of what was happening and how they attempted to manipulate the elements that contributed to these processes.[6]

The first encounters took place on the individual and human level as individuals began to venture to the edges of their own group and look across at the other. None of these was a truly *first* encounter, as all parties had had previous experience of transatlantic others. Moreover the natives' oral tradition asserted they had had foreknowledge that strange people would come from across the sea. Uttamatomakkin, who accompanied his sister-in-law Pocahontas to London, told his hearers there that the God Okeus had warned the Powhatan priests that the English were coming. Nineteenth-century Narragansett historian Thomas Commuck wrote that his people "had a tradition" that they had heard a tune in the air many years before they first saw Europeans, and had later recognized that melody when they first attended church services in Plymouth; he included it in his book, *Indian Melodies*, and wrote that the tune had been preserved because of its prophetic role. In the twentieth century the Mohegan scholar Gladys Tantaquidgeon recorded the Gay Head Indians' memory that their dying chief had warned about the imminent arrival of a light-skinned people, and a similar oral tradition was told at Mashpee.[7] The oral history record also maintained memories of Americans' first impressions of the newcomers. A Massachusett told William Wood early in the 1630s that his people had thought the first ship was a floating island, and that they were going out to pick strawberries on it when the ship's guns fired on them. As the anthropologist William Simmons points out, indigenous Americans had many traditions of floating islands and were thus incorporating the novel into the familiar.[8]

Yet many early English accounts do retain much of the immediacy and curiosity on both sides that typified a first encounter. Whether the writer was aware of it or not, we can see that the Indians actively shaped both the narratives and the actions they describe through their own ways of knowing. A particularly good example comes from the exploring expedition of Bartholomew Gosnold to New England in 1602, of which there are reports by Gabriel Archer and by Reverend John Brereton, who traveled with the expedition as chaplain. When the expedition arrived in May, touching the American coast in Maine, Archer wrote that the first people they saw sailed toward them in a "Biscay shallop." Because it was a European boat, the English assumed the eight men in it were "Christians distressed," but as the boat drew near they realized the occupants were Indians. These came aboard the English ship; most were wearing skins, but the man Archer called the "Commander" had on European clothes, and several had "some few things made by some Christians."[9] The Indians took up a piece of chalk and proceeded to draw a map of the coast for the newly arrived sailors, speaking "divers Christian words, and seemed to understand much more than we, for want of Language could comprehend." These Indians were Micmacs from the north who had had extensive contact with European fishermen who came to Newfoundland every summer. So much for virgin encounters.

The expedition moved down the coast, naming Cape Cod because they caught so much cod there; Brereton wrote that in five or six hours' fishing the ship was "pestered" with so much fish that they threw some of the catch overboard. A young Indian man came to the captain and showed a willingness to help, but neither Archer nor Brereton said much about this encounter. As they continued their southward journey, Archer wrote, they were approached by several canoes at once with natives indicating their readiness to trade. As before, Archer recorded their self-presentation and attire, particularly the copper and other items of value they wore. He mentioned, without supporting detail, that these natives were more "timerous" than ones seen previously "yet very theevish," possibly reflecting American attempts to enforce their own standards of reciprocity in gift giving. These Indians tracked the expedition, running along the shore as the ship navigated along the coastline, "as men much admiring at us."

A few days later they named Martha's Vineyard (Gosnold's daughter was named Martha, and they found "incredible store of Vines" there) and encountered "fast running thirteene Savages apparelled as aforesaid, and armed with Bowes and Arrowes without any feare." These brought tobacco, deerskins, and cooked fish, and they "offered themselves unto us in great familiaritie." Archer noted that they had even more copper than any of the others. Brereton praised their tobacco and described their pipes; he remarked that the English gave the Indians "certain trifles, as knives, points, and such like, which they much esteemed."

Finally the expedition settled on Cuttyhunk Island, called Elizabeth's Isle by them, which they planned to make their headquarters. Two days after their arrival, Archer reported that an Indian man and two women of "countenance sweet and pleasant"—his wife and daughter, the English thought—came to them. The man, controlling the terms of the encounter, gave the women "heedfull attendance" and would allow no one to touch them. Gosnold explored the island with a small party and seized a canoe left by some Indians who had fled in fear; the English kept it and brought it back to England.

Next day Captain Gosnold sailed across Buzzard's Bay to the mainland opposite. Almost immediately a group of men, women, and children approached "who with all curteous kindness entertayned him, giving him certaine skinnes of wilde beasts, which may be rich Furres, Tobacco,

Turtles, Hempe, artificiall Strings coloured, Chaines, and such like things as at the instant they had with them. These are a faire conditioned people." The men continued work on the fort in which some of them were expected to spend the winter. A few days later a canoe came out to the island with "their Lord or chiefe Commander," who pointed to the sun to indicate that he would come again the next day.

The next day fifty "stout and lustie men" came and "amongst them there seemed to be one of authoritie because the rest made an inclining respect unto him." Most of the English were on the ship, which was anchored some distance off; Archer had only eight men with him, and so he had to improvise. The Indians who approached him were probably Pokanokets, and the chief would have been the father of Massasoit, the man who was an ally of the later Plymouth colony. Although the Pokanokets obviously had procedures for dealing with the English, Archer had to improvise some English ceremony of greeting. He walked forward from his company and "clapt my hands first on the sides of mine head, then on my breast, and after presented my Musket with a threatning countenance, thereby to signifie unto them, either a choice of Peace or Warre." The chief, humoring Archer, also put his hands on his head and breast, and Archer "stept forth and imbraced him," after which everyone began trading. When Gosnold arrived, he put on another ceremony to show that he outranked Archer, which left "the Seignior" unimpressed.

Gosnold gave the chief two knives and a straw hat. The chief wore the hat briefly, but he admired the knives very much. Archer thought this treatment "made them all in love with us."

Two days later "the Seignior" and all his men came back and were invited to midday dinner. They ate bacalao, or dried cod, with mustard and drank beer; "the Mustard nipping them in their noses they could not indure: it was a sport to behold their faces made being bitten therewith." While they were eating someone stole an English shield, and, when the chief was told this, "with feare and great trembling they restored it againe" and the party went on. When the Indians departed, four stayed to help dig sassafras, but they refused entreaties to go on the ship.

A few days later a single Indian came and did stay all night on shipboard; the English decided he was a spy. He "filched our Pot-hookes, thinking he had not done any ill therein," and the English ignored the provocation just as the Indians had ignored their stealing of a canoe. Then, when Gosnold and the main party were again away on the ship, Archer sent out four men to look for food. These were attacked by Indians whose identity is unknown, and one was wounded. It was only

This engraving of New England natives eager for trade greeting Bartholomew Gosnold and his men was published in the multivolume collection of narratives of America, the *Great Voyages*, created by Theodor de Bry and his sons in Frankfurt. The coastal Algonquians offered the English strings of wampum, beads made from shells, but the European artist, who apparently had never seen wampum, misread the description and drew whole shells strung together. The English gave knives in return; one native American has a European hat, so this portrayal may represent the moment when Gosnold made a gift a straw hat. Both Indians and English came to this encounter armed. The John Carter Brown Library at Brown University.

two weeks after the initial encounter at their chosen site, and those who had promised to stay now made "revolt"; supplies were much lower than anticipated, and everyone insisted on being taken home.

An Indian oral tradition recorded in the early nineteenth century in the region of the Taunton River might refer to this or any of a number of other voyages. The tradition describes Europeans who, arriving in a large bird, took some Indians into the bird as hostages. When the Europeans went looking for water at a spring, they were set upon, and some were killed; then, despite the thunder and lightning that "issued from the bird," the hostages escaped back to the land. The event was commemorated by the name White Man's Brook.[10]

Like the native account, the English narratives of Gosnold's voyage contain the emblematic elements of the encounter story. By their own account the English, attempting to do too much with too few men and resources, were constantly seeking to disguise their vulnerability while trying to find out what valuable commodities the Indians had and what it would take to get them to part with them. The least sign of friendliness was taken for admiration, love, or reverence, and hostility and stealing were expected constantly; when an Indian was too friendly, they expected treachery. When the English stole the canoe, they saw no reason to make recompense, nor did they apparently think of it as something to disguise, even though they talked frequently of the thievish nature of the Indians. Even Archer's report, written by a man whose principal consideration was exploration and promotion of colonization, shows English curiosity about the Indians and their arrangements. Acher consistently noted their clothing and ornamentation and commented on their physiques, and he was very attentive to evidence of political and social relationships. At the same time he demonstrated that the Indians took the initiative time and again in these early relationships; they dictated when and where meetings would take place and set up the way they would be conducted. The man he called the "Seignior" clearly came to inspect the encampment within his own territory, and, although the English may not have realized it, set forth the terms on which they would stay. And Archer frequently hinted at tensions within the English camp, another constant element.

Brereton's report offers interesting and instructive contrasts; he gave fuller descriptions of the appearance of the Indians he saw and argued that their "perfect constitution of body" demonstrated "the holsomnesse and temperature of this Climat." As in the case of tobacco pipes, he provided detailed information on their copper work, and inquired about their source of copper. More important, he included more personal vignettes, particularly ones that demonstrated the Indians' own standards of behavior. For example, when describing the large party that came to the island, he wrote that one of the natives, recognizing Brereton as the man who had given him a knife a few days before on the mainland, spoke to his chief, who then "rose up and tooke a large Beaver skin from one that stood about him and gave it unto me, which I requited for that time the best I could." Brereton wrote that when the group left they paused their canoes and "made huge cries & shouts of joy unto us; and we with our trumpet and cornet, and casting up our cappes into the aire, made them the best farewell we could." But while Brereton provided these windows into the personal level of experience, he also minimized the Indians' own agency in the story, and several events that Archer presented as fortuitous Brereton depicted as the result of English planning and manipulation. For example, he wrote that Gosnold had deliberately set up the incident of the stolen shield in order to test the chief's authority over his people. Like Archer, he thought stealing was endemic among them: "some of the meaner sort given to filching, which the very name of Salvages (not weighing their ignorance in good or evill) may easily excuse." But Brereton seemed to understand that the native system involved reciprocity and exchange rather than the "bartering" that Archer saw. On the other hand in Brereton's account the English always satisfied the Indians with "trifles," not fair exchange, even though the value of the knives given was actually great. And, chillingly, in the margin next to Brereton's description of the Indians' joyful farewell, are the words: "Indians apt for service."

Comparing these two accounts, which here stand in for countless others, we can draw important lessons for thinking about the mutual scrutiny and interpretation that went on all up and down the coast in the late sixteenth and early seventeenth centuries. One is that close and comprehensive reading is necessary. Archer and Brereton described the same brief period, and their accounts match in many ways, down to the "sowre face" the Indians made at English mustard. But they also differ in crucial respects, and in using them it is important to think not only about the overall structure and purpose of the document but also about the particular words chosen. What does "Indians apt for service" mean? Why was it placed next to the passage on the Indians' friendly leave-taking, and was it written by Brereton or the printer? Was Archer's or Brereton's report more favorable to Indian culture? Is that a question we should ask? Drawing quotes from either of these accounts, one could "prove" that the English admired the Indians, that they had contempt for the Indians, that the Indians were childlike, that they were savage, that they were noble, that the English treated the Indians well, that they treated the Indians badly, and so on. A close and thorough analysis of a broad range of texts, including the natives' own traditions, is essential to understanding the true quality of the early interpretation. Only through such scrutiny, which brings together all the threads, can a meaningful argument be constructed.

Assiduous and wide reading also offers us the possibility of thinking about the Americans' response to the European element that became more insistent and unavoidable in their lives over the period under study here. Because we often have several English accounts of the same events, and because elements of the Indians' oral tradition figure prominently in those accounts and in later records, we can gain an inkling of the American response and their manipulation of new opportunities. Through comprehensive reading we can also build a picture of the range of English responses. It is important to realize that, just as the Americans and their culture are remote and foreign to us, so the English are as well. It is a mistake to think that we can easily and directly understand the minds of English actors. Their purposes and meanings are alien and require imaginative reconstruction just as native American purposes and meanings do; and it is too easy to fall into the trap of thinking we know what they mean because their words appear to say something a modern person might say. These are often just the places where the import is utterly different.

Sources written by people closest to events deserve the most attention. As the case of Archer and Brereton shows, no source can simply be taken straight. In reporting their experiences, both of them struggled to describe unfamiliar circumstances, and their effort and their choices of what to include open windows into events and relationships. The writings of those who stayed in England often offer the best "sound bite" quotes; it was far easier to be sure of what you thought, and especially of your own superiority, in the comfort of England than in the villages, woods, and streams of America. Books written by armchair travelers, whose epithets are so clear and striking, form a goldmine for modern authors who portray the English as overconfident imperialists, pushing the Americans out of the way without a second thought. But no writer who actually went to America and had direct experience of Indians and their culture wrote in such a simple way. The writing of eyewitnesses shows the strain of their struggle to explain to an uncomprehending English audience just what kind of challenge and opportunity America presented. The level of difficulty was such that as soon as smugness surfaced it was quickly submerged again by doubt and hesitancy. We need to restore the complexity, the uncertainty, and the fear to the story of the English in earliest America.

The record analyzed here grew out of the first wave of English colonialism in America. It spans the period from the earliest ventures, which involved multiple frustrating failures, to the firm establishment of permanent settlements. Put another way, the period extends from a time when few would have predicted much future for an English American empire to a point where a continuing presence looked likely. Sir Walter Ralegh—a favorite on whom Queen Elizabeth showered resources—tried several times to found a colony at Roanoke within the Carolina Outer Banks in the 1580s. Like many leaders at the time, he believed that

England would remain a weak, impotent country unless it emulated the great superpower Spain with its rich American empire. The colony's site, hidden within the banks but close to Atlantic shipping lines, was chosen partly so that the colony could function as a privateering base, harboring ships that would prey on ships carrying American treasure to Seville.

Roanoke was a poor location for a colony, and its choice showed how little the English understood colonial realities. Ralegh sent two colonies, one in 1585 and the other in 1587. The first, composed of young men under military leadership, went home after one winter; they had clashed with the neighboring Indians on whom they relied for food, and their situation had become increasingly untenable. The second was made up of families who intended to grow their own food. But all colonies needed constant infusion of supplies from England. When the threat of the Spanish Armada caused the government to detain all ships, Ralegh and his backers could not resupply the colony in 1588. When a ship did arrive in 1590, the colonists were gone. They had left in an orderly fashion, and had not posted the agreed distress signal, so it was supposed at the time and ever since that they amalgamated with one or several native communities. Other, more lucrative and promising, interests diverted English leaders from American schemes for the next twenty years.

In 1607 the time was right for renewed interest in America, but the new king James I forbade the anti-Spanish thrust of Roanoke's design. The entire coast had been designated Virginia in Elizabeth's time, and two Virginia Companies founded colonies in 1607. The one in Maine, Sagadahoc, folded in just a few months after an exceptionally hard winter. The other, Jamestown, went through years of discouragement but held on. Both were like the first Roanoke contingent in having a relatively small company of young men under military leadership; Jamestown began with just over a hundred. Like Roanoke, Jamestown was actually abandoned in 1610, but the defeated colonists going downriver met the supply ships coming upriver, and the colony lived on. Luckily leaders had prevented the disgruntled men from burning down the fort as they left.

Everything was done on a shoestring, and as the drama of Jamestown's near abandonment suggests, the tolerances between success and failure were often thin. Funding a colony and keeping it alive over the long difficult years required more than the resources of one or a few rich men, and English promoters began to understand what was required. Jamestown's sponsors hit on the idea of selling relatively inexpensive shares in the Virginia Company so that its membership, and its pockets, became broad rather than deep.

But for English entrepreneurs of empire, the central question remained: what was a colony for? The first answer was easy—to obtain gold. Archer and Brereton's reports of Gosnold's 1602 voyage, with their constant discussion of the copper and other minerals they saw Americans wearing, were typical of all early reports. But backers quickly discovered that there was a good reason why North America's Atlantic coast lay unsettled by Europeans more than a century after Spain had begun to spread over the lands to the south. Other than furs, which were better farther north, and sassafras and other wood products, venturers could not find the commodities that would bring riches to investors and settlers. Worse, they could not even feed themselves; in fact they were barely able to cope at all with the environment.

Military regimes, initiated by Captain John Smith in Jamestown and later authorized by the company in London, kept the colonists alive and functioning, but they did not create genuine societies. If the ventures were to be more than short-term military outposts, other ways of motivating colonists had to be found. Slowly planners began to realize that the settlements needed to replicate English society as much as possible; women were sent to Virginia, and the later colonies began with families. They also understood that the commodities whose sale would repay investors would have to be produced, not acquired, and that old-world labor would be necessary to make that happen. Land of their own was offered to prospective settlers, something they would never achieve at home, and, partly because of hard times in England, many took the chance. The development of tobacco as a marketable crop in Virginia was the lynchpin that made the land attractive.

New England, seen as even less promising than Virginia, was settled later and profited from the lessons of Jamestown. Plymouth colony, 1620, and Massachusetts Bay, 1630, began with families. The later colony also began with a very large number of colonists, many times greater than the usual hundred or so of earlier ventures. Both were puritan colonies, and their founding grew partly out of fear of an approaching religious oppression in England; Maryland was also founded as a religious refuge, this one for Roman Catholics, in 1635. New England's colonies grew rapidly from their larger foundations and quickly spun off colonies into Rhode Island and Connecticut. The Chesapeake Bay colonies, Virginia and Maryland, also grew rapidly in the 1620s and 1630s.

The Indian experience of colonialism was in many ways the mirror image of the English. Strong native leaders, looking at the pathetic early plantations, understood that the English were utterly dependent and therefore controllable. Although the newcomers were erratic and apt to strike out wildly and unexpectedly if they thought they had been crossed or challenged, Indian commanders knew that this pattern was also an expression of weakness. The central question is, Why did American leadership allow the colonies to exist in the early years? The Americans could have finished off the colonies, as Powhatan, the paramount chief in Virginia at Jamestown's founding, pointed out to Captain John Smith, by pulling away and sequestering their food supply. If the Americans were pressed too hard, Powhatan asserted, "we can hide our provisions and fly to the woods," and then the Jamestown colonists "must famish by wronging us your friends."[11] The margin between success and failure was so thin that, even though colonial leaders used strong-arm tactics such as capturing hostages and terrorized neighbors into feeding them, the colonies would probably all have been abandoned (as so many were) without some willingness on the Americans' part to keep them alive.

One answer to the question is that leaders such as Powhatan realized that having the colonists as neighbors could be useful. The English brought tools made of iron and steel to communities that had previously had only stone and bone tools. Those people situated near the settlements could, by becoming middlemen in the trade in native and European-produced equipment, become powerful, thus intensifying a process of consolidation that preceded colonization. Immensely rich and powerful tribes and paramount chiefdoms emerged in the early years of colonization. But these also came to be seen by the English as stumbling blocks as the colonies grew. As the English presence became larger and more assured, the newcomers put increasing pressure on the very tribes and leaders who had made settlement possible and to whose eminence they had contributed. The growth in English control, especially as the numbers of settlers grew and they spread over the land, spelled dissolution or diminution of power for those leaders the English had called emperors.

Indians and English seeks to recover this early period as it was lived, erasing as much as possible our knowledge of the ultimate growth of the settlements. This means seeing the English as supplicants rather than conquerors, doubtful and insecure rather than self-assured and dominant. And it means understanding the Americans as active, setting the agenda for encounters and controlling colonists' actions, rather than simply as victims. English colonists wrote these documents to convince people at home that they should continue to put money into supporting American projects, so the writers usually claimed success. Like Archer and Brereton, they constantly said the Indians loved them, sometimes even that they worshipped the English as gods, but they also as constantly told of their hardships. Ultimately, like Gosnold's men, many ran for home.

Each of the colonies, even the failed ones, produced myriad documents—reports, letters, and company and government deliberations.

Because the sponsoring companies were always seeking investment and other support, many of the reports and letters were published as books at the time, sometimes even without their writers' consent or knowledge. And there were massive collections. Richard Hakluyt in the sixteenth century and Samuel Purchas in the early seventeenth collected and published reports of travel and settlement all over the world in huge multivolume editions. Thus, a surprising number of accounts and perspectives on early English colonialism in America survive.

Despite the propagandistic nature of these writings, the Indians' responses and strategies come through. As recent work on the postcolonial world has reminded us, all documents of colonialism are the result of dialogue, and the voice of the colonized is always there, shaping and focusing the statement despite the writers' own determination to control the story. This insight applies even more in the tentative world of early America, where writers not only did not know how to build colonies and live in that environment, they did not know what the shape of a colonial narrative was supposed to be.[12] The identity of the other was not even always clear for these writers—sometimes the other seemed to be the actor's own treacherous compatriots. At times religious affiliation or social status seemed a more important dividing line than ethnicity or nationality. Clear lines of division came later; our task here is to avoid reading those later demarcations back into the early period and to recapture the process of figuring out in that universe full of questions.

The line of interpretation presented here does not presuppose good will all around, and *Indians and English* does not seek to find and celebrate the "good" voices among the English writers. Suspicion, hostility, and armed clashes suffuse the record from first to last. No author wrote in a humane way as we would define humaneness; even the most sympathetic writers easily moved into chilling denigration or worse. Some of the most intricate and sensitive accounts of native life were written by men on military expeditions, men who would carry out the most barbaric campaigns if they felt threatened or challenged. Those who saw the Indians as hostile opponents often took the most care to try to understand them. People who remained in England and wrote at second hand could pen dismissive accounts of pathetically primitive savages, but those on the front lines in America, whose lives depended on their knowledge, knew better. This book offers an analysis of the struggle of all those involved to come to terms with the new realities.

1 Mirror Images

When the English belatedly began to try to build colonies in North America, the encounters up and down the coast were between sets of peoples all of whom were caught up in multilayered processes of change. American Indian societies had already felt massively the effects of the contact between two long-separated biological and cultural worlds, and these effects accelerated and redirected long-range lines of development within native cultures. At the same time the carriers of English culture reflected great and destabilizing changes occurring at home, changes which, though welcomed by many, were also threatening. Thus members of two developing groups of systems interacted on North America's east coast and tried to make sense of each other.

The confrontation between English and Indians in America has often been represented as the striding forward of a confident, burgeoning, literate culture into a world of no less confident but technologically disadvantaged societies. In reality the English who pushed out their own frontiers were deeply ambivalent members of a culture marked by fears and misgivings as much as confidence. Ambivalence pervaded the whole project of expanding into world trade and establishing colonies in America. English men and women feared the effects of such new ventures as much as they were excited by the prospects of the changes those ventures would bring.

In England, as in North America, great and fundamental transformations were occurring in the way society and the nation's economy were organized. The consolidation of power in the hands of the royal government and its representatives and the emergence of powerful merchant groups had contributed to the growth of cities, particularly London, and increased the riches and importance of the kingdom among the nations of Europe. The Reformation and the belief of many that England was destined to leadership of the Protestant nations enhanced the widespread sense that the nation's direction was important in a cosmic sense and fed the fires of religious controversy at home. England had a providential part to play, and America, hidden by God until the time for the rupture of Rome's control of Christendom had come, was an essential stage for that action.

At the same time England was ill equipped to take up its ordained role. The royal income was paltry in comparison to that of rival monarchs of France and Spain, and therefore Elizabeth, last of the Tudors, and James I, first of the Stuart line of monarchs who succeeded her in 1603, were cautious, even timid, in their commitments. Moreover, the effects of population explosion and inflation meant that the country seemed unable to feed and employ all its people. Resurgence of plague, which reached epidemic proportions in some years of the 1620s and 1630s, led to the conclusion that God was punishing the country for its sins. Many commentators felt that the country was under siege from the "wandering poor" who roamed the countryside and converged on the cities. The presence of unattached and unemployed men and women, like the rise of powerful merchant families and new kinds of capitalist organizations, fed the belief that the social order was being distorted, that it was becoming shapeless and disorderly. An important role for England on the world stage was both attractive and dangerous.

The English thought of themselves as insular, inhabiting a poor country on the margins of Europe, the "Suburbs of the old world" as John Donne called it.[1] Much of the colonization literature poured out lavish descriptions of the riches colonization would bring to England, allowing it to rival the vaunted wealth of the Spanish and assume its rightful position as the leader of the Protestant nations. But these same pamphlets and books vibrated with tension over the dangers to the country's moral fiber posed by wealth and cosmopolitanism. England's insularity and the simplicity and straightforwardness of English people were the sources of its strength and virtue. It was a commonplace that these were already being lost, and anyone with eyes to see knew that opening up the land to further foreign influences would only accelerate the degeneration.

In 1592 the playwright John Lyly pictured the English as mad for new sensations in the prologue to his play *Midas*, which was performed before Queen Elizabeth. The play opened with an apology arguing that "so nice is the world"—"nice" meaning overrefined or elegant—that in music, writing, food, and clothing every new fashion "breedeth society [satiety] before noone, and contempt before night." Not only did society race frantically after novel fashions, but the country's culture was becoming hopelessly mixed. Playing on England's key industry, the manufacture of plain sturdy woolen cloth, Lyly wrote that "Trafficke and travell hath woven the nature of all Nations into ours." Such mixing spelled the end of the old values; England was now "like Arras [tapestry], full of devise, which was Broade-cloth, full of workemanshippe." The "whole worlde is become an Hodge-podge."[2]

Social boundaries and their demarcators mattered to early modern English men and women. As foreign influences were increasingly felt through "apish and servile Imitation," commentators worried that categories were becoming blurred, and the foundations of good order undermined. Gender distinctions were crucial; they were determined by nature but required visible and emphatic demarcation. It was a commonplace that in countries such as France, which was considerably farther along in the descent into luxury and sophistication, fashionable dress blurred the sexual division of society. Class and status, equally given by nature, were also vital categories necessary to the maintenance of civility and good order in society. As travelers to America reported their experiences, their criterion for civility was the degree to which the Indians recognized male-female distinctions and a hereditary hierarchy, and maintained these demarcations by outward signs.

English commentators feared their own society was breaking down and that crucial distinctions of social rank and gender were being elided. Elegantly dressed men seemed effeminate, and women, "suting their light feminine skirts with manlike doublets," were too masculine.[3] This period saw an unparalleled "rage for novelty and bizarre experimentation in dress," including wearing items of clothing associated with the opposite sex, that defied all attempts to control it.[4] As the fundamental distinction between the sexes was elided, the visible demarcation between social ranks was also threatened; the two processes were interrelated because expansion was bringing wealth and power into the hands of people who lacked the lineage and background of the "better sort." If rank was not honored, then authority and respect, absolutely necessary to the commonwealth, would also go. The literature of this period was shot through with concern for the need to maintain categories and their visible signs. And these writers were keenly aware that trade and contact with the world only hastened dangerous blurring as it brought disproportionate riches to some, and the authority conferred by experience to others.[5]

People at the bottom of the social scale, even in England, were considered cultureless and uninteresting. Poet Michael Drayton assumed that the Indians would all be like the "meaner sort" of English people. In his poem "To Master George Sandys, Treasurer for the English Colony in Virginia" (1622), he listed the news he and his fellow writers who stayed home hoped to receive from Sandys in Virginia. He then went on to say:

> But you may save your labour if you please,
> To write me ought of your savages.
> As savage slaves be in great *Britaine* here,
> As any one that you can shew me there.[6]

Drayton demonstrated in the most direct way his assumption that even savagery is a constructed category, dependent on social status as much as ethnicity.

Writers who actually went to America proved Drayton wrong—not about the English poor but about the Indians—because they were in no doubt that the latter lived in highly organized societies and recognized key categorical boundaries. The more direct experience a colonist had, the more complex became the description and its lessons. For practical as well as intellectual reasons, their reports tended to focus on the elites and on how they maintained order and distinction. Their writings held the Indians up as a mirror in which English readers could examine their own society.

Study of the Indians as a previously isolated branch of the human family offered a way of answering the questions that were uppermost in many minds at home: were gender and status distinctions primary, timeless, and inherent? Did these categories, as commentators on English life asserted, represent the natural order of things? An affirmative answer would help to settle debates about social control in England and support those who favored rigidly enforced markers. Lessons could be drawn from Indian lifeways to reestablish fundamental order and virtue as the basis of life.

Moreover, a positive report would mean that a relationship of mutual benefit and understanding would be achieved quickly and easily in America. If the Indians recognized the same distinctions and observed the same codes of conduct as the English, the gap could be bridged easily and peacefully. Reflecting the doubleness of vision they brought to their task, writers assured their audiences that the American natives would benefit from exposure to the sophistication and learning that the English would bring them, especially knowledge of the Bible; only intermittently did they acknowledge that they also brought the corrupting influences they saw with dismay in their own world.

Ambivalence—the mixture of fear and anticipation that characterized English culture as Elizabeth's long reign drew to a close and James I and his son Charles I began the new dynasty—shaped the context in which ideas of the American Indians were formed, and conceptions of the Indians reflected that mental dividedness. Sometimes writers celebrated their compatriots' sophistication and attainments, castigating the Americans as primitive savages. But then again the very same writers turned and praised the Americans' vigor, simplicity, and primary virtue, contrasting that virtue with the luxurious degeneracy of England. Many observers saw in the Indians the lost world of their own past with all its roughness and its strength, and these writers asked their readers to reflect on the losses and gains England had made along the way to wealth and sophistication.[7] This split way of thinking emerged most strongly in those writers who actually spent time in America. The more direct experience a colonist had, the more complex became the description and its lessons.

The double vision with which the English approached America can be seen in two words in common use: "wonder" and "curiosity." "Wonder" meant something closely akin to our word "awe," but it imparted spiritual meaning beyond the modern concept. Certain kinds of experiences were sought for their ability to evoke the experience of "wonder," conveying values and ideas that could not be grasped in mere words. English monarchs and great nobles presented themselves and their courts in elaborate masques and pageants designed to convey majesty and grandeur and to produce wonder in those who saw them. People flocked to these displays or avidly read about them in order to experience wonder. Occurrences out of the ordinary, showing the range and power of earthly and divine authority, attracted huge audiences.[8] Robert Burton suggested that melancholia could be cured by study of marvelous books, maps, and pictures from around the world including "Indian pictures made of feathers" and "Those parts of America, set out, and curiously cut in Pictures by Fratres à Bry."[9]

America added immensely to the store of wonderful things, and there was a ready market for news of rarities. Richard Hakluyt, one of the earliest promoters of American projects, devoted his life to collecting and publishing narratives of voyages to newly revealed places for an avid public. Others collected and displayed items brought from around the world in "cabinets of curiosities" in which the paying public could see exotic displays and marvel at the range of phenomena in the world. Hakluyt wrote of how he had been "as it were ravished" in seeing the materials

gathered "with no small cost" in the "excellent Cabinets" of two antiquaries, Richard Garthe and Walter Cope.[10] Although some of the
world's great museums had their origins in such cabinets, the early modern displays were organized to produce a different effect than in modern
institutions. The cabinets grouped items by the materials of which they
were made, or the uses to which they could be put, rather than by the
cultures from which they came, thus preserving their status as exotic.
Each was seen as an isolated thing, strange and completely cut off from
its context.[11]

In 1599 a German traveler in England, Thomas Platter, visited the cabinet of curiosities created by Walter Cope and saw a collection of "queer
foreign objects in every corner." He compiled a list of the fifty most interesting items, which ran from the mummified corpse of a child to
"Heathen idols," and finished with the canoe that Cope had hung from
the ceiling. Platter recorded seeing a live camel in another London house.

This engraving of Ole Worm's Cabinet of Curiosities in Copenhagen shows every surface covered with items chosen for their strangeness and grouped to emphasis their awe-
inspiring qualities. The John Carter Brown Library at Brown University.

That canoe, or possibly the one Gosnold brought from Cuttyhunk, was apparently pressed into service four years later when Cope arranged for some "Virginians" who had been brought to England to give a demonstration of American canoe-handling on the Thames near the Strand in London.[12]

The two John Tradescants, father and son, were gardeners who sought exotic plants from newly revealed sources, as did many others all over Europe. In the middle of the sixteenth century, when plant hunting began in earnest, European herbals described about five hundred plants, a number basically unchanged from compilations known in the ancient world. By the end of the seventeenth century, the number of known plants ready for cataloging had leaped to an astonishing twenty thousand. No wonder people believed they lived in a awe-inspiring times. The senior Tradescant designed the gardens at Hatfield House and rose to be the king's gardener; he and his son made numerous trips to Europe, North Africa, and America seeking exotic specimens, and their interests grew to include all kinds of artifacts, which they presented to the world in their cabinet of curiosities (significantly named The Ark), charging sixpence per visit. Their collection included about a hundred items from America as well as specimens from all over the world. Peter Mundy recorded in 1634 that he spent an entire day seeing all of it, and remarked that in one day a man might see in such a cabinet more than in a lifetime of travel. The Tradescant cabinet formed the basis for the collection of the Ashmolean Museum in Oxford, where some of it can still be seen.[13]

People flocked to the theater as to the cabinets of curiosities. The theater fed the lust for the new while it contributed to the blurring of crucial distinctions between people. English theatergoers, men and women of all ranks jostling together, learned about foreign lands and events, and playwrights incorporated news items into their plays.[14] Shakespeare's play *The Tempest* drew on dramatic accounts of the great hurricane that wrecked a Virginia-bound fleet on Bermuda in 1609, and when the witches in *Macbeth* vowed to torment the master of the *Tiger* and his crew by tossing them in a tempest for nine times nine weeks or 567 days, they referred to a recently returned ship and its disastrous 567-day voyage.[15] Maria's comparison of Malvolio's fiercely smiling face to "the new map with the augmentation of the Indies" in *Twelfth Night* relied on audience knowledge of Edward Wright's just-published map using the converging lines of the Mercator projection.[16]

Wonder-producing experiences could convey a vision of the world and spiritual uplift unreachable by ordinary descriptions, yet such hungering after sensations of the new, the dramatic, and the strange fed the very appetite for superficial novelty that so many commentators feared threatened the core of English values. In this view wonder became translated into mere curiosity, often written as "needless curiosity." Writers portrayed the English as flocking to see monsters as they neglected their own heritage and roles. Henry Farley, who campaigned for the repair of St. Paul's cathedral in London, wrote disparagingly of the values displayed by his fellow citizens:

> To see a strange out-landish Fowle,
> A quaint Baboon, an Ape, an Owle,
> A Dancing Beare, a Gyants bone,
> A foolish Ingin [Engine] move alone,
> A Morris-dance, a Puppit play,
> Mad Tom to sing a Roundelay,
> A Woman dancing on a Rope,
> Bull-baiting also at the Hope;
> A Rimers Jests, a Juglers cheats,
> A Tumbler shewing cunning feats,
> Or Players acting on the Stage,
> There goes the bounty of our Age:
>   But unto any pious motion,
>   There's little coine, and lesse devotion.[17]

Farley's complaint matches the more famous sentiment voiced by Trinculo in *The Tempest:* "when they will not give a doit to a lame beggar, they will lay out ten to see a dead Indian."[18] Henry Farley ironically drew the lesson that others would draw more thoughtfully, when he concluded, "Farewell Britania, For I will goe unto Virginia, To see what Salvages will doe."[19]

Many writers, reflecting on American experience, wondered seriously if the Americans did not retain the honest simplicity they feared England had lost. Thomas Harriot, for example, wrote that the Indians he knew were "verye sober in their eatinge, and drinkinge, and consequentlye verye longe lived because they doe not oppress nature." A few pages later he returned to his praise of Indian moderation and went on, "I would to god wee would followe their exemple. For wee should bee free from many kynes of diseasyes which wee fall into by sumptwous and unseasonable banketts, continuallye devisinge new sawces, and provocation of gluttonye to satisfie our unsatiable appetite."[20] The restless, greedy search for new food sensations was symbolic of all that was wrong with English society; the need for "variety of Sauces to procure appetite" showed how jaded they had become.[21]

VIII.
Variety of Rarities.

Indian morris-bells of ſhells and fruits.
Indian muſicall Inſtruments.

Indian Idol made of Feathers, in ſhape of a Dog.

Indian fiddle.

Spaniſh Timbrell.

Inſtrument which the Indians ſound at Sun-riſing.

Portugall muſicall Inſtrument like a hoop, with divers braſſe plates.

A choice piece of perſpective in a black Ivory caſe.

A Canow & Picture of an Indian with his Bow and Dart, taken 10 leagues at Sea. *An°.* —76.

A bundle of Tobacco, *Amazonian.*

Birds-neſts from *China.*

Indian Conjurers rattle, wherewith he calls up Spirits.

Indian *Pa* God.

The Idol *Oſiris. Anubis,* the Sheep, the Beetle, the Dog, which the Ægyptians worſhipped.   Mr. *Sandys.*

A Gamaha with *Jeſus, Joſeph* and *Mary,* in Italian capitall letters.

A Gamaha with a Fiſh in it.

A

John Tradescant published a catalog of the Tradescant Collection in 1656. These pages show American items mixed in with rarities from other places and grouped by type. Brown University Library.

X.
Garments, Vestures, Habits, Ornaments.

AN Arabian vest.
A Russian vest.
A Portugall habit.
A Turkish vest.
A Brackmans vest of Leaves of Aloes.
A Virginian habit of Beares-skin.
A Babylonian vest.
A Greinland-habit.

A Match-coat from —— *Virginia* of { Feathers. / Deer-skin. } *Canada*.

Match-coat from *Greenland* of the Intrails of Fishes.

Pohatan, King of *Virginia*'s habit all embroidered with shells, or Roanoke.

A Match-coat of *Virginia* made of Racoune-skins.

Crownes { Indian. / Amazonian. }

Swabes suit.

Henry the 8 his { Stirrups. / Haukes-hoods. / Gloves. }

Barbary

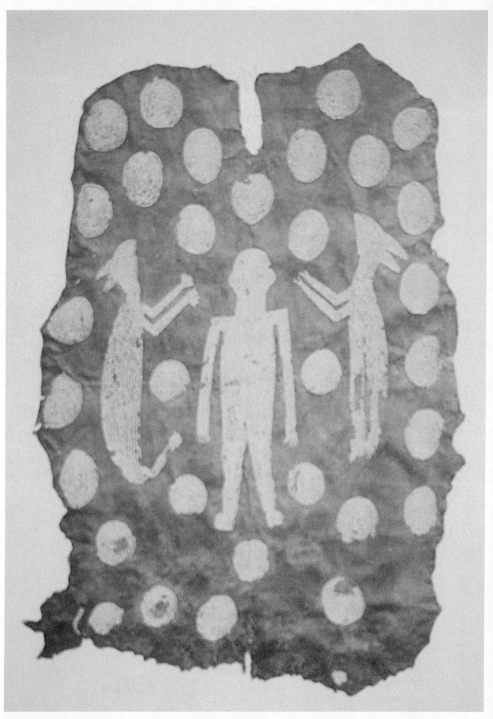

This deerskin decorated with shells is very probably the "King of Virginia's habit all embroidered with shells, or Roanoke" listed in the Tradescant catalogue. Although it is called Powhatan's mantle, some anthropologists think it may represent a map or diagram of the various tribes or villages over which Powhatan ruled rather than a garment. Ashmolean Museum, Oxford.

Appetite was emblematic of the more serious greed that was destroying English life, while wealth was dissipated on "soft, unprofitable pleasures."[22] On all sides virtue was dissipated. Blurring of categories meant not only that the lower orders failed to honor authority but also that the rich, who should have been the "better sort," failed to live up to the responsibilities of their positions. In a series of sermons and books commissioned to support renewed effort after the initial setbacks in the newly founded Virginia colony, ministers thundered on the theme that English selfishness was destroying the values that had made the country strong. William Crashaw compared those who put their own comfort before contributing to the great work of conversion in Virginia to "Sowes" wallowing in their own pleasure.[23]

The curious search for the new was unsettling partly because the humanist education of the times looked to the past, to ancient times, for lessons to guide the present. Lessons derived from study of the classics and the Bible warned of the danger in which the English nation stood from increasing wealth and cosmopolitanism. The years when the English first planted colonies in America were a time of renewed interest in Roman history, whose lessons seemed particularly applicable to early modern England. Parallels between ancient Rome and contemporary England were so common that they "had become a habit of mind."[24] Virtue had taken its place alongside lineage as the essence of true nobility; the historian John Speed, in reconstructing British origins, warned his readers to remember that "true British nobilitie is more in vertue than in Auncestors."[25] Poets, playwrights, and historians painted virtue in classical forms, but the corruption and plotting endemic among leaders of the Roman Empire also provided vivid warnings of the dangers into which many feared the English court was falling.

Plutarch and Livy, who earlier had been the favorite Romans, were now supplanted by Tacitus, who was the most popular ancient author in the first half of the seventeenth century. His writings seemed to reach across the centuries and were peculiarly applicable to the new challenges and choices the English faced as their place in the world changed. "Tacitus was both ancient and modern": his histories offered insights into the workings, especially the hidden workings, of power and were therefore relevant to the political manipulations rumor said were common at court.[26] Tacitus taught prudence and restraint, and his works warned against the enervating effects of luxury. Thus they struck a chord with those who believed that England was being undermined by "pride and flattery, mesmerised by false values of outward display and extravagance," and who blamed the nation's perceived degeneration on contamination by foreign influences. Under Charles I, particularly, some feared infiltration of the court by Spanish intrigues which they linked to the contemporary vogue for newsmongering, needless curiosity.[27] Ironically, those who promoted a larger role for England in the world and colonization of America also betrayed their own uneasiness over the consequences of more porous cultural and economic boundaries. Ultimately a leader such as John Milton would come to feel that the desire for empire had distorted England's own polity irreparably.[28]

Readers of Tacitus set his Roman history against his portrait of the ancient Germans and the ancient Britons as simple, even barbaric, yet strong and admirable peoples, and that picture was clearly in the consciousness of many who wrote about the Americans. The honest, straightforward Germans, "neither craftie nor subtle," formed a striking contrast to the sophisticated and manipulative Romans and, in the minds of readers of Richard Greneway's English translation at the end of the sixteenth century, to the destructive striving and competition of the contemporary court, which too many had come to accept as inevitable. Tacitus's Germans prized honor. A dishonored man or woman had no place among them, and they did not take dishonesty lightly: "No man laugheth at vices: neither when any is corrupted, or doth corrupt, do they say, it is the time." Men attained leadership roles not through manipulation and flattery but by their own valor, and women were courageous and chaste. The Germans of Tacitus's day were robust and warlike. They had no interest in gold and silver and freely offered hospitality to all. The Germans loved liberty, and important matters were decided by meetings in which "all in generall consult." They had no need of complicated laws and lawyers, because theirs was a communal society.[29]

Tacitus's portrait of the ancient Germans had special resonance for English readers, because they believed he was describing their own ancestors. Increasingly through the sixteenth century and into the seventeenth antiquarians sought in old documents and practices the true roots of English life and institutions. As Ralegh sent out ships to found their first American colony at Roanoke in the 1580s, William Camden was presenting a sustained argument for England's Saxon origins, and in the 1590s his colleagues Richard Greneway and Sir Henry Savile translated the key texts for this analysis, the writings of Tacitus. Camden titled his history of the reign of Elizabeth *Annals*, an echo of Tacitus's history. In asserting their Saxon origins, English writers portrayed the ancient Germans as a singular people, not subject to the kind of mixing produced by population movements in the ancient world. The Saxons were manly and vigorous, warlike when necessary, and Tacitus, according to Richard Verstegan, was the best "witnesse of their woorthynesse."

Moreover, in a theme that was developed by parliamentary champions in the seventeenth century, the Saxons were said to have possessed the most free institutions on earth. Champions such as Sir Edward Coke, John Pym, and Sir Dudley Digges traced the English parliament back to the Saxon witenagemot, and argued that in ancient times the king had been chosen from among the council of leading nobles and was answerable to them. Although the argument for Saxon origins of English institutions enjoyed royal patronage early in the reign of James I, interest in Tacitus soon became so much the badge of those who sought to turn England back from the path of luxury and corruption; and the implied criticism of royal policy became so pointed that in late 1627 Cambridge University officials intervened to stop the inaugural course of lectures on Tacitus by Isaac Dorislaus, the university's first professor of history. Dorislaus's lectures justified the resistance of his native Netherlands to the tyranny of Spain, a popular but dangerous argument. The order prohibiting the lectures was issued in the name of Charles I, and the government soon had ample illustration of the danger. In the debates over the Petition of Right a few months later, members of parliament rested their case on the Saxon polity as described by Tacitus and the unbroken tradition of English institutions that they argued were traceable to it.[30]

The Britons who resisted imperial Roman legions were also English ancestors. Tacitus depicted the Britons as a hardy, liberty-loving people not softened by prolonged peace. They preferred death to slavery under a corrupt regime, and their own way of life to the sophistication the Romans offered. Seventeenth-century English readers could measure both their own gains in civility and their decline in primitive vigor and virtue against Tacitus's portrayal. And the connection to the new imperial course on which England had embarked was obvious. Voyagers to America described the Indians in Tacitean terms. And the assumption that in looking at the Indians English men and women were looking at their own forebears became a commonplace in England: the early inhabitants of both Britain and Germany were, as Nathanael Carpenter wrote, "little different from the present Americans."[31]

Greneway's and Savile's English translations were reprinted many times and must have struck a deep chord of understanding in many readers. The puritan movement was one among many responses to the widespread feeling that English society had declined from the simplicity and virtue that had characterized it. Formerly, communities had taken care of their own, and people had worked for the common good; openhanded hospitality had been the hallmark of the great. Now the sharpest at cutting corners came out on top, and anyone who cared about integrity or the welfare of others was counted a fool. Simplicity had given way to a dangerous sophistication. Travelers and their audiences saw the Americans through this veil of nostalgia, and although they thought the Indians' life crude and deprived by European standards, they recognized that it constituted a living reproach to England.[32]

But the roles were now reversed. In a further twist writers on America likened themselves and the English enterprise in America to the Romans' invasion of England. Though the simple English had resisted subjugation, their descendants realized that that conquest, which brought Christianity to a pagan land, had brought a new life and the possibility of true virtue. Citing Tacitus, William Strachey wrote that "Had not this violence, and this Injury, bene offred unto us by the Romanis" the English "might yet have lyved overgowne Satyrs, rude, and untutred, wandring in the woodes, dwelling in Caves, and hunting for our dynners, (as the wyld beasts in the forrests for their prey,)." Playing on the theme of the English nation's Anglo-Saxon origins, he argued that "Angli" should play the part of "Angells" in converting the Americans.[33] And Robert Burton made the connection clear: "see but what Caesar reports of us, & Tacitus of those old Germans, they were once as uncivill as they in Virginia, yet by planting of Colonies & good lawes, they became from barbarous outlawes, to be full of rich and populous Cities, as now they are, and most flourishing kingdomes."[34] Again the colonization literature exhibits its characteristic double vision: the primitive peoples of whom Tacitus wrote and the invaders who conquered them were both ancestor models to the early modern English.

Every letter, broadside, and book about America by a writer with transatlantic experience was steeped in ambivalence. England was proud of its accomplishments as a nation and looked forward to a greater role in the world, and the English people valued their civility and refinement in comparison to even the very recent past. They loved the magnificence of the court and demanded displays of sovereignty of their local rulers. Yet at the same time they felt profound unease over what they saw as the consequences of sophistication, luxury, and commerce. They read all the signs of decline around them and feared that England had lost its special vigor and virtue forever. Descriptions of the American natives that, appealing to this ambivalence, described them as "civil savages" must be set in this context.[35]

Promotional tracts for American colonies offered readers a solution to the problem posed by the desire for opening to the wider world without losing England's distinctive culture and virtue. America was a field for endeavors that would reinvigorate and enrich the English nation and restore its vitality through Baconian engagement in productive work. The greatness of the nation depended on a large population fully committed to work contributing to the common good. Andrew Fitzmaurice argues that the very rhetorical form in which English promotional tracts were cast conveyed the message of civic humanism by proposing involvement in American enterprise as an avenue to the life of active engagement that virtue required.[36]

Thus colonization offered a way out of the conundrum. England could expand in wealth and power without loss of virtue or vigor, because the creation of new commonwealths was a field of action which would absorb and revitalize the marginal and irresolute elements of the population and would offer scope and direction to the great. Such creation required the kind of dedication that civic humanism called for. At the same time American enterprises could increase the nation's wealth and make possible the openhanded largess appropriate to greatness.

Religious ferment was another spur to action. Many English men and women found in puritanism a way not only to understand what they saw happening to their country but also, as with civic humanism, a call to action that put an end to feelings of fear, confusion, and irresolution. God had opened the way to America just at the time when it was needed. "If it should please God to punish his people in the Christian countries of Europe, for their coldness, carnality, wanton abuse of the Gospel, contention, etc., either by Turkish slavery, or by popish tyranny," wrote Robert Cushman in Plymouth colony, "here is a way opened for such as have wings to fly into this wilderness."[37] But even more important, America offered the godly an opportunity, not just to save themselves, but to do God's work.

Writers who sought to direct the energies of the godly to America pointed out that religious controversies at home were unproductive and smacked of pride. In the mid-1620s Edmund Garrard castigated both "insolent" Roman Catholics and extreme Protestants who, "with their insolencie and boldnesse, have much prejudiced the Common-wealth."[38] One ship to America was more vexing to "Papists," according to John Donne, than twenty "Lectures in Matters of Controversie." And Alexander Whitaker, writing from America to report the conversion and baptism of Pocahontas, marveled that so few of the English ministers "that were so hot against the Surplis and subscription : come hither where neither spoken of." He wondered if they "keepe themselves at home for feare of loosing a few pleasures?"[39] The truly godly would seize the opportunity God had sent, and bring new dedication both to their own lives and to their country.

Early accounts of American life were much more than simply mirrors in which English readers could see their own virtues and vices reflected.

They are our best source of information about native life because they relied so heavily on the Indians' own testimony about their lives and traditions. Many of the writers were keen observers, but none would have been able to write so compellingly and fully if they had not been the beneficiaries of American instruction. Not only did English eyewitness accounts incorporate the natives' oral tradition, as Neil Whitehead has argued for Ralegh's *Discoverie of Guiana,* but in their form and wording they also often transmitted, consciously or unconsciously, the Indians' own voices.[40]

English writers emphasized that they conveyed the Indians' own local knowledge. Thomas Harriot, who was able to learn coastal Carolina Algonquian before he went to Roanoke, emphasized that his knowledge came from his "special familiarity with some of their priestes."[41] Others acknowledged that many early sources contained errors because of the difficulty of learning American languages on the spot. The British Library copy of John Smith's *True Relation* has this handwritten marginal note: "This author I find in many errors, which they do impute to his not well understanding the language." Early writers also came to understand that the Indians could and did manipulate them for their own purposes with "false reports."[42] Thomas Morton in New England, writing in the 1630s, argued that the English were now able to correct former errors. For example, they had believed that Indians had told them of monstrous humans when actually they described great hairy beasts, a mistake made because "wee were but slender proficients in the language of the Natives."[43] Edward Winslow of Plymouth corrected his own underestimation of American religious beliefs: "therein I erred, though we could then gather no better."[44] True understanding came through learning from native tutors.

Later Indian leaders, such as the Pequot William Apess in the early nineteenth century, recognized that their own oral tradition was embedded in these early sources. In his *Eulogy on King Philip* he drew on them to shape his account of the relationship between the New England natives and the English newcomers, and of the reactions and motivations on both sides. Mohegan scholar Gladys Tantaquidgeon also cites the early sources, particularly Roger Williams's *Key into the Language of America,* for information about native life at the time of colonization. Nanepashemet disputed archaeological theories by pointing to the early accounts and arguing that modern scholars failed to recognize the authentic American information embedded in them.[45]

The Americans maintained their own histories, passing on knowledge from generation to generation through oral transmission. Formal modes of learning the stories of their past were recorded in all regions; children

worked at this learning until it was perfect. Sites maintained on the landscape also commemorated important events and occasioned retelling of
their stories. William Kendall, traveling south from Plymouth in the first
decade of the nineteenth century, found the landscape alive with memories of King Philip; every landmark provoked another association in his
hosts' minds.[46] These modes of maintaining the oral tradition continued. Deeds and other documents, many written in the Massachusett language, relied on participants' ability to remember relationships and
arrangements from many generations past, and often on their ability to
repeat conversations verbatim. The written documents supported the
oral tradition rather than replacing it. Other kinds of lore were treated
similarly. Tantaquidgeon was herself the recipient of such knowledge
from her Mohegan community in the twentieth century, and she
recorded similar transmission techniques among Gay Head Indians.
Thomas Commuck recorded several Narragansett words in the mid-
nineteenth century and noted how specific members of his family had
passed them on.[47]

In addition to the early written sources and the oral tradition they contain, our understanding has been enhanced in recent times through archaeology. In some cases, as with the Mashantucket Pequots of
Connecticut, archaeological investigation has been sponsored by the
tribes themselves, who seek to broaden their understanding of the
changes and continuities from the contact period.[48] Because the soils in
the East are damp and often acidic, little physical evidence remains in
the ground, but modern techniques, such as the analysis of stains and
other variations left in the soil, yield evidence of things that no longer
exist. In many cases the scientific results have shown the contemporary
accounts to be more accurate than past ethnographic analysis.

On occasion the oral tradition as it has come down and as it is embedded in the early accounts conflicts with the findings of archaeologists. One example, the question of the origins of the Pequots and
Mohegans, offers a good illustration of how the oral tradition has been
transmitted. Seventeenth-century English documents record the natives'
memory that the Mohegans and Pequots came from the west, from the
region of the Hudson River. Modern archaeological evidence has been
interpreted as indicating the tribes originated in Connecticut, where they
were when the English arrived. The Mohegans' oral tradition, however,
supports the testimony in the early accounts and maintains that they
did come from the west, and this memory illustrates how the lore was
maintained. Emma Fielding Baker, who was born in 1828, recorded in
the early twentieth century memories from the early nineteenth: "When
a child of seven years my great, great aunt [Martha Uncas] used to take

my sister, brother, cousin and myself on the hill near where the Church now stands and say that was where her folks came from . . . away to the hills of Taughannick." Fidelia Fielding, the last fluent speaker of the Mohegan language, also told this oral tradition stretching through Martha Uncas, who was born in 1761, back to the colonial period.[49]

Like English society, native cultures were undergoing dramatic change at the time when the two spheres began to interact. Until recently scholars have believed that the changes reported by contemporaries and confirmed by the archaeological record were the result of the coming of European trade followed by settlement. Certainly the Americans, presented with the effects of European intrusion across a huge range of experiences, were developing new patterns in response to those challenges. In North America these effects had been going on for almost a century by the time sustained colonies were founded, so most of our accounts describe people whose entire lives had been lived in the changing environment. Hundreds of fishing and trading voyages, which have left only ghostly trails, had already introduced Americans to European ways and products. By the middle of the sixteenth century several hundred ships a year went to the Newfoundland Banks for the rich summer fishing and some ventured down the New England coast. Many shipwrecked or simply jettisoned Europeans must be added to the famous Lost Colonists of Roanoke, left in 1587, so that hundreds must have joined Indian societies all along the coast. The first Roanoke venturers were actually told of two shipwrecks that had happened decades earlier. Every so often an early explorer, thinking he was in uncharted territory, was startled to see Indians wearing European shirts or hats, or using a shirt as a makeshift sail for their canoe as Archer and Brereton were in their first encounter off the Maine coast with Indians skillfully sailing "a Baskeshallop," a large sailing boat obtained from Basque fishermen in Newfoundland or Cape Breton. And imagine the response of the Pilgrims when Samoset, the first Indian they saw up close, began his speech by saying, "Welcome."[50]

Not only had Indians had ample opportunity to learn about Europeans, but their social and political arrangements had been irrevocably altered. First and foremost, the massive impact of imported diseases to which the formerly isolated Americans had no acquired immunity mowed down Indians in their hundreds of thousands; many of these epidemics occurred in the sixteenth century, so communities were weakened by European contact well before colonization. One great wave swept through New England in 1616. Thomas Dermer traveled along the New England coast in 1619 and saw "antient Plantations, not long since populous, now utterly void." Measles and the common cold joined plague and typhus as killers. Estimates of the size of the pre-Columbian population vary widely, but scholars think that the native population along the east coast may have been reduced by as much as 90 percent during the first century of systematic contact. Robert Cushman of Plymouth colony wrote, "I think the twentieth person is scarce left alive." Thomas Morton wrote that as he traveled near the villages of the Massachusett Indians, "it seemed to me a new found Golgotha." A second great wave of disease in 1634, after the colonies were well established in New England, wreaked havoc among groups relatively untouched by the first.[51]

Deaths on this scale led to disarray at all levels. Psychologically the course of the biological onslaught enormously enhanced the Europeans' apparent strength. Europeans all had a degree of acquired immunity because these diseases were part of their environment and many had been exposed in childhood. The adults who ventured to America thus seemed to be exempt from the scourge, although other diseases such as scurvy presented huge problems in the early settlements. As we shall see, both Europeans and Americans looked to supernatural explanations, and many Indians as well as Europeans were led to believe that God or the gods had somehow directed that the land was to go to the newcomers.

Thomas Shepard recorded one native's memory of God's hand in the epidemic that preceded Plymouth's settlement. This man said he had had a dream during the "great mortality among the Indians" two years before the English arrived. In his dream "he did think he saw a great many men come to those parts in cloths, just as the English now are apparelled, and among them there arose up a man all in black, with a thing in his hand which hee now sees was all one English mans book; this black man he said stood upon a higher place then all the rest, and on the one side of him were the English, on the other a great number of Indians: this man told all the Indians that God was *moosquantum* or angry with them, and that he would kill them for their sinnes." In the dream the black man assured the Indian that he and his "Papooses" would be safe, but Shepard could not persuade him to come to church.[52]

The epidemics were so devastating in part because the Indians' coping mechanisms did not work. Shamans found their healing techniques powerless; such practices as sweatbaths, leading to dehydration, may even have made some diseases worse. Communities were often struck all at once, so traditional modes of caring for the sick were necessarily foregone; no one was able to carry them out. William Bradford wrote of terrible mortality along the Connecticut River caused, he thought, by smallpox. Because everyone became sick simultaneously, the people struggled to make fires, burning even their dishes and bows and arrows, and crawled out of their homes on their hands and knees to try to bring in water. Traders along the river, Bradford wrote, took pity on the suffering and built fires and brought water, but to little avail. Proper burial of the dead was often impossible; Bradford wrote of corpses rotting on the ground in places. Failure to observe their own rituals then contributed to the Indians' feeling that they were somehow bringing this terrible disaster on themselves.[53]

Disruption of native life was also the product of underlying environmental factors. Recent work on the reconstruction of climate has demonstrated that the entire northern hemisphere was in the grip of a period of cold so intense it has been dubbed the Little Ice Age. Europe and Asia were affected as well as America. The greater cold led to shortened growing seasons, and to changes in wind and rainfall patterns. These conditions probably led to the intense drought conditions researchers have found in the Chesapeake and along the Carolina Outer Banks at the end of the sixteenth century and beginning of the seventeenth, which they have labeled the worst conditions in eight hundred years. The early colonial record contains plenty of evidence of drought and competition over the ability to bring rain through supernatural means. The colonists, none of whom produced their own food in the early years, must have created intolerable burdens on native food supplies.[54]

Politically and socially the effect of all these disruptions was massive. Remnants of villages and bands came together in new political groupings, and catastrophic depopulation created opportunities for "big men" to consolidate positions of power and to add lands and lineages to their traditional holdings. When combined with the presence of the Europeans and their trade goods, these new political arrangements created unprecedentedly powerful chiefs, and English leaders channeled their trade goods to enhance the power of chosen allies. John Pory, secretary of the Virginia colony, gave a revealing glimpse of such attempted manipulation as he reported his conversation with Womanato, who was a subchief to his brother Namenacus, "King of Pawtuxents." Pory asked Womanato "if he desired to bee great and rich." The answer was, according to Pory, "They were things all men aspired to." Pory told Womanato that "he should be, if he would follow my counsell."[55]

Some ethnohistorians believe that the village or band had been the key unit for many coastal Algonquians in precontact times and that political processes within the community rested on the consensus-building skills of the chief rather than coercion. Tribes, incorporating several villages, may have grown up partially as a response to colonization and the demands of the newcomers to have certified representatives with whom they could deal. Tribes with consolidated political authority may also have been a response to the new foreign products in their midst. Leaders who found themselves situated near the newcomers had prime access to desirable trade goods, especially metal tools and weapons; because they could become the middlemen between the other tribes and the colonists, chiefs such as Powhatan in the Chesapeake, Wingina in Roanoke, Bashabes of Mawooshen among the Eastern Abenakis, Miantonomi of the Narragansetts, and Uncas among the Mohegans emerged as very powerful.

At the same time the military threat presented by the newcomers, and by other chiefdoms growing in strength through consolidation in the wake of epidemics and opportunities, may have fostered concentration of power among the natives of each coastal region, enabling them to field armies capable of confronting the challenge. With their wealth from the new trade they could attract warriors, so the two processes were mutually reinforcing.[56] This portrait—of a precontact society organized politically at the village level governed by leaders who worked through consensus—has been supported by some archaeological work on New England.[57] In this model consolidation and the emergence of tribes with powerful leaders was a result of the challenges presented by the Europeans and the trade they instituted.

A competing way of describing and analyzing how and why the Americans were undergoing dramatic change has emerged from other archaeological findings. This interpretation agrees that native societies were moving in the direction of greater consolidation, both in enhanced territoriality and in concentration of power in the hands of chiefly lineages. But natives were not just reacting to the dynamic European presence. Rather, the processes of change are seen in the archaeological record before colonization and therefore were an internal development within native culture which may have been intensified by the European presence but were not created by it.[58] The Susquehannocks provide a good example of this process. Archaeological evidence suggests that sometime in the mid-sixteenth century, they moved their location three hundred kilometers down the Susquehanna River closer to the centers of trade, and instead of replicating their scattered villages, they built a single large fortified town at the new site. The trade in native-produced commodities that they controlled began to include European goods as these became available. When Jamestown was settled, the Susquehannocks approached the colonists about opening a trade relationship and including the English in their network.[59]

Ethnohistorians argue that the strong Powhatan chiefdom at the head of a highly complex society began to emerge in the Chesapeake in the sixteenth century well before European influence was felt in a prolonged or systematic way. Even in the 1580s the Roanoke colonists were warned that on a great bay to the north there was a powerful king who was able to field an army with "a greate many of men." Archaeologists find European goods showing up only in seventeenth-century contexts, contemporaneously with the settlement of Jamestown, and evidence of large-scale epidemics before 1600 is also missing. Helen Rountree argues that the process of consolidation was occurring on differing scales throughout the mid-Atlantic region; a less highly developed system was seen among the Roanokes on the North Carolina Outer Banks. This interpretation argues that war and intimidation were essential parts of native life, led by a hereditary elite or "noble" class with a strong urge toward consolidation of power.[60]

In New England as well, archaeologists emphasize processes internal to American culture in fostering consolidation of political and economic life. Kathleen Bragdon, drawing on a wide variety of findings, argues that probably from the fifteenth century the introduction of maize agriculture and rising population had combined with a new long-range trade (in which wampum manufactured from coastal shells played a prominent role) to create more hierarchical social structures with increasingly powerful chiefly lineages and more clearly defined specialist roles. Powerful outsiders may have played a part in this transformation, but these outsiders would have been the native Hopewellian state in the interior and its Iroquois intermediaries. Although European elements were present in these trade networks, they were far less important than indigenous developments and their dissemination was entirely in the hands of native middlemen. Management of the trade and production, as well as competition, led to centralization of authority. This process of consolidation and differentiation was then magnified by the massive impact of European traders and settlers in the sixteenth and seventeenth centuries, especially as epidemics disrupted chiefly lineages.[61]

Archaeological evidence thus directly challenges the widely accepted view that American life was egalitarian and native political systems were consensual at the time of contact, and problematizes the picture of communitarian Indians being overwhelmed by individualistic Europeans as romantic. The first colonists transmitted reports of powerful rulers, at least among some Indians, set apart in an elite class from those they governed and prepared to use force to sustain their territorial and trade claims, but scholars rejected these descriptions as simply reflecting the naive preconceptions of ethnocentric Europeans. Now the Indians' own traditions, new archaeological findings, and restudy of the documents support a picture closer to that taught to the early colonists than we have been accustomed to accept. Schaghticoke historian Trudie Lamb Richmond describes leadership in very similar terms. Both lines of interpretation present Indians as actively and creatively responding to changing circumstances; the difference lies in whether the European presence inaugurated that change. Neither is content to see the Indians as passive victims of forces over which they had no control, and both argue for ongoing change at the time English colonization began.[62]

English observers attempting to describe the American societies they encountered, then, were struggling with their own preconceptions about "normal" human society and its foundations and feared the degeneration of their own culture. The cultures they described were, as many of them were dimly aware, undergoing profound change of their own. The cultures of the precontact native Americans and of the sixteenth- and seventeenth-century English are both remote from modern experience. In the construction of American reports, much depended on the kinds of relationships English and native individuals forged and the circumstances in which they talked of their own histories and cultures. Friendships, professional relationships, rivalries, even captivities could lead to illuminating discussions that found their way into these early accounts.

English colonists and their readers at home studied the Americans, especially those of the "better sort," as a guide to figuring out just what God and nature intended for the human race. Everyone whose description of America included discussions of Indian life was concerned to fit them into prevailing notions about how human society was organized, and their descriptions followed an implicit template, almost a checklist of questions to be answered when describing another society. Deep and fundamental issues could be addressed by learning about American societies. If the Indians recognized the same kind of status and gender distinctions that English people valued, for example, then that would be evidence these were natural and foundational to human society and would contribute to debates raging at home. If, as many believed, the Americans were descended from the Lost Tribes of Israel, then the providential revelation of these long-hidden continents would mean that the culmination of history foretold in the Book of Revelation was near. If, as others argued, they resembled England's Saxon ancestors as described by Tacitus, then conclusions about the origins and development of national political and social structures could be drawn. Venturers were aware that they played a small part in the great ingathering of knowledge that flowed from the revelation of hidden worlds and the early stirrings of the scientific spirit, and they consciously sought to make a contribution to it.

The English were interested in the Indians in part because they wanted to understand more about themselves. In looking at the meeting of English and native cultures in America we are examining societies on all sides whose assumptions and attitudes are foreign to us. The English observed Americans and wrote about them partly as a way of learning more about themselves, as all travelers do, but many were also interested in learning about the natives and how they functioned. For their part, many Americans saw the possibility of shaping the newcomers' understanding of themselves, the land, and relationships in America and actively participated in that process. That these writings are still the best source of knowledge about American Indians in the period of first contact and settlement is a tribute to how seriously both parties undertook the task.

2 Reading Indian Bodies

There is a puzzle in early English discussion of American Indian appearance, best seen in the strange career of the watercolors of John White. White, a London painter, was teamed with Thomas Harriot, a recent Oxford graduate trained in mathematics and geography, and together they were sent in 1585 to create a full-scale natural history of Sir Walter Ralegh's Virginia, including people, plants, animals, and landscape.[1] White produced a remarkable portfolio of paintings of the Indians and their daily life. He was meticulous in attempting to render an exact and sympathetic likeness of the people he had come to know. His Indians were tanned, they assumed postures that looked ungainly in European eyes, and their faces seemed to reflect Asian origins. Their hair was straight and black. Their bodies were ornamented with tattoos or painting, and their clothing, made of animal skins, was minimal.

White's paintings were seen by few contemporaries; they were not published until the twentieth century. His Indians became famous, though, through copperplate engravings of them done in the workshop of the Flemish engraver Theodore de Bry. Harriot's overview of his findings, *A Briefe and True Report of the New Found Land of Virginia*, had been rushed into print in 1588 in order to keep interest in the Roanoke colony alive. In 1590 de Bry, at the urging of Richard Hakluyt, reprinted the *Briefe and True Report* in his multivolume collection titled *The Great Voyages* with engravings done from a set of paintings White had prepared especially for him, and with notes by Harriot explaining each picture.

Comparison of the de Bry engravings with White's paintings presents a puzzling contrast. De Bry and his assistants meticulously recreated the patterns of tattoos, jewelry, and other decorations and also followed White exactly in the figures' clothing. But they completely changed their faces, postures, bodily proportions. The faces were sweetened, softened and Europeanized. With their new high foreheads, puckered mouths, and ringleted hair, they resembled classical figures in the German engraving tradition. Long, thin feet and hands became small and chubby, and postures were rendered more graceful to European eyes.[2] The artists simply put American garments and decorations on stock figures from their repertoire.

In many ways it is easier to understand the artists' use of standard figures than to explain their exacting care in replicating clothing, jewelry, and body paint. Why were some aspects of White's paintings more crucial than others? The answer is not that de Bry sought to make the Indians look more acceptable to European viewers. White, the eyewitness, was trying to render accurately what he saw, but he had no desire to make the Indians seem repugnant to his European audience; in fact he spent much of the rest of his life trying to encourage interest in America and was one of the very few who signed up for a second tour of duty in Roanoke. De Bry, who never went to America, evidently thought he and his assistants *were* making accurate copies of White's paintings. We can conclude, then, that de Bry and his workshop followed familiar models in rendering native faces and bodies—rather than White's versions—because they considered variations in those features unimportant.

The engravings gave an accurate portrayal of those aspects of appearance that are manipulable, that is, in a person's control. De Bry knew that his audience wanted to know who the Indians were, and early modern people answered such questions by looking at the way one presented oneself. Announcing one's status and placing others in theirs, even on casual contact, was a regular feature of English life. People needed to know where they stood in relation to those around them. Contemporary writing on portraiture held that presentation of the person's role and place in society was the goal of portrait painting, not an exact representation of the sitter's face and figure.[3]

A modern description of previously unknown alien peoples would reverse these priorities, on the assumption that the manipulable can more easily be made to lie. To convey the truth, descriptions would have to focus on those intrinsic aspects of face and body over which the individual has little immediate control, and that would therefore reflect the true character of the person being described.[4] Moderns would want to know, in their terms, the reality, not what someone was trying to make them believe through clever self-presentation.

Early modern usage cut across the concept of race as modern people customarily use it; they thought in terms of socially and culturally created categories. Like modern people, they expected the body to be emblematic of these categories; but color, posture, and other features were interesting to them because they were "accidental" rather than inborn. Climate was clearly, in their view, one causative factor in human differences, and English people who went to the Caribbean and the southern parts of America feared losing their distinctive Englishness through a change of environment.[5] They sought information in realities of the flesh, as when the Virginia Company instructed its first settlers to look carefully at natives' bodies in choosing a site. They were to avoid low-lying coastal places that "have their people blear Eyed and with Swollen bellies and Legs." Where "the naturals be Srong and Clean made it is a true sign of a wholesome Soil."[6]

But as to character, English observers sought their truth in consciously assumed markers. As they wrote about the Indians in the first decades of contact and colonization, they attempted to "read" the bodies, the self-presentation of the people they met, in order to understand the underlying qualities of their culture and the prospects for cultural convergence. Thomas Bavin, a draftsman who was appointed to sail with an abortive expedition in 1582–83, received detailed instructions about how to create accurate charts and maps. His instructions concluded, "Drawe the figures and shapes of men and women in their apparell as also of their manner of wepons in every place as you shall finde them differing."[7] Most eyewitnesses included a description of the Indians' appearance in their accounts of America, and these almost always followed the same pattern: they began with stature and then moved on to color of hair, skin, and eyes. The other elements of a successful description were clothing, jewelry and other forms of decoration, and, often at great length, the way natives dressed their hair.

Looking at American Indian life, the reporters were gratified to find the same social and cultural concerns that motivated the English, and the same distinguished bearing that set the "better sort" apart. William Strachey—his choice of words emphasizing conscious performance—was surprised to find "so much presentment of Civility."[8] Moreover, because elite Americans distinguished themselves and maintained distance from ordinary people through display as English leaders did, these writers reported that the Indians were simultaneously attempting to read English bodies and behavior with the same issues in mind.

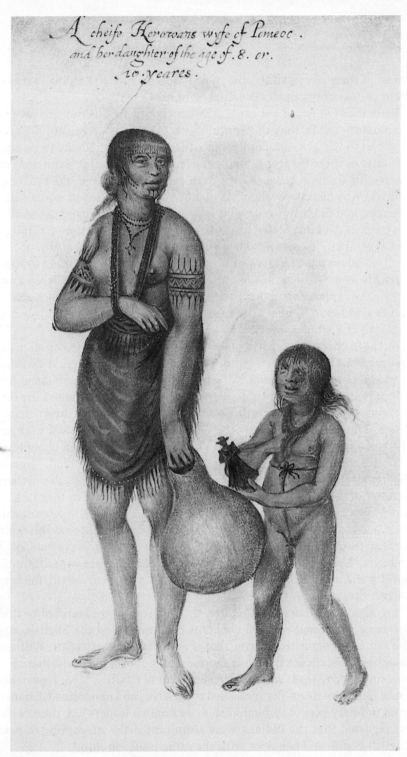

A cheife Herowans wyfe of Pomeoc.
and her daughter of the age of .8. or.
10. yeares.

This comparison of a painting by John White, depicting a mother (the wife of the chief of Pomeiooc) and daughter, with the copperplate that Theodor de Bry's artists created from it shows how images from America were received in Europe. Although some aspects of the figures were carefully preserved, others, particularly body shape and postures, were modified to fit old-world expectations. Both pictures show the

beginnings of cross-cultural exchanges in the doll the little girl carries; she is said to have been eight or ten years old. Thomas Harriot's note to this picture said that Indian children were delighted with such toys. © The British Museum, British Museum Press; The John Carter Brown Library at Brown University.

Physique and carriage provided valuable indicators of one's place in the world. Countless manuals informed the European gentry and those who aspired to gentle status about how they should act and conduct their lives, and these emphasized proper deportment and presentation of one's body in society. Gait, posture, and clothing all occupied central roles in this literature, whose authors included writers as eminent as Erasmus. The shape and presentation of the body reflected the reality of the inner self.[9]

Thus when English colonists described the Indians, their descriptions began with physique, and it is noteworthy that Indian bodies were universally praised. Readers steeped in the manuals of gentility would have seen their ideal reflected in these descriptions. Their "perfect constitution," wrote John Brereton of the New Englanders he met, was seen in their strength, agility, and straight posture as well as in the complete absence of the physical problems that so troubled Europeans of the time. William Wood, also writing from New England, agreed: "I have been in many places, yet did I never see one that was borne either in redundance or defect a monster, or any that sicknesse had deformed, or casualitie made decrepit, saving one that had a bleared eye, and an other that had a wenne on his cheeke."[10]

Many writers considered the Indians well proportioned, but there was a wide range of opinions about their typical height. The English thought of themselves as generally of medium height, and some put the Indians into the same category. More often, though, the Indians were deemed tall, taller than Europeans. Opinions also differed on how lean they were; some wrote that women were shorter and fatter than men, an indication of good health and fruitfulness. There was no controversy about the admirable erect posture of the Indians, as "straite as arrowes" according to John Underhill. Thomas Morton, who, like Underhill, wrote of southern New England, thought the Indians' straight spines were a cultural product, the result of being carried on their mothers' backs "by the help of a cradle made of a board forket at both ends, whereon the childe is fast bound, and wrapped in furres." He summed up his impressions: "to give their character in a worde, they are as proper men and women for feature and limbes as can be found, for flesh and bloud as active." John Smith similarly described the Susquehannocks, who "seemed like Giants to the English." One he met at the head of Chesapeake Bay was "the goodliest man that ever we beheld."[11] Descriptions of Indians the writers knew "experimentally" all portrayed the Indians as admirable physical specimens, more perfect examples of European bodies. And, as in Europe, the "better sort" were seen as more attractive, their physical beauty reflecting their inner qualities.

Eyewitnesses did not dip into the inherited bag containing archetypes of human monsters—people with one large foot, or with no heads and eyes in the middle of their chests, or with huge ears used as sunshades— that readers knew from the medieval and classical writers.[12] Monstrous Indians, though, sometimes entered such accounts when writers were transmitting stories of those who lived beyond the frontier of contact. These writers had never seen the monsters they wrote of, but they always claimed reliance on unimpeachable sources. Such sources were Indian informants, who were usually describing their own traditional enemies, or occasionally other Europeans. The reported characteristics of these monstrous people always served to make them seem stronger and more fearsome than the Indians the colonists knew, and these enemies were usually described as absolutely fearless fighters.

One of the earliest accounts, that of David Ingram, reported the existence of cannibals in North America. Ingram was one of a hundred sailors set ashore by John Hawkins in the Gulf of Mexico. He claimed to have walked with two other men from there to Acadia in one year, 1568–69, where they were picked up by fishermen. His *Relation*, apparently a mixture of genuine observations and remembered stories and experiences of other areas, was mentioned by George Peckham in his *True Reporte*, and was printed in the first edition of Hakluyt's *Principall Navigations*. Ingram reported that the Indians he had come to know were enemies of the "Canibals or meneaters," who "have teeth like dogs teeth, and thereby you may know them." Peckham made use of Ingram's report, urging support of overseas ventures to "ayde the Savages against the Canniballs" with their doglike teeth. Samuel Purchas's *Pilgrimage* passed on rumors from the short-lived Sagadahoc colony in Maine of cannibals with teeth three inches long, but admitted that the colonists had not seen these monsters.[13]

New England colonists, all of whose informants were Algonquian speakers, gathered reports of two such fierce groups: the Iroquoian Mohawks of the Hudson River region and the Tarrentines, who were the Wabanakis of western Maine. Philip Vincent wrote that "Mowhacks" were "cruell Bloody Canniballs," and that all other Indians were afraid of them. During the Pequot War of 1636–37, the "cruell but wily" Mohawks mutilated some Pequots who had fled to them seeking refuge and sent parts of them back to the English. William Wood began his discussion of the New England Indians with the "cruell bloody " Mohawks who "come down upon their poore neighbours with more than bruitish savagenesse." Wood wrote that he had interviewed a man who had been a Mohawk captive and examined his scarred arm. This man recollected having been painted and "hem'd in with a ring of bare skinned morris dancers" every morning while in captivity. Later, "when they had sported enough about this walking Maypole, a rough hewne satyre cutteth a gobbit of flcsh from his brawnie arme, eating it in his view." The Mohawks were said to be as strong as they were cruel. Wood heard from "an honest gentleman" that he saw one of them "with a fillippe with his finger kill a dogge." They were also portrayed as desperate fighters, with their war cry of "*Hadree Hadree succomee, succomee*, we come we come to sucke your blood" and their style of fighting using "Tamahaukes" and javelins, disdaining bows and arrows as cowardly. Wood transmitted native testimony that the Tarrentines were almost as fearsome: "saving that they eate not mans flesh, are little lesse savage, and cruell than these Canniballs."[14]

Even while passing on these reports of monstrous peoples, editors in England raised doubts about them. Ingram's *Relation* was dropped from the second edition of Hakluyt's *Principal Navigations*, as Samuel Purchas later wrote, because of "some incredibilities of his reports." Purchas himself cast doubt on the veracity of the Sagadahoc report of cannibals with three-inch teeth. He printed the story, but added a marginal note: "These seem to be the deformed Armouchiquois made in the telling more dreadfull." And Wood concluded his discussion of the Mohawks and Tarrentines by reiterating that he was passing on hearsay: "But to leave strangers, and come to declare what is experimentally knowne of the Indians, amongst whom we live. . . ." He affirmed that he had not seen any vicious monsters.[15]

Roger Williams repeatedly referred to savage cannibals, whose food was the bark of trees mixed with the fat of animals or people, and who were "the terrour of the neighbour Natives." He wrote that they made "a delicious monstrous dish of the head and brains of their enemies." Yet these discussions always included a metaphorical wave of the hand, as Williams conveyed their remoteness by saying they lived "up into the west two, three, or foure hundred miles from us." And even they were not permanently set apart but were potentially reclaimable: "and yet these Rebells, the Sonne of God may in time subdue." They might even turn out to love God more fully: "great sinners forgiven love much."[16]

Descriptions quickly moved on from Indian bodies to the clothes that covered them. Because attire played such a key role in maintaining categories in England, colonists assumed that Indian dress and hairstyles would be the society's most important markers, and even brief accounts sometimes devoted more than a page to elaborate descriptions of all the various hair and apparel fashionings the author had seen. Discussions concentrated on details of clothing that changed with seasons, with age or marital status, or that marked higher or lower rank. Readers took sat-isfaction from knowing that dress performed such social functions.

On the other hand, everyone "knew" that savages are naked. The naked savage, a staple of European assumption, is found even in eye-witness accounts. Some writers gave detailed descriptions of Indian dress; others flatly spoke of the Indians as naked. Often writers presented one kind of portrait in one context and used the single adjective naked in others. "Naked" was thus a complex word, conveying a variety of lev-els of meaning and would have been read in that way. Clearly it did not mean completely without clothes, which would have been rendered by the phrase "stark naked." For many, it seems to have implied that Indian clothing was less elaborate than European, lacking the layers so com-mon at home. English men and women wore, when sleeping as well as awake, a long shirtlike shift over which their other clothes were tied or buttoned on. A person wearing only a shift was described as naked.[17]

John Speed, who wrote one of the earliest authentic histories of Britain in 1611, drew on reports from America and ancient chronicles in dis-cussing whether the ancient British went naked. He based his analysis on Julius Caesar's account "(as being auncientest)" to refute reports of literal nakedness, "as neglective either of weathers iniurie, or of civill modesty." Even the most primitive wore animal skins, but all the ancient inhabitants of England wore little, a practice supported by their hardi-ness: "The like patience we find even now not onely in the wilder Irish, and Virgineans, but in rogues and Wanderers of our owne Countrey."[18]

Writers who used the term naked often tied it to simplicity in cloth-ing, as when William Bradford and Edward Winslow wrote that south-ern New England Indians were naked, wearing "onely a skin around their middles." Similarly, George Percy portrayed the Indians in Virginia as "altogether naked, but their privities are covered with Beasts skinnes beset commonly with little bones, or beasts teeth."[19] But even those who wrote of the Indians in this way often emphasized their modesty, another attribute the conduct manuals associated with virtuous carriage. William Wood, for example commended the modesty of Indian women, though several times he referred to the Indians as naked, and Roger Williams warned against associating nakedness with immodesty. Thomas Morton repeatedly praised the modesty of Indian men and women, and wrote "they seeme to have as much modesty as civilized people, and deserve to be applauded for it," while Bradford and Winslow at Plymouth went further, saying that Indian women were "more mod-est then some of our English women."[20]

Williams, throughout his *Key into the Language of America*, insisted on a pervasive and literal nakedness among the Indians and presented a more nuanced account. There were two sorts of nakedness. Children, he wrote, went stark naked until age ten or twelve, although girls' genitals were covered from infancy, a claim corroborated by John White's painting of an Indian girl. Adults wore a kind of apron "after the pattern of their and our first Parents" and a long mantle of skins or English wool. Inside their houses the mantle was cast aside and only the apron worn, but "I have never seen that wantonesse amongst them, as, (with griefe) I have heard of in Europe." Old men made cloaks of fine turkey feathers comparable to English velvet.[21]

"Naked" was one of those words that seemed automatically to go with the word savage"; and promoters without any experience of America used it freely in their writing. The armchair traveler Samuel Purchas even "corrected" James Rosier's eyewitness description of Indian women wearing beaver skins, substituting the single word "naked" when he reprinted Rosier's account of New England.[22] The word's rhetorical use evoked a complex set of meanings with little relation to what travelers actually saw. For some writers, particularly those whose direct experience was limited or nonexistent, the presumed nakedness of the Indians served a utilitarian purpose. Writers drew conclusions about the American climate, arguing that it must be mild if the natives lived comfortably without elaborate clothing.[23] Others, citing the support that would flow to the English textile industry from sales to the naked savages of America, argued, as did Richard Hakluyt, that "great multitudes of course clothes" would be sold to those who lived in regions with "sharpe and nippinge winters."[24] The poor of England could be employed providing warm coverings for the deprived people of America.

"Naked" also hinted at a more pervasive vulnerability to some writers. To be naked was to be weak and defenseless against both the weapons and the ideas of Europeans. Indians, they implied, lacked a hard shell of complex culture and were therefore open to the new. As Richard Eden wrote in transmitting early Spanish reports and before direct English experience, "these simple gentiles lyvinge only after the lawe of nature, may well bee lykened to a smoothe and bare table unpainted, or a white paper unwritten, upon." The nakedness of the Indians was the guarantee of English superiority. Promoters, especially of early projects, argued, as did Sir George Peckham in 1583, that settlement would be easy, "these Savages, beeing a naked kinde of people, voyde of the knowledge of the discipline of warre." Similarly, Edward Hayes said the Indians were "simple, naked, and unarmed."[25] The poor simple Indians presented by these writers would welcome the English and their way of life; those few who might attempt to resist could easily be dealt with.

Yet another connotation of "naked" reversed the equation. Some readers drew the conclusion that the simplicity of the Indians represented a kind of superiority, because they were content with little rather than constantly seeking novelty and excess as so many Christians did. Adam and Eve were naked in Eden, clothed only in "Originall purity" until they sinned and became aware of their shame. Adam could not answer God's question, "Who tolde thee, that thou was naked?" Their need to cover their bodies was the visible emblem of their sinfulness, and God "made coates of skinnes, and clothed them" before expelling Adam and Eve from the garden.[26]

Arthur Barlowe, in the initial report from Roanoke, played with the theologically dangerous idea that the Indians might live in prelapsarian innocence, that they might not have participated in Adam's sin and the sentence of God: "in the sweat of thy face shalt thou eat bread." Barlowe wrote, "Wee found the people most gentle, loving, and faithfull, void of all guile, and treason, and such as lived after the manner of the golden age. The earth bringeth foorth all things in aboundance, as in the first creation, without toile or labour." Richard Hakluyt published Barlowe's account in the first edition of his great collection, *The Principall Navigations, Voiages, Traffiques, and Discoveries of the English Nation*, in 1589, but when he reprinted it in the second edition of 1598–1600, Hakluyt omitted the claim that the Indians reaped the earth's bounty without labor. By then the Roanoke colonists had been abandoned in America; no attempt to reach them had been made for almost a decade, and early hopes of an easy settlement had vanished. Moreover, Hakluyt's patron Sir Walter Ralegh had been forced to defend himself against a charge of atheism before the Court of High Commission in 1594, and Thomas Harriot and others interested in colonization had been mentioned as sources of dangerous thoughts. Hakluyt may have decided it was safer or more politic to eliminate the theologically questionable observation. Ten years after Hakluyt's new edition began to come out, Harriot, who never published another word after his *Briefe and True Report*, wrote to Johannes Kepler, saying, "Our situation is such that I still may not philosophize freely; we are still stuck in the mud."[27]

The association of nakedness with innocence continued to be problematic. The Reverend Alexander Whitaker, while he was instructing the captive Pocahontas in the Christian faith, exhorted the English to contribute to missionary efforts, calling the Indians "naked slaves of the divell." His book is a festival of plays on the word naked. Whitaker, a puritan and the son of a Regius professor of divinity at Cambridge University, attempted to subvert the lesson of Genesis, writing that "they live naked in bodie, as if their shame of their sinne deserved no covering." And, he went on, "Their names are as naked as their bodies." But his book also offered proof that nakedness really meant simplicity, even virtue. In his opening he addressed the book's readers, exhorting them to remember that "none other be worthie of God, but those that lightly esteeme of riches. Nakednesse is the riches of nature, vertue is the only thing that makes us rich and hounourable in the eyes of wise men." His friend, William Crashaw, stated in the book's preface that Whitaker had not written it for publication. If he had, he would have "written it in Latine or in Greeke, and so to have decked it for phrase and stile, and other ornaments of learning and language" as to show his attainments. But the Virginia Company decided to publish it nonetheless "so the naked and plaine truth may give a just affront to the cunning and coloured falshoods devised by the enimies of the Plantation."[28] Direct prose, naked in its simplicity, was the best way to confront clever, sophisticated enemies. What did this suggest to readers about the primitive simplicity of the Americans confronting English sophistication?[29]

As the colonies became established and new Euramericans tried to explain themselves to English readers, simplicity became a positive virtue. The tradition enunciated by Alexander Whitaker's editors, that America proudly expressed itself in a plain, direct style, so unadorned as to appear naked, was appropriated as the essence of Euramerican identity. Early on, Robert Cushman, in publishing the sermon he had preached in Plymouth colony, refused to apologize for his unadorned prose: "To paint out the Gospel in plain and flat English, amongst a company of plain Englishmen (as we are,)is the best and most profitable teaching; and we will study plainness, not curiosity, neither in things human nor heavenly." Proudly proclaiming "I am an Indian" at the end of the century, Virginian Robert Beverley compared American directness and sincerity to European convolution in his *History and Present State of Virginia*, where he celebrated "the Plainness of my Dress." His preface set forth the difference: "Truth desires only to be understood, and never affects the Reputation of being finely equipp'd. It depends upon its own intrinsick Value, and, like Beauty, is rather conceal'd, than set off, by Ornament."[30]

Even in the 1630s some commended the simplicity, even the nakedness, they found in the Indians without going so far as Barlowe, especially two men writing of their New England experiences. One was William Wood, who wrote to promote the puritan colony of Massachusetts Bay, and the other was Thomas Morton, the most persistent thorn in the puritans' side. Morton evoked the Genesis story of the expulsion from Eden when he wrote: "Now since it is but foode and rayment that men that live needeth (though not all alike,) why should not the Natives of New England be sayd to live richly having no want of either: Cloathes are the badge of sinne, and the more variety of fashions is but the greater abuse of the Creature."

Both Morton and Wood argued that the clothes the Indians wore were better suited to their bodies and way of life than English clothing would be. Because of their superior adaptation to the American environment, the Indians, they wrote, should not be encouraged to abandon their traditional ways of dressing. Morton concluded, "In this kinde of ornament, (they doe seeme to me) to be hansomer, then when they are in English apparrell, their gesture being answerable to their one habit and not unto ours." Wood agreed in transmitting what native friends had told him: the Americans did not want English coverings except "a good course blanket, thorough which they cannot see" or a piece of "broade cloth . . . they love not to be imprisoned in our English fashion." Moreover Wood judged them "more amiable to behold (though only in Adam's livery) than many a compounded phantasticke in the newest fashion." Indians told him they rejected the imported apparel partly because they refused to spend extra time dressing themselves, and partly "because their women cannot wash them when they bee soyled, and their meanes will not reach to buy new when they have done with their old . . . therefore they had rather goe naked than be lousie and bring their bodies out of their old tune, making them more tender by a new acquired habit, which poverty would constraine them to leave."[31] Wearing the same clothes day after day with infrequent cleaning did not bother the English unduly, and most were accustomed to the lice and fleas that shared their lives.[32] Thus, Wood implied that Indian simplicity involved a higher standard of cleanliness and hardiness.

English and Indians both considered clothing a fundamental demarcator as well as the most immediate emblem of the difference between the two peoples. Right from the beginning the Indians were as interested in English clothing as the voyagers were in the Indians' dress. Arthur Barlowe, writing of the initial encounter on his reconnoitering voyage to Roanoke, said that the native name for the region was "Wingandacoa." But the colony's sponsor, Sir Walter Ralegh, later wrote that the Indians' reply to the explorers' question actually meant, "you weare good clothes, or gay clothes." Ralegh, embarrassed, appealed to Queen Elizabeth, who allowed the entire area she had granted him, from Florida to Newfoundland, to be renamed Virginia in her honor.[33]

Roger Williams reported that the Narragansetts' word for Europeans meant "Coat-men, or clothed." Williams told them that Christians had been given clothes by God, apparently without mentioning the circum-

stances. In chapter-ending verses he represented the Indians musing on
the crimes they had heard were committed in Europe, and on the oaths
they heard Christians in America utter, and asking, "If such doe goe in
Cloaths, And Whether God they know?" The Indians, for their part,
averred in Williams's rendition:

> We weare no Cloaths, have many Gods,
>   And yet our sinnes are lesse:
> You are Barbarians, Pagans wild,
>   Your Land's the Wildernesse.

He reminded his readers that Indians and English would both appear
naked before God at the Last Judgment.[34]

The social functions of clothes were exemplified in details that were
of consuming interest to many observers, such as whether Americans
wore skins with the hair on the inside or outside. Often a writer simply
affirmed that Indians' genitals were decently covered. Some described
Indian clothing in detail, and these reports focused on whether clothes
reflected gender and age differences. New England writers described deer-
skin leggings—"long hosen up to their groynes, close made; and above
their groynes to their wast another leather"— that attached to belts or
loincloths and extended to their moccasins, and compared these to "Irish
trousers." William Strachey, writing of Virginia, also likened these leggings to "the fashion of the Turkes or Irish Trouses."[35] Virginia observers
compared native skin cloaks to "Irish mantels," as did William Wood
and Martin Pringe in New England.[36]

In instances where the markers worn failed to communicate accurately, both Indians and English were perplexed and frustrated in trying
to "read" a person's self-presentation. A Jesuit report from Maryland,
though asserting that Indian leaders had "absolute power of life or death
over their people," a power far beyond that of English monarchs, remarked that they should not be compared to European princes, because,
in the writer's view, they were not sufficiently distinguished from the
common sort of people in their dress and ornaments. Actual power mattered less for this writer than visible effect.[37]

This preoccupation with clothes as symbols and with the need to get
them right is most graphically demonstrated in the case of Thomas or
Thomasine Hall, whose self-presentation was both male and female. The
case came before the Virginia authorities in 1629 because several
colonists, hearing that Hall sometimes dressed as a woman and sometimes as a man, had tried to find out the truth by forcibly examining
Hall's body. Hall testified to having been christened Thomasine and
being brought up as a girl. At age twelve, with adolescence approaching,

Hall was sent to live with an aunt in London, and continued to live as a woman up to the age of twenty-two. When Hall's brother was pressed for service in the English expedition to the Isle of Rhe in France, Hall designed a new short-haired identity and signed up to go with him as a soldier. Upon returning to England, Hall once again put on women's clothes and lived in Plymouth doing needlework, until, deciding to go to Virginia, Thomasine resumed men's clothes and shipped out as Thomas Hall. Because the specter of a person alternately assuming male and female dress comfortably was so disturbing, the General Court of Virginia set out to determine Hall's true gender, in order to dictate proper dress. After hearing sworn statements from men and women who had carried out the examinations, the court accepted Hall's claim to be both male and female, and decreed mixed clothing expressive of this double gender. Hall was ordered to dress as a man, but to wear a woman's cap and apron; the court also decreed that Hall's dual nature was to be "published" in the "plantacion where the said Hall lyveth . . . that all the Inhabitants there may take notice thereof."[38]

As engrossing as clothing was, much more ink was spent describing the way Indians wore their hair, a subject of intense interest. Hair and its dressing were ideologically charged subjects in England, as the Civil War epithets Roundhead and Cavalier demonstrate.[39] Although many writers faulted the Americans' dress because, like the Irish, it appeared to embody few discriminations between men and women, hairstyles were perceived as involving key distinctions.[40] Generally, Indian men were said to shave the hair on one side of their heads, with that on the other side growing long. Some writers said the long hair was allowed to hang down but others portrayed it as tied up at the back of the head in "an arteficiall and well laboured knott." The knots were then ornamented with "feathers of fowles, in fashion of a crownet." Wood learned that "their black haire is naturall, yet it is brought to a more jetty colour by oyling, dying, and daily dressing. Sometimes they weare it very long, hanging down in a loose dishevel'd womanish manner; otherwhile tied up hard and short like a horse taile, bound close with a fillet, which they say makes it grow the faster: they are not a little phantasticall or customsick in this particular." Wood was told that boys were not allowed to wear their hair in this way till they were sixteen. Meanwhile, as they approached manhood, boys experimented with cuts "which would torture the wits of a curious Barber to imitate."

Henry Spelman, who had intimate knowledge of native life in the Chesapeake, argued that the dominant hairstyle was utilitarian. Although men allowed the hair on the left side of their heads to grow long, that on the right side was cut short "that it might not hinder them by flappinge about ther bow stringe, when they draw it to shoott." But when Samuel Purchas interviewed Pocahontas's brother-in-law Tomocomo (Uttamatomakkin) in England, he extracted an ideologically charged explanation. Uttamatomakkin told Purchas that the Virginians' God, Okeus, appeared to the priests and chief men "in the forme of a personable Virginian, with a long blacke lock on the left side, hanging downe neere to the foote," and it was in imitation of Okeus that "Virginians wear these sinister locks." Hair and its cut was as important to Indian culture as to English. Uttamatomakkin told Purchas that he could not accept the Christian God because of "this defect, that he had not taught us so to weare our haire."[41] Their distinctive long male hairstyle as a marker of identity has persisted among Chesapeake area Indians through the intervening centuries and into the twentieth century.[42]

Among the Indians, as with the English, significant life changes were marked by transformations of hair. In both cultures women changed their hair at marriage. Virgins could be distinguished, according to Williams, "by a bashfull falling downe of their haire over their eyes." Morton wrote that when a girl came to marriageable age, she wore a red cap for a year to make her eligibility known. Other writers reported that married women cut their hair differently from "maides."[43] Chopping off the hair could be a sign of humiliation. Connecticut leaders complained to Roger Williams that some captive Pequot women who were placed with other tribes following the Pequot War had been "wronged (as their hair cut of etc)." Edward Winslow of Plymouth reported that the father of a dead child would "cut his hair, and disfigure himself very much in token of sorrow."[44]

But one distinction common in Europe was lacking; even mature men rarely had beards. Because Indians' beards were sparse, many reporters wrote, they plucked the hair from their chins. So firmly established was this perception that when the Jamestown colonists were joined in their explorations by Mosco, "We supposed him some French mans sonne, because he had a thicke blacke bush beard." The Indians also called anyone among them with "but the appearance of a beard" an "English mans bastard."[45] John Brereton wrote that the New England Indians he met wore artificial beards "of the haire of beasts: and one of them offered a beard of their making to one of our sailers, for his that grew on his face, which because it was of a red colour, they judged to be none of his owne."[46]

Observers worked hard to convey what they had seen and the meaning of hair, eye, and skin color. Accounts agreed that Indian hair was black, although some writers thought that children's hair could be

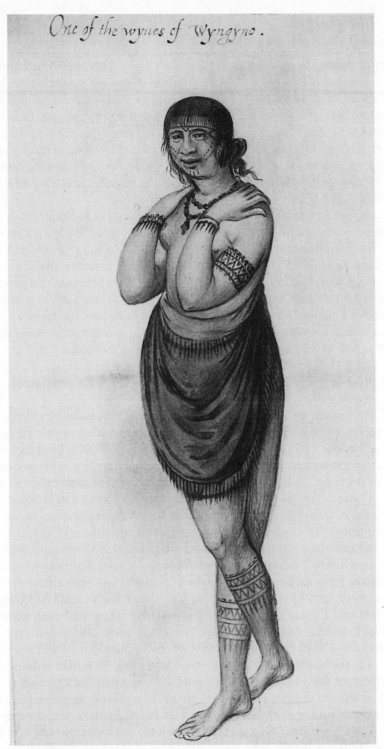

This painting by John White is labeled "One of the wyves of Wyngyno." Harriot wrote that women often put their hands on their shoulders as a gesture of modesty. © The British Museum, British Museum Press.

lighter. Arthur Barlowe reported seeing children with "very fine aburne, and chestnut colour haire."[47] The Pilgrims were deeply puzzled by their discovery of an adult male skeleton wrapped with "a great quantity of fine and perfect red powder" in a European sailor's cassock and breeches whose skull had "fine yellow haire." There was a "varietie of opinions" as to who the dead man could be. "Some thought it was an Indian Lord and King. Others sayd, the Indians have all blacke hayre, and never any was seene with browne or yellow hayre; some thought, it was a Christian of some speciall note."[48]

Very rarely English writers turned the lens around and conveyed Indian interest in the newcomers' appearance. Arthur Barlowe, describing the first reconnaissance voyage to Roanoke in 1584, wrote that the Indians "wondered mervelously when we were amongst them, at the whitenes of our skinnes, ever coveting to touch our breastes, and to view the same." Indian tradition maintained that twenty-six years before Barlowe's voyage some "white people" had been rescued from a shipwreck, but they had died trying to sail back to Europe on makeshift boats. And as we have seen native oral traditions maintained that farseeing leaders had predicted the coming of light-skinned people; sometimes the prophecy was said to have been occasioned by the appearance of a white whale.[49]

Color presented a puzzle to these observers. Indians were never said to be red in this early period; they were almost always described as tanned or tawny. But their darker color was an artificially produced cultural badge. As such, it was far more interesting than it would have been as an inherited, inborn characteristic. Martin Pringe presented the formula "swart, tawnie or Chestnut." John Brereton compared Indian color to "a darke Olive" and William Strachey said they were tawny, "as a sodden quince is of, (to lyken yt to the neerest coulour I can)."[50]

But these descriptions carried no implication that the Indians were of a different race, because the writers hastened to add that they were naturally as light skinned as the English. English observers affirmed that they were, as William Strachey wrote, "from the woumb indifferent white" and Captain John Smith wrote flatly, "they are borne white." Gabriel Archer affirmed that the Virginians were tawny, but "not so borne," and William Wood said of the New Englanders, "Their swarthinesse is the Sun's livery, for they are borne faire."[51] Indian color was a cultural artifact, self-consciously produced on a pale background.

The writers did not doubt that one of themselves, immersed in that culture, would appear the same. In fact Ralph Hamor, accompanying Captain Christopher Newport on a state visit to Powhatan, was startled to see William Parker, who had been captured three years before: he had "growen so like both in complexion and habite to the Indians, that I onely knew him by his tongue to be an Englishman."[52]

Because they believed the Indians were naturally white, observers agreed that Indian skin color was "accidental," the result of manipulation. Some assumed, with William Wood, that the Indians' darker skin was the "Sun's livery," but others learned that the Indians colored their skin with walnut juice or dyes made from roots and minerals. Indian contacts explained that they did so partly because it rendered them more resistant or less attractive to mosquitoes and other biting insects. More important, they enhanced their skin color because they liked the way it made them look; coloring their skin was a deliberate act of self-presentation. As Martin Pringe wrote of New England, the natives were tawny "not by nature but accidentally." William Strachey found that both men and women "dye and disguise themselves into this tawny colour," the women especially "esteeming yt the best beauty, to be neerest such a kynd of Murrey," by which he meant mulberry colored. But he also drew a comparison with the ancient "Britaynes" who "died themselves redd with woad."[53]

Not only did the ancient Britons dye their skin—blue, not red—but John Speed argued that the very names Briton and Pict meant *painted or stained.*" His description of the designs painted or tattooed on ancestral English male and female bodies carried a marginal note to "Hariot's Virginia" as a source, and Speed illustrated his book with de Bry's engravings of White's ancient Picts and Britons. John White's portfolio of paintings of Carolina Algonquians concluded with paintings of ancient Picts and Britons that portrayed the English ancestors with garishly decorated bodies and holding the dripping severed heads of their enemies. Speed argued that a desire not to cover the "painting and damasking" they put on their bodies may have accounted for the British habit of going naked. He cited Caesar's opinion that men applied designs of ferocious beasts "because it made them looke more terrible in warre."[54]

Although skin color as a cultural artifact was a subject of great interest, it made many observers nervous because such manipulation involved the possibility of deception. Color, especially when linked with manipulation, was a word filled with possible meanings. Often it referred to the presentation or appearance of actions, especially hidden or disgraceful acts. Bradford and Winslow, for example, castigated the unscrupulous ship captain Thomas Hunt who, "under colour of truking [trading] with them," kidnapped twenty Pawtuxets and seven Nausets from New England, including Squanto, and sold them into slavery in Spain. Or, as in William Crashaw's preface to Whitaker's *Good Newes from Virginia,* it could mean presentation that cleverly disguised real-

John White closed his portfolio of portraits of the men and women of Roanoke, Secoton, and Pomeiooc with depictions of England's savage ancestors, and de Bry followed suit. This tat-tooed ancient British man, his landscape littered with the severed heads of savage war, and this lav-

ishly painted Pictish woman were included in the *Great Voyages*. The John Carter Brown Library at Brown University.

ity: "cunning and coloured falshoods." Father Andrew White, however, evoked a more benign sense when he wrote that Maryland's leaders "bought the space of thirtie miles of ground" from the Indians "To avoid all occasion of dislike, and Colour of wrong," meaning that they wanted to avoid even the undeserved appearance of unscrupulous dealing.[55]

Partly because of the implication of constructed reality, Indian manipulation of skin color was troubling. Father White acknowledged the conventional wisdom that the natives painted themselves dark red to keep away gnats, but went on: "wherein I confesse there is more ease than honesty," employing honesty in the now obsolete sense of decorum or comeliness. Even more problematic was the Indian practice of painting designs on the faces and bodies of both men and women. Strachey wrote that "he is the most gallant who is the most monstrous and ugly to behold." Father White found the red and blue painted faces "gastly."[56] Roger Williams learned from his Narragansett teachers words by which English emissaries could dissuade Indians from painting themselves: "Mat pitch cowáhick Manìt keesiteónckqus," meaning "The God that made you wil not know you." But Williams also reminded his readers that "our Fore-Fathers in this Nation" similarly painted themselves like "all barbarous Nations." He wondered why Indians wanted mirrors, having "no beauty but a swarfish colour." In times of grief, he wrote, they did not paint themselves for beauty, "but for mourning."[57]

Reporters and their readers in England saw ties between American and European practices. Strachey linked Indian "annoyn[ting]" of their bodies with colored dyes to domestic concern over "our great Ladies" in England with their "oyle of Talchum, and other Paynting white and redd." Part of the danger of such practice was its happening behind closed doors out of sight of the unsuspecting public. On the other hand, reflecting the many-layered debate over face painting in England, Strachey implicitly criticized English women who refused to share the empowerment locked in their cosmetics, saying that Indian women who perfected a cosmetic did not keep it secret as in England, "but they freindly comunicate the secrett and teach yt one another."[58] Captain John Smith was quoted without attribution in an anti-Leveller pamphlet of the English Civil War; the Levellers thought their actions made them seem gallant, but sober and rational people found them "monstrous and hateful" according to John Canne as "amongst the Virginians, they use to dye themselves with the juice of diverse Hearbs, and he is held the gallantest man, that is most monstrous to behold."[59]

Some writers admired the Indians' art. As descriptions moved from preparation of the canvas, dyeing the skin, to painting designs on it, the writers' emphasis tended to shift away from the virtuous simplicity of

Indian life broadly to the equally important theme of the sophisticated ways that the "better sort" manipulated their self-presentation in the style of European elites. George Percy, the younger brother of the earl of Northumberland and therefore a man used to aristocratic display, wrote, "some paint their bodies blacke, some red, with artificiall knots of sundry lively colours, very beautifull and pleasing to the eye, in a braver fashion then they in the West Indies." He gave a long description of the "Werowance [chief] of Rapahanna" and his train—"as goodly men as any I have seene of Savages or Christians:

> The Werowance comming before them playing on a Flute made of a Reed, with a Crown of Deares haire colloured red, in fashion of a Rose fastened about his knot of haire, and a great Plate of Copper on the other side of his head, with two long Feathers in fashion of a paire of Hornes placed in the midst of his Crown. His body was painted all with Crimson, with a Chaine of Beads about his necke, his face painted blew, besprinkled with silver Ore as wee thought, his eares all behung with Braslets of Pearle, and in either eare a Birds Claw through it beset with fine Copper or Gold, he entertained us in so modest a proud fashion, as though he had beene a Prince of Civil government, holding his countenance without laughter or any such ill behaviour.

Percy also described the Indian women's practice of tattooing themselves, imprinting designs of "sundry lively colours . . . which will never be taken away."[60]

Painting and dyeing, combined with artful hair dressing, served the function, according to many of these writers, of delineating differences of status, origin, and role. Such demarcation was absolutely crucial in English society, where knowledgeable men and women learned to read presentations of the self. Portraits contained such obvious markers as the insignia of the Order of the Garter, but also many more hidden references to heraldry or to the subject's roles or office. The number and placement of pearls and other ornaments, the colors and shape of the feathers decorating a person's hat, even the length of the draperies behind the sitter in a portrait, indicated the level of regard due him or her.[61]

Posture as well as decoration conveyed one's position in society as can be seen in new trends in portraiture, especially of elite men and women. Representation of men in positions of power and authority changed in the direction of bolder presentation of the body. The classic pose was of an armed figure, with one arm akimbo and one leg extended. This is a pose of great arrogance, reserved for those who could command respect, and northern European portraiture in the early seventeenth century "experienced an explosion of male elbows."[62] Many objected to such aggressive postures. In his *Chironomia,* a guide to gestures for orators, John Bulwer warned that "to set the arms agambo or aprank, and to rest the turned-in back of the hand upon the side is an action of pride and ostentation, unbeseeming the hand of an orator."[63] This stance was proscribed to any but the "better sort." A particularly telling example comes from Massachusetts Bay where Captain John Endecott admitted in 1631 that he had been "too rash" in striking "goodman Dexter"; only later, he argued, did he learn that it was "not lawfull for a justice of peace to strike." "But," he wrote to Governor Winthrop, "if you had seen the manner of his carriage, with such daring of me with his arms on kembow etc. It would have provoked a very patient man."[64] Gestures, as Francis Bacon wrote, are "a kind of emblem."[65]

Sir Walter Ralegh and his son Wat were painted in this arrogant posture. Ralegh's employee John White painted a Carolina Algonquian leader in the same aristocratic attitude, and Theodor de Bry's engraving of the painting with a note by Thomas Harriot identifying him as one of "The Princes of Virginia" was published and republished as emblematic of Indian authority.

Other conventions of portraying highborn women as well as men were extended to American elites. Renaissance painters proclaimed the modesty of their elite female subjects by showing them with their arms in a "self-enclosing gesture," and White linked the American "better sort" to the European by employing this convention in his portraits of Carolina Algonquian women.[66] White painted separate portraits of a coastal Carolina Algonquian chief and a werowance's wife, each standing with arms folded. Thomas Harriot's notes, in explaining this stance, evoked the European language of civility: "They fold their armes together as they walke, or as they talke one with another in signe of wisdome." When Pocahontas was in London, Smith reported, the courtiers who saw her thought "many English Ladies worse favoured, proportioned, and behavioured."[67]

As they looked at Indian culture English observers believed they saw a society that recognized the same kinds of gender and status distinctions as their own. Reports of graded status markers in badges, body painting, and tattooing were reassuring, because they indicated impressively sophisticated social and communal distinctions and an orderly society. White's paintings and Harriot's explanations of the engravings created from them made this point again and again, transmitting the intricate knowledge natives had imparted to them of differences in patterns of tattooing and hair dressing from village to village, and various badges of rank, occupation, and origin. Harriot wrote that most men had marks "rased" on their backs "Wherby yt may be knowen what Princes

Portrait of Sir Walter Ralegh and his son Wat, both taking the arrogant posture of the aristo-cratic gentleman. By courtesy of the National Portrait Gallery, London.

The manner of their attire and painting them selues when they goe to their generall huntings or at theirs Solemne feasts.

This famous painting was labeled a "great Lorde of Virginia." John White's notation indicated that this state and demeanor was reserved for great occasions. © The British Museum, British Museum Press.

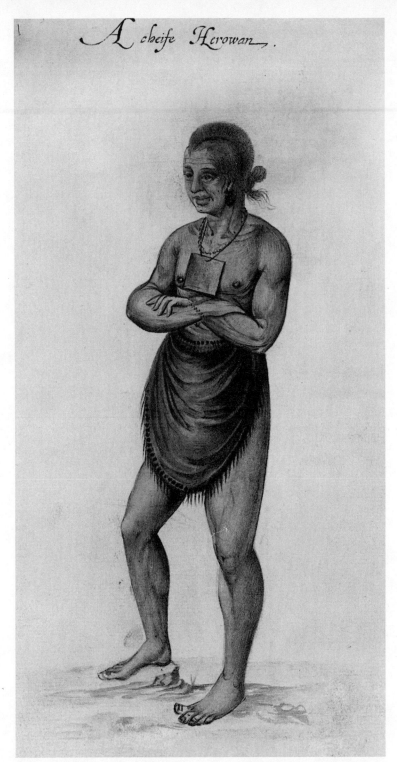

A cheife Herowan.

This is John White's painting of the Roanoke chief Wingina. Harriot's note said that leading men "fold their armes together as they walke, or as they talke one with another in signe of wisdome." The copper gorget he wears offers evidence that the coastal Algonquians participated in long-distance trade networks. © The British Museum, British Museum Press.

The wyfe of an Herowan of Secotan.

This coastal Carolina Algonquian woman, known only as the wife of a chief of Secoton, appears in the same dignified posture as Wingina. © The British Museum, British Museum Press.

subjects they bee, or of what place they have their originall." White drew a figure surrounded by all the region's marks, with an identifying list by Harriot "that they might more easelye be discerned."[68] Arthur Barlowe, writing about the same society, described an initial scene of general trading between his mariners and the Indians, "but when Granganimeo, the kings brother was present, none durst to trade but himselfe, except such as weare redde peeces of copper on their heades, like himselfe: for that is the difference betweene the Noble men and Governours of Countries, and the meaner sort."[69]

White's paintings of Indian leaders showed them wearing badges of office, and assuming postures appropriate to their dignity. The portrait of Wingina, chief of the Roanokes, was reproduced as a woodcut for de Bry's *America* with a note by Thomas Harriot. Harriot wrote of the "cheefe men" that "in token of authoritye, and honor, they wear a chaine of great pearls, or copper beades or smoothe bones abowt their necks, and a plate of copper [hung] upon a stringe."[70] Williams reported such use of tokens in New England as well, where men, women, and children hung strings of wampum on their necks and wrists. Some wore heavy girdles or collars of wampum, and "Princes" wore "rich Caps and Aprons (or small breeches) of these Beads thus curiously strung into many formes and figures: their blacke and white finely mixt together."[71]

Some men flaunted exotic adornments in holes punched in their earlobes, like the bejeweled bird claws George Percy saw in the Rappahannock werowance's ears. John Smith said he had seen men wearing "a smal greene and yellow coloured snake, near halfe a yard in length, which crawling and lapping her selfe about his necke often times familiarly would kisse his lips. Others wear a dead Rat tied by the tail." Their heads were adorned with various emblems, some as elaborate as a stuffed skin of a hawk with the wings outspread, and including such things as "the hand of their enemy dryed."[72] Wood described ear pendants carved in the shapes of animals complementing tattooed "pourtraitures of beasts" that the "better sort" wore on their cheeks, and wrote: "a Sagamore with a Humberd in his eare for a pendant, a black hawke on his occiput for his plume, Mowhackees for his gold chaine, good store of Wampompeage begirting his loynes, his bow in his hand, his quiver at his back, with six naked Indian spatterlashes at his heeles for his guard, thinkes himselfe little inferiour to the great Cham; hee will not stick to say, hee is all one with King Charles. He thinkes hee can blow downe Castles with his breath, and conquer kingdomes with his conceit."[73]

Elite women exhibited the same emblems of rank. In Virginia Gabriel Archer saw a woman leader, whose name he rendered as "Queene Apumatecs." She came to meet his exploring party in "state" preceded

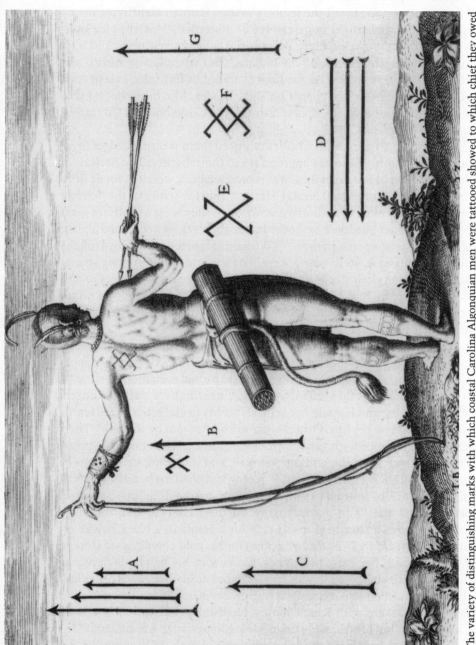

The variety of distinguishing marks with which coastal Carolina Algonquian men were tattooed showed to which chief they owed allegiance, and Thomas Harriot identified each of these marks in his accompanying note. The John Carter Brown Library at Brown University.

by an usher. She had "much Copper about her neck, a Crownet of Copper upon her hed." Her female attendants were "adorned much like her selfe (save they Wanted the Copper)." Her posture also bespoke her dignity. She sat "with a stayed Countenance," and permitted "none to stand or sitt neere her."[74]

Acting the part was a reciprocal process. Not only did the early modern English believe that identity is created, or assumed, or assigned and communicated to the world through signs, but they also believed in the psychological power of donning a role. Once a role was taken up, and one's outward aspect tailored to the part, a person's actions were subtly molded to its demands. English writers describing colonial life constantly attested to their belief in the link between changes in clothing and in personality.[75] The promoter Richard Hakluyt quoted a very early chronicle recording the three Newfoundland men brought to the court of Henry VII by John Cabot: "These were clothed in beasts skins, & did eate raw flesh, and spake such speach that no man could understand them, and in their demeanour like to bruite beastes, whom the King kept a time after. Of the which upon two yeeres after, I saw two apparelled after the maner of Englishmen in Westminster pallace, which that time I could not discerne from Englishmen, til I was learned what they were, but as for speach, I heard none of them utter one word."[76] As with the captive Englishman William Parker in Virginia, language, a culturally constructed indicator, was a surer guide to identity than appearance. The Indians were equally aware of the role-enforcing power of clothes. Powhatan, for example, was extremely reluctant to put on the "scarlet cloake and apparel" that the English sent him until his close adviser Namontacke, who had actually been in England, convinced him "they would doe him no hurt."[77]

Powhatan may have been right to worry because changes of heart were often signaled or effected by changes in clothes. Indians and English alike associated the wearing of European clothes with Christianity, and it seemed clear that one moved closer to being a Christian by dressing as one. Roger Williams told the Narragansetts that it was God who had given the English "Clothes, Books, &c."[78] When Edward Howes in England heard that there was good hope to convert "John Sagamore," he suggested to John Winthrop, Jr., that the Massachusetts Bay colony give him and other "petty kings" among the Indians "a scarlet coate I mean a red coate to wear" as a mark of "respect and honor." Scarlet was an extremely expensive kind of fine woolen cloth, which could be of any color. Scarlet coats for Massachusett chiefs, like the Virginia Company's gift of a scarlet cloak to Powhatan, were extravagant gifts fit for aristocrats. In 1639 the Jesuit missionaries in Maryland reported that the Tayac, a title they translated as emperor, had asked to be baptized, and had "exchanged the skins, with which he was heretofore clothed, for a garment made in our fashion." Earlier Father Andrew White, unselfconsciously conflating European dress and Christian values, had written that the Indians "exceedingly desire civill life and Christian apparrell."[79] Robert Cushman wrote of the Plymouth venture that the younger Indians were ripe for conversion "if we had the means to apparel them, and wholly to retain them with us, (as their desire is,)."[80] Attiring the Indians was not necessarily the complete transformation the English hoped for, though. The Narragansetts Williams knew wore English clothes only while they were actually with English people and took them off as soon as they returned home.[81]

Among the Chickahominies of Virginia the eight-man council of "elders" was the governing body. This "stout and warlike nation," loosely allied with Powhatan but anxious not to be drawn fully into his empire, had agreed to become English allies, thus becoming "King James his men," the first king they had ever acknowledged. Both sides honored the power of self-definition through clothing, as the Chickahominy elders, "no longer naturalls," donned red coats, which were to be sent them annually, and "each of them the picture of his Majesty, engraven in Copper, with a chaine of Copper to hang it about his necke wherby they shall be known to be King JAMES his noble Men." These adornments signified their change of identity, but the English took care to make the copper medal similar to the gorgets worn by werowances. Henceforth the Chickahominies would call themselves "Tassentasses," which the colonists understood was their name for the English. The entire relationship was shaped and managed by the Chickahominies. Finally the elders, pointing out that governor Sir Thomas Dale was extremely busy, suggested that they should continue to "injoy their own laws and liberties" and to be governed by their eight elders "as his substitutes and councellors." They would supply corn to Jamestown, which would be paid for in trade goods. While the English presented all this in terms of sovereignty and tribute, the negotiations actually produced an alliance and trading pact under which the Chickahominies governed themselves as before. So successful were they at managing relationships that they maintain a thriving community in the twentieth century.[82]

All parties to the multicultural exchange of the early years were engaged in learning new languages of presentment and attempting to influence the others' behavior. When the Powhatans desired peace following the great Indian attack of 1622 in Virginia, they sent home a captive, Mrs. Boyce, "(the Chiefe of the prisoners) . . . appareled like one of theire Queens, which they desired wee should take notice of."

Similarly, a Plymouth expedition seeking a lost boy, ten-year-old John Billington, conferred with Iyanough, the Cummaquid sachem, whom they described as "indeed not like a Savage save for his attyre." Iyanough, shaping this encounter, directed them to the Nausets who, although they remained "ill disposed to the English" because of the "wretched" Hunt, brought John Billington to the search party "behung with beades" in another symbolic gesture. As they returned, the Plymouth party again met Iyanough, whose people showed them "all the kindnes they could, Iyanough himselfe taking a bracelet from about his necke, and hanging it upon one of us."[83] Both parties to this encounter understood a powerful language of social symbols involving magnanimity and hospitality.

Both English and Americans also picked up items from the other's culture and adapted them to their own purposes. Roger Williams reminded his English readers that the furs worn by queens and princes were first in "foule hands (in smoakie houses)."[84] Just as Queen Elizabeth sought pearls from America to create the elaborate displays she wore as emblems of her greatness, so Indian leaders adapted items from England to the same purpose. Arthur Barlowe wrote of the venturers' bemusement at Roanoke when Granganimeo claimed "a bright tinne dishe" from among the array of trade goods. He then "made a hole in the brimme thereof, & hung it about his necke," in imitation of English armor, they thought.[85] In actuality, he was fashioning the English dish into a gorget, a badge of authority. And Powhatan, who was crowned on orders of the Virginia Company as a vassal of King James, adapted his new crown to his own purposes and reinforced the exercise of his power. Henry Spelman described the annual coming together of the people to plant corn for the king. When they were finished, Powhatan donned the crown sent him by King James and walked among the planters throwing out beads or placing them in the hands of favored people. Whereas the harvested corn and other offerings from his own people were stored by Powhatan in a specially created building and overseen by an idol, the crown, beads, and other presents from the king of England were stored "in the gods house at Oropikes," the mortuary for the royal line.[86]

While Powhatan deployed his crown, the symbol of his recognition by King James, as he presented himself to his clients, in England cosmopolitan men and women adopted and adapted—played with—aspects of Indian identity. George Chapman's *Masque of the Middle Temple and Lincoln's Inn* (1613), performed to celebrate the marriage of the princess Elizabeth, was set in Virginia. The principal masquers, the court's most prominent aristocrats, took the parts of "Virginian Princes," and Inigo Jones's designs played on the correspondence between the noble English and the "noblest Virginians," the reality underneath the disguise. The

1615 wedding portrait of Elizabeth Pope, daughter of Virginia Company investor Sir Thomas Watson, is filled with references to Virginia. As in Chapman's masque, white ostrich feathers denoted the noblest connections, pearls the riches of the new world. This Elizabeth, passing from virginity to fruitfulness, was portrayed as America.[87]

Francis Higginson reported speculation that the style of wearing one long lock of hair among fashionable young men in England was conscious imitation of the asymmetrical Powhatan male cut. In 1617 Samuel Purchas quoted Sir Thomas Dale and Pocahontas's husband, John Rolfe, on the colonists' belief that the fashion had been "borrowed from these Salvages" by the returning Roanoke colonists over thirty years earlier. In the 1590s both the earls of Essex and of Southampton were painted wearing lovelocks. Southampton's hair was extremely provocative. In an altercation at court he struck Ambrose Willoughby, who, in reply, "puld of some of his locke." Clearly, the earl's "locke" conveyed his arrogant stance. Purchas, informed by Uttamatomakkin that his people wore this style in imitation of their God, was indignant: "(a faire unlovely generation of the Love-locke, Christians imitating Salvages, and they the Divell)."[88] Nevertheless, the fashion continued. In 1631 Richard Brathwait ridiculed London's "young Green-wits" and their shallow affectations: "A long Locke he has got, and the art to frizle it."[89]

Frivolous playing with an Indian identity by London gallants opened the possibility, unwelcome in this optimistic early period, of influence moving in the wrong direction and tapped deep fears among the insular English of how the pursuit of commerce and exchange with the whole world, and the wealth it brought to some, were changing and distorting English society. William Prynne in England and Roger Williams from New England denounced the wearing of lovelocks copied from America, which Prynne characterized as "Effeminate, Proud, Lascivious, Exorbitant, and Fantastique." These and other elaborate fashions threatened to break down the essential division of English society into two unequivocal genders. Prynne argued that in these "Degenerous, Unnaturall, and Unmanly times," women were being "Hermaphrodited" by "Odious if not Whorish Cutting, and Crisping of their Haire." Men likewise were "wholy degenerated and metamorphosed into women" in their "Womanish, Sinful, and Unmanly, Crisping, Curling, Frouncing, Powdring, and nourishing of their Lockes and Hairie excrements." Prynne saw no difference between this importation and the consumption of French frippery: "Are not many degenerated into Virginians, Frenchmen, Ruffians?" Williams denied that any Indian would so "forget nature it selfe in such excessive length and monstrous fashion, as to the shame of the *English* Nation, I now (with griefe) see my Countrey-men in England are degenerated unto." Indian hairstyles and painted faces were foul, he wrote, but "More foule such Haire, such Face in Israel. England so calls her selfe, yet there's Absoloms foule Haire and Face of Jesabell."[90]

Prynne's concern was for his own society and the damage he feared was being done by its opening to new influences and affluence. Not only was society's division into two unqualified genders threatened by the rage for new fashions, but rank and hierarchy were also becoming prob-lematic as wealth brought status to families lacking in lineage. England needed a rationale for controlling these effects. Eyewitnesses who wrote about the American Indians reflected their compatriots' concerns. Those with a degree of knowledge and experience of Indian cultures, intrigued by what they saw, seized the opportunity to instruct their readers on burning issues involving the course and future of English society; cul-tural priorities shared across the Atlantic could be construed as autho-rized by nature.

When English venturers looked at America's natives they assumed they were looking at people who came from a common stock with them-selves. English colonists in the first period of settlement saw Indians as well within the sphere of normal human beings. "Their correspondency of disposition with us, argueth all to be of the same constitution, & the sons of Adam, and that we had the same Maker, the same matter, the same mould."[91] Roger Williams, fortifying his claims with biblical ci-tations, was particularly clear on this point: "Nature knowes no differ-ence between Europe and Americans in blood, birth, bodies, &c. God having of one blood made all mankind, Acts 17. and all by nature being children of wrath, Ephes. 2." He cautioned, "Boast not proud English . . . Thy brother Indian is by birth as Good."[92]

The evidence suggests that the American natives, like the English, were curious about the nature of these newly revealed people and that both interpreted the newcomers and their goods in terms of traditional categories. Everyone involved was concerned to fit these other people and their trappings into their own sense of the normal. Partly because status was so important in English thinking, their lines of analysis cut across the categories we expect them to employ; race, and the exclu-sionary thinking that went with it, came later.

As writers who ventured to America struggled to report their authen-tic experience of Indian cultures, they communicated a picture of grace-ful figures who presented themselves in ways that recognized and pre-served all the distinctions English society considered important. These distinctions bespoke a structured society, one in which Europeans could see "presentment of civility." So close were the Indians to European norms, in fact, that commentators assured their readers that only a series of short steps—aimed at the creation of a favorable context—separated them from achieving full civility. Certainly they were of the same stock and origins as the English themselves. The Reverend William Crashaw, though he never went to America, confirmed this contention from his own experience. He reported that he had seen a "Virginean" living in England whose skin "was so farre from a Morres or East or West Indians, that it was little more blacke or tawnie, then one of ours would be if he should go naked in the South of England."[93] All these reports generated tremendous optimism about the future of American colonialism: the task of bringing together English and Indians, always by "raising" the Indians to English levels, would be easy to accomplish, and soon the two groups would be indistinguishable. Such were the hopes of the early years, informed by the belief that environment was more important than inheritance in determining human character and values, and based on the assumption that the Indians, accustomed to manipulating their self-presentation, would naturally seek to transform themselves into Europeans.[94]

3 Indian Polities

Henry Spelman was a boy of fourteen when he was sent to America in August of 1609, possibly because his mother, a widow with eight young children, found him uncontrollable. He described himself as "in displeasuer of my frendes, and desirous to see other cuntryes." He was "a young Gentleman well descended"; his uncle was the noted antiquarian Sir Henry Spelman. Almost as soon as he had arrived, he was selected to accompany the new president of the Virginia council, Captain John Smith, on a voyage to the falls of the James River for the purpose of bringing peace between the small outpost of settlers there and the natives. Much to his surprise, young Henry was given to Parahunt, an adult son of Powhatan who presided over the region, when the truce was made; Spelman thought Smith had sold him in exchange for an Indian village. He became one of a small group of teenagers on both sides, including Pocahontas and another English boy named Thomas Savage, who served as emissaries and interpreters in Virginia. Apparently they were able to go into situations where adults would have aroused feelings of mistrust.

Back in England after several years in Virginia, Spelman wrote an account of Indian culture based on his year of experiences with the Patawomecks on the Potomac River. He wrote that he had not attempted to learn anything about Indian government and laws, because of his youth, but even more because "I thought that Infidels wear lawless." The only action of the law he could recount was the execution of several people for murder and theft.[1]

Henry Spelman's childish assumption that Indians had neither law nor government, even though he had lived and worked alongside several chiefs, opens another of those categories that early moderns automatically associated with "savages." Lawlessness, like nakedness, could simply be assumed; they were part of the definition of savagery. Some of these automatic assumptions came out of the great classical and medieval tradition of fabulous natural history accounts of foreign lands begun by the Roman author Pliny. Medieval Europe also had its own tradition of the Wild Man, the subject of popular legend reinforced by rumors of actual wild men found living deep in the woods. The Wild Man was a renegade from human society. He lived alone or with his mate only. Since he lived out of society, he needed no government. As he had no need to communicate with other human beings, he had no language. And, because he was ignorant and incurious about the place of human beings in the universe, he had no religion. As his deformed hair-covered body made visible, he was indeed more brute than human.[2]

Some writers contended that the American Indians could be fitted into this stereotype. For example, Robert Johnson, a Virginia Company promoter who never crossed the ocean, wrote this description of America: "It is inhabited with wild and savage people, that live and lie up and downe in troupes like heards of Deare in a Forrest: they have no law but nature, their apparell skinnes of beasts, but most goe naked: the better sort have houses, but poore ones, they have no Arts nor Science, yet they live under superior command such as it is."[3] As wild people, then, the Americans would have been nomads ranging over the land in search of game; they would have resembled the beasts they hunted. They would have lacked law or proper government. And their understanding of the world would have been simple and possibly defective.

But no one who actually came to America and described personal experience of Indians ever projected such an image. We have already seen that the Americans were never presented as hairy, as the Wild Man was, and their straight, agile bodies elicited only the highest praise; they had none of the Wild Man's physical characteristics.[4] Nor did they share his social deficits. English observers came with a set of criteria by which any society should be judged, and eyewitnesses all agreed that the Indians passed, that they lived in civil society. These tests included having a complex language, government by a hereditary hierarchy, organization of society in towns, and agriculture that implied care to provide for the morrow. Religion was also required for true societies.

Humans, the English thought, were above all social beings, and town life was superior to any kind of scattered life. All the other attributes they looked for were in support of this main one. In order to live comfortably together, people had to have the power of complex communication. Moreover, they had to be able to regulate relationships, not only to settle disputes but also to set forth the functions and responsibilities of each member of society. An orderly life was the sign of a healthy society, and order was best achieved by government based on a hereditary structure of royalty, aristocracy, and commons, so that people would not be moved to question their assigned place in the great structure. These were the issues that observers wrote about, and the books that were issued and reissued demonstrate that the reading public wanted to know whether and how the natives of America fulfilled these criteria.

Language was absolutely fundamental to civil society, and many of the colonists displayed tremendous interest in Indian languages. The humanist education of the times centered on rhetoric and taught, following Cicero, that language alone made society possible and separated human beings from animals. Thomas Wilson's extremely popular *Arte of Rhetorique* went through many editions in the second half of the sixteenth century. It was a manual that drew on classical authors, conveying the importance of speaking effectively. Although weak in body, humans excelled "all other Creatures livynge" in one thing: their power of language. In his paraphrase of Cicero, Wilson wrote that humans would never have consented to submerge their own private desires to work for a common goal without the power of persuasive speech. Henry Peacham, author of another popular work on rhetoric, argued that in the past it was eloquence combined with wisdom that "made savage nations civil, wild people tame." Without "apt utterance" wisdom is silent and ineffective.[5]

Eyewitness descriptions strove to represent Indian speech accurately. Much of the interest in Indian languages was purely practical, because cross-cultural communication was impossible without some understanding of the other's language. Thomas Harriot learned Carolina Algonquian from two Indians, Manteo and Wanchese, who were brought back to England by the expedition Ralegh sent out to seek a good location for his colony in 1584, and they learned English from him. Thus when all three went to Roanoke in 1585, the English could learn a great deal about the Indians and the environment, just as the Algonquians would understand English culture. Harriot, who used his ability to gather native knowledge in writing one of the earliest and most sophisticated reports, responded to English interest by including the Indian name for each plant or animal he described, and he demonstrated how to form the plural of coastal Carolina Algonquian words. He stressed that full understanding of Indian culture, especially religion, could not come without even greater competence in Indian tongues.[6]

The later Jamestown colonists used total immersion to prepare people such as Henry Spelman to be interpreters, and in New England ministers and military leaders learned the Algonquian dialects spoken there in order to function as intermediaries. Tribal leaders fostered such learning so that their own voice would be heard in the records, and English leaders understood that the natives were the most important source of information about the geography and natural resources of America. Pressed hard by their backers in England, the colonists needed accurate information about the "commodities" they might produce or procure in trade and about the waterways and land. Promoters continued to hope that native friends would lead some English group to a passage through the continent to the Pacific Ocean. Roger Williams titled his work on the Narragansett language *A Key into the Language of America,* and he spun out the image, saying that it could "open a Box, where lies a bunch of Keyes" and these in turn gave entrance "into the secrets of those Countries." Without a key, he and others had made "grosse mis-takes."[7]

More fundamental issues underlay the study of languages. The diversity of languages in the world had been visited on humans at Babel as a punishment by God for their "pride and vainglorie" in attempting to build a tower that would reach to the heavens "that we may get us a name, lest we be scatred upon the whole earth." God did scatter the people and "confound[ed]" their language.[8] He had even kept the two halves of the world hidden from each other. Now that God had revealed the existence of these hitherto hidden continents, there was to be a great ingathering of knowledge on both sides. As European scholars began to study unknown species of plants and animals, they evolved new ways of thinking about the natural world, and the problem of classifying all this new information led some to see deficiencies in European languages. Study of peoples and languages was part of this knowledge explosion. Some scholars, thinking that God's revelation of the existence of the hidden continents meant that the culmination of human history might be near, studied Indian languages to find elements of that lost universal language people had spoken before Babel. Each language as it had evolved was only an approximation of that great first language. God had bestowed the original language on Adam, and that language had actually been knowledge; each word had conveyed the inner truth about the thing described. Contemporary languages only conveyed the outward impression of the thing and were dependent on context and therefore inexact.[9]

Thomas Harriot, though in his mid-twenties, was the most scientifically educated English traveler to America in this early period, and his report is of the greatest significance for natural history. He went on to a distinguished career as a scientist, although, because he published almost nothing beyond his short treatise on Roanoke, the true distinction of his work was not known until his papers were studied in the twentieth century. Not only had Harriot studied coastal Carolina Algonquian with Manteo and Wanchese and achieved some proficiency before he went to America, but he also created an unprecedented way of recording unfamiliar languages for use in America.

The problem Harriot set out to solve stemmed from colonists' practice of writing down Indian words phonetically, as they also wrote even English words: each person used the combination of vowels and consonants that seemed to render best the sounds heard. Thus for any given word, the records contained wildly different spellings, and one could only guess at the pronunciation based on what the reader thought the writer's own speech might sound like. And yet contemporary scholars believed, as Roger Williams wrote, "the Life of all Language is in the Pronuntiation." Williams tried to deal with this problem by writing his Indian words with diacritical marks to indicate pronunciation.[10] Harriot went much farther, as he set out to create a new phonetic alphabet for which the sounds would be standardized, and to record Indian words in this writing. Then anyone who knew the system could pronounce any word written in it, whether the language was known or not. Harriot titled it "An universall Alphabet conteyninge six & thirty letters, whereby may be expressed the lively image of mans voyce in what language soever; first devised upon occasion to seeke for fit letters to expresse the Virginian speche. 1585"; and historical linguist Vivian Salmon calls it "an astonishing feat for his time."[11]

Finding a way to record all languages so they could be pronounced by nonnative speakers was a practical problem that linguists of the time worked on, but Harriot was also searching for the underlying reality of language, the principles that all languages, however different, had in common. That might be the first step toward recovery of the one great language everyone had spoken before God's anger confounded that knowledge. Presumably every language spoken on earth retained some elements of that original language, though in corrupt form. Harriot knew that Indian languages would be changed through contact with Europeans and that traces of that primary language, if they were present, would be lost forever. Therefore he sought a way to preserve native languages as they were spoken at contact for future study.

Because he was working alone and his attention was divided among many interests, Harriot did not develop his system's potential. In the 1630s interest in Harriot's work revived, and the usefulness of his system for recording Indian languages was again perceived. Early in the 1630s Edward Howes wrote that "by a special providence" he had acquired "a book of Characters, grounded upon infallible rules of Syntax and Rhetorick" as well as an "Accidence and grammer of such a rare method that it is admirable to conceive" both created by "an excellent scholar and a linguist." These were probably Harriot's; Howes wrote of the author that "a prophet hath small honour in his owne Contrie," and he said the system had been "in obscuritie at least this 14 yeares." In 1635 Samuel Hartlib, a promoter of projects to pool and disseminate knowledge, noted that Walter Warner had Harriot's manuscripts and was hoping to publish them. Harriot and Warner were both in the circle around Henry Percy, the earl of Northumberland, and were maintained by him. Harriot's pension was equal to that paid by the earl to his younger brother, the Jamestown colonist George Percy. Harriot's system was never published and there is no evidence that Howes sent it to New England. Later in the seventeenth century a fellow mathematician, John Pell, saw a sheet of Harriot's symbols and called it "an alphabet that he had contrived for the American language, like Devills."[12]

The enterprise of determining the underlying principles on which all languages were based continued, however, and many scholars in the generation following Harriot worked to create a new universal language with created characters like his. Although this "philosophical language" would be created by human beings rather than by God, it would be guided by rational principles that reflected the order God had created in nature. Jan Comenius, a leader in the campaign to bring together all knowledge in a rational system, published a plan for systematizing languages whose English title was *The Gate of Tongues Unlocked and Opened, Or else A Seminarie or seed-plot of all Tongues and Sciences.* Comenius believed that rectification of the confusion of languages would lead to universal salvation for the world. Such endeavors would clearly make a difference; the authors of *New Englands First Fruits,* published in 1643 to celebrate early missionary successes in Massachusetts, wrote that conversion was slowed because of the difficulty of learning Algonquian languages and teaching English, "there being no Rules to learne either by." The diversity of languages in New England was also a problem, "every part of that Countrey having its own Dialect differing much from the other."

Cave Beck sought to continue Harriot's search for *The Universal* Character, *By which all the Nations in the World may understand one anothers Conceptions.* The frontispiece of Beck's book showed representatives of Europe, India, and Africa sitting around a table, with an American in feathered skirt and headdress standing beside it pointing a huge arrow at the floor and holding up his hand in greeting. Beck's preface said for the last century scholars had sought a way out of "this

Laborinth of Languages" and argued that elimination of "all Equivocal words, Anomalous variations, and superfluous Synonomas" would further both commerce and true religion. The result, one of his friends wrote, would be "*Babel* revers'd."[13] Mathematics was thought to be such a universal language, describing an external reality that was the same for all people in all cultures. What had been done with numbers could also be done with words, and the scholars who hoped to create the philosophical language sought as close a correspondence between words and the things and thoughts they described as was possible.[14]

Other scholars developed the notion that a universal and natural language of gestures tied together peoples of all regions. This natural language of signs allowed communication in situations where no spoken language was possible.[15] Practical demonstrations dotted accounts of early voyages, as in James Rosier's report of George Waymouth's 1605 expedition to New England, then called the north part of Virginia. Rosier "signed" to the first Indians the party met, suggesting that they would trade knives "and such things as I saw they most like" in exchange for furs. So successful was this mode of communication that they agreed the time and place of the next day's trade, as Archer's hosts had done three years earlier by pointing to the sun. After several days' trading, when the Americans became "verie merrie and bold," Rosier began to write down the names of things as they were told to him. When the Indians realized what he was doing, they went to get various things and then would "stand by me to see me write their names."[16]

In Virginia similar exchanges were recorded. On an early exploring trip up the James River, George Percy was aided by a high-ranking native named Navirans. Percy wrote that Navirans "had learned me so much of the Languadg, & was so excellently ingenious in signing out his meaning, that I could make him understand me, and perceive him also wellny in any thing." John Bulwer published a combined guide to gestures for the use of public speakers in 1644 called *Chirologia: Of the Naturall Language of the Hand . . . Whereunto is added Chironomia: Or, the Art of Manuall Rhetorique*. A friend who signed himself "Jo. Harmarus, Physician at Oxford" attested to the use of signs in Virginia:

> "In this garb long ago
> We spake with the Indian Apochankano."[17]

Roger Williams began his book on the Narragansett language with gesture, saying the Indians he knew were of "two sorts, (as the English are)" in their mode of greeting. Some were "Rude and Clownish" because, although they would return a salute, they would not initiate it. "Others, and the generall, are sober and grave, and yet chearfull in a meane, and as ready to begin a Salutation as to Resalute, which yet the English generally begin, out of desire to Civilize them." He reported that subjects demonstrated their reverence for the sachem by stroking both his shoulders.[18]

Samuel Purchas collected other kinds of nonverbal communication. He wrote, quoting the Spanish author Gomara, that "there were some in Mexico, that understood each other by whistling." He went on: "Yea, in *our Virginia* (so I hope and desire) Captaine *Smith* told me that there are some, which the spacious divorce of the wilde streame notwithstanding, will by hallows and howps understand each other, and entertaine conference."[19]

Observers in America and their audiences were interested in the peculiarities of particular languages, because language was a prime indicator of a people's culture. The playwright Ben Jonson, like many people at the time, kept a commonplace book, a notebook in which he recorded passages he found interesting or important in other authors. Unlike most, Jonson often rewrote the passages in his own words, making the thoughts his own. In one of these passages he reflected the common opinion that language was the best indicator of inner truth. "Language . . . springs out of the most retired and inmost parts of us, and is the Image of the Parent of it, the mind. No glasse renders a mans forme, or likenesse so true as his speech."[20] Scholars thought that analysis of native languages would be the best way to determine what old-world culture the Americans most closely resembled. Some believed that American speech resembled Welsh, reflecting belief in the legendary voyage of the Welsh prince Madoc and his followers across the Atlantic centuries earlier. Shortly after Jamestown was established, leaders of an expedition to the Siouan-speaking Monacans to the west, recognizing that they spoke "a farr differing languge from the subiectes of Powaton," and finding "theyr pronunciation being very like Welch," asked Captain Peter Wynne, a native of Wales, to interpret their speech.[21]

Many observers tried to learn about the qualities of Indian languages, to judge how complex and subtle they were, as a means to understanding Indian culture. One set of issues concerned their level of completeness and comprehensiveness. Harriot wrote that "every government" spoke a different language and that the degree of difference increased with distance; English writers translated this into a picture of "confused tongues."[22] But as soon as the subject was raised, eyewitnesses quickly moved to place it in context. Christopher Levett recorded that the New England Indians he knew had learned to speak to each other in broken English because they lacked any other common language. But then he brought the point home: "Their Language differs as English and Welsh." William Wood also reminded his readers of the differences in dialect in the north, south, and west of England that sometimes prevented understanding.[23] Very few would have joined the three-week New England resident Robert Cushman in dismissing "their barbarous tongue." And even Cushman's comment can be put in European context; William Bradford who, like Cushman and the other Pilgrims, had accepted many years of hospitality and refuge in the Netherlands, found the Dutch language "strange and uncouth."[24]

English readers would have understood all these arguments against the background of intellectual currents in Europe. The period of early contact and colonization was also the time when European states were taking steps toward creating unified national cultures. Standard English, French, and German were only coming into being; most people spoke regional dialects and thought of themselves as citizens of regions as much as nations. Europe's relationship with America began contemporaneously with efforts to standardize the vernacular, the language of the people, across Europe. In Spain, for example, Elio Antonio de Nebrija created the first grammar of a contemporary vernacular language in his Spanish *Gramática*, written in 1492. Queen Isabella asked what it was for, and the bishop of Avila answered, "Language is the perfect instrument of empire." Nebrija himself called it the "companion of empire." This exchange took place before Columbus had returned with news of unknown lands across the sea, so empire here meant mastery over the provinces of Spain itself.[25]

The English language had been formed through successive waves of invasions—Roman, Germanic, and Norman French—and some in the seventeenth century worried about its porousness, its propensity to absorb foreign words, and its lack of a central core. English was less elegant and unified than other, Latin-based, languages, and some called it barbarous. In 1577, just at the time some Englishmen were beginning to think of venturing to America, William Harrison wrote *An Historical Description of the Island of Britain*. He chronicled the successive incursions by conquerors who brought new tongues, with the result that English had become a multilayered language, and wrote that although he found English speech commodious and fine, "some have affirmed us rather to bark as dogs than talk like men, because the most of our words (as they do indeed) incline unto one syllable." He also noted that five separate languages were still spoken in the Britain of Queen Elizabeth. Richard Verstegan, a principal proponent of the argument that the English were Saxon in origin, was distressed by the habit of borrowing words from Latin languages. The practice brought English into contempt, "some saying that it is of it self no language at all, but the scum of many languages, others that it is most barren, and that wee are dayly faine to borrow woords for it (as though it lacked making) out of other languages to patche it up withall."[26] So vulnerable was English to absorbing new linguistic forms that Richard Eburne recommended Newfoundland as best for colonization because its Indian population was small and therefore the English language ran less danger of being corrupted there.[27]

The notion that Indian languages were simple, less complex and sophisticated than European, was floated in early reports. Captain John Smith wrote, for example, that around Chesapeake Bay the single word *werowance* was used for all "commanders"; therefore, he argued, their language had "but fewe words."[28] As modern linguistic analysis has confirmed, the languages that English venturers learned were in fact simple, but only because the Indians deliberately fashioned them thus in order to shape what the newcomers learned about them. They taught the colonists pidgins, simplified forms of highly complex tongues, that sheared off complexities of verb and pronoun inflections and gender designations and other grammatical categories and offered reduced vocabularies. A pidgin was a "distinct, conventionalized contact language, a language that all its speakers had to learn." Historical linguist Ives Goddard has demonstrated, by examining the regularity with which certain forms were used in the pidgins while others were systematically excluded, that these trade languages were fashioned and taught to Europeans by Indians who thus protected their own languages and their ability to communicate with one another without being understood by the newcomers.[29]

Some colonists realized that they were offered something less than the language spoken by the Indians among themselves. The Reverend Jonas Michaëlius, the first minister in New Netherland, contradicted colonists who considered the Indians' tongue "an easy language, which is soon learned," and he averred that they knew only what was necessary for trading, which relied on gestures as much as words. As for the Americans, "they rather design to conceal their language from us than to properly communicate it, except in things which happen in daily trade; saying that it is sufficient; and then they speak only in half sentences, shortened words, . . . and all things which have only a rude resemblance to each other, they frequently call by the same name. In truth it is a made-up childish language; so that even those who can best of all speak with the savages, and get along well in trade, are nevertheless wholly in the dark and bewildered when they hear the savages talking among themselves."[30]

Edward Winslow of Plymouth wrote that the natives' language was "copious, large, and difficult." He said that the English "as yet . . . cannot attain to any great measure thereof," but that they could understand and make themselves understood "by the help of those that daily converse with us," presumably using the local pidgin.[31] William Harrison had written that foreigners found English difficult to pronounce, although John Brereton wrote of a startling experience when a New England native repeated a question in English back perfectly to him "as if he had beene a long scholar in the language." Others said that New England natives found the letters *r* and *l* unpronounceable. On the other hand William Wood reported that Massachusett was "hard to learne; few of the English being able to speake any of it, or capable of the right pronunciation, which is the chiefe grace of their tongue."[32]

Several writers included lists of native words or phrases and their English equivalents, and these lists provide modern linguists with evidence for the design and creation of pidgins. Early modern language theorists looking for underlying structures concentrated on concepts basic to human life: abstractions such as love, friendship, or beauty and relationships between people, and those who transmitted wordlists tended to focus on these as well as practical words.[33] Lists gave the names for parts of the body, often in minute detail, and plants and animals. Terms for bargaining and establishing value followed numbers and their equivalents, and mercantile terms included praise or blame words. Longer lists told of how to ask for directions and how to make social distinctions. Other lists, though shorter, tried to perform similar tasks. John Smith concluded his pidgin vocabulary with a window into the developing relationship: "*Kekaten pokahontas patiaquagh ningh tanks manotyens neer mowchick rawrenock audowgh.* Bid Pokahontas bring hither two little Baskets, and I wil give her white beads to make her a chaine."[34]

Some sources offer evidence that a pidgin English was also in use, such as Christopher Levett's remark about the Indians communicating in broken English. Wood also noted that Indians were "not a little proud that they can speake the English tongue," and that they used it in front of "stranger Indians . . . from more remote places" who could not understand—just as they used their own languages before English speakers who knew only the pidgin.[35]

Most of the Algonquian words and phrases embedded in early accounts offer proof that the writer had learned a pidgin rather than a native language. But some—like Roger Williams, who made an intensive study of Narragansett—achieved real progress in learning the authentic complex language. He wrote that it was "exceeding copious," sometimes having five or six words for one thing. For example one word for soul came from the word for sleep, because the soul "operates" during sleep. Another had affinity with a looking glass or clear image, "which indeed seemes very well to suit with the nature of it."[36] Chapter 1 of Williams's *Key into the Language of America* opened with the phrase "What cheare Nétop?" and explained that "Nétop" meant friend. The chapter continued with directions for inquiring after all sorts of social ties. The book then presented chapters, each "an Implicite Dialogue," on entertainment, housing, marriage, Indian knowledge of the natural world, flora and fauna, government, religion, and all aspects of their spiritual and social life as well as terms for trading. Williams demonstrated how plural words were formed and sentences put together. He also included words for discussing Christianity to help any who had opportunity to talk with "these their wild brethren and Sisters" about religion and the creation of the world.

Williams began studying native languages from his 1631 arrival in Massachusetts and by 1634 Wood reported that "he can speake to their. understanding, and they to his." Wood said the Indians "love any man that can utter his minde in their words." Williams, who began to concentrate on Narragansett after his forced removal to Rhode Island in 1635, agreed, saying the Americans, like the English, loved to hear news, so much so that "a stranger that can relate newes in their owne language, they will stile him Manittóo, a God." When someone arrived with news, the Indians would gather and sit smoking and listening gravely. They especially esteemed eloquence in their "princes." The rhetorical forms in which Massachusett leaders couched formal speech are preserved in deeds, wills and other documents written in Massachusett. Williams concluded his long chapter on terms for news and discussing news with a reflection on Europe: "The whole race of mankind is generally infected with an itching desire of hearing Newes."[37]

For civil society to exist recording the past was more important than hearing the news. A people with no certain sense of its own past would be like nomads, rootless and free-floating, occupying space rather than living on a land. Readers wondered how the Americans maintained memory of their great events and traditions and of their personal histories, especially in the absence of written language. As James Rosier reported, Indians were intrigued when they saw the English writing; they quickly saw the possibilities of making words concrete by writing them down. Captain John Smith, while a captive, had written a note to be carried to Jamestown. He lied about the note's contents, leading his captors to think he was sending for a special medicine while actually warning those at the fort of an impending attack, but he also specified items that should be sent to aid his release. The main lesson the Indians drew was that the English could make paper "speake" and that intentions could be recorded. Later Ralph Hamor, on an embassy to Powhatan, was amazed when the werowance pulled out a "table-booke he had" and told

Hamor to record exactly what Powhatan expected the Jamestown authorities to send him. Because the notebook was "a fair one," Hamor asked to have it, "it being of no use to him," but Powhatan refused, saying "it did him much good to shew it to strangers." So Hamor made his notes in his own "Table booke."[38]

Reports that the Indians calculated using the same principles of arithmetic as in Europe reinforced European scholars' notion that mathematics actually was a universal language because it represented an abstract reality that was true by definition rather than culturally constructed. George Percy reported a demonstration of American ability to count by tens as well as by ones when Captain Christopher Newport asked a Virginia Indian named Navirans the age of "a lustye olde man." Newport took a branch and dropped the leaves one by one saying "caische which is .10. so first Navirans tooke . 11. beanes and told them to us. pointing to this olde fellow, then 110 beanes; by which he awnsered to our demaund for .10. yeres a beane, and also every yere by it selfe."[39] Roger Williams wrote that the Indians had both feminine and masculine numbers. He was amazed at how quickly the Narragansetts calculated using grains of corn and wondered whether "Tradition of ancient Forefathers, or Nature" had taught them "Europe's Arithmaticke." He also wrote that their games involved "a kind of Arithmatick." Several writers reported that the Indians kept track of seasons; some writers thought the great ages claimed by elders were a result of counting each summer and winter separately. They observed the night sky and had names for the constellations, including naming the Bear as Europeans did, and they recorded the phases of the moon. Edward Winslow of Plymouth wrote that they were "very ingenious and observative" and could predict the weather "by observations in the heavens."[40]

Writing may have been intriguing to the Indians because they analogized it to their own systems for keeping track of events and the passage of time. In addition to records woven into wampum belts and symbolic designs in beadwork, painted bark and skins, and other decoration, the Indians kept track of their promises with little sticks "as by a tally." Tomocomo, who accompanied Pocahontas to London, was said to have carried a stick on which he planned to make a notch for every person he saw so that he could report back to Powhatan on the population of England.[41]

English observers linked American techniques for recording and shaping memory to familiar European modes, and some scholars found in them echoes of England's Saxon ancestors as described by Tacitus.[42] Early modern people learned methods of constructing mental edifices as an aid to memory, and the ancient Saxons maintained memories through verses. Although, as Thomas Harriot pointed out, reliance on "tradition from father to son" meant that people did not know exactly how many years passed since any event, some observers found that native Americans had a prodigious ability to remember. John Lederer, writing of western Carolina, was able to describe the "ancient Manners and Customs" of the Indians because these were passed on "from father to son" in "long Tales" memorized by the children. John Lawson also recounted the orations describing great leaders and events from times past, which "serve instead of our Traditional Notes" and through which "younger Fry" learned their people's history. New England's oral tradition holds that the lore keepers were very carefully chosen for this role, and that the male line of transmission was matched by a female chain. These practices would have been familiar to English readers; in villages throughout England the annual peregrination of the boundaries by the people with their priest reinforced physically as well as intellectually the corporate sense of the community and its place.[43]

Tacitus recorded the ancient German practice of covering the dead lying on the field of battle with blocks of earth, so that high hills grew up, especially in the case of important men. In England physical monuments like the "statues, Trophees and ensignes of honour" created in "fore-spent tymes" served both to aid memory in those who saw them and to "drive them on, to a greater excellency of fame and vertues." Observers saw similar mechanisms in use among the Indians.[44] Edward Bland, who traveled in the region of the Virginia–North Carolina border in 1650, asked the meaning of the great heap of sticks and green boughs by the path. His guides told him that it was the grave of a great man who had died in battle, and that when they went to war, "they relate his, and others valorous, Loyall Acts, to their yong men, to annimate them to doe the like when occasion requires." Bland witnessed another commemoration practice when his Appamatuck guide Pyancha stopped and cleared the western end of a path that ran across their way; he refused to explain why he did this, "sighing very much." Then the expedition's Nottaway guide, Oyeocker, came up and, clearing the east end of the path, "prepared himselfe in a most serious manner to require our attentions." He told of a quarrel between the "King of Pawhatan" and the "King of Chawan" over a stolen consort that ended with the Powhatan chief, who was accompanying "their late great Emperour Appachancano" on a war mission, treacherously killing the other at an ostensibly friendly meeting. The path was maintained and the ends cleared by the friends of either tribe whenever they passed "in memoriall of this."[45] Lawson encountered "Heaps of Stones" at places where an Indian was slain by the enemy and wrote "to this Memorial, every Indian that passes by, adds a Stone, to augment the Heap, in Respect to the deceas'd Hero."

New England also provided such monuments, and Edward Winslow of Plymouth described their effect on the English:

> Instead of records and chronicles, they take this course. Where any remarkable act is done, in memory of it, either in the place, or by some pathway near adjoining, they make a round hole in the ground, about a foot deep, and as much over; which when others passing by behold, they inquire the cause and occasion of the same, which being once known, they are careful to acquaint all men, as occasion serveth, therewith; and lest such holes should be filled or grown up by any accident, as men pass by, they will oft renew the same; by which means many things of great antiquity are fresh in memory. So that as a man travelleth, if he can understand his guide, his journey will be the less tedious, by reason of the many historical discourses will be related unto him.[46]

The tradition of commemorating important events by placing branches on their sites was passed on in New England as well as the south. In 1802 natives of Mashpee performed such rites, and William Kendall was told of similar practices near Plymouth at about the same time; the tradition in Mashpee has persisted to the present.[47] The dedicated missionary Thomas Mayhew, Jr., was commemorated by a pile of stones at the place where he last spoke, and each passerby added a stone; this memorial can still be seen.[48] Such monuments, like today's Vietnam War memorial, became a "symbolic collective text" for the society, linking people to "prototypical persons and events" and shaping their communal memory.[49]

Language and memory were considered prior to government, which was the foundation of civic order. The best government was based on law, which guaranteed the people's ancient rights but was characterized by a high degree of authority and command. Weak authority led to disorder and was a sign of decay, but strong government not based on consent would degenerate into tyranny. English colonists, following the Tacitean tradition, reflected widespread feelings about their own society and government when they wrote about Indian leadership. Thus it is significant that colonial observers lavished high praise on the way Indian societies were governed, particularly the great authority of the leaders and the reverence paid them by their people. All who actually saw native communities functioning affirmed that the Americans lived in well-governed civil societies. Such accounts were particularly striking in the 1610s and 1620s against the background of the constant flow of reports of extreme disorder, degeneracy, and ineffective government among English colonists in Jamestown.[50]

Again and again the writers offered portrayals of Indian leaders, usually using a native word—*sachem, sagamore, mamanatowick, bashabes, werowance*—along with an English equivalent—king, lord, commander, prince, or emperor. Roger Williams compared the American order of king, priest, and prophet to that of ancient Israel.[51] The Virginia Company sternly objected to colonists' calling Powhatan a king, saying that Virginians could recognize no king but King James, and investors chided the colonists for seeming to recognize the sovereignty of Opechancanough, Powhatan's successor. But the colonists could not afford to indulge such fantasies. Indian leaders functioned as kings in their eyes, and they used the word constantly.[52]

What did it mean to call an Indian leader a king or queen? As venturers began to report on their experiences in America, their portrayals of native leaders reflected their understanding of the nature of leadership. In England aristocrats and monarchs, knowing that government rested more on honor and credit than on law or force, took care to surround themselves with visual emblems of magnificence, great state, presenting their persons in ways that affirmed their place atop the hierarchy. They staged lavish public spectacles such as coronations, weddings, and investitures. Other displays occurred within the court or noble house, and the most magnificent of these were the masques performed at the Stuart court. The masques, in which the king and courtiers took part, showed royal power bringing harmony to a disordered world, and gave visual form to the divine order underlying proper human relationships. They were designed to convey ideas that mortal minds could not grasp directly; their desired effect was to evoke in the affirming audience a sense of wonder or awe.[53]

It is against this backdrop that we should read reports like that of William Strachey, a member of the London literary world. Strachey related that Powhatan conveyed "such Majestie . . . which oftentimes strykes awe and sufficient wonder in our people" that, although Powhatan was a heathen, he seemed to possess "an infused kynd of divinenes." Captain John Smith was similarly awestruck. When first brought into Powhatan's presence, he found the "Emperour proudly lying uppon a Bedstead" with "such a grave and Majesticall countenance, as drave me into admiration to see such state in a naked Salvage."[54] The performance of magnificence required an affirming audience, and Smith and Strachey fell naturally into that role.[55] When Smith returned to Powhatan with Captain Christopher Newport, he again experienced the effect of majesty: "This proude salvage, having his finest women, and the principall of his chiefe men assembled, sate in rankes as before is expressed, himselfe as upon a Throne at the upper ende of the house, with such a Majestie as I cannot expresse, nor yet have often seene, either in Pagan or Christian."[56] Later, when Smith was president in Jamestown and visited Powhatan on an official embassy, he sharpened the comparison by describing the welcoming dance presented by Pocahontas and thirty young women as "A Virginia Maske."[57]

Lineage and high birth were traditionally the sources of authority and eminence in English society, but increasingly aristocrats and gentry came to value the virtues embodied in Christian humanism, acquired through education and displayed in conduct and carriage, and it was by these standards that they came to be judged. As James Cleland wrote in *Propaideia, or The Institution of a Young Noble Man,* honor "is not in his hand who is honoured, but in the hearts and opinion of other men."[58] The great were wise, steadfast, courteous, and gave freely of their largesse, and leaders must be seen to be great. As Thomas Gainsford advised English leaders, "Though curtesy, moderatt behaviour, affabillity, and other vertues enoble the name of a Prince: yett are the common people caried away with outward shoes: so that a Prince had the better maintaine his estate with ornaments of majesty, pompous attendancy, and all other observations of greatnes."[59]

Reports from every region echoed the language of English aristocratic self-presentation. John Winthrop's embassy to the Narragansett leader Canonicus "observed in the Sachem muche state, great Commande over his men: & mervaylous wisdome in his answears."[60] Massasoit's great dignity similarly impressed the Pilgrim leaders: "in his person he is a very lusty man, in his best years, an able body, grave of countenance, and spare of speech," while the younger Iyanough, "a man not exceeding twentie-six yeeres of age," was described by them as "very personable, gentle, courteous, and fayre conditioned."[61] William Wood repeatedly praised the New England Indians' courtesy and self-possession, writing that "they are no way sooner dis-joynted than by ingratitude." They hated "a churlish disposition" or "dissimulation." "Of all things they love not to be laught at upon any occasion."[62] Reverend William Morrell, noting the great state of Indian leaders, wrote that they "Keep just promises and love equitie."[63] The Jesuit Father Andrew White wrote of the Chesapeake area Indians in the same vein: "they are generally so noble, as you can doe them noe favour, but they will returne it."[64] In short the Indians exhibited the same natural courtesy, virtue, and care for their reputations that characterized England's nobility. Indian kings acted like kings, "in their behaviour as mannerly, and civill, as any of Europe."[65]

Noble women created similar effects. "Queene Apumatecs" astonished the first Jamestown colonists: "we saw the Queene of this Country comminge in self same fashion of state as Pawatah or Arahatec; yea rather with more Majesty." After exchange of gifts, she asked the English party to demonstrate a gun, "whereat (wee noted) she shewed not neere the like feare as Arahatec [a neighboring chief] though he be a goodly man." Like other chiefs in the region she was under Powhatan, "yet within herselfe of as great authority as any of her neighbour Wyroances." In recognizing strong female leaders the Indians echoed England's British ancestors who followed Boudicca, and of whom Tacitus reported that "in matter of governing in chiefe they make no distinction of sexe."[66]

When William Strachey described the beloved "consort" of a deposed werowance, she was not the most handsome woman he had seen in America, "yet with a kynd of pride can take upon her a shew of greatnes." Her attendants dressed her in "a faire white drest deare-skyn," adding a collar, necklaces, and earrings of white coral, pearl, and copper and finished with a mantle of blue feathers "so arteficially and thick sowed togither, that yt showes like a deepe purple Satten, and is very smooth and sleek." When elite native women were fully decked out, "they seeme as debonayre, quaynt, and well pleased, as (I wis) a daughter of the howse of Austria behoung with all her Jewells." The sense conveyed by these words has evolved. In Strachey's day "debonair" meant gracious or courteous, and "quaint" meant beautiful, handsome, fashionably elegant. Strachey justified this "digression . . . synce these were Ceremonies which I did little looke for carrying so much presentment of Civility."[67]

Pocahontas in London likewise conveyed majesty through her comportment. As Rebecca Rolfe, she "still carried herselfe as the Daughter of a King, and was accordingly respected."[68] When Pocahontas and Smith met in England, she insisted that she would call him father while she was in his country, but, Smith wrote, "I durst not allow of that title, because she was a Kings daughter." She was incredulous: "Were you not afraid to come into my fathers Countrie, and caused feare in him and all his people (but mee) and feare you here I should call you father." But Smith, who was by his own account fearless in Virginia, was not bold enough to countervene social boundaries in England.[69]

These portrayals and references were not created frivolously or ironically in an age when every detail of clothing and other forms of display was carefully regulated according to rank. The splendid urban mansions of the English nobility, some more magnificent than the king's residence, were always called houses, never palaces.[70] Thus the Jesuit official report from Maryland for the year 1639 created a powerful picture when it described Father Andrew White as living "in the metropolis of Pascatoa . . . in the palace with the Emperor himself of the place."[71] Similarly, a colonist's story about Powhatan described him acting in the mode of English monarchs. The story began: "The greate Werowance Powhawtan in his annuall progress through his pettye provinces . . ." Others talked of events in "Opochancano's courte."[72] These words carried clear implications. Henry VIII adopted the closed imperial crown when he broke with Rome, exemplifying his status as a king under no authority but God's. "Your Majesty" then became the normal mode of address to the English monarch, replacing "your grace," as symbolic of a new level of sovereignty in the throne.[73]

Erasmus advised kings to go among their people, showing themselves and learning about their domains. New Englander William Wood also wrote of Indian chiefs making annual progresses to inspect their domains; those with "large Dominions" used this occasion to judge the behavior of their "Viceroyes." When the king entered, he was greeted by "an Oration gratulatory to his Majesty for his love; and the many good things they enjoy under his peacefull government."[74] And Roger Williams actually traveled "with a great Prince, and his Queene and Children in company, with a Guard of neere two hundred" He wrote that the prince's house was both larger and finer than others.[75]

Indian nobility, like European, were portrayed as proudly holding themselves apart, refusing "to be importuned against their own likings . . . nor to condiscend to every request." Christopher Levett observed in New England that "Sagamores will scarce speake to an ordinary man," just as Ralph Hamor reported that when some Indians approached the captive Pocahontas she would talk to "them of the best sort, and to them onely."[76]

Indians of the "better sort" were fully cognizant of their own standing and dignity. When the Virginia Company ordered that Powhatan was to be crowned as a vassal of King James, the colonists found great difficulty in persuading him to see it as an honor. Smith was sent to lure him to Jamestown with the promise of presents. Powhatan's reply was full of admirable pride: "If your king have sent me presents, I also am a king, and this my land, 8 daies I will stay to receave them. Your father is to come to me, not I to him; nor yet to your fort: neither will I bite at such a baite:" Even after presents and crown were brought to Powhatan, who understood well the language of gesture and posture, "a fowle trouble there was to make him kneele to receave his crowne."[77]

American prestige, like English, required recognition. Thomas Morton was told of a dispute between two New England sachems over an escort of honor. The "Sachem or Sagamore of Sagus" had married "a Lady of noble discent, Daughter to Papasiquineo: the Sachem or Sagamore of the territories neare Merrimack River a man of the best note and estimation in all those parts." After the wedding, the bride's father sent her to her new home with traveling attendants chosen from among his men. Soon she desired to visit her father, and her husband sent her along with "a number of his owne men," who, like the earlier escort, then returned home. When she wanted to return to her husband, her father sent him a message that "desired the younge Lord to send a convoy for her." He refused, "standing upon tearmes of honor, and the maintaining of his reputation," saying that it was up to her father to provide an escort "and that it stood not with his reputation to make himself or his men so servile, to fetch her againe." The outraged father-in-law rejected this slight, so his daughter stayed with him. Morton found his reaction admirable, noting that it "is a thinge worth the noting, that Salvage people should seeke to maintaine their reputation so much as they doe."[78] Readers would have seen this episode as reminiscent of countless disputes between elite men over precedence and honor in England.[79]

Anyone, English or Indian, who tried to assume status or dignity without true worth risked being held up to ridicule. King James knighted George Yeardley, "a meane fellow," in order to enhance his status when he was named governor of Virginia. According to a commentator, John Chamberlain, the honor went to his head while he was still in London and "set him up so high that he flaunts yt up and downe the streets in extraordinarie braverie, with fowrteen or fifteen fayre liveries after him."[80] As with Yeardley, sometimes the pride of a "Savage Seignior" was presented as ridiculous. But more often observers saw proud carriage as proceeding from the genuine qualities of Indian leaders, comparable to those of true European nobility.[81] Not only did Indian leaders maintain a dignified state, but English observers were almost always impressed by the awe in which they were held by their people. As Arthur Barlowe wrote of his experiences in Roanoke, "no people in the worlde carry more respect to their King, Nobilitie, and Governours, then these doe."[82] John Smith wrote that when Powhatan "listeth, his will is a law and must bee obeyed: not only as a king but as halfe a God they esteem him."[83] In New England William Wood wrote that though leaders did not have "Kingly Robes, to make him glorious in the view of his Subjects . . . nor sumptuous Pallaces; yet doe they yeeld all submissive subjection to him."[84] Absolute obedience, and the majesty to command it, were held up as a mirror to England, a society many believed was degenerating into a cockpit of competing particular interests marked by disrespect for authority.

Many writers went beyond general statements of the authority and state of Indian leaders and tried to exemplify how government actually worked in America. They wrote of paramount chiefs as emperors, in an effort to convey their overlordship of client groups. Captain John Smith began his description "Of the manner of the Virginians governement" in this way:

> Although the countrie people be very barbarous, yet have they amongst them such governement, as that their Magistrats for good commanding, and their people for du subjection, and obeying, excell many places that would be counted very civill. The forme of their Common wealth is a monarchicall governement, one as Emperour ruleth over many kings or governours. Their chiefe ruler is called Powhatan, and taketh his name of the principall place of dwelling called Powhatan. But his proper name is Wahunsonacock. Some countries he hath which have been his ancestors, and came unto him by inheritance. . . . All the rest of his Territories expressed in the Map, they report have beene his severall conquests.

Strachey reported that the land Wahunsonacock ruled was called Tsenacommacah, which may have meant "densely inhabited land," and that his title was Mamanatowick, although the colonists always called him Powhatan. Modern analyses agree that the Powhatans had a complex governing structure; in fact, they are considered "the largest and most complex tribal society that existed east of the Appalachians at the time of the arrival of Europeans."[85]

Judgments matching those of Smith and Strachey were also made by writers who were hostile to the Indians. In 1622, after the great Indian attack directed by Opechancanough had wreaked havoc on the burgeoning Virginia colony, John Martin composed a plan for making Virginia a royal colony. He portrayed Indian Virginia as a series of towns with their surrounding fields resembling shires in England. He wrote that the "revolted Indian Kinge . . . Commaundeth 32" of these small kingdoms.[86]

Smith wrote that every group under Powhatan controlled its own lands, but they paid annual tribute to the paramount chief in corn, game, skins, pearls, and copper.[87] Ethnohistorians differ in their judgments of how large the tribute payments were, and Powhatan may not have taken everything offered to him, though Henry Spelman said he had a storehouse to hold the "goods and presents that are sent him, as the Cornne." The fields planted and harvested for him may have been more important than whatever goods were offered.[88] Because of this system, some ethnohistorians characterize the Powhatans as a classic chiefdom because of the centralization of activities under a hierarchical organization with formal, ascribed leadership positions in both government and religion and "incipient hereditary class ranking" all fueled by "complex redistribution / tribute systems."[89]

Roger Williams reported a layered system in New England similar to those the English found in Virginia: the Indians were "very exact and punctuall in the bounds of their Lands, belonging to this or that Prince or People." Sachems presided over undersachems and the people gave presents to both. When necessary, subjects could call on the undersachems who were their particular protectors to avenge any injury for them. When a deer was killed in water, its skin was given as tribute to "the Sachim or Prince" in whose territory it was slain.[90]

Although they were powerful, the kings and emperors portrayed by English observers were said to govern with councils made up of their great men whose advice they were bound to follow—a system many leaders wished to institute in England in the early seventeenth century. Councilors, who achieved that station through their accomplishments in war, were the "better sort" that English observers thought constituted a hereditary nobility. Narragansett leaders told Samuel Gorton that they had ruled their territory "time out of mind" when they appointed him and other colonists to act as their attorneys in dealings with the government of England. Deeds written in the Massachusett language and petitions to colonial governments confirm this picture; their terminology calls on long chains of oral transmission, and they testify that only transactions witnessed and confirmed by the leading men were considered valid.[91]

Restraints on chiefly power echoed the picture conveyed by Tacitus of the ancient Germans, which parliamentary leaders claimed as the source of English political traditions. Among the ancient Germans important matters were presented in the form of arguments by orators, after which the leading men of the council indicated their decision. Tacitus wrote that judgments were made "using rather perswasion then authoritie of commaunding." Study of rhetoric prepared early modern English gentry and aristocrats for public life; the orator, able to persuade the commonwealth to proper action, was the ideal citizen. English portraits of Indian leaders confirmed their reliance on eloquence.[92] Williams reported that although sachems were absolute monarchs, they would not take action on matters that concerned all—laws, taxation, or wars—unless the people agreed; American leaders also used only "gentle perswasion." Drawing upon her knowledge of her Schaghticoke tribe's oral tradition, Trudie Lamb Richmond affirms that although chiefs had great

Captain John Smith's map of Ould Virginia, 1624, with scenes of Smith's own exploits. Smith wrote that much of his geographical knowledge came from Indian sources. The scenes at top right and bottom left show Smith facing down powerful Indian leaders, but those at top left and bottom right show him as a captive. At the lower right he shows the young Pocahontas interceding in the ceremony which he expected to end in his death. These engravings show the way in which de Bry's engravings of John White's figures quickly became the standard images of Indians. The John Carter Brown Library at Brown University.

powers, actual command was always dependent on the leader's political skills.[93] Early in the eighteenth century John Lawson found the same respect for the general interest among the natives of western Carolina. He described the councils of leaders in which matters of war and peace, trade and hunting were debated without selfishness: "They discharge their Duty with all the Integrity imaginable, never looking towards their Own Interest, before the Publick Good." After discussion, decisions were made by majority vote.[94]

English observers who witnessed Indian councils in operation were impressed by the dignity of the proceedings. The Jesuit Father Andrew White wrote of the Chesapeake area Indians: "They use in discourse of great affaires to be silent, after a question asked, and then after a little studdie to answere in a few words, and stand constant to their resolution." The *Relation of Maryland*, possibly also by Father White, transmitted a more pointed comment. The author marveled at the way Indian assemblies were conducted without rancor. Indian friends told him of attending the assembly at Jamestown and being scandalized to find "that they all talke at once, but wee doe not so in our *Match-comaco*." William Wood in New England seconded White: "he that speakes seldome, and opportunely, being as good as his word, is the onely man they love." The Stockbridge Mohican Hendrick Aupaumut, writing about 1790, described the teaching received by the children of his tribe from their fathers, which included prohibition on loud, frivolous, and quarrelsome speech. Aupaumut confirmed Roger Williams's judgment: "I have found lesse noyse, more peace in wilde America."[95]

Chiefly power was handed on in ways that English readers could recognize and approve. Management of inheritance was a subject of great interest to English writers: orderly passing of estates was a mark of civility. Some writers asserted that Indian inheritance matched the European custom—the eldest son inheriting, followed by other sons in succession, and finally by daughters. Others insisted that inheritance went through the female line. Lines of descent were not easy to comprehend clearly. John Smith, for example, wrote in his *True Relation*, published just a year after Jamestown's founding, that the heirs of the king's sisters inherited. Four years later, he wrote that the king's brothers inherited first, followed by his sisters or their heirs, "but never to the heires of the males."[96] Most Indian societies along the east coast were probably matrilineal, so the writers were struggling to present an accurate picture of an unfamiliar system. *A Relation of Maryland* reported that the royal line passed first to the werowance's sons in turn and then to his daughters' sons, "for they hold that the issue of the daughters hath more of his blood in them than the issue of his sonnes."[97]

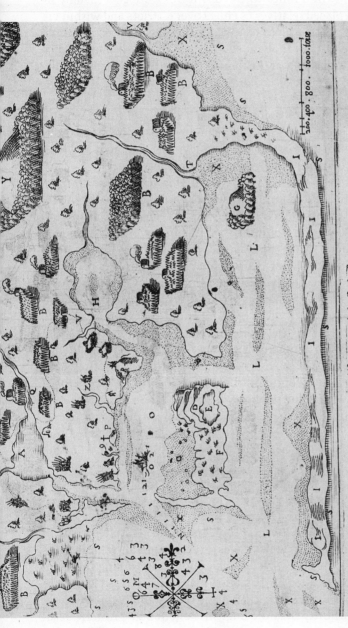

200. 400. 800. 1000. toise

Les chifres monstrent les brasses d'eau.

A Estang d'eau salée.	I Dunes de sable sur vne languette de terre.	Q petis ruisseau.
B Les cabannes des sauuages & leurs terres où ils labourent.	L Cul de sac.	R Montaigne qui descoure de fort loin.
C Prairies où il y a 2. petis ruisseaux.	M Rade ou mouillasmes l'ancre deuant le port.	S La coste de la mer.
D Petis costaux de montaignes où l'isle est plis de bois. vignes.	N Entrée du port.	T Petite riuiere.
	O Le port & lieu où estoit nostre barque.	V Chemin que nous fismes en leur pais autour de leurs logement, il est plein de petits
E & pruniers.	P La croix que l'on planta.	X Bans & baze.
E Estang d'eau douce, où il y a quantité de gibier.		Y Petite montaigne qui paroit dans les terres.
F Manieres de prairies en l'isle.		Z Petis ruisseaux.
G Isle remplie de bois dedans vn grand cul de sac.		9 L'endroit où nos gens furent tués par les sauuages prés la Croix.
H Maniere d'estang d'eau salée & où il y a force coquillages, entre autres quantité d'huitres.		

Champlain's Map of Port Fortuné, modern Stage Harbor, Cape Cod, 1613. The engraving shows well-settled Indian dwellings and productive land. The John Carter Brown Library at Brown University.

Orderly transmission of power, a key element of civility, was also indicated by reports of child kings whose territories were governed by regents. Werowances placed relatives as chiefs over districts and within villages.[98] In some cases, when close relatives challenged a leader, territories could be divided. John Pory thought such a division had occurred when the friendly "laughing King at Accomack" gave his younger brother Kiptopeke, who was "more affected by the people than himselfe," the largest portion of his territory on the eastern shore. Roger Williams reported a similarly amicable division of power between "Caunoúnicus, of about foure score yeeres old" and his nephew, the "younger sachem, Miantunnômu." Williams marveled at their level of agreement and their mutual unwillingness either to give or to take offense.

In these accounts the colonists were struggling to describe an unfamiliar system of dual chiefdoms: an inside chief responsible for the internal affairs of the group and a commander or war chief who dealt with outsiders. When Powhatan voluntarily handed over chiefly power in 1617, a year before his death, he was succeeded by both Itoyatan and Opechancanough, in the roles of "paramount chief, the head of the council," and war chief respectively. Because the war chief dealt with outsiders, the colonists saw Opechancanough as the more powerful and important.[99]

Colonists reported other, less amicable, assumptions of power, as in the case of Powhatan's acquisition of more than twenty chiefdoms. Leonard Calvert, the governor of Maryland, wrote his brother Lord Baltimore, the Maryland proprietor, that "Porttobacco now Emperor of Paskattaway" had within the previous two years "stept into" power by killing the "old Emperor," his eldest brother. Calvert, however, recognized Porttobacco's rule as legitimate and, using the language that European rulers reserved for one another, wrote of him as "my Brother Porttobacco."[100]

Some firsthand observers offered complex pictures of Indian government in operation. They were interested in the questions that raised concern in own their society: How were disputes resolved? How were proper distance and relationships between people maintained? Above all, they wanted to know if Indian society was orderly, and how order was achieved. Although they portrayed Indian culture as lacking the complicated set of written rules for behavior that characterized European polities, most writers argued that the Indians were actually more orderly and respectful of authority than the English. Functionally, American society was worthy of respect.

Law was a subject that exposed the ambivalence many felt in writing about the Indians. Since the Indians had no written laws, some observers wrote that they lacked law completely, or had, as Christopher Levett wrote, "Club Law." Modern scholars have assumed that because colonists wrote that Indians lacked law, they were judging them incapable of producing true polities. But in fact English writers were placing American polities within the proudest traditions of the English nation. Captain John Smith, asserting that Indian law "is custome," implicitly linked Indian and English legal culture. England's legal system rested on the huge body of customary and unwritten common law, which, reinforced by local knowledge, made up the constitution and guaranteed English liberties. Sir Dudley Digges, presenting the case of the House of Commons in the debates on the Petition of Right in 1628, argued that "the laws of England were grounded upon reason more ancient than books, consisting much in unwritten customs." Digges asserted that the roots of the common law, and of parliament itself, were the Saxon traditions as described by Tacitus.[101] Customary law was a higher form of law to these writers. Ralph Hamor confirmed this when he wrote that the Chickahominies were governed by a set of laws.[102]

Experienced observers wrote most about crime and punishment because that is what they saw in operation, but also because customary law was most often expressed in judicial decisions at home.[103] Most argued that Indians punished few crimes—murder, theft, and, some thought, adultery—and that the punishment was death, sometimes carried out by the chief himself. Henry Spelman's assumption that Indians were lawless was overturned by the punishments he witnessed. Thomas Harriot, one of the few writers with a real command of an Indian language, offered a much more sophisticated description of criminal law, with a range of punishments graded in severity to fit the crime.[104] Roger Williams, also a linguist, marveled at the quiet resignation with which punishments were accepted, although occasionally secret executioners were sent "when they have feared Mutiny by publike execution."[105]

Customary law in England rested on agreed traditions as construed and expressed by society's leaders under the watchful gaze of the people. Written law was least necessary where the area of agreement was broadest, and an orderly acceptance of relationships indicated a healthy society. English writers bemoaned the litigiousness of their own society, where the lawyers with their private language, having wrested control of affairs away from the domain of local knowledge, tied people up in "tedious pleas in law to consume us with their many years disputations for Justice."[106] The Indians, as perceived by early English writers, lived on terms of honest accord, thus eliminating the need for written law that forced human relationships in Europe into an alienating labyrinth of rules. Oral transmission of relationships based on deep wells of local knowledge remained central to American life; later written documents supported but did not replace such oral tradition.

Writers of all religious persuasions believed they were seeing human life as it was lived in earlier, less sinful times. The Roman Catholic writer of the *Relation of Maryland* was filled with admiration for the unforced orderliness of native societies: "hee that sees them, may know how men lived whilest the world was under the Law of Nature; and, as by nature, so amongst them, all men are free, but yet subject to command for the publike defence." The Church of England minister William Morrell, who traveled in New England, also claimed that the Indians needed no bonds to keep their promises because they "love equitie." And William Wood, who went to New England in the vanguard of the puritan migration, evoked images of the infancy of the world when natural virtue had made laws unnecessary: "For their Lawes, as their evill courses come short of many other Nations, so they have not so many Lawes, though they be not without some." Roger Williams also wrote that fewer gross crimes were committed among the Indians than in England: "I conceive that the glorious Sunne of so much truth as shines in england, hardens our English hearts."[107] In presenting the Indians in this way the writers recalled Tacitus's approval of the natural courtesy of the ancient Germans: "Good manners are of greater authoritie and force among them, then elsewhere good lawes."[108]

When English commentators discussed what was happening to their own society, much of the concern centered on the decay of hospitality, a term with very broad implications in early modern England. The concept of hospitality was suffused with emotional content, and it encapsulated much: the duty of Christians to help one another, the responsibility of the great and rich to care for the less fortunate and the traveler, and the sense that all ranks agreed on the justness of society's structure because none would be forgotten. Many writers measured the degeneracy of their own times, the unraveling of the social fabric, by the prevailing failure to live up to the demands of hospitality.[109]

The decay of hospitality was linked to the massive changes wrought by England's opening to the world and to feared assaults on the powers and separate role of the aristocracy. In the idealized past it had been necessary for the great to garner wealth and maintain lavish establishments in order to serve the whole society. Now the colonization literature rang with the charge that rich men, especially those to whom riches had come lately through new mercantile enterprises, were distorting England's pattern of social harmony stretching back to the earliest days. Wealth and power, formerly used for the good of society in this version of the past, were now instruments of oppression in England where the rule had become "tush! thrust the beggar out of dores." Alexander Whitaker wrote from Virginia that those who neglected their duties to the poor, orphans, and widows were actually thieves hoarding the riches that God had only lent to them. And Daniel Price made the most dramatic accusation of all when he charged those who sought riches at the cost of others with cannibalism, the emblematic crime of the savage. The bread you eat, he preached, is "the flesh of man," and your wine is "the bloud of man, thou art a Canibal."[110] The Indians' example was superior. Roger Williams reported that "there are no beggars amongst them, nor fatherlesse children unprovided for," and the newly widowed were taken in by friends. Readers knew that England could make no such claim; in fact the colonies had provided a dumping ground for orphans. In 1618 John Chamberlain had reported a Virginia Company bargain with the city of London, for example: "The citie is now shipping thether an hundred younge boyes and girles that lay starving in the streetes."[111]

On hospitality and the social contract it implied, as on so many other subjects, the Germans of Tacitus furnished the template: "Greater hospitality and entertainment is no where more bountiful than there, being a cursed deed to barre any man his house."[112] American reporters wrote that among the Indians, as in England in former times, the chief was the fount of hospitality and generosity for all comers to the village. Like England's ancient ancestors the Indians lived up to the ideal better than the contemporary English: "It is a strange *truth*, that a man shall generally finde more free entertainment and refreshing amongst these *Barbarians*, then amongst thousands that call themselves *Christians*."[113] Edward Winslow of Plymouth wrote that "All travelers or strangers for the most part lodge at the sachim's."[114] While they stayed "they receive entertainment, according to their persons, but want not." All the people contributed corn to the sachem to make this hospitality possible and the chief, in return, "bestoweth many gifts on them." Ordinary people gave up their other activities to go and care for sick friends.[115] William Wood wrote that the Indians were "as free as Emperours, both to their Country-men and English, be he stranger, or neare acquaintance." English travelers far from home had been welcomed, and the Indians gave them the "best roomes" and the "best victuals they could." Nor did the hosts grumble if visitors stayed even two or three weeks. Wood also reported instances where the Indians had taken great pains to rescue English people lost in the woods, particularly one "selfe-helplesse person" whom they found almost frozen to death and carried twenty miles to his home. At the end of the eighteenth century Hendrick Aupaumut wrote that fathers still taught their children that they must always welcome strangers.

Like many of the early observers, Wood was particularly struck by the Indians' ethic of sharing, and he presented it in terms that evoked the teachings of Jesus: "They are as willing to part with their Mite in poverty, as treasure in plenty." If an Indian received "but a piece of bread from an English hand," it was "parted equally" among all comrades and eaten "lovingly." They hated ingratitude above all. Thomas Morton also cited the practice of dividing up even the most humble "bisket cake" among the whole company and concluded "Platoes Commonwealth is so much practised by these people."[116]

Similar reports came from the south, where the Indians were reported to have helped the English "as any neighbor or friend uses to doe in the most Civill parts of Christendome."[117] One of the earliest eyewitness accounts, that of Arthur Barlowe's reconnaissance voyage to Roanoke in 1584, described their hospitable reception in an Indian village they happened upon. Although guests had not been expected, the women of the village, whose men were away, produced an elaborate meal presented "with as much bountie, after their manner, as they could possibly devise."[118]

Hospitality was ordained by natural law, and Indians were seen as understanding other ramifications of that law which is common to all human society. Some observers asserted that the Americans, like Europeans, recognized a set of fundamental principles that should govern relationships between nations. In European writings these principles, identified variously as the law of nature or of nations, were considered evident to all people possessing reason and a moral sense. Roger Williams described the operation of international law in America: if a robbery occurred "between Persons of diverse States, the offended State sends for Justice."[119] The governor and council of Virginia implicitly argued that international law operated in America when they discussed the invitation of Opechancanough to join in punishing a tribe to the west that had reportedly killed some Powhatan women "Contrary to ye law of Nations."[120]

The Americans had mechanisms short of war for settling serious conflict. In Maryland, Indian leaders offered to make restitution for the deaths of some colonists in their accustomed way, by payment of "100. armes length of Roanoke (which is a sort of Beades that they make, and use for money)" for each slain person, rather than delivering up the killers as the English demanded. The native emissary argued "since that you are heere strangers, and come into our Countrey, you should rather conforme your selves to the Customes of our Countrey, then impose yours upon us." Lawson wrote that Carolina natives also accepted useful items to satisfy revenge.[121] Educated readers would again have called to mind Tacitus's portrait of their ancestors, the Germans, who accepted a set number of animals in compensation for deaths. Tacitus wrote that the "common good" is served by such a system, "for where libertie is, there private enmities are dangerous." For lesser offenses fines were levied and divided between the injured party and the king or city.[122]

Peacekeeping systems sometimes failed, as in Europe, and war resulted. "Warlike" was another of those words that fitted naturally with "savage." Europeans assumed that Indians would be devoted to war and preparation for war, and that much of the presumed savagery of native life was a result of immersion in constant and unreasoning war.[123] English observers did make war a central theme in their portrayals of the Indians, and when they attempted to estimate populations, they counted only men capable of fighting. Gabriel Archer from Jamestown, for example, wrote that Indian warfare was "violent Cruell and full of Celerity," but he was actually describing a sham battle put on as an after-dinner show.[124] Picturing Indians as involved in continuous warfare offered a way of conceptualizing the English relationship to the Indians. Policy makers assumed, for example, that chiefs could be induced to allow or even welcome settlement because of the prospect of having technologically advanced European neighbors as allies. Similarly, Indians would be amenable to control, they thought, as the intruding English offered alliance and aid to one or the other side in nearby conflicts. Those for whom war was a way of life lost a portion of their autonomy.

Feelings about war and its place in civilized life provoked, as with many other subjects, division in the minds of English writers. The English watched with fascinated horror the destruction and atrocities in Germany during the Thirty Years' War (1618–48) and feared a "German war" in England. They hated the effects that flowed from having soldiers billeted among the populace, and found standing armies dangerous. Whereas war and savagery seemed to go together, the blessings of peace allowed a flourishing life and culture. At the same time, however, English writers like Ben Jonson and Sir Francis Bacon, who thought their own society was declining from an earlier vigor and purity, argued that prolonged peace sapped the masculine vitality of the population, and bred effeminacy and corruption.[125] This theme reverberated through the writings of Tacitus, who contrasted the ancient British and French. The warlike Britons were strong, "not mollified yet by long peace," but through prolonged peace the French had become cowards, so that "shipwrack was made both of manhood and libertie togither."[126]

Given the general assumption that native life involved unceasing war and vengeful cruelty, it is surprising to see that most English observers found Indian warfare to be understated, almost trivial; Captain John Mason said the Indians fought in the Pequot War "after their feeble manner." Roger Williams wrote that "Their Warres are farre lesse bloudy and devouring then the cruell Warres of Europe; and seldome twenty slaine in a pitcht field." Captain John Underhill, who led English forces in the Pequot War agreed: "they might fight seven years and not kill seven men." Their warfare was "more for pastime, then to conquer and sub-due enemies."[127]

The Pequots were pursued to what the English thought was their ex-tinction, and this forms a striking contrast to native modes of warfare. Opechancanough led devastating attacks on the English settlements in Virginia in 1622 and 1644, and both times the colonists were reeling in their aftermath, but neither was followed up by continued assaults. Thus the opportunity to destroy the plantations altogether was foregone. American war was premised on the assumption that a defeated enemy would withdraw. Earlier in Virginia Henry Spelman had seen a battle be-tween the Patawomecks and the Massawomecks that ended as soon as the Massawomecks had shot all their arrows without much result. Williams said that battles usually ended as soon as some were wounded.[128]

Large-scale attacks occurred—Sir Thomas Dale said that Powhatan could assemble a thousand warriors in two or three days—but these were rare; most battles were more like ambushes or raids. American warfare differed because typically its purpose was not to establish dominion over lands, as European countries sought to do, but rather to add or punish clients and to take captives. As John Smith wrote, "They seldome make warre for lands or goods, but for women and children, and principally for revenge." Women taken as captives were incorporated into the village, because, as Edward Winslow was told in New England, those with the most women were the most wealthy. Williams reported that the Narra-gansetts hid their women and children deep in the swamps in time of war, and compared this to the Irish use of bogs.[129]

Indians attempted to terrify their enemies. John Smith mentioned an instrument like a recorder and a drum for use in war, "But their chiefe instruments are Rattels made of small gourds or Pumions shels. Of these they have Base, Tenor, Countertenor, Meane and Trible." The purposed effect of these instruments, together with a chorus of twenty or thirty men, was "a terrible noise as would rather affright then delight any man." William Strachey also reported the use of singing to intimidate. He had heard a "kynd of angry song against us in their homely rymes" appealing for their God's aid in vanquishing the English.[130] In fact Roger Williams was informed that mocking "(between their great ones) is a great kindling of Warres amongst them." Yet he also wrote that they were often reluctant to light a fire whose spread they could not control "for the barking of a Dog."[131]

Some observers also reported that Indians who could achieve their aims without war preferred to avoid it, and several affirmed that gambling and gaming had some of the same functions as war. As among the ancient Germans depicted by Tacitus, meets involved great gatherings in which the Indians sang, danced, and feasted, and then played games with the seriousness accorded war. Roger Williams said he had heard of events attended by "hundreds; sometimes thousands" where huge strings of wampum hung from the rafters in "great stakings, towne against towne." William Wood described football matches on which Americans gambled so heavily that participants sometimes lost all they owned, echoing Tacitus's descriptions of Germans who, "when all else is lost," wagered even "their libertie and body upon the last throw." So serious were these games that "they paint themselves, even as when they goe to warre, in pollicie to prevent future mischiefe, because no man should know him that moved his patience or accidentally hurt his person, taking away the occasion of studying revenge." Wood also described a game of skill played with dice-like bones called Hubbub, and Puim, a game of "many strange whimseyes." While the men played "the boyes pipe, and the women dance and sing trophies of their husbands conquests; all being done a feast summons their departure." Despite the high stakes, the participants separated peacefully: "there is no seeking of revenge, no quarreling, no bloody noses, scratched faces, blacke eyes, broken shinnes, no brused members, or crushed ribs."[132]

William Strachey in Virginia thought one sport might be similiar to an ancient game of "scipping and frisking at the Ball" that Virgil had described the Trojans teaching to the Romans. He wrote that the Americans refused to trip each other in football as the English did, "not accompting that praise worthy to purchase a goale by such advantage." Henry Spelman also compared the sportsmanship in these great feasts and games favorably to English: "They make ther Gooles as ours only they never fight nor pull one another doune." He compared their dancing to "our darbysher Hornepipe."[133]

Other sources speak of great gatherings of Indians from all over for religious festivals, particularly the annual ceremony of renewal and thanksgiving, the Green Corn Festival, and this picture is sustained in the native oral tradition.[134] Clearly, modes of coming together as perceived by the English involved displays of authority and largess, dominance and submission. War, a principal concern in Europe, figures prominently in these accounts because colonizers hoped to build alliances and relationships of native dependence. But the accounts registered even more the great majesty of Indian leaders, male and female, and the admirable orderliness of Indian civil life. The civil savages of America constituted a living reproach to England.

4   The Names of God

As Indians and English came to know each other all along America's east coast, nothing mattered more than religion. Religious beliefs were fundamentally important to all the cultures, and every participant was therefore vitally interested in knowing about the beliefs of the others. Curiosity operated on many levels. Since religion was the key to cultural systems, learning about religious beliefs would lead to full understanding of the others' cultures. Moreover, religion was also the principal source of power and knowledge, and therefore understanding relationships to divine authority was absolutely necessary. Up and down the coast, both Indians and English staged demonstrations of the power of their God and their ability to call forth that power in efforts to overawe the other side. And of course many people were just plain curious.

An early encounter shows this curiosity about relationships to the divine. Owen Griffin, a member of an expedition to New England in 1605, spent the night among a group of Wabanakis in northern New England in exchange for a "young Salvage" who came aboard the English ship, and Griffin witnessed "the ceremonies of their idolatry." The oldest person stood up "and looking about, suddenly cried with a loud voice, Baugh, Waugh." Then the women lay on the ground while the men began stamping the earth, "making the ground shake" and giving "sundry outcries, and change of voice and sound." Many took "fire-sticks, and thrust them into the earth, and then rest silent a while, of a sudden beginning as before, they looke round about, as though they expected the comming of something (as hee verily supposed) and continue stamping till the

yonger sort fetch from the shoare Stones, of which every man take one."
They beat on the stones with the sticks, and then beat the earth with
the stones "with all their strength." The ceremony continued, Griffin
thought, for two hours, and he counted 283 participants.

Shakespeare's play *The Tempest*, first performed in 1611 six years after
James Rosier's account of Owen Griffin's experience was published, offers an intriguing hint of how such descriptions were received in
England. After uttering the incantation "Baugh, Waugh," the Wabanakis
seemed to be looking for a spirit or an apparition, so in *The Tempest*
Ariel, a spirit invisible to all but Prospero, sings a song whose refrain is
"bowgh-wawgh."[1]

Griffin's account also offered hints of how the Americans were struggling to make sense of English religious beliefs as he tried to record
theirs. During a pause in their ceremonies, the Indians had heard the
watch onboard the English ship singing, so they asked Griffin to sing for
them, which he did while holding up his hands and eyes toward heaven.
"Then they pointed to the Moone, as if they imagined hee worshipped
that, which when he with signes denied, they pointed to the Sunne rising, which he likewise disliked, lifting up his hands againe, then they
looked about, as though they would see what Starre it might be, laughing one to another."[2]

English men and women approached discussion of religion from a variety of fiercely held religious positions. Even though Christianity had
been split by the Reformation of the sixteenth century, Europeans still
believed that there could be just one true church. Only one among all
the competing Christian denominations was true; all others, like Indian
religions, were false in their view. Protestants and Roman Catholics in
Europe readily called each other atheists or worse; Ralph Lane, governor
of the Roanoke colony, called the pope "that Antychryste of Rome," and
Reverend William Symonds commended the Virginia Company for not
allowing in any "papists that depend on the Great *Whore.*" Edward
Howes, a friend of John Winthrop, Jr., referred to the Roman Catholic
missionaries in Canada as "vermine."[3] And at the time the English
colonies were being founded, Protestants and Catholics in Europe fought
devastating wars over religious allegiance. On all kinds of other issues,
writers might come with open minds and be prepared to be amused or
enlightened by American practices, but on religion only one way—that
represented by the writer's own commitment—could be considered acceptable. Discussion of Indian religious belief and practice was deadly
serious.

Because European beliefs were so ideologically charged, the first question was whether the Indians had any religion at all. Some of the earliest

Spanish reports had alleged that the Americans lived without any idea of God. If that were true, such knowledge might bring the entire colonization enterprise into question. Could the land be suitable for habitation if it was not capable of sustaining the most basic human requirements?

Acknowledgment of a higher power was considered a fundamental attribute of human consciousness, attainable without the divine revelation that was the foundation of the Judeo-Christian tradition. John Calvin had summed up orthodox Christian opinion when he wrote, citing Cicero: "We lay it down as a position not to be controverted that the human mind, even by natural instinct, possesses some sense of a deity." Roger Williams followed Calvin: "The Sunne and Moone, and Starres and seasons of the yeere doe preach a God to all the sonnes of men." Captain John Smith affirmed it out of his own experience that "There is yet in Virginia no place discovered to bee so Savage in which the Savages have not a religion, Deare, and Bow, and Arrowes." And William Morrell asserted the same for New England: "all feare some God, some God they worship all."[4] Although, of course, the Indian belief system would have to be eradicated—a latitudinarian position would have been considered profoundly immoral—it would be something to build on. That the Indians understood human life had a purpose beyond the simple gratification of the moment, and aspired to organize their lives in honor of a power beyond themselves, was evidence not only of culture, but also of a hunger for the truth. Christianity was revealed religion; there was no access except through God's own words in the Bible, so the Indians would never have been able to satisfy their spiritual longing without the coming of Europeans. Their own religious beliefs and aspirations would provide the foundation from which they could be brought to understand the great gift they were being offered.

Once the Indians' religious sensibility had been acknowledged, English observers varied widely in their ability to tolerate and examine the particulars of American beliefs. Many dismissed American worship outright as "Paganisme and Idolatrie." Some of these later corrected themselves or were corrected by others. John Smith's first book, *A True Relation of such occurrences and accidents of noate as hath hapned in Virginia*, was published in 1608 in a badly edited form while he was still in Virginia. The same reader who denounced Smith for his ignorance of the language was particularly indignant about his underestimating the content of Virginia Algonquian religious beliefs: "This Author I fynde in many errors which they doe impute to his not well understandinge the language for they doe Acknowledge both God & the Devill and that after thei are out of this world they shall rise agayne in another world where they shall live at ease and have great store of bread and venison & other ———."[5]

Edward Winslow corrected his own error. Like Smith, he found that an early letter of his, in which he alleged that "they are a people without any religion or knowledge of any God," had been printed "against my will and knowledge." In a later book he acknowledged his error and wrote that "we could then gather no better."[6] Father Andrew White, writing from the Roman Catholic Maryland colony, explained that he would have to write tentatively about Indian religion as the only interpreters available to them were Protestants. He assumed Protestants could not or would not describe it accurately.[7]

Early writers, especially those who had not gone to America, assumed that if the Indians had a religious life, it would inevitably center on human sacrifice. For example, Sir George Peckham, a Roman Catholic and a backer of the earliest serious English attempt at American colonization, argued that the Indians would gain more than the English, partly because "their poore innocent children" would be saved from "the bloody knife of the sacrificer."[8] Human sacrifice was the mark of the savage regardless of time or place; William Strachey even asserted that the ancient Britons had sacrificed their children and that the Scots had ritually eaten theirs before the Romans had lifted them from savagery. Expectations of American horrors had been reinforced by translations of Spanish accounts of Aztec sacrifices, "wherein they surmounted all the Nations of the World in beastly butchery."[9]

The notion that eastern Algonquians were forced by their religion to sacrifice children persisted in the early years of settlement through confused reports of the *huskanaw* from the Chesapeake and its environs. The *huskanaw*, which the colonists called the black-boy ceremony, was a rite through which Algonquian boys symbolically passed from childhood to adulthood. Samuel Purchas pieced together an account of the ceremony from Captain John Smith and William White, a Jamestown colonist who had lived some time with the Indians, and presented it in his *Pilgrimage* of 1614. The ceremony began with a ritual dance and a feast in which the entire village participated. On the first day the teenage initiates, painted white and guided and protected by specially chosen men, ran several gauntlets through rows of men striking them with bundles of sticks, while the women of the village mourned and lamented and prepared funeral trappings. Once the initial events were over, the boys were taken into the woods, where they were taught the secrets shared by the men. Early observers, misled by the grieving women, by the apparent violence, and by seeing the boys lying under trees seemingly lifeless, believed that at least some of them had been sacrificed, especially as they were not seen again for several weeks or months. Henry Spelman, who had lived among the Chesapeake Algonquians when he

was of the age to be *huskana*wed, wrote that two or three children designated by "ther god" were sacrificed annually by being bound and cast
into a fire. After the ceremony, according to Spelman, "the men depart
merily, the weomen weaping."[10]

Almost as soon a these reports were circulated, however, doubts began
to emerge. William White acknowledged even in his first report that
most of the missing boys reappeared in nine months, and that they were
destined to become "Priests, and conjurers." When Purchas published a
new edition of the *Pilgrimage* in 1617, he reprinted White's report, but
cast further doubt on it. White had been affected by the sight of a woman
"mourning for yong Paspiha, sacrificed at the town of Rapahanna," but,
three years later Purchas wrote: "this Paspiha is now alive, as Mr Rolph
hath since related to me: and the mourning of the women is not for their
childrens death, but because they are for divers moneths detained from
them, as we shall after see. Yea, the Virginians themselves, by false reports might delude our Men, and say they were sacrificed when they
were not." Each time he mentioned the black-boy ceremony in his 1617
edition of the *Pilgrimage*, Purchas stressed that reports of sacrifice had
been in error. Even earlier, Alexander Whitaker hedged in reporting that
children were sacrificed to the devil in Virginia, adding, "(as I have heere
heard)."[11]

The *huskanaw* made sense as an initiation rite and a symbolic death.
The boys ended their lives as children and emerged as adult men, full
members of the society; and their mothers grieved over the lost relationship with their children. The ceremony in which the captive John
Smith believed Powhatan priests had been stopped from bashing out his
brains only by the intervention of Pocahontas may have been such a
symbolic death preparatory to his entrance into Powhatan's entourage.
Two days later, in return for cannon and grindstones, Powhatan, painted
to look like the God Oke, offered to give Smith the "Country of
Capahowosick" to govern as a sub-werowance, "and for ever esteeme
him as his sonne Nantaquoud." The idea that Smith had gone through
something like the black-boy ceremony and had been reborn as a member of Powhatan's family is supported by Pocahontas's addressing him
as father when they met, many years later, in London.[12]

Edward Winslow of Plymouth in New England wrote without elabo-
ration that the Indians made sacrifices and in some cases children were
killed. But the sacrifices he actually described involved the burning of
large piles of worldly goods.[13]

As observers moved beyond the stereotypical attributes of the savage,
some were profoundly interested in the tenets of Indian belief.
Renditions of the creation of the world were fundamental to the reli-

gious sensibility, and the curiosity of both the English and the Indians about the other's ideas emerges from a story told by Henry Spelman. Spelman was living with the Patawomecks at Mattchipongo when an English ship from Jamestown under Captain Samuel Argall arrived there to trade with "Iopassus [or Iapazeus] the great kings brother" at Christmas 1610. Iopassus came aboard the ship and was sitting with Argall "by the fire upon a harth in the Hold" where one of the men was reading a Bible. Iopassus "gave a very attent eare and looked with a very wish't eye upon him as if he desired to understand what he read," so Argall took the book and, turning to the picture of the creation of the world at the front, asked Spelman to "enterprett yt in his language, which the boy did, and which the king seemed to like well of."

In return Iopassus offered to tell his own people's creation story, "which was a pretty fabulous tale indeed." Iopassus said they had five gods, the chief of which appeared in the shape of a "mightie great Hare." The other four were the four winds; Iopassus sectioned out the world into quarters with his hands to indicate their location. The hare decided to make other creatures and created men and women, but kept them temporarily in a great bag. Some spirits like great giants came to the hare's home near the rising sun and tried to take the men and women to eat them, but the hare drove them away. At this point Argall wanted to know what substance the people and other creatures were made of, but Spelman refused to offend Iopassus by interrupting him. "That godlike hare" made the water and the land and stocked the water with fish and put a great deer on the land. Then the other four gods, envious, killed the deer and ate it, so the hare "in despight of this their mallice to him, tooke all the haires of the slayne deare and spredd them upon the earth with many powerfull wordes and charmes whereby every haire became a deare and then he opened the great bag, wherein the men and women were, and placed them upon the earth," each country receiving one couple.[14]

Such elaborate accounts, necessarily acquired by discussion rather than observation, were offered by those who had achieved some facility in an Algonquian language. Thomas Harriot told the Carolina Algonquian creation story: the "one onely chiefe and great God, which hath bene from all eternitie" first made other gods to assist in the creation and government of the world. The waters of earth were then made, and all creatures "visible or invisible." Among humans, a woman was created first "which by the working of one of the goddes, conceived and brought foorth children," but Harriot was unable to determine how many ages had passed since this all happened.[15]

Henry Spelman reported that the chief deity lived in the east; more commonly the residence of the great God was said to be the southwest, toward the setting rather than the rising sun, and the direction from which corn had come to the eastern woodland Indians. Roger Williams, after offering future missionaries a sentence-by-sentence translation of the biblical creation story, reported that his Narragansett informants had been told by their fathers that "Kautántowwit made one man and woman of a stone, which disliking, he broke them in pieces, and made another man and woman of a Tree, which were the Fountaines of all mankind."[16]

As colonists gained more experience of Indian religious life, they added complexity and detail to the basic account, beginning with the nature of the deities the Indians worshipped. Writers agreed that the Indians acknowledged a large body of supernatural forces collectively known as Manitou or Montóac. Roger Williams wrote that the Narragansetts call "Manittóoes, that is, Gods, Spirits or Divine powers, . . . every thing which they cannot comprehend." In fact, "at the apprehension of any Excellency in Men, Women, Birds, Beasts, Fish, &c, they cry out *Manittóo* A God."[17] Using a slightly different spelling, Reverend Jonas Michaëlius of New Netherland wrote of "Menetto; under which title they comprehend everything that is subtle and crafty and beyond human skill and power."[18] The Massachusett leaders who worked with John Eliot in translating the Bible into their language rendered the phrase "he is God" by the term Manittóo, and Williams also used Manit for the Christian God. These Indians thus indicated the affinity they saw between the God of the Bible and their own conception of Manitou.[19] In the twentieth century Fidelia Fielding, who wrote her diary in Mohegan, began each entry with "Mándu is good." As a member of the Christian church at Mohegan, she also saw affinities between the two conceptions of divinity; in one entry she wrote, "Mándu is good because he knows all things."[20]

But within this collective force, reporters asserted that the Americans acknowledged two preeminent gods, one good but remote and the other potentially harmful and intimately involved in daily life. The benevolent God was named Tanto, Kiehtan, or Cautàntouwit in New England sources (the central syllable *tan* occurred in all forms, and Edward Winslow wrote that the prefix *kieh* "hath reference to antiquity") and Ahone in southern sources. The fear-inspiring deity, analogized to the devil by Europeans, was named as Okeus or Okee in reports from the south and in Samuel de Champlain's report from Canada, but New England writers recorded him as Squanto or Hobbomock (Abbomocho) or Cheepi.[21] Squanto, as Reverend Francis Higginson wrote, was an "evill God whom they feare will doe them hurt." Similarly, Pilgrim Edward Winslow said that Hobbomock "as far as we can conceive, is the devil."[22] The eighteenth-century Mohegan preacher Samson Occum wrote in much the same manner of the traditional beliefs of the Montauk Indians, among whom he served as minister, and of the powers claimed by the powwows. Hobbomock appeared to powwows and communicated with them in dreams; he seemed to evoke images of the underworld, death, and the cold northeast wind.[23]

Manitou contained many beings and forces that could be called upon in a variety of ways. Thomas Harriot wrote that the temples contained carved and painted idols called *kewasówak* (singular *kewás*), and that the common people thought these idols were gods. Samuel Purchas remarked that the Reverend Alexander Whitaker had sent one of these "ill favouredly made" images to England "painted on a Toadstool (fit shrine for such a deitie)."[24] Roger Williams wrote that he had been told the names of thirty-seven separate gods for different directions, places, and natural phenomena, and this is confirmed by Gladys Tantaquidgeon. Even individual Indians might have their own personal deities who had appeared to them in dreams. Comparing this multiplicity of gods to "the Papists" with their "He and Shee Saint Protectors," Williams wrote that there were also a women's god and one for children. He argued that the conviction that God exists and "all Excellencies dwell in God and proceed from him "was "naturall in the soule of man."[25]

Not everyone agreed that what English reporters saw could be dignified by the name of religion. Thomas Morton, who had extensive and sympathetic contact with Indian culture and who wrote one of the fullest insider's accounts based on his friendships with Massachusett speakers, flatly denied that they had religion. Morton lived in an easy relationship with natives at his little settlement at Merrymount, near present-day Saugus, and he ridiculed the godly pretensions of the puritans around him, especially the Pilgrims who tried to expel him from New England and to bring the Indians into their way of thinking.

Morton's denunciation of Indian religion occurred in a chapter in which he gave a very full account of that religion and discussed its bearing on important issues in Europe. He began his chapter "Of their Religion" with the "common receaved opinion from Cicero, that there is no people so barbarous, but have some worshipp" and went on to say that if Cicero had spent as much time among the Indians as Morton had, he would have reversed his opinion. Morton ridiculed Massachusetts Bay colonist William Wood, whose *New Englands Prospect* had recently been published, saying he did not need to climb up on a "wodden prospect" to get at the truth. His authority was Sir William Alexander, a nobleman and a colonial promoter who never actually came to America, and Morton quoted Alexander's formula—*sine fide, sine lege, et sine rege*—

with approval, saying he had confirmed it by his own experience. In asserting that "the Natives of New England have no worship nor religion at all," he argued that it was "absurd" for colonists to claim Americans had religion but that they did not know "whome or what it is they are accustomed to worship." One might as well conclude that elephants "(which are reported to be the most intelligible of all beasts) doe worship the moone," he wrote.

A few pages on in his book, Morton returned to the subject. After again affirming, with reference to Sir William Alexander, that the Indians lacked religion, he wrote, "yet are they not altogether without the knowledge of God (historically) for they have it amongst them by tradition, that God made one man and one woman, and bad them live together, and get children, kill deare, beasts, birds, fish, and fowle, and what they would at their pleasure; and that their posterity was full of evil, and made God so angry: that hee let in the sea upon them, & drowned the greatest part of them, that were naughty men, (the Lord destroyed so.)"[26] Ironically, then, Morton's *New English Canaan*, while vehemently maintaining that the Indians had no religion, gave an account of their religious beliefs that matched other reports.

Morton's account is important because, with its apparent reference to Noah's flood, it contributed to a momentous debate among these writers over whether Indian religious beliefs showed any trace of the Judeo-Christian tradition. Many writers, including the nineteenth-century Pequot activist William Apess, believed that the Indians were descended from the Lost Tribes of Israel.[27] If this were true, they would once have had access to biblical knowledge. Was their religion, so simple and defective (to European eyes), a dimly remembered version of the truth, or was it a groping toward true religion from total ignorance? Were the Indians on a descending or an ascending plane in their religious knowledge?

Some writers were confident that the traces of biblical knowledge remained in American consciousness. The Reverend Alexander Whitaker (the puritan minister who converted Pocahontas) and the Jesuit priest Andrew White in Maryland both believed that the remote benevolent deity only dimly perceived by the Americans was the Judeo-Christian God. Both men also argued that although the Indians longed to know and honor God, they were constrained by their fears to worship the devil. Whitaker wrote, "They acknowledge that there is a great good God, but know him not, having the eyes of their understanding as yet blinded; wherefore they serve the divell for feare." And yet they retained "so many footsteps of Gods image." Virginia colonists continued to find "motiones of religione" in the natives.[28] John White, a puritan leader in

England, was pleased to transmit reports that the Indians emulated the
Jews in practices such as seclusion of menstruating women and that "in
some place may be discoved some foot-steps of the knowledge of God,
of the Creation, and of some Legall Observations." John White asserted
that the native name for Salem had been Nahum Keike, which he said
was "perfect Hebrew." Father Andrew White also reported, like Morton,
that "they have notice by tradition of Noah his flood."[29]

Roger Williams, one of the most learned puritans, went even further.
He argued that the Indians' culture obviously derived from an old-world
model and presented the evidence in the preface to his *Key into the
Language of America* so that his readers could draw their own conclusions. He agreed that the Americans seemed to share many culture traits
with the ancient Hebrews: many of their words "hold affinitie with the
Hebrew"; they also "constantly annoint their heads as the Jewes did";
and the practice of giving dowries for their wives also echoed ancient
Jewish practice, as did menstrual seclusion. In explaining these the
Indians cited "Nature and Tradition." Even more strikingly, Williams
argued that the Indians might have some knowledge of Jesus. His evidence was: "They have many strange Relations of one Wétucks, a man
that wrought great Miracles amongst them, and walking upon the waters, &c. with some kind of broken Resemblance to the Sonne of God."
Although they were "lost," Williams hoped that "(in the Lords holy season) some of the wildest of them shall be found to share in the blood of
the Son of God."

Toward the end of his book, Williams returned to this theme in his
discussion of Narragansett religious life: "They have an exact forme of
King, Priest, and Prophet, as was in Israel typicall of old in that holy Land
of Canaan, and as the Lord Jesus ordained in his spirituall Land of Canaan
his Church throughout the whole World." On the other hand, as he had
written in the preface, he believed the Narragansett language had more
affinity with Greek than Hebrew, and their names for constellations
seemed to echo the Greeks'. As we have seen he thought the Indians
knew "Europe's Arithmaticke" and wondered whether "Tradition of ancient Forefathers, or Nature" had taught them.[30] William Wood agreed
that language was not a good indicator of origins because, although some
words resembled Hebrew, others "sound after the Greeke, Latine,
French, and other tongues."

Thomas Harriot of Roanoke matched New Englander Roger
Williams—both were university men and each had studied a native language thoroughly—and Harriot's report on Roanoke religious beliefs and
practices was no less sophisticated than Williams's on the Narragansetts.
Harriot asserted that the Indians believed in "one onely chiefe and great

God, which hath bene from all eternitie," and this God created the world
and all the other gods. Of the Roanoke religion he remarked that "although it be farre from the truth, yet beyng as it is, there is hope it may
bee the easier and sooner reformed." Harriot was especially encouraged
because native priests were most interested in the Christian religion,
having been "brought into great doubts of their owne."[31]

The possibility that the Indians had some dim recollection of biblical
knowledge and religious truth opened a new understanding of the
planters' mission. Everyone who reads the literature of colonization is
struck by the constant use of the word *reduction* for the proposed relationship with the Indians. Writers from all over Europe asserted that the
Americans must be reduced to civility and Christianity; to modern readers this language seems to indicate absolute self-confidence on the
Europeans' part and their expectation that they would impose harsh humiliation on America's proud savages. But another meaning of "reduction"—to restore, to lead back—complicates the picture and neatly en-
capsulates the mysteriousness of America in these early years. With its
dual implications, the term reflected the uncertainty, as well as the arrogance, with which Europeans approached the newly revealed peoples.[32]

If the Americans had once known of the Judeo-Christian God, and especially if they still had some slight remembrance of that religion, then
the newcomers' role would indeed be to lead them back from error to
truth rather than simply to impose an alien creed on them. Thus Richard
Hakluyt, demonstrating the layered nature of these sentiments, could
write in one place that England could "*reduce* many Pagans to the faith
of Christ" and, in another, praise Ralegh's plan "to *recall* the savage and
the pagan to civility." Certainly, according to Hakluyt, the American natives were "waiting to be discovered and subdued, quickly and easily."[33]

Writers readily accepted the idea that the Indians worshipped their
own deities, particularly the harmful one that was so easily analogized
to the devil, out of fear and ignorance alone. So fundamental was fear to
their religious sensibility that many writers said the Indians worshipped
anything that they could not understand or control. Giambattista Vico
drew on this literature and on Tacitus in arguing that in early times "ignorance, the mother of wonder, made everything wonderful to men who
were ignorant of everything" so that "they imagined the causes of the
things they felt and wondered at to be gods. (This is now confirmed by
the American Indians, who call gods all the things that surpass their
small understanding. . . .)" And it was true of the Germans described by
Tacitus. Vico said that the ancient Greeks had thirty thousand gods and
compared them to the Indians of America.[34]

It became a commonplace that the Indians longed for the love of the true God, but that apprehension prevented them from making the leap of faith. The Jesuit father Andrew White, echoing the archpuritan Roger Williams, reported that the Indians worshipped, as beneficial, wheat and fire and acknowledged one great good God, "But use all their might to please an Okee which signifies a frantique spirit, for feare of harme from him." Captain John Smith also wrote that the Indians worshipped anything able to hurt them "beyond their prevention." He asserted that English artillery and horses were now worshipped in Virginia along with fire, water, and lightning and thunder. "But their chiefe God they worship is the Divell. Him they call Oke and serve him more of feare then love." Drawing on the recently published compendium of classical verse by Martin Fotherby, *Atheomastix; clearing foure truthes, against atheists*, he presented the same notion in a couplet: "Feare was the first their Gods begot: / Till feare began, their Gods were not."[35] Christopher Levett wrote that the New England natives hated Tanto and that when any "evill fortunes" befell them, "then they say Tanto is hoggry, that is angry," and at death "they say Tanto carries them to his wigwam." Sometimes Hobbomock carried people away bodily. John Winthrop recorded that during a great hurricane in March 1639, "The Indians near Aquiday being pawwawing in this tempest, the devil came and fetched away five of them." William Wood wrote that the Indians would not go out of their houses at night "for feare of their Abamacho (the Devill) whom they much fear"; he would sometimes "carrie away their wives and children" in order to reinforce his authority over them.[36]

Hobbomock's reign was coming to an end, however. Wood asserted that the Indians were deserting "his colours," and that they were much less fearful now that the English had settled. The deity fought back in the face of the Christian challenge and became very active in trying to keep his followers from being too curious about imported English methods and beliefs. Reports from Sagadahoc in Maine, the earliest attempt to found a colony in New England, state that although the neighboring Indians were attracted to the English deity, their God Tanto made dire threats that kept them in line: "Hee commanded them not to dwell neere, or come among the English, threatning to kill some and inflict sicknesse on others, beginning with two of their Sagamos children, saying he had power and would doe the like to the English the next Moone, to wit, in December."[37] In 1638 John Winthrop recorded that "the Indians, which were in our families, were much frightened with Hobbamack (as they call the devil) appearing to them in divers shapes, and persuading them to forsake the English, and not to come at the assemblies, nor to learn to read, etc." Abamacho had also tried to scare away the English, according to Wood, with "horrible apparitions, feare-full roarings, thundering and lightning."[38]

In 1643 "a very strange Disease" broke out among the Indians on Martha's Vineyard. "They ran up and down as if delerious, till they could run no longer; they would make their Faces as black as a Coal and snatch up any Weapon, as tho they would do Mischief with it, and speak great swelling Words, but yet they did no Harm." The Indians attributed "this, and all other Calamities . . . to the Departure of some of them from their own heathenish Ways and Customs." Nineteenth-century Wampanoag oral traditions reported frequent encounters with spirits.[39]

Christians stood before their God in fear, but they also approached God with love, and God returned love to believers. As they came to under-stand the Christian religion and felt its power in their hearts, the Americans, so the English rationale went, would enter into the assur-ance of a loving relationship with God, and the terror induced by Okee or Hobbomock would lose its power. They would learn to fear God's just punishment for sins, not the capricious and arbitrary vengeance of their own trickster deity. Virginia priests, according to William Strachey, "feare and tremble, lest the knowledge of god and of our Saviour Jesus Christ should be taught in those parts."[40]

This neat and clear-cut agenda and rationale began to unravel as soon as thoughtful and knowledgeable observers explored in more depth. Many writers were forced to acknowledge that the simple model was wrong on a variety of counts. For one thing, they realized that the Indians' "spirituall Pharao" possessed powers that even the English could see and was not so easily vanquished. For another, this God was not wholly evil like the Judeo-Christian devil; his persona included many aspects associated with God the creator. America's natives loved Okee or Hobbomock as well as fearing him, and they loved him because of the benefits they received from him. Hobbomock or Okee, within Manitou, gave Americans the means to control their environment and enhance their lives. Champlain wrote of the Montagnais or Algonquins of the north, "When they see a man doing something extraordinary, or cleverer than the average, a valiant warrior, or infuriated and beside himself, they call him Oqui, as we should say, a great spirit, or a great devil." He wrote that some natives "act as Oquis or Manitous"; not only could they heal, they also foretold the future.

These powers were also seen in the colonists. William Wood reported the Indians' astonishment when they saw an English plow at work; they "told the plow-man, hee was almost Abamocho, almost as cunning as the Devill." Because of the association of Hobbomock and his power with the sacred color black, some Indians, encountering an African man

DeBry's engraving of a statue of Kiwasa shows the deity as an Algonquian man. The white and black painted figure was said to be four feet high. According to Harriot, it was placed in a dark corner of the temple, and its mysteriousness held the people in awe. The John Carter Brown Library at Brown University.

who had lost his way, were extremely fearful, thinking him an apparition of the deity, and asked the English to "conjure" him "to his owne place."[41]

Uttamatomakkin, also known as Tomocomo, was a leading man and a priest among the Powhatans of the Chesapeake. He was married to Powhatan's daughter Matachanna, and he was chosen to accompany Pocahontas, now Rebecca Rolfe, on her trip to England. While they were in London, Samuel Purchas interviewed him, and Uttamatomakkin disputed the idea that Okeus was worshipped out of fear. Rather it was "hee which made Heaven and Earth, had taught them to plant so many kinds of Corne, was the author of their good; had prophesied to them before of our mens comming; knew all our Country." Thus, Uttamatomakkin claimed that, through Okeus, he and other Powhatan leaders not only had foreknowledge of the arrival of the English but knew everything about them. Although Okeus spoke directly only to the priests and leading men, he indicated his will to common people through signs and directed them to game when they went hunting. In a later work Purchas shortened this report, saying simply he "beleeved that this Okee or Devil had taught them their husbandry, &c." In his report of New England, Thomas Morton wrote that Kytan lives near the setting sun and "hee . . . makes corne growe, trees growe, and all manner of fruits."[42]

William Strachey was told of another of Okeus's roles: judging human sin. Strachey reported that Okeus visited harm on "these wretched Miscreants" after "looking into all mens accions and examyning the same according to the severe Scale of Justice."[43] Okee's intervention in human life could be helpful or harmful depending on his pleasure; many observers presented the Indians as seeking to placate or win over this spirit through elaborate shows of allegiance. The earliest report from Roanoke acknowledged that the coastal Carolina Algonquians claimed "incredible things" of "their Idoll," although it was "a meere illusion of the Devill," In the early days of the Jamestown colony, the men vividly experienced the Indians' regard for their image of Okee. John Smith was "scorned" when he tried to obtain corn at Kekoughtan for the hungry colonists. When his party of six or seven men then forced their way in, they were confronted by sixty or seventy Americans painted red, black, and white who made "a most hydeous noyse" as they "came in a square order, singing and dauncing out of the woods, with their Okee (which was an Idoll made of skinnes, stuffed with mosse, all painted and hung with chaines and copper)" and charged the English. When the latter replied with their muskets, the Indians fled, dropping the Okee. "One of their Quiyoughkasoucks," a priest, soon came and offered peace to get their Okee back; Smith reported that he was conciliatory, restoring their Okee and giving gifts as the Indians loaded his boat with corn and "Venison, Turkies, wild foule, bread, and what they had."[44]

Roger Williams wrote that the chief gamesters among the Americans, as among the English, "much desire to make their Gods side with them in their Games," and therefore keep "a piece of Thunderbolt, which is like unto a Chrystall, which they dig out of the ground under some tree. Thunder-smitten." They believed it would bring them success, and indeed Williams said he had not heard that anyone who possessed such a charm had ever lost, "which I conceive may be Satans policie and Gods holy Justice to harden them." The Penobscot oral tradition maintains that "thunder stones" dug out of the ground bring good luck.[45]

Native religious practitioners, who endured deprivation and long training in their youths, seem to have been of at least two sorts, or at least had two kinds of roles. One set of roles involved worship and healing; the other seems to have combined military and spiritual leadership. John

White painted two men with supernatural powers. The first, labeled "One of their Religious men," was older; Harriot's note said he was "well stricken in yeers, and as yt seemeth of more experience then the comon sorte." These priests were "notable enchaunters." The other, younger, man was variously labeled "The flyer" or "The conjuror." These men, Harriot said, were "verye familiar with devils," from which they gained information about their enemies, and they were "often contrarie to nature in their enchantments." The people gave "great credit" to what they said because their information was so often accurate. Harriot called them "juglers," which meant wizards or magicians and carried overtones of trickery. Ironically, back in England, Harriot, who became known for his unorthodox thinking, was later called a juggler, and many found his scientific and linguistic work disturbing.[46]

In New England, the priests who specialized in healing and conducting worship were called powwows; the spiritual / military leaders were called pnieses. Accounts of all regions reported that native religious practitioners of both sorts had direct access to the gods, especially to Okee or Hobbomock, and could even make him appear.[47] And these religious leaders were very quickly identified as central to the maintenance of cultural integrity by besieged native societies; they were the most powerful individuals in America. Their centrality, and their strength, came from their capacity to cross lines, to summon spirits and to visit spirit worlds and return with impunity. They advertised their abilities partly through such visible signs as hairstyle and badges of office, and they had command of a special language known only to them. They were the principal advisors to chiefs, and their advice determined issues such as peace and war.

According to Captain John Smith, the Chesapeake area Algonquian priests could summon Oke, "say they have conference with him, and fashion themselves as neare to his shape as they can imagine." Ordinary people saw "his image evill favouredly carved" in their temples.[48] Uttamatomakkin recounted to Purchas that Okeus appeared when four priests came together in a sacred space and spoke special words understood neither by the English interpreter nor by the "Common-people" among the Virginia Algonquians. When the deity appeared, he first called for the presence of eight more "principle persons" and then walked up and down telling the twelve what he wanted done. When he was finished talking, he disappeared into the air from which he had come. Purchas was frustrated because Uttamatomakkin was "very zealous in his superstition, and will heare no persuasions to the truth." Saying he was too old to learn a new religion, Uttamatomakkin suggested the English should try to talk to the boys and girls.[49]

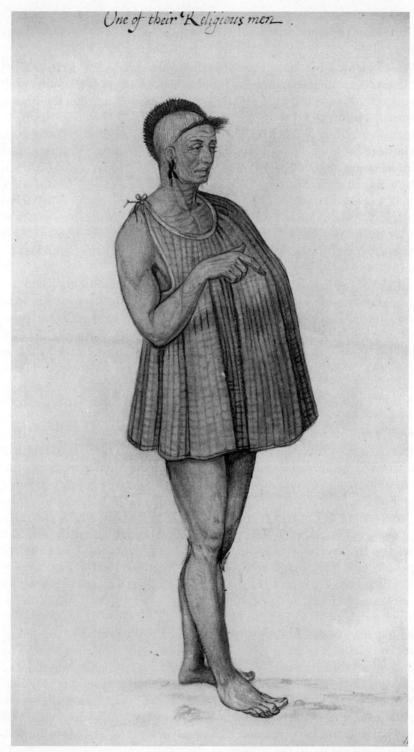

One of their Religious men

John White's painting of a Carolina Algonquian priest. Harriot noted that the priests wore a special cloak of quilted rabbit pelts. © The British Museum, British Museum Press.

The flyer.

White's painting of a conjurer, "the flyer," shows a young man whose bird headdress and animal pelt may have signified his special powers; Harriot called the bird the "badge of their office." © The British Museum, British Museum Press.

Other writers reported that religious leaders saw the gods and brought back messages from them. Edward Winslow of Plymouth described the training of "the most forward and likeliest boys," who were destined to the priesthood. These boys went through sustained hardships "to make them hardy and acceptable to the devil, that in time he may appear unto them." Winslow wrote that Kiehtan, the remote benevolent deity, never appeared to human beings. Hobbomock manifested himself in various shapes only to the "chiefest and most judicious amongst them; though all of them strive to attain to that hellish height of honor," and he never appeared when the English were present.[50]

Alexander Whitaker wrote of the priests in Virginia, "a generation of vipers even of Sathans owne brood," that they lived apart in special houses like "popish Hermits," waited upon by the village people. In return the priest used his power for them. "If they would have raine, or have lost any thing, they have their recourse to him, who conjureth for them, and many times prevaileth. If they be sicke, he is their Physition, if they bee wounded he sucketh them." No "thing of moment" was decided without consulting the Quiokosough, or priest.[51] Despite their insistence on seeing Hobbomock as evil, then, English writers acknowledged in a variety of ways that he supported Indian life.

Episodes of crossing between the mundane and spiritual planes were not wholly foreign to the Christian experience. Thomas Shepard, who was active in early efforts to convert members of the Massachusett tribe, said that in prayer "I have seen God himself, and I have been ravished to behold him." And Cotton Mather recorded of one of his sermons that "A Spirit who with a wondrous Lustre, made his Descent into my Study, declaring himself to be a good Angel of God, and expressing his Desire to have Act. IX. 5. preach'd upon, was the occasion of my preaching it." Years later Mather, still pondering that visitation, "entreated of the Lord, that I might understand the Meaning of the Descent from the Invisible World, which nineteen years ago produced in a Sermon from me, a good part of what is now published."[52]

Most often Indian priests visited the spirit world in dreams. Roger Williams reported that one of the Indian words for soul was derived from the word for sleep, because "it works and operates when the body sleepes." A bad dream was considered "a threatning from God," and on wakening from a nightmare, Indians immediately began earnest prayers, reminding Williams of the example of the biblical King David. Earnest Christians, English or Indian, also experienced dreams in this way. The Mohegan preacher Joseph Johnson wrote in his diary for December 27, 1771 of just such a dramatic dream that caused him to redouble his commitment to Christianity. Christians also received messages in dreams;

John Rolfe, in explaining his decision to marry Pocahontas, wrote that God's spirit came to him in his sleep, "even waking mee to astonishment . . . pulling mee by the eare, and crying: why dost not thou indeavour to make her a Christian?"[53]

Father Andrew White discovered that traditional belief in dreams made the Pascatoans more interested in his Christian message. Having failed to convert Maquacomen, "the King of Patuxent," White moved farther into the Maryland interior to "Kittamaquund, the metropolis of Pascatoa." There he was welcomed with "the greatest love and veneration" by the Tayac (the "emperor," as White called him) because of two dreams, "unless you [that is, White's Jesuit superiors] may deem it proper to honor them with another name." One dream, in which Father White and another priest, Father Gravener, appeared, had come to the chief's predecessor. The second was dreamed by the Tayac himself, and poignantly encapsulated the challenge posed by the newcomers and the forces between which the Indians were caught. It comprised three vignettes. The first was the emperor's own dead father accompanied by "a god of a dim color, whom he worshipped, and who was beseeching him that he would not desert him." The second was an English heretic [Protestant], "one Snow," and his companion was "a most hideous god." The final group was Maryland's governor, Father White, and a beautiful God "seeming gently to beckon the Emperor to him." From that time on, the Tayac treated both the governor and Father White "with the greatest affection."[54]

Christopher Levett, writing of his experiences in New England, reported that only "pawwaws" saw Squanto or Tanto, and that was in dreams. Every sagamore depended on his pawwaw for guidance, because the priest was able to foretell, perhaps even to control, events. Levett recounted noticing a marten's skin in a sagamore's house, which he tried to buy. He was refused because the pawwaw laid this skin under his head when he dreamed "and if he wanted that, he could do nothing; thus we may perceive how the devil deludes those poor people, and keeps them in blindness."[55]

So powwows and pnieses had access to the spirit world, and were able to cross over into that world in dreams and even summon its beings into the human environment. To accomplish this they employed secret words and used items reserved for themselves. Their manipulation of the dangerous spirit realm won them great honor among their people. Prophecies promulgated by the priests were taken very seriously. William Strachey wrote of two prophecies circulating in Jamestown's early years. Powhatan's priests had convinced him that among the peoples on Chesapeake Bay "a Nation should arise, which should dissolve and give end to his Empier." In reaction, according to Strachey, Powhatan had wiped out the Chesapeake Indians, an independent tribe that had been visited by a party from the earlier Roanoke colony and that may have sheltered some members of the Lost Colony from two decades before. Such wholesale destruction was not characteristic of Indian warfare. Another prophecy concerned the English colonists directly, and predicted that the Powhatans would twice overthrow and "dishearten" strangers attempting to invade or settle among them, but that "the third tyme they themselves should fall into their Subjection and under their Conquest." Strachey wrote of "straunge whispers (indeed) and secrett" running through the Indian villages, and promised he would "expresse the particulers" in "another place."[56]

Occasionally English visitors witnessed Indian religious ceremonies. George Percy described a ceremony of welcome when the first Virginia fleet arrived at Kecoughtan: "They made a dolefull noise, laying their faces to the ground, scratching the earth with their nailes. We did thinke that they had beene at their Idolatry." When the newcomers had eaten the food offered by the village, the Indians gave them tobacco and then danced before them "shouting howling, and stamping against the ground, with many Anticke tricks and faces, making noise like so many wolves or devils." Percy was intrigued by the way they kept time with their feet. He thought they worshipped the sun, and asserted that they would keep an oath sworn on the sun better than a Christian. He said they performed a ceremony morning and evening in a circle of dried tobacco. He described their prayer: "many Devillish gestures with a Hellish noise foaming at the mouth, staring with their eyes, wagging their heads and hands in such a fashion and deformitie as it was monstrous to behold."[57]

When Captain John Smith was captured not long after Jamestown was founded, Powhatan priests performed a three-day divination ceremony before he was taken into the presence of the emperor, "to know if any more of his countrymen would arive there, and what he there intended." He was placed in a longhouse on a mat before a "great fire"; another mat was placed opposite him and "presently came skipping in a great grim fellow, all painted over with coale, mingled with oyle; and many Snakes and Wesels skins stuffed with mosse, and all their tayles tyed together, so as they met on the crowne of his head in a tassell; and round about the tassell was as a Coronet of feathers, the skins hanging round about his head, backe, and shoulders, and in a manner covered his face; with a hellish voyce and a rattle in his hand. With most strange gestures and passions he began his invocation." After he had made a circle of meal around the fire, "three more such like devils came rushing in with the like antique trickes." These were painted in red, white, and black. Soon

three more entered, "as ugly as the rest." When they were finished dancing, they sat with the chief priest in the middle and sang accompanied
by their rattles until the chief priest "layd downe five wheat cornes: then
strayning his armes and hands with such violence that he sweat, and his
veynes swelled, he began a short Oration." The ceremony continued
with the setting of corn punctuated with groans and further orations
until "they had twice incirculed the fire." Then they began to lay small
sticks in the same fashion. While the ceremony continued they all fasted
all day, but "feasted merrily" in the evenings. They explained to Smith
that "the circles of meale signified their Country, the circles of corne the
bounds of the Sea, and the stickes his Country. They imagined the world
to be flat and round, like a trencher, and they in the middest." Only when
the ceremony had been completed was Smith brought into Powhatan's
presence.[58]

Roger Williams had opportunities to witness many Narragansett religious ceremonies, but he testified in the most meaningful way that he
considered them true acts of worship by refusing even to watch priests
conduct a service. Williams had broken with the Massachusetts Bay puritans over his contention that being present at any worship with a person who had not received God's grace was a sin, and he not only demanded that the colonists denounce their former attendance at Church
of England services, but he refused to be silenced. Therefore, just as he
would not enter an Anglican church during services, so, after acknowledging that the Narragansetts had a fully realized religion, "I durst never
bee an eye witnesse, Spectatour, or looker on, least I should have been a
partaker of Sathans Inventions and Worships, contrary to Ephes. 5, 14."

Because of his refusal to attend, Williams wrote that most of his information came "by their owne Relation." He described a great thanksgiving service of call and response between the priests and the congregation; for the priests it involved "a laborious bodily service, unto
sweatings" with "strange Antick Gestures, and Actions even unto fainting." Williams himself attended feasts for twenty, fifty, a hundred, even
near a thousand people; and, besides the food, the hosts gave the guests
"a great quantity of money, and all sort of their goods." Williams saw it
all as the devil's doing, encouraging people to give and attend feasts
through "plausible Earthly Arguments," and recalled "(as the Turk sai-
eth of the Christian rather the Antichristians,) they run mad once a
yeare) [sic] in their kind of Christmas feasting."[59]

Edward Winslow also wrote of the great feasts of the Narragansetts
who, because they "exceed in their blind devotion," brought "almost all
the riches they have to their gods"; all the goods were cast on a great fire
and burned to ashes. Winslow's account was written before Williams

came to New England and, having learned the Narragansett language, presented his own detailed account. Despite the dismissive phrase "blind devotion," Winslow asserted that the sacrifice was effective; Indians and Pilgrims alike noted the Narragansetts' freedom from the European-introduced diseases that plagued others and attributed it to this observance.[60]

Earlier southern reports had also affirmed that the Indians, collectively and individually, offered thanks to a supreme being. Thomas Harriot's early report from Roanoke described the Carolina Algonquians offering tobacco, *Uppówoc*, both for thanks and for supplication, and "they thinke their gods are marvelously delighted therwith." He wrote that it was accompanied with "strange gestures," dancing, stamping, and clapping their hands and holding them up to heaven, "uttering therewithal and chattering strange words & noises." He also described large thanksgiving ceremonies, some involving several villages, after the harvest or when they had escaped any "great danger." Harriot felt none of Williams's scruples, and noted that he witnessed these ceremonies, "For it is a strange custome, and worth the observation."[61] Henry Spelman recorded that each person "mumbleth" a grace before eating in Virginia, and Gabriel Archer reported that they sprinkled tobacco on the water before they washed in the morning.[62] In the twentieth century the Mohegan Harold Tantaquidgeon continued this tradition of offering a pinch of tobacco.[63]

One of the most sympathetic accounts of the native mode of giving thanks was written by the anonymous, probably Roman Catholic, writer of the *Relation of Maryland*.

> These People acknowledge a God, who is the giver of al the good things, wherewith their life is maintained; and to him they sacrifice of the first fruits of their Corne, and of that which they get by hunting and fishing: The sacrifice is performed by an Ancient man, who makes a speech unto their God (not without something of Barbarisme) which being ended, hee burnes part of the sacrifice, and then eates of the rest, then the People that are present, eate also, and untill the Ceremony be performed, they will not touch one bit thereof.[64]

Sickness and its treatment was a central religious issue. All observers were keenly interested in how the Americans cured disease, and especially in the priests' role, and in how these techniques compared to familiar European methods. English ministers often doubled as healers. And as illness reflected divine will, either testing or (more often) punishing the weak characters of sinners, healing in Europe relied heavily on prayers and invocations. Inevitably some healers, neighborhood "cunning men" or "wise women," were thought to have appealed to the devil for aid. Thus there was still an uncertain line between straightforward herbal and other medicine, much of which involved purging in one way or another, and the use of charms, prayers, and sympathetic magic; and even educated people accepted the usefulness of conjuring and charms. When English writers analogized American powwows to "our English witches," the comparison was meaningful. Samson Occum, writing his observations of the Montauk Indians to whom he ministered, and presumably drawing on his own Mohegan oral tradition, said powwows drew their powers from dreams. After describing some of the powwows' feats, he remarked, "And I don't see for my part, why it is not as true, as the English or other nation's witchcraft, but is a great mystery of darkness, &c."[65]

American priests orchestrated treatments in which the entire village participated. In the case of great leaders, people came from miles around; Roger Williams said that more than a thousand men had gathered at the deathbed of a Narragansett great man. Williams described how Indian priests threatened and conjured the sickness out of the person and reported that they believed divine powers resided in the human body: "In his pulse, his heart, his Lungs, &c." Friends came to be with the sick person, and they would join the priest "(like a Quire) in prayer to their Gods for them." The priests undeniably did accomplish "great Cures," although Williams was sure that was with the help of the devil, and he was scornful of the great gifts the afflicted lavished on the priests for their cures. Williams said the Narragansetts were forced to save up against times of sickness because of the priests' greed, and he thought the common people usually died in their care "for alas, they administer nothing but howle and roare, and hollow over them." Williams compared them to Simon Magus in the Bible, a great magician of "the citie of Samaria," who became a Christian and, seeing the curing powers of the Apostles, offered them money to be given the like powers, "that on whomesoever I lay the hands, he may receive the holie Gost." Simon was spurned by the Apostles, and Williams, who believed that ministers should not even collect salaries (he contemptuously called those who did a "hireling ministry"), may have been reflecting contemporary English controversy over ministers who supplemented their income by collecting fees for medical treatment.[66]

William Wood also described the sick or lame being brought to the powwow, who performed his rites before the assembled people, pausing in his "imprecations and invocations" and "many a hideous bellowing and groaning" for "a short Canto" from the onlookers. Then the powwow resumed, "somtimes roaring like a Beare, other times groaning like a dying horse, foaming at the mouth like a chased bore, smiting on his

naked brest and thighs with such violence, as if he were madde." Often
the priest would spend half a day "in this diabolicall worship," and sometimes the devil "recovers the partie, to nuzzle them up in their divell-
ish Religion."

Wood had no doubt that the powwows possessed genuine powers. The
Indians assured him that one in particular, called Pissacannawa, could
"make the water burne, the rocks move, the trees dance, metamorphize
himselfe into a flaming man." He could also burn a dead leaf to ashes
and produce a new green one in the middle of winter, or turn a snakeskin into a living writhing snake. All these miracles were reported by
the Indians, but Wood, who believed in them, pressed his readers to see
that "by Gods permission, thorough the Devils helpe" these powwows
did produce "effects of wonderment." He passed on the eyewitness account of an "honest Gentle-man" who was present at the cure of a man
with "the stumpe of some small tree run through his foote." The powwow wrapped the foot in a piece of cloth and over that a beaver skin.
Then, putting his mouth to the beaver skin, "by his sucking charmes he
brought out the stumpe, which he spat into a tray of water, returning
the foote as whole as its fellow in a short time."[67]

The Reverend Alexander Whitaker described from Virginia the wonders produced by the priests, described as great witches with powers over
nature. He wrote that "the principall amongst them beinge bound with
stronge Irons and kept with great watch" still have managed to escape
"wihout our knowledge or prevention."[68]

Edward Winslow described the villagers' response to the powwow's
invocations, comparing it to an "Amen." In his account the powwow
was accompanied by a snake and an eagle that were invisible to all but
him; these sucked the wound to draw out the harm. The powwows were
"eager and free in speech, fierce in countenance" and performed many
"antic and labourious gestures"; they promised to sacrifice many precious goods to "the fiend" if he would come and help with the cure, "but
whether they perform it, I know not."[69]

Henry Spelman described priests in the Chesapeake curing by stroking
the body of the sick and sprinkling them with water after a ceremony of
chanting and shaking a rattle; if the person was wounded, the powwow
would also cut the wound and suck out the poison, after which he applied a powdered root to the sore.[70]

Thomas Morton applied his famous skepticism to the "pretty conjuring tricks" of the powwows, whom he termed "but weake witches." One
in particular, called Papasiquineo (which may be the same name as
Wood's Pissacannawa), was said to have swum underwater across a broad
river. Morton believed that he had not really done this, but rather that

he had befuddled the onlookers by "casting a mist before their eies" so they could not see him coming up for air (Morton apparently considered creating a mist a relatively easy task). Papasiquineo also made a piece of ice appear in a bowl of water on a hot summer day in front of an English audience; as he intoned an incantation, a thick cloud suddenly appeared, a thunderclap was heard, and the ice was seen in the water. Morton's judgment was that it "doubtles was done by the agility of Satan his consort."

Like Roger Williams, Morton was filled with indignation over the reverence in which priests were held and the gifts that the ordinary people bestowed on them in return for their services, particularly in curing. But he also told of an Englishman who availed himself of the services of a powwow who "quickly recovered him," although Morton assumed it must have been "with the helpe of the devill (as may be conjectured,)."[71]

Some, of course, did not recover, and English observers were also keenly interested in burial and mourning practices among the Indians. The partnership of the scientist Thomas Harriot and the artist John White at Roanoke produced a remarkable depiction of mortuary customs for the Carolina coastal Algonquians. John White painted a temple in which a carved wooden idol and a priest kept watch over the remains of their "Weroans or cheefe lordes." Thomas Harriot explained the procedure in his notes to the engraved version: the bodies were opened and the flesh removed from the bones, and the skeletons, "still fastened together with the ligaments whole and uncorrupted," were covered with leather and with the skin again as if they had not been disturbed. The dried flesh was placed in baskets at their feet, and the bodies were laid side by side on a high platform under which lived a priest who "Mumbleth his prayers nighte and day." Harriot ended his discussion with the kind of remark that made him seem dangerous to the establishment in England: "Thes poore soules are thus instructed by natu[r]e to reverence their princes even after their death."[72]

John Smith reported similar burial customs along the Chesapeake, adding that chains of copper and pearls were placed around the necks of the corpses, and "their inwards they stuffe with copper beads . . . hatchets and such trash." They were wrapped "very carefully in white skins" and then in mats. Additional wealth was added to the baskets at their feet. Ordinary people, according to Smith, were buried wrapped in skins and with their "jewels" in the ground on platforms of sticks.[73] Thomas Morton in New England also wrote of distinctions between the burials of "persons of noble, and of ignoble, or obscure, or inferior discent," although all were buried in the earth. The noble dead were placed on a "planck" somewhat in the manner of the stick platform Smith wrote of,

The Tombe of their Cherounes or cheife personages, their flesh clene taken of from the bones save the skynn and heare of theire heads, w flesh is dried and enfolded in matts laide at theire feete. their bones also being made dry ar couered wth deare skynns not altering their forme or proporcion. With theire Kewash which is an Image of woode keeping the deade.

John White's painting of a Carolina Algonquian mortuary. © The British Museum, British Museum Press.

and other boards were placed on the sides and top of the body, "in forme of a chest." A monument was then placed over the grave "in forme of a hearse cloth."[74]

Indian burial customs echoed English practices, which involved strikingly different treatment of "better sort" and common dead. Ordinary people were often buried in a shroud into which flowers were wrapped if the season allowed. Coffins were just coming into widespread use in England, and they were sometimes assembled at the burial site from planks, just as Morton described for Indian burials. Sometimes an English parish owned one coffin, used only for carrying the shrouded corpse to the place of burial. Only the wealthy had the luxury of both shroud and coffin.[75] The Massachusetts puritans departed from traditional English practice and erected no monuments over graves. Morton wrote that the Indians, seeing these bare graves, thought no high-ranking person had yet come to New England.[76]

English writers were struck by the mourners and their grief, especially because they wanted to know if Indian religion offered hope of meeting loved ones again in an afterlife. Many described extravagant expressions of grief by the bereaved. John Smith wrote that women in Virginia painted their faces with charcoal and oil, and for twenty-four hours mourned "with such yelling and howling as may expresse their great passions." William Wood was particularly impressed by the anguish he saw: "to behold and heare their throbbing sobs and deepe-fetcht sighes, their griefe-wrung hands, and teare-dewed cheekes, their dolefull cries, would draw teares from Adamantine eyes, that be but spectators of their mournefull Obsequies." He said they spent a long time at the grave in their "Irish-like howlings" and returned annually, painting their faces "with a blacke stiffe paint," and concluded: "These are the Mourners without hope."[77]

But, they were not strictly without any hope. Wood went on to say that the Indians did believe that the soul is immortal and, after death, went to "the South-west Elysium, concerning which their Indian faith jumps much with the Turkish Alchoran, holding it to be a kinde of Paradise, wherein they shall everlastingly abide." Enemies or "loose livers, whom they account unworthy of this imaginary happines" go to "the infernall dwelling of Abamocho, to be tortured according to the fictions of the ancient Heathen." Thomas Morton also wrote that the souls of the good go to the Southwest to "live with Kytan for ever in all manner of pleasure," whereas the "naughty" go to the "habitation of the Devill" in the center of the earth.[78]

Roger Williams reported a long and strict period of mourning, with lavish expressions of grief: "I have seen teares run downe the cheekes of stoutest Captaines." The possessions of the dead person were laid in and on the grave, "to rot with the dead." He compared the practice of mourners blackening their faces with charcoal to the English custom of wearing black mourning clothes, and he admired the way friends came together to console the relatives of the dead. The name of the dead person was not used after this, and anyone with the same name assumed a new one. As Samson Occum noted, Indians of the southern New England region continued to honor the interdiction on using the name of dead persons; even title deeds use formulas such as "he that was sachem" to avoid mentioning a name directly.[79] Williams wrote that the Narragansetts believed in the soul's immortality, but not in a resurrection to come. Like Wood, he compared their idea of paradise to his notion of a Muslim model: "where they have hopes (as the Turkes have) of carnall Joyes." Williams argued that they located "Cautàntouwit his House" in the southwest because the best weather comes with the southwest wind. The souls of murderers, thieves, and liars wander "restless abroad."[80]

Southern reports varied the location of paradise and hell. William Strachey offered two versions from Virginia, his own and that collected by Henry Spelman. Spelman reported that the souls of the good went to the top of a high tree from which they could "espie a faire plaine broad pathe waye" lined by fruit bushes. They followed this path toward the rising sun, stopping for refreshment midway at the home of a "woman goddesse," until they came to the house of the great Hare God, where they lived "in great pleasure in a goodly feild." They lived there until they grew to be "starke old men" in that world, after which they died there "and come into the world againe." Strachey asserted that the common people had no immortality, but the priests and werowances traveled to the place where the sun set to live in luxury until they were old, at which time they would die "and come into a woman's womb againe, and so be a new borne unto the world not unlike the heathen Pythagoras his opinion and fable of Metempsychosis." Nor was this belief any more "ridiculous or Savage," according to Strachey, than Epicurus's teaching that the soul was simply the "vitall power."[81]

Thomas Harriot collected the stories of two people who, through near-death experiences, had actually visited those spirit worlds. One, a "wicked man," was disinterred when the earth over his grave was seen to move. He told his rescuers that he had been on the threshold of Popogusso, the place of torment, which was a great pit near the setting sun where people burned continuously. One of the gods intervened and gave him permission to return to this world, so that he could "teach his friends what they should doe to avoid that terrible place of torment."

Another, also disinterred from the grave, had traveled along the broad way lined with fruit trees that Spelman told of. When he arrived at a settlement of "most brave and faire houses," he met his dead father, who "gave him great charge" that he must go back and urge his friends to live good lives so they could "enjoy the pleasures of that place." His father promised him that he would eventually be able to return himself. Samuel Purchas, in reprinting Harriot's account, compared these near-death experiences to "the Popish Legends."[82]

Harriot, referring to the "subtilty" of the "Wiroances and Priestes," pointed to the social utility of reports of punishment after death for keeping the "common and simple sort of people" in line. Everything depended on the priests, whom the colonists saw as their chief antagonists, the principal guardians of the Indians' culture. Harriot attributed his extraordinary knowledge to his friendship with Carolina priests; William Strachey, giving the same admission a more sinister twist, wrote that further understanding of "their unhallowed misteryes" could not be achieved "untill we can make surprize of some of their Quiyough-quisocks."[83] As time went by some found the vitality of native religion and the high regard in which the priests were held created daunting obstacles to English plans. The Reverend Jonas Stockham, writing from Virginia in 1621, was angry at "lasie servants" and "Italiannated and Spaniolized Englishmen" who thought only of themselves, but mainly he was fed up with his ongoing contest with American priests. Although they had "endevoured by all the meanes they could by kindnesse to convert them," in return the English got only "derision and ridiculous answers." His solution was to take out the competition: "till their Priests and Ancients have their throats cut, there is no hope to bring them to conversion." Stockham had been driven to admit that the lure of Christianity (at least as presented by him) was not sufficient against deeply held American religious beliefs.[84]

In targeting priests, even in the most bloodthirsty versions, English colonists were acknowledging that native societies were tightly organized around a core of religious beliefs and that these beliefs made those cultures strong and vibrant. English writers who became truly knowledgeable about these cultures recognized many elements in common with familiar old-world models; so clear were these resemblances that some thought the Indians retained elements of former Jewish identity. The gods the Indians worshipped were false to European eyes, and that worship was paganism, but they lay in "Ethnick darkness" because they had not had access to the truth. Moreover, the devil was active in human affairs only because God allowed it, and the future Jesuit James Rosier argued that it was God who had elected to "darken" the Americans' "understanding," making them a "purblind generation."[85] English Christians would provide an example of true religion that would draw the Indians from their paganism. Testifying to both the strength of American religious beliefs and their readiness for conversion, John Rolfe wrote that "they meerely through ignorance of God and Christ, doe runn headlong, yea with joy into distruccion and perpetuall damnation."[86] The very vitality of their beliefs made them readier for the truth. The principal challenge to this agenda lay in the Americans' religious leaders, the central and most powerful figures in native life.

Many Indians were interested in Christianity, but not in the way English leaders hoped. Even open acceptance of Christianity did not mean that converts stripped away one identity and replaced it with another. Rather, converts sought to take control of their Christianity and fashion their worship according to their own lights; where they could they prohibited Euramerican Christians from interfering. Mohegan preachers Samson Occum and Joseph Johnson, together with the Montauk David Fowler, ultimately led seven Indian congregations away from New England onto Oneida lands in western New York to found Brothertown, where they could worship without interference just after the American Revolution.[87] Even those who stayed behind in Mohegan maintained their own traditions, as Fidelia Fielding's daily invocation of Mándu in the early twentieth century indicates.

Some Indians found their own routes to the power and teachings of God. During King Philip's War, the colonists were opposed in the Northeast by "Squando, the sagamore of Saco," and Madocawando, "the chief Commander of the Indians Eastward about Penobscot." Squando's enmity stemmed from the callous mistreatment of his wife and child by some English mariners, which had resulted in the child's death. But Squando and Madocawando were "a strange kinde of moralized Salvages," who "pretend to have received some Visions and Revelations." They were "Grave and serious" and worshipped "the great God," abstaining from work on the sabbath. The English thought they discerned the influence of "some Papist" who had led these Indians to the devil, but the sachems were secure in their own religiosity.[88]

One particularly revealing exchange—between would-be missionary Richard Treat and a group of Indians at Middletown, Connecticut, in 1734—indicates the complexity of the native response to Christianity. When Treat preached about the resurrection, one of his hearers "(in a scoffing and ridiculing manner)" pointed to a pig and asked "whether that pig would rise again after it was dead as well as wee." Treat silenced the man with difficulty, but every time he preached he was subject to

"their objections and little Slouffles." Hearing of a great gathering to conclude the mourning period for a man who had died and to determine by
conjuration whether he had been poisoned, Treat went to the dance
ground on Saturday, where he was greeted angrily: "One of them, with
no little fury, told me that I was Come to see if I might not preach to
them the next day, which he said I should not do." To make peace "a
number of Nahantick and moheegan Indians" told Treat that if he would
leave, they would gather nearby to hear him preach on Sunday, but no
one showed up at the appointed time. Treat heard that a child was very
sick and, as he had no congregation, thought he would visit the child,
but he was driven away. Peacemakers again interposed and told Treat to
go to a little grove of apple trees nearby, saying "they would Speedily
Come to me and they would hear me preach." As he waited under the
apple trees, Treat heard the noise of the "paw wawe," "the most Dolfull
noise that Can be thought of." Because he believed the Indians were raising the devil, Treat repeatedly intervened to try to break them up, although he thought he might be killed for doing so. He told his story in
an unsuccessful effort to get compensation from the Connecticut
Assembly.[89]

Treat's story demonstrates what colonial leaders feared: America's natives were determined to maintain control of their own worship.
Christianity did not represent a package that they accepted entire; rather,
they unpacked it and reassembled its parts in conjunction with their own
traditions. Reverend Joseph Fish, who preached to the Narragansetts in
the eighteenth century, was horrified by a conversation with Tobe
Cowyass, who incorporated traditional Narragansett modes of crossing
over into the spirit world into the Christianity Fish preached. Cowyass
told Fish he had traveled to heaven, where he had seen God, "a Great
Gentleman," Jesus, "A handsome Man," and many folks "Resembling
Butterflies of Many Colours." But Fish faced a more fundamental challenge; his greatest antagonist was not a priest of the native religion but
a Narragansett Christian preacher, Samuel Niles, whom the Indians
themselves had ordained. Although Fish viewed the nearly illiterate
"Father Sam" and his style of preaching with disdain, he had to face the
fact that the congregation preferred him.[90]

The early colonization literature had held out the hope that Indian religions would be a foundation on which Christian teaching could be laid.
They were right in many cases, but the result, native appropriation and
fashioning of Christianity, was far different from their expectation. For
American Indians, such fashioning offered the possibility of sustaining
a religious life that was satisfying to them while holding unwanted control at arm's length.

5   Village Life

Daily life, relations between men and women, parents and children—these were central to any real understanding of the Americans. They were also essential topics for those commentators who hoped to use these accounts to determine what kinds of relationships were natural and fundamental to all human life. But village-level connections required intimate knowledge if they were to be presented properly, and wildly varying portraits were penned, as lack of experience was no bar to publication. Writers who remained in England sometimes portrayed the Indians as moving over the land like deer, living from hand to mouth and having a kind of herd instinct rather than any larger sense of structure. Those who transmitted their authentic American experience and drew on the lore of the natives they talked with, on the other hand, strove to convey both the complex nature of American village life and its similarity to familiar English forms.

Such a clear division, however, is too simple. Even within a single book, varying contexts elicited differing portraits, and we look in vain for a voice presenting an unambiguous interpretation of American social relationships and daily life. Many writers who presented full and nuanced pictures of Indian life also sometimes indulged in rhetorical denunciations that played to European preconceptions, and, although these statements often occurred when venturers were explaining their own failures, modern readers sometimes mistake these flourishes for the whole picture.

John Smith wrote extensively on native technology and relationships and unabashedly described English reliance on them. Yet, stung by the "worlds blind ignorant censure" of the Jamestown colonists for not finding and sending back rich commodities as Spanish venturers had done in Mexico and Peru, he hit back by blaming the Indians, not the unrealistic predictions of colonial promoters. He explained that the Spanish conquistadors had stumbled, through no skill of their own, on technologically advanced natives who could be forced to provide the items they wanted: "But had those fruitfull Countries, beene as Salvage as barbarous, as ill peopled, as little planted, laboured and manured as Virginia, their proper labours (it is likely) would have produced as small profit as ours. . . . But we chanced in a lande, even as God made it. Where we found only an idle improvident, scattered people; ignorant of the knowledge of gold, or silver, or any commodities; and carelesse of any thing but from hand to mouth." This judgment was contradicted by Smith's own careful account of Indian life, and especially of their technology, and by his frank admission of the colonists' total dependence on native supplies for food.[1]

Similarly, James Rosier alleged that New England's soil must contain rich ores and other possibilities but that these were not available because the Indians had not developed them. He wrote that God had thus far denied them the capacity to "discerne, use, or rightly esteeme the unvaluable riches in middest whereof they live sensually content with the barke and outward rinde." But in other places Rosier wrote enthusiastically of the Indians' "exceeding good invention, quicke understanding and readie capacitie" and praised their "kinde civility."[2]

The first requirement for modern readers, then, is to go beyond the telling quote and look at the fully rounded picture presented by those who took the trouble to investigate—and to deal with the inevitable internal contradictions. The picture presented to early modern readers in full accounts written by people with real experience offered Americans with all the marks of civility. And the widely circulated copperplates made from the paintings of John White together with Thomas Harriot's notes left no room for doubt. White's portfolio of American pictures, and the engravings created from them in the workshop of Theodor de Bry, included two village scenes. One, the village of Pomeiooc, was surrounded by a palisade. The other, Secoton, was open, and Harriot said the open villages were "commonlye fayrer." Within the villages, White depicted and Harriot took care to note, people involved in all kinds of activities that supported civil life. White depicted Secoton with cornfields in three stages of growth, as well as other crops, and portrayed

Americans preparing and eating food. Each village contained a religious temple, and Pomeiooc also held the chief's lodge. White included a religious ceremony, the Green Corn Festival, in Secoton. Each of the vignettes within the village pictures was also the subject of a separate painting, and the engraving made from each painting carried a note by Harriot reinforcing the lessons of the images.

White and Harriot together argued in the most forceful and effective way that the American natives were social beings, possessing all the characteristics necessary to civility: community life and the family structure, hierarchy, and orderliness that made it possible; care for the morrow by cultivating and preserving foods; and all informed by a religious sensibility that honored the human dependence on supernatural forces in the universe. White and Harriot also portrayed individuals and conveyed the meaning of relationships within the family and the village through these sympathetic portrayals. After Thomas Harriot's *Briefe and True Report of the new found land of Virginia* was reprinted in 1590 with engravings of White's paintings accompanied by Harriot's explanation of each picture, these copperplates become the standard pictures of Indians in Europe and were used to illustrate books on all kinds of topics. The coastal Carolina Algonquians as rendered by this Roanoke team were *the* Indians throughout the colonial period, and White's lesson of native civility was available in countless contexts.

Others did with words what White achieved through his pictures. The basic message—expressed with varying degrees of approval or hostility— was always the same: the Indians lived settled civil lives in villages led by both political and religious figures. To those who saw with approving eyes, this message meant that the Indians were, in their own way, admirable, and these writers always had classical models partially in mind.

Writers who were hostile or wary about settling with the Indians, however, also emphasized the Americans' competence. They had to get people in England to see that the Indians were not inconsequential. Although promoters at home might daydream of easily overawed native peoples, the Indians were the only people who knew how to make the land productive and how to negotiate the landscape in search of the valuable products that the colonists were supposed to be sending home. Everything, in fact, depended on the Indians. No one actually in America could afford to trivialize the people who occupied the land.

Descriptions followed a template that corresponded to early modern English notions of a society's essential building blocks; often the template echoed Tacitus's description of the ancient Germans. The family was the most fundamental unit in America as in England, and the process of family formation was found to be strikingly similar. Marriage

The following text labels appear within the illustration:

Their rype corne.

Their greene corne.

Corne newly sprong.

Their sitting at meate.

The place of solemne prayer.

The howse wherin the Tombe of their Herounds standeth.

SECOTON

A. Ceremony in their prayers w strange iestures and songs dansing abowt posts carued on the topps lyke mens faces.

Secoton. A villager sits on the platform in the middle of the cornfield to keep away crows and other scavengers. The depicted village would have been reassuringly familiar to English readers. © The British Museum, British Museum Press.

The towne of Pomeiock and true forme of their howses, couered and enclosed some with matts, and some with barcks of trees. All compassed about with smale poles stock thick together in stedd of a wall.

Pomeiooc. Harriot's notes drew attention to the temple with the peaked roof, the larger house of the chief, and the pond, which the inhabitants had dug for water. He also remarked on the ingenious system of mats that covered the house frames allowing control of ventilation and light. © The British Museum, British Museum Press.

alliances, as described by these writers, were approached formally within the sight of the whole community. The prospective husband, after obtaining "the good-will of the Maide or Widdow," sought the consent of the bride's parents or guardian, and a dowry was paid, although the sources varied on which party received the payment. Among the ancient Germans, according to Tacitus, the husband had paid a dowry to the bride's family, and Roger Williams reported the same practice, comparing it not to the Germans but to ancient Israel. When Samson Occum described the Montauks' culture, he devoted the longest section of his

report to four ways of contracting marriages. Reports from all regions described festive weddings where the friends and families of the bride and
groom came together to witness their union and to feast and dance.[3]

Distinctions operated in marriage according to these reports, and many
writers argued that the "better sort" married only within their own status. John Pory, the colony secretary in Virginia, traveled to the eastern
shore "betwixt the Bay and the maine Ocean," and found the Indians
there the "most civill and tractable people we have met with." His reasons included that they produced enough corn to last all year, and that
they had a system of reckoning. Moreover they respected incest taboos
in marriage: "they observe a large distance, as well in affinitie as con-
sanguinitie." In New England, James Rosier reported that the Indians
were discreet: "They lie with their wives secretly." A related sign of
order was women's observance of strict menstrual seclusion.[4]

Sexual relations outside of marriage were described in a variety of
ways. Many authors asserted that young men and women were allowed
sexual freedom before marriage. John Smith was disturbed when, following the dance of welcome to Powhatan's village by thirty painted
young women that he labeled "A Virginia Maske," the young "Nymphes
. . . tormented" him by "crowding, pressing, and hanging about him,
most tediously crying, Love you not me? love you not me?" Some argued the Americans allowed sexual license even within marriage; "and
uncredible yt is, with what heat both Sexes of them are given over to
those Intemperances, and the men to preposterous Venus." Edward
Maria Wingfield was reported to have told Samuel Purchas that same-
sex relationships were included in such freedom. Moreover, reports from
Virginia and New England asserted that prostitutes practiced their trade
in Indian villages.[5]

A related question, and one that struck deep chords of association with
the exotic, was whether polygamy was practiced among the Indians.
Many of the earliest accounts simply affirmed that polygamy was allowed, but that husbands were constant to their wives. As time went by
and more evidence was gathered, the reports became more qualified and
maintained, as Tacitus had written of the Germans, that only kings or
the very wealthy were allowed more than one wife. As Christopher
Levett wrote from New England, "he that hath the most wives is the
bravest fellow" (brave here meaning splendid or ostentatious).[6]

Later reports moved to downplay the sensationalism implicit in the
notion of polygamy. William Wood wrote that "the kings or great
Powwowes, alias Conjurers, may have two or three Wives, but seldome
use it. Men of ordinary Ranke, having but one; which disproves the report, that they had eight or tenne Wives apeece." The Reverend William

Morrell, who traveled in New England, even argued that polygamy made sense in that society: because women were the primary agriculturists, the food supply was guaranteed where men had multiple wives. Corn, as he reminded his readers, was the most valuable item in Indian society. Roger Williams echoed this thinking, arguing that Narragansett men, most of whom had only one wife, justified polygamy by pointing to both the agricultural wealth women produced and their long withdrawal from sexual relations after the birth of children.[7]

Christopher Levett tried to convince "one of their sagamores" that having many wives was "no good fashion," so the chief asked how many wives King James had. When told that James I had had one wife and that she was now dead, the sagamore "wondered" and asked Levett how the king got his work done. "You may imagine he thought their fashion was universal, and that no king had any to work for them but their wives." The Pilgrims also reported Indian amazement that the English king lived without a wife.[8]

The main theme the writers sought to convey was that marriage was entered into in an orderly way and was an honored state among the Indians. The ancient Saxon model presented by Tacitus and avidly read during this period portrayed a society in which constancy in marriage was the "most commendable" attribute, and married women lived "in most straite chastitie, uncorrupted with the allurements of shewes and spectacles" Marriage was between mature people and adultery was taken very seriously.[9] Adultery was also severely punished among the Indians, according to many reports, and commitment in marriage was prized— which demonstrated, according to Roger Williams, that marriage was a natural state commonly revered by all people.[10]

Most observers, however, saw Indian women as little more than slaves. Although English writers in America admired the perceived orderliness of family formation, they were indignant about the division of labor on gender lines. Indian women were seen as doing all the real work in their villages, and the writers unanimously censored Indian society for this inexcusable exploitation.

Early reports from Jamestown set the standard line. Gabriel Archer wrote that the women "do all the labour and the men hunt and goe at their plesure," while John Smith said "the women be verie painefull and the men often idle."[11] Smith, Archer, and virtually every other early colonial leader wrote copiously about their frustration over the colonists' idleness and leaders' inability to command them to labor, but when they wrote of the Indians, they thought in terms of ideal English traditional work categories. Agricultural labor in England was men's work, even though women pitched in at harvest time. It was considered demeaning and unjust to expect women to work in the fields as part of their regular duties. Other occupations, such as laundering, were as strenuous and demanding as farm work, but, since they were defined as female, placing women in them was not exploitation.[12]

American roles were assigned on very different lines according to eyewitness reports. Women planted, tended, harvested, and preserved the food crops, and they constructed and maintained the houses—even carrying the mats and poles of which houses were built when the village moved. The chief occupations of Indian men, echoing Tacitus's depiction of the ancient Germans, were war and hunting, as well as spiritual/ceremonial duties. In their disdain for idle Indian men, the observers drew on class as well as work categories; hunting was reserved for gentlemen at home, and ordinary Indian men were thus appropriating undeserved roles.[13] The problem lay in what kinds of tasks were defined as work and in their gender assignments.

Much depended on the context, and on the subject under discussion. When the topic was gender inequality, English writers were indignant, but when they attempted to portray the relative social equality they saw in Indian societies, they drew a different picture. Both John Smith and the author of the *Relation of Maryland* wrote that the werowance did the same work as other adult men, and they offered an expanded catalogue of that work: "For the King himselfe will make his owne robes, shooes, bowes, arrowes, pots; plant, hunt, or doe anything so well as the rest." The *Relation of Maryland* asserted that he made his own equipment "as any other common Indian."[14] Roger Williams, while agreeing with the general picture of idle men and painful women, softened it somewhat by reporting that sometimes men out of love for their wives or care for their children would help with the crops "which (by the custome of the Countrey) they are not bound to," and also that the entire village and its neighbors would combine to clear new fields for planting, "a very loving sociable speedy way to dispatch it." He wrote that a single woman could raise two or three heaps of twelve, fifteene, or twentie bushells a heap . . . and if she have helpe of her children or friends, much more." This picture of cooperative agriculture in which ingenuity made up for the lack of tools was confirmed in the oral tradition, and was told to "A. Holmes" in 1804. Williams wrote that women continued to use "naturall Howes of shells and Wood" even when European metal tools were available. Older and poorer women were especially "fearfull to leave the old tradition." On the other hand Henry Spelman wrote that native tools had been abandoned in favor of imported "scavels and spades" in the Chesapeake.[15]

Outrage over the exploitation of American women reached a crescendo with William Wood in the 1630s. He devoted a chapter of his book to

Indian women, whom he found "more excellent" than their "lazie husbands." He directed this chapter to women readers "who otherwise
might think their sex forgotten, or not worthy a record," and recommended that English women read "these few lines" to "see their own
happinesse." Wood's chapter outlined the responsibilities of Indian
women. First they constructed the houses, covering the frames with
"close-wrought mats of their own weaving." When, according to Wood,
their husbands decided to move for fishing or hunting, the women were
forced "like snailes, to carrie their houses on their backs."

He also described their agricultural work, saying their fields were more
like gardens than farm plots, they "not suffering a choaking weede to advance his audacious head above their infant corne, or an undermining
worme to spoile his spurnes." They had to contrive special means to
keep the harvested corn safe from their "gurmandizing husbands," who
would eat up even the seed corn. They also fished. If the men went fishing, according to Wood, they dumped the catch on the shore and the
women had to go and get it and then clean and prepare it. When fish were
plentiful, the women dried them for storage. Once the food was prepared,
the men ate while the women "dance a Spaniell-like attendance at their
backes for their bony fragments."

Neither pregnancy nor motherhood lessened these duties. By the time
the baby was three or four days old, according to Wood, its mother was
back at work in the "Icie Clammbankes" with the newcomer strapped
to her back on a cradleboard, while she dug the shellfish "Whereby her
lazie husbands guts shee cramms." He contrasted the civility, mildness,
and modesty of Indian women with the "customarie churlishnesse and
salvage inhumanitie" of their husbands.[16]

This theme of the contrast between the gender equality in English life
and the cruel exploitation of Indian women, was dear to the hearts of
English men.[17] Unbalanced gender roles was another distinguishing
mark of the savage, and it was a trope that served key purposes. It enhanced the self-confidence of English venturers and bolstered their own
conviction of civility. Moreover, like the universal assumption that
Indians who welcomed settlers were beleaguered victims of other more
warlike and dominant natives, it opened the door to a blanket justifica-
tion for colonization. The coming of the English would help Indian men
to see their errors, and, as they became civilized, they would learn to esteem the contributions of their wives. Only large-scale settlement, with
a full representation of English society, would allow such learning to
take place.

Many writers responded to the fear that influence might in fact go the
other way, and that American conditions might cause immigrants to

treat their wives with less respect than at home. Reports vehemently denied that rough colonial conditions necessitated hard work for English women, or that men, freed from the constraints of society, "usurpe over their Wives and keepe them in servile subjection."[18] Rather, Wood reported, the wholesome example of immigrant wives was transforming the consciousness of Indian women. He described scenes of cross-cultural exchange in English kitchens, where the native women poured out their troubles. "If her husband come to seeke for his Squaw and beginne to bluster, the English woman betakes her to her armes which are the warlike Ladle, and the scalding liquors, threatning blistering to the naked runnaway who is soone expelled by such liquid comminations." Wood's conclusion to "this womans historie" was the love of the American women for their counterparts and the precious gifts of rare foods they brought to show their esteem.[19] Wood's account, contrasting self-confident English women against servile American "Squaws" and their bullying but cowardly and defenseless husbands, evoked a world to which hearty English common sense would quickly bring order and stability. On the other hand Lion Gardiner answered Pequot bravado about killing English men and capturing their women with the retort that "it would do them no good, but hurt, for English women are lazy, and can't do their work."[20]

Modern analysis argues that English observers erred in their depictions of native women's exploitation; they did not see a connection between the matrilineal pattern of descent and inheritance they tried to describe and the powerful economic role of women in Indian societies. What they described as exploitation the natives' own tradition and ethnohistorians have presented in terms of authority and centrality. Since the group's wealth was measured in corn, and the houses belonged to the women who made them, they were the producers and owners of the village's assets. Recent studies argue that the roles of men and women were balanced and reciprocal.[21]

Moreover, it is clear that life in the early colonies forced English men to think about the essential role of women in their own society. Writers analyzing the irresolution and discouragement of Jamestown's early years came to understand that part of the blame lay in planners' decision to make it an all-male society initially. John Pory's report of the Virginia Assembly's first meeting made the need for women very clear, saying, "In a new plantation, it is not known whether man or woman be more necessary."[22] The Virginia Company quickly moved to send single women, acknowledging that the way to "tie and root the Planters' minds to Virginia" was through "the bonds of wives and children": "by long experience we have found that the Minds of our people in Virginia are much dejected, and their hearts enflamed with a desire to return for England only through the wants of the comforts without which God saw that Man could not live contentedly, no not in Paradise." The company resolved to send "young, handsome, and honestly educated Maids to Virginia."[23] And gendered labor assignments were affected by American conditions. Whatever promoters may have written in their pamphlets, English women in the Chesapeake did perform hard physical labor, including field work, that they would not have done at home.[24]

Although their view of gender relations among the Americans made English men certain of their superior civility, these reports also reflected their uncertainty and dividedness about changing male and female roles in England. While they castigated the perceived brutish subjugation of Indian wives, the writers admired the cool humility of these women in accepting their place without complaint or rebellion, and drew lessons about disintegrating distinctions in their own society, especially the phenomenon of mannish assertive women. William Wood, who celebrated the powerful English women who drove bullying Indian husbands from their kitchens, was forced to see things very differently by the vivid testimony of a native man:

> An Indian Sagomore once hearing an English woman scold with her husband, her quicke utterance exceeding his apprehension, her active lungs thundering in his eares, expelled him the house; from whence he went to the next neighbour, where he related the unseemelinesse of her behaviour; her language being strange to him, hee expressed it as strangely, telling them how she cryed Nannana Nannana Nannana Nan, saying he was a great foole to give her the audience, and no correction for usurping his charter, and abusing him by her tongue.

Ballads, comic plays, and village rituals in England ridiculed the dominated husband with savage humor, but they also had a serious point. A husband who failed to keep his wife's respect as Indian husbands were said to do was responsible for the subversion of good order. Wood and his fellow reporters could save the conception of their civilizing mission because breaches of harmony were always seen as exceptional when they occurred in English communities.[25]

Not only did Indian women accept their gendered position gracefully, they enhanced the life of the village aesthetically, as in their fine feather cloaks and woven mats. Wood was particularly taken with the "curious baskets with intermixed colours and protractures of antique Imagerie" made by Indian women. He also praised their beautiful singing: "To heare one of these Indians unseene, a good eare might easily mistake their untaught voyce for the warbling of a well tuned instrument."[26]

Moreover, the labor Indian women did, far from unsuiting them for feminine roles, seemed to make them better adapted for their natural role of bearing children. Hard work made them able to bear children in a "wonderfull more speedy and easie Travell, and delivery then the Women of Europe." Their quick return to normal life following delivery was less emblematic of their slavery than of the superior conditioning of their bodies.[27]

Sociability was a key attribute of human beings, and the Indians were no exception: Roger Williams wrote that they "love societie," and they were especially fond of their families and hated to be separated from them.[28] Relationships between generations were another sphere in which English observers saw dangerous decay in their own society, and through their description of the Indians they sought to instruct their readers. The Americans were universally described as affectionate parents: "they love their children verie dearly." As among the uncorrupted ancient Germans, mothers nursed their own children, a course strongly urged on English mothers. William Wood wrote that Indian children were cared for tenderly and "generally as quiet as if they had neither spleene or lungs."

Some thought tenderness was carried too far: Indian children were spoiled. Roger Williams reported his fruitless efforts to get an Indian father to discipline his "sawcie, bold, and undutifull" son. But writers also reported strict preparation for adult life from an early age, such as bathing babies in special mixtures so that "no weather will hurt them." Christopher Levett wrote that children were buried in snowbanks up to their faces "to make them the better to endure cold." Training for adult life began at the earliest age; boys learned to use bow and arrow from two years on.[29]

Indian parents could not bear separation from their children, according to these reports. Whereas in England most children left home in early adolescence, Indian parents kept them at home until they were adults. Promoters' plans for conversion and assimilation were often based on the assumption that children could be taken and brought up in English homes and then returned fully acculturated to their villages. But the immigrants found that they could rarely persuade parents to part with their offspring. Job Kattenanit, a Christian Indian, risked his life to retrieve his children from the enemy during King Philip's War in the late seventeenth century because he could not bear the separation. The Jesuits in Maryland did induce chiefs in their region to agree that "some of their children may be brought up amongst the English." Thomas Morton in New England reported that an Indian man who had lived with Morton before he married asked to have his son brought up in Morton's house "and that he might be taught to reade in that booke [the Book of Common Prayer]." When Morton agreed, the Indian was "joyfull" because then his son would "(as hee said) become an English-man; and then hee would be a good man."[30]

English and Indians both attempted to manipulate political relationships by using the other side's interest in children. Opechancanough, a successor to Powhatan, proposed a joint expedition against Indians living to the west to punish them for killing Powhatan women. Among other inducements, he offered to share "all the booty of male and female Children." The Virginia Council was interested because the children could serve "particular persons" and could also be educated in the college the Virginia Company proposed to create, "this beinge a fayer opportunitye for the Advancement of this blessed worke seinge those Indians are in noe sort willinge to sell or by fayer meanes to part with their Children."[31]

Knowing the strong bonds between parents and children, English exploring parties routinely kidnapped the children of chiefs to ensure that the Indians among whom they traveled would cooperate with them. Ralph Lane, governor of the Roanoke colony, for example, knew that Menatonon would give him guides "for I had his best beloved sonne prisoner with me." In a passage marked by the marginal note, "How to deale with the Salvages," John Smith's technique was described. As he entered a village, he always seized "some childe for hostage" to back up his demands.[32] Many Indians were kidnapped and taken to Europe, and few were as lucky as Squanto, who returned to America; ultimately he went to live with the Pilgrims at Plymouth. The Pilgrim leaders were chagrined when confronted by an old woman "whom we judged to be not less than a hundred years old" whose three sons had been kidnapped with Squanto by the unscrupulous Captain Thomas Hunt. She came to see them "weeping and crying excessively" but despite their distress they were powerless to help her recover them.[33] Colonists rarely saw so vividly what the coming of the Europeans meant to many Americans.

The most famous kidnapping was that of Pocahontas, whose loss was mourned by her affectionate father. Powhatan refused to send a second daughter to live among the English because he could not bear so much separation. Similarly, the chief of Rappahannock, when asked for his son as a pledge of peace, refused because "having no more but him he could not live without him." Indians also developed strong affectionate relationships with English boys who were left with them.[34]

The grief of Indian fathers who had lost a child to death was terrible. Edward Winslow wrote that in such a case the father will "put his own most special jewels and ornaments in the earth with it, also will cut his hair, and disfigure himself very much, in token of sorrow." Roger

Williams wrote of the lamentations of "a poore Indian" over the loss of a child, rising at daybreak to plead that divine anger would turn away from him "and spare the rest of my children." Williams himself witnessed the grief of the Narragansett chief Canonicus who, after burying his son, "burn'd his owne Palace, and all his goods in it, (amongst them to a great value) in a sollemne remembrance of his sonne, and in a kind of humble Expiation to the Gods, who (as they believe) had taken his sonne from him."[35]

The generations were bound together by ties of respect and obedience. Just as mothers and fathers cared tenderly for their children, so the younger generation voluntarily treated their elders with respect and love, as Hendrick Aupaumut testified at the end of the eighteenth century. Thomas Morton suggested that "some of our irregular young people of civlized Nations" should study the Indians and copy their "better manners." Since so many "divine and humane authors" studied in Europe enjoined such "duetyfull" behavior, it seemed strange to Morton that "yet uncivilized" people should live up to their precepts better.[36]

Communities, composed of families, were the next level of social organization that marked civil life. White's drawings and Harriot's accompanying commentary set the tone, and English observers overwhelmingly presented Indians living a recognizably settled community life. The *Relation of Maryland* compared Indian towns to "Countrey Villages in England." And Thomas Morton resorted to irony to refute the notion that the Indians' movement from agricultural to fishing to hunting grounds constituted nomadism; he compared them to "the gentry of the Civilized natives," that is, the English elite who moved between their town and country residences. He also pointed out that moving allowed the Indians to maintain the supply of fuel in each place and was thus a sign of providence and forethought.[37] Most accounts of Indian towns described them as collections of twenty to fifty houses, but William Strachey said the town of Kecoughtan sometimes held a thousand people in three hundred houses. The overwhelming picture presented by early writings was of Americans living in settled communities sustained by formal agriculture; as Ralph Lane of Roanoke put it, America was "very wel peopled and towned, though savagelie."[38]

Thomas Harriot was the first English writer to describe a North American Indian house, and his description became the standard one for all regions throughout the colonial period. Explaining John White's very clear renderings of various types of houses, Harriot said they were made of small poles or saplings driven into the ground and bound together at the top to make a rounded roof. The frame was then covered with bark or woven mats. According to Harriot, houses were usually twice as long

as they were wide, with the length varying from twelve to twenty-four
yards. Other writers offered various estimates of standard sizes, some asserting that longhouses could be up to a hundred feet long. Mats could
be rolled up or down to make windows and doorways, and to regulate
ventilation. The longhouse had a fire burning in the center and smoke
hole above. The Indians slept on benches or a raised platform around the
perimeter, and the houses were described as smoky but warm. Gladys
Tantaquidgeon recalls the Mohegans building such structures for ceremonial occasions into the twentieth century.

The colonists would not have found such houses as primitive as modern readers might think. Chimneys were only at this time becoming normal for houses in England, and Father Andrew White reminded his readers that "the ancient halls of England" had central fires and smoke holes
above. Henry VIII's great banqueting hall at Hampton Court, the most
sumptuous of its day, was heated by fires along its center with the smoke
escaping through holes in the ceiling. Moreover, Harriot compared
Indian houses to "arbories in our gardens of England," and his comparison, like his general description, was employed again and again by other
writers. Drawing such resemblances reinforced the idea that these
houses were "homely," as Francis Higginson called them.[39]

Descriptions of Indian houses were usually presented simply, without
much praise or criticism, although their limitations might be indicated
by phrases such as William Strachey's who said they were "like gardein
arbours, (at best like our sheppardes Cottages,) made yet handsomely
enough." One exception was Edward Waterhouse, who, as secretary
of the Virginia Company in London, wrote the official account of the
great Indian attack of 1622. In that attack the Powhatans, led by
Opechancanough, reacted to the sudden dramatic growth of the colony
and the Indians' eviction from their best lands by attacking the plantations simultaneously and killing about a third of the settlers.
Waterhouse, who never went to Virginia himself, contemptuously referred to Opechancanough's "denne or Hog-stye." When Captain John
Smith reprinted this description of the great attack in his *Generall
Historie of Virginia, New-England and the Summer Isles*, he edited out
Waterhouse's offensive slur.[40]

Waterhouse wrote that the colonists had built for Opechancanough "a
fayre house according to the English fashion, in which hee tooke such
joy, especially in his locke and key, which hee so admired, as locking and
unlocking his doore an hundred times a day, hee thought no device in
all the world was comparable to it." Roger Williams wrote that the
Indians had begun to make doors for their houses in imitation of English
dwellings, which were secured from inside with a rope, so the last per-

son to leave climbed out through the chimney.[41] But emulation also went the other way. New Englanders, surprised to find such winter cold in a land so far to the south of England, were challenged to build sufficiently warm houses. William Wood reported admiration for the closely woven mats that formed the walls and roof of Indian houses. Not only were these mats "handsome," but they were proof against "any drop of raine, though it come both fierce and long, neither can the piercing North winde finde a crannie, through which he can conveigh his cooling breath, they be warmer than our English houses." Early Jamestown sources reported that the colonists had taken to covering their houses with mats and bark "according to the fashion of the Indians." William Strachey said the colonists avidly sought the "delicate wrought fine kinde of Mat the Indians make." If they could not be bought, they were "snatched up," and colonists decorated their chambers with them, "which make their houses so much the more handsome." He reported that they also covered their houses with tree bark in imitation of the Indians, which was as good as the "best Tyle" and kept them warm in winter and cool in summer, "which before in sultry weather would be like Stoves."[42]

White's paintings of Secoton showed the cornfields and gardens lying among the houses. The agricultural fields were the economic heart of village life, and the entire family was involved. Despite the assertions of their laziness, the accounts make clear that men took on the labor of clearing the fields when new plots were opened up. Women then did the planting, cultivating, and harvesting, and the entire village or sometimes several villages would come together to celebrate the successful harvest. For English observers trying to make readers at home understand Indian life, the essential point was that agriculture provided the Indians' principal food supply, and that food was preserved and stored for winter use.

The crops illustrated in White's painting of Secoton were maize in three stages of growth, patches of tobacco, a group of sunflowers, a pumpkin patch, and a vegetable garden. The Indians' diet was based on corn and beans which, when eaten together, form complete proteins supplying the eight amino acids the human body cannot synthesize. Although White depicted each crop growing separately in rows, Harriot's *Briefe and True Report* described the classic method of planting corn in hills of several stalks with beans and pulses growing around them and using the stalks for support. Beans fix nitrogen in the soil as they grow, thus the corn was fertilized continuously. Roger Williams transmitted the Indians' belief that a crow first taught them to plant and eat these together; it brought them a grain of Indian corn in one ear and "an Indian or French beane" in the other "from the Great God Kautántouwits field in the Southwest, from whence they hold came all their Corne and Beanes." Samson Occum confirmed that beans and corn and other food crops were believed to have come from the west, and Penobscot Indians told Frank Speck in the twentieth century that crows were the original owners of corn. Because of the crows' role in bringing their crops, the Indians did not kill these birds; Williams and Harriot reported that they erected a platform in the fields on which a villager sat to scare away the scavenging birds.[43]

Indian fields did not look as regimented as White depicted them. When new fields were to be opened up, the men killed the trees by girdling them, and then the crops were planted around the dead tree trunks. Once the crops were in the ground, however, the women were remarkably assiduous in keeping them weed free. Writers from all regions discussed Indian cultivation methods at great length, focusing on how the soil was prepared, the cultivation of the crops, and their harvesting and storage. Some had personally seen fields that extended to several hundred acres. There was certainly no doubt that the Indians were settled agriculturalists.

Extended descriptions of Indian cultivation techniques fitted into a growing concern in England, where landowners were researching methods of improving their land and experimenting with new crops with the goal of increasing agricultural yields. Much of the impetus stemmed from the revival of interest in classical literature. Ancient authors such as Virgil, Cato, and especially Columella offered advice that was newly available in translation and was incorporated into English manuals in the sixteenth century. Indian methods were laudable in terms of this new literature. In growing beans and other legumes together with the maize crop, the Indians were replicating Columella's insight that legumes enrich the soil.[44]

Writers who had learned about American practice had astonishing news to report to those interested in the latest techniques for improving harvests, because American yields of maize, variously called Turkey or Guinie wheat, were said to be stupendous. Maize was superior to old-world grains, both in increase—"the Plentifullest encrease of any Corne in the World"—and in the variety of uses to which it could be put. English writers tried various formulas to convey the information that one grain of maize produced a very large stalk with several ears and that each ear was covered with hundreds of kernels. Gabriel Archer, for example, wrote that each stalk bore two or three ears each "above a spann longe, besett with cornes at the least 300 upon an eare for the most part 5, 6, & 700." His account was printed with a marginal note that said simply: "infinit increase." Thomas Harriot called maize "a graine of marveillous great increase; of a thousand, fifteene hundred and some two thousand fold." After describing American planting methods, he reported colonists' own experimental results: an English acre yielded "at the least two hundred London bushelles" of corn and legumes, not counting other plants such as sunflowers. The contrast could not have been more dramatic: "in England fourtie bushelles of our wheate yeelded out of such an acre is thought to be much."[45]

Maize was also considered extraordinary in its variety of uses. Not only was bread made of it in the Indian fashion, but several writers affirmed they had also experimented with malting it and brewing beer. Ralph Lane wrote that the Roanoke colonists ate bread made of corn "and the Cane maketh very good and perfect suger." Sir Thomas Gates was quoted as saying cornstalks contained a juice so sweet the colonists in Virginia drank it as a cordial.[46]

Maize was beautiful, with its variety of colors, white, red, yellow, and blue, "a very goodly sight." Indian fields were also attractive, "the goodliest Corne fieldes that ever was seene in any Countrey."[47] Many eyewitnesses affirmed that maize was the best grain in the world. But it did not simply grow; as Metacom would remind his English foes later in the seventeenth century, the English needed training in its cultivation. William Wood's rendition of this education demonstrated how complicated and laborious maize culture was: "Many wayes hath their advice and endeavour beene advantagious unto us; they being our first instructers for the planting of their Indian Corne, by teaching us to cull out the finest seede, to observe the fittest season, to keepe distance for holes, and fit measure for hills, to worme it, and weede it; to prune it, and dresse it as occasion shall require." The newcomers also learned about a wide variety of new food crops and their use. Despite this tutelage the English yield, as the Pilgrims complained, was sometimes lower probably because they were using fields Indians had previously used and abandoned rather than spending the labor to clear new fields every few years as the Americans did.[48] English farmers may also have been reluctant to plant crops intermixed and, in aiming to create more orderly fields of segregated crops, missed the nitrogen-fixing properties of their legumes.

When the harvest was in, as the oral tradition and the documents say, the Indians stored their produce in "their barnes," great pits lined with bark or mats in which sun-dried corn was kept in large baskets, a practice English readers would have known from the newly available translation of Tacitus. The pits were covered with logs and earth. William Strachey, citing Pliny, compared this mode to the ancient Roman practice of storing treasure in underground cellars. Fish and meat were also dried for winter storage over smoky fires.[49]

Reports of Indian production of an agricultural surplus and its storage for use during the winter exposed the double, even self-contradictory, vision of the English travelers' layered response. The central issue was providence, an essential attribute of civil life. When writers portrayed the Indians tending their fields and preserving their harvest, they endorsed American life as civil in their terms. Such passages occurred within detailed examinations of native culture and were designed in part to reassure English readers that food was plentiful and sustenance would not be a problem for newcomers.

But in other sections of their books, often in introductory chapters where they adopted a more self-consciously literary mode, writers sometimes wrote that the Indians lacked any concern about saving. Sometimes these passages lauded the openhanded hospitality that English observers valued so highly. But at the same time they denigrated American culture as below the level of civil concern. Captain John Smith, for example, concluded his detailed discussion of Indian agriculture and food preservation with the statement that "for near three parts of the yeare" the Indians "live of what the Country naturally affordeth from hand to mouth, &c." Describing scarce times of the year, Smith wrote, "It is strange to see how their bodies alter with their diet, even as the deare and wilde beastes they seeme fat and leane, strong and weak." However, he added that those "that are provident" dried food for later consumption.

Smith's portrait of alternating fat and lean times may reflect the pressure under which the Chesapeake Bay Algonquians were suffering at the time Jamestown was founded, especially the unprecedented drought conditions recently revealed by tree-ring analysis. Gathered wild foods were a staple of the Indian diet, however, not a sign of desperation, and the mixture of cultivated and wild foods made their food supply more drought resistant than the English system. Coping with drought was certainly compounded by the demands of the colonists, who produced little or no food of their own and relied on native sources. In fact, Smith spent much of his time in Jamestown commandeering corn from Indians around Chesapeake Bay, and he admitted that "the whole colony had starved" without the corn he obtained. He also remarked of the Americans that "victuals" was "all there wealth." Smith also set the hungry Jamestown colonists to learn how to gather wild foods from native hosts.[50]

William Wood loved the generous hospitality he experienced among the Indians, and offered long detailed stories to illustrate it, yet he judged their lavish feasting in terms that fed English preconceptions: "wise Providence being a stranger to their wilder wayes: they be right Infidels, neither caring for the morrow, or providing for their owne families." This statement followed a description of their diet in the various seasons emphasizing the use of stored agricultural produce.[51] In their layered presentation of their own perceptions , English observers in America were caught between the lore they had been told and the preconceptions of their readers. They wanted to be read and believed, and the rhetorical flourishes were designed to attract readers. They also wanted to support schemes for colonization, and to portray the land as healthy and productive. These agendas competed for dominance throughout the various accounts.

Thomas Morton followed a third path, comparing Indian strategies to natural phenomena. Saying that "these people are not without providence, though they be uncivilized," he described their methods of food storage for winter use, comparing them to the one really congenial model from nature, that of the industrious "Ant and the Bee."[52]

The Indians' crops were supplemented by a wide variety of foods gathered in various environments and available for extended periods of the year, and by hunting. Ethnohistorians, drawing on both the archaeological and the written record, assert that their diet may have been superior in variety and nutritional value to that of the Europeans. Certainly, English settlers avidly incorporated native crops into their diets. European grains proved to be difficult to transplant to the American environment, and Indian crops became the mainstays of the early planters.[53]

English writers portrayed the Indians as enjoying their food and eating, when at home, with gusto: "they eat often and that liberally." They tended to be much more modest when eating in the English houses, although William Strachey reported that Indian laborers in Jamestown ate double English portions.[54] James Rosier described an experiment in which Captain George Waymouth invited two Indians to dine with him in his cabin "to see their demeanure." The English were delighted to find that their guests "behaved themselves very civilly," and "fed not like men of rude education." In Virginia the newly arrived Jamestown colonists were offered bread and "such dainties as they had," but the Indians did not want them eaten rudely: "they would not suffer us to eat unlesse we sate down."[55] Readers were interested in this subject partly because they were concerned about how English men and women would fare in America, but also because they associated straightforward enjoyment of simple food with good health and the old virtues. Moralists at home decried the constant search for new sauces and fantastic cooking methods that seemed necessary to tempt the jaded appetites of the novelty-seeking English.

Discussions of Indian presentation and consumption of food were read against the background of the new concern for manners and the emerging code of "civility" in Europe, where advice books included instructions on how to take food with the fingers from the common dish; individual plates were rare, and forks were just being introduced. Diners carried their own knives and speared food from the serving dish with them, and the manuals directed that they should be wiped beforehand. Thus the *Relation of Maryland*'s description of a great feast in which two hundred guests were served in their own individual bowls would have set a standard met in few households in England. Henry Spelman also wrote that "the better sort never eates togither in one dish." Depictions of feasts with everyone, high and low, eating together would have found an approving audience in England.[56]

Most descriptions of Indian food focused on the mixtures of maize, beans, sunflower seeds, and other vegetables with meat and fish. Most popular was a kind of stew in which meat and vegetables were "seethed" or "sodden" together. Some writers liked this "sweete, and savorie" stew, but William Wood complained that the Americans insisted that everyone partake of their "high-conceited delicates" with "some remaining raw, the rest converted by over-much seething to a loathed mash, not halfe so good as Irish Boniclapper." Wood's picture was very different from that conveyed by the *Relation of Maryland*. He said the Indians ate only every two or three days, and were so hungry that they ate without "trenchers, napkins or knives" on the "verdent carpet of the earth which Nature spreads them" and consumed enormous amounts "till their bellies stand south, ready to split with fulnesse." But Roger Williams reported that there was no drunkenness or gluttony. They did take tobacco, he wrote, "because they want the refreshing of Beare and Wine, which God hath vouchsafed Europe."[57]

In rounding out their picture of native life, many of the writers described preparation of food. Civil people ate their food cooked, and James Rosier, describing how his party offered their New Englander guests various foods, wrote: "and this I noted, they would eat nothing raw, either fish or flesh." A few years later governor Sir Thomas Gates watched in horror the "incredible example" of the troubled Jamestown colonists who ate fish raw "rather than they would go a stones cast to fetch wood" with which to cook it.[58]

Observers were fascinated by the technology of creating fire. Gosnold's party in New England requested a demonstration of how the natives lighted a flame, and both Archer and Brereton included the episode in their accounts. Their native guest took out of a leather bag at his waist an "Emerald stone" or "Emerie Stone (wherewith Glasiers cut glasse . . .)" which he struck against a "Minerall stone," capturing the "sparkles" on a piece of soft wood that he carried with the stones. Captain John Smith

This painting by John White was labeled "Their sittinge at meate." In his notes Harriot praised the soberness and restraint Americans showed in their diet. © The British Museum, British Museum Press.

wrote that the Indians rubbed a pointed stick in a hole made in a block of wood until they produced sufficient heat to ignite bits of moss or dry leaves, and William Strachey used this description in his own account, adding that women worked assiduously to maintain the fire in their homes and considered an extinguished fire an "evil signe"[59]

Food was then either cooked as a stew in great pots or broiled on racks over the fire. What the colonists called green corn was an ingredient in the stews, and dried mature corn was ground and used to make bread or cakes; the colonists sought instruction in making cornbread for themselves. On their travels Indians carried cornmeal, which was mixed with water when they needed to eat. William Wood found this *Nocake* dry eating: "If it be in Winter, and Snow be on the ground, they can eate when they please, stopping Snow after their dusty victuals, which otherwise would feed them little better than a Tiburne halter [a hangman's noose]. In summer they must stay till they meete with a Springe or Brooke, where they may have water to prevent the imminent danger of choaking." But Roger Williams said the English made this cornmeal up with milk and butter into a tasty dish called *samp*. Modern Indians throughout the east preserve fond memories of eating *nocake* or *yokeag* and *samp*, especially on ceremonial occasions. Williams thought the American diet was far more healthful than that of the English, largely because cornmeal was, as he put it, "an admirable cleanser and opener." He thought that thousands of lives could be saved if corn were introduced into England, balancing the "binding nature" of wheat with "the Indian Corne keeping the body in a constant moderate loosenesse."[60]

Some writers described the seasoning of native foods. Richard Whitbourne reported that the Indians used dried egg yolk in cooking "as Sugar is used in some meates." James Rosier learned that the northern New Englanders hung whale meat in their houses and flavored their corn and beans with the blubber. Thomas Harriot reported that the Indians taught him to make oil from acorns. England's textile industry needed a good source of oil for the soap used in cloth manufacture, so such reports were more than curiosities. Salt, essential for the preservation of fish caught in America for sale in Europe, was another commodity backers had hoped to find or to make, so reports that the Indians did not know about the use of salt were disappointing. Thomas Morton said his native friends "would begge Salte of mee." Harriot found the Roanoke Indians had a herb whose ashes were used as a seasoning like salt, but not as a preservative.[61]

English writers enthusiastically praised the strength and versatility of Indian pottery which, although the walls were as thin as English iron pots, could be used over an open fire because of the "special Cunninge" with which they were made. John White provided a picture of such a pot upright in a fire. Others mentioned dishes of bark and of wood.[62] New England reports said that each group had its distinctive pottery and wooden bowl designs, which were traded from village to village. But despite the high quality and aesthetic integrity of native dishes, the sources chronicled the effect of the European presence; Americans were seeking to acquire English metal kettles.[63]

English writers pictured the Indians as superbly adapted to their environment in their agriculture and in hunting and fishing. Moccasins were among the marvels they reported. Roger Williams praised their versatility and they way they could be dried after soaking without harm. When the Powhatans invited the Jamestown colonists to join them in attacking their enemies to the west, they offered to provide the English with moccasins for the march.[64]

The single most popular products of Indian technology were canoes, which were infinitely superior to the clumsy boats the English had brought with them. Extensive descriptions usually began with how they were made. Sources from Virginia and southern New England described dugout canoes. White painted a picture of a log being turned into a canoe, and Harriot's note began simply: "The manner of makinge their boates in Virginia is verye wonderfull." He described the coastal Carolinians' method of alternately burning and scraping out the center with sea shells, completely eliminating the need for metal tools, and argued that this demonstrated that "god indueth this savage people with sufficient reason to make thinges necessarie to serve their turnes." The Roanoke

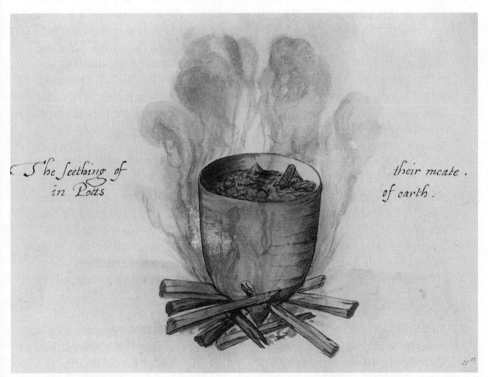

"The seething of their meate in Potts of earth." © The British Museum, British Museum Press.

sources described canoes capable of carrying up to twenty people, and John Smith, writing of Virginia, said that he had seen a few with capacities of forty. Roger Williams echoed these estimates for southern New England canoes and said that he had seen a lone man make one in ten or twelve days.[65]

Birchbark canoes, seen on the northern coast and overlapping with dugouts in southern New England, were regarded as even more marvelous; they could hold, according to John Winthrop, as many as eighty men. Martin Pringe presented a detailed description, saying they were "made of the Barke of a Birch-tree, farre exceeding in bignesse those of England: it was sowed together with strong and tough Oziers or twigs, and the seames covered over with Rozen or Turpentine little inferiour in sweetnesse to Frankincense . . . it was also open like a Wherrie, and sharpe at both ends, saving that the beake was a little bending roundly upward. And though it carried nine men standing upright, yet it weighed not at the most above sixtie pounds in weight, a thing almost incredible in regard of the largeness and capacitie thereof." Pringe brought a canoe back with him to Bristol.[66] American canoes were large, but the form was not unknown in Britain, where small boats consisting of a leather covering over a wicker framework were used in the far west and north.[67]

Canoes were so well adapted to America because they were light and swift. Colonists in English boats were often stymied by shallow and rocky places in American streams, but the Indians simply alighted, picked up their canoe, and went around the rapids. Moreover, they could carry their boats cross-country from stream to stream. John Guy reported from Newfoundland, "every place is to them a harborough; where they can goe ashoare themselves, they take aland with them their Canoa." John Smith wrote home scornfully of the Virginia Company's solution to the problem of impassable rivers, a boat in four pieces that the explorers were to carry and assemble above the falls. Smith's comment was, "If he had burnt her to ashes, one might have carried her in a bag; but as she is, five hundred cannot, to a navigable place above the Falles." Smith's quip stung when read against New England claims that one or two men could carry a canoe that would hold ten or twelve.[68]

Canoes simply handled much better than anything produced by European technology. Indians could take their canoes out on open waters when English boats were unsafe: "In these cockling fly-boates . . . they will venture to Sea, when an English Shallope dare not beare a knot of sayle; scudding over the overgrowne waves as fast as a winde-driven Ship, being driven by their padles; being much like battle doores; if a crosse wave (as is seldome) turn her keele up-side downe, they by swimming free her, and scramble into her againe." New England Indians gave

Calling the Carolina Algonquian method of making canoes "verye wonderfull," Harriot marveled at the way they used fire and seashells in place of metal tools. In the background, some men are using fire to bring down a tree and others to cut a large tree to the desired length. In the foreground, Carolina Algonquians are shown building fires in the interior of the log they are shaping. Burned sections were scraped out, and then the process was repeated. The John Carter Brown Library at Brown University.

one particularly humiliating illustration of their canoe's handling ability; three Indians in a canoe circled constantly around an English boat "when we rowed with eight oares strong; such was their swiftnesse, by reason of the lightnesse and artificiall composition of their Canoa and oares." In addition to their superior paddling speed, Williams wrote that "their owne reason" had taught them to rig a sail with "a Coat or two" on a small pole.[69]

Indian technology figured significantly in the fishing and hunting that supplemented agriculture as food sources. Reports from southern colonies described Indian-made weirs or traps, which the English admired greatly: "Ther was never seene amongst us soe cunninge a way to take fish withall." These weirs, which were illustrated by John White, lured the fish into "a Labourinth or Maze" made of reeds. Ralph Lane's Roanoke colonists tried to make such weirs, but lacked the skill. The Indians were persuaded to build weirs for the colonists, but Lane then lived in fear that they might return and deliberately break them; the colonists could not even repair existing weirs. English writers also described natives fishing with lines and nets. Thomas Harriot praised their ingenuity in using a crab's tail for a hook. William Wood of New England argued that the Indians were successful in fishing because they studied the habits of their prey and adapted their techniques to the season and the fish, and Roger Williams similarly marveled at the "exceeding great paines" they took in fishing even in the coldest weather. Williams also noted the influence of European imports; just as metal tools facilitated traditional modes of canoe making, so the Indians had begun to tip their fishing spears with metal points.[70]

Williams wrote that large-scale projects such as hunting and fishing expeditions were done "With friendly joyning." John Smith, comparing Indians to Tartars, was typical in portraying the entire village embarking on the hunt, or sometimes several villages together, with assemblages that could amount to several hundred men. Houses were dismantled, and the mats and equipment necessary to recreate them at the hunting site were carried by the women. In hunting the men surrounded the deer and then, using fires and torches, drove them into a narrower and narrower space where they were easily killed. A single hunter covered his head and arms with a deerskin so that he could approach, all the time imitating the characteristic stance and movements of the deer until he was close enough to shoot an arrow. The deer's cunning lay in their highly developed senses, according to Roger Williams, because they could smell the human scent on hidden traps. Therefore the hunter had to be extremely careful in setting and checking snares. William Wood in New England described Indians hunting beavers, saying that their knowl-

The manner of their fishing.

John White's painting of Indian fish weirs is a compendium of information. The weir is full of fish, indicating the efficiency of this system. White also offers a picture of fishing from a canoe; the fire, which drew the fish to the light, indicates that the scene took place at night. He included carefully drawn images of various fishes and birds he had seen and, in the foreground, exact representations of coastal Carolina's interesting flora. © The British Museum, British Museum Press.

edge of the animal and its habits were what made them effective. "These beasts are too cunning for the English, who seldome or never catch any of them, therefore we leave them to those skilfull hunters whose time is not so precious, whose experience bought-skill hath made them practicall and usefull in that particular."[71]

Thomas Morton believed that Indians were personally adapted to their environment as well. He asserted that they had developed their senses to an extraordinary degree; if he had not read the same things in French sources about Canada, he said he would have been reluctant to put down what he had witnessed, "which is a thinge that I should not easily have bin induced, to beleeve, if I my selfe, had not bin an eie witnesse, of what I shall relate." He wrote that Indians could sight a ship at sea two hours before an Englishman watching for the ship could see it. Their "sight is so excellent," Morton wrote, that "one would allmost beleeve they had intelligence of the Devill, sometimes," and he attributed this excellence to the blackness of their eyes. "And as they excell us in this particular so much noted, so I thinke they excell us in all the rest." French sources told him that Indians could distinguish between a Frenchman and a Spaniard just by the smell of their hands. Moreover, Morton had himself accompanied a hunter who tracked a deer and distinguished old from new tracks just by sight and smell, "and I did eate part of it with him: such is their perfection in these two sences." Williams also reported that Indians knew the country so well that they could guide the English forty miles in a straight line through the woods.[72] In the Pequot War soldiers marching without native aid found the woods baffling and forbidding. John Mason wrote that the soldiers marched in extreme heat, some fainting, "in an uncoath and unknown Path to the English, though much frequented by Indians." God, he wrote, showed them the way.[73]

Modern popular culture portrays the Indians as in tune with nature and far more ecologically sensitive than the Europeans who intruded on their lives, and the emblem of the destruction brought by the newcomers is the ruthless depletion of the beaver population in the decades following colonization.[74] Certainly the English, following the book of Genesis, believed that the natural world had been given to human beings by God for their use. Not to develop and use nature would have been regarded as sinful. Moreover, nature had to be tended or it would degenerate, become "savage." Human beings were part of nature, with a God-given role; their exploitation did not diminish the landscape, but developed and enriched it. Nature could not reach its full potential without human intervention. Even the Garden of Eden required tending; the Virginia Company averred that "Adam himselfe might not live in paridice without dressing the garden."[75]

English venturers clearly shared this presumption. In a telling inversion of modern norms, they considered "artificial" to be a word of the highest praise, indicating the application of artifice and skill to raw materials, while "natural" could mean simple or refer to a simple-minded person. John Brereton was so taken with the beauty of the New England coast that he wrote it was "as if Nature would shew her selfe above her power, artificall." George Withers, in a congratulatory verse to John Smith, pictured New England as a "rude Garden" where the English would "order Nature's fruitfulnesse." And Smith himself argued against the notion that New England was less promising than the greatest countries by saying, in words very similar to those he had previously used of Virginia, "They are beautified by the long labor and dilligence of industrious people and Art. This is onely as God made it, when he created the worlde."[76]

George Hakewill presented this thesis clearly in his *Apology for the Power and Providence of God*: "all things by labour and industry may bee made better than Nature produces them. And it is certaine that God so ordained it, that the industry of man should in all things concurre with the workes of Nature, both for the bringing of them to their perfection, and for the keeping of them therein being brought unto it."[77] Just as the bee in its exploitation of the flower performs a role crucial to the plant, so human beings' use of nature was equally necessary. Seventeenth-century people were fascinated by other animals whose destiny it was to work and develop the world around them; in their view a beaver dam was an artificial structure.

Both the English and the Americans changed the natural environment as they lived in it and moved over it. Historians Richard White and William Cronon argue that the idea that the Indians made no impact on the land is demeaning, implying that they lacked culture and history: "To regard Indians as primal ecologists is a crude view." Like the English, they used the environment; they differed, according to White and Cronon, in the reciprocity built into their relationship with the land and the animals they hunted—in the virtually social correspondence between the Indians and their environment.[78]

English writers, steeped in their own view of the proper and responsible correspondence between humans and the land, sometimes criticized the Indians as reckless or wasteful of natural resources. One subject of controversy was the practice of burning the underbrush in the woods to facilitate hunting.[79] Many English observers were struck by the open, parklike quality of American woods, saying that one could ride a horse at a gallop or even take a coach and horses through them. Modern studies have also argued that controlled burning increased the variety of food-producing plants and therefore of animals in the woods, and may have driven away some unwanted animals.[80]

Generally this firing of the woods destroyed underbrush but not large trees. It could not be strictly controlled, however, and colonists such as Thomas Morton pointed out how dangerous it was. He asserted that the only trees in New England not damaged by fire were in the swampy lowlands. He wrote that he carefully burned the area around his own house to make it more secure from runaway fires, "For when the fire is once kindled, it dilates and spreads it selfe as well against, as with the winde; burning continually night and day, untill a shower of raine falls to quench it."[81]

These early English travelers were concerned about depleting the animal population, and some of them faulted Indian hunting practices as wasteful. Ralph Hamor argued the fecundity of America was a special providence of God, because if the land were not so productive "the Naturalls would assuredly starve." He wrote that the Indians took deer "all the yeer long, neither sparing yong nor olde, no not the Does readie to fawne, not the yong fawnes, if but two daies ould." So many were killed in hunting that, according to Thomas Harriot, the English could trade for thousands of skins annually without raising the toll. New Englanders reported finding carcasses with only the horns taken and the rest left. So prolific was the hunt that Thomas Morton said the Indians "have bestowed six or seaven at a time, upon one English man whome they have borne affection to." Such a gift, in fact, was the genesis of the first thanksgiving at Plymouth. Edward Winslow wrote that Massasoit and ninety of his men came to the Pilgrims just as the English had brought in their harvest; the Indian guests killed five deer which they "bestowed on our governor, and upon the captain and others" and the company feasted together.[82]

These descriptions thus came full circle back to the village in its natural setting, its inhabitants enjoying the bounty produced by the cooperative effort of environment and people. English writers who described American life for readers at home were dedicated to presenting these unknown societies going about their daily life; they sought to delineate the relationships within them and the strategies by which they lived. The Indian societies they depicted recognized distinctions important to Europeans, and maintained lines of order at least as well as old-world peoples. The portrait they transmitted was above all recognizable as human, and well within the circle of the civil and the normal. They accomplished their job of gathering local knowledge and reporting their own observations so well that these accounts, incorporating native voices, are still our main ethnographic resource for understanding

American societies at contact. And eyewitness writers—sympathetic or hostile—insisted that their experience and relationships gave them a new kind of authority: they were the only authors whose words should be trusted. They knew how formidable and competent native American societies were and how dependent and wary the English settlers were, and they were furious at armchair travelers who trivialized their situation by portraying the Indians as simple. John Smith spoke for all these writers and their authorial claims when he wrote:

> there is a great difference, betwixt the directions and judgement of experimentall knowledge, and the superficiall conjecture of variable relation: wherein rumor, humor, or misprision have such power, that oft times one is enough to beguile twentie, but twentie, not sufficient to keep one from being deceived. Therefore I know no reason but to beleeve my own eies, before any mans imagination, that is but wrested from the conceits of my owne projects, and indeavours.[83]

6   Incorporating the Other

The first impulse of native leaders was to incorporate the English settlers as clients, and to understand their presence in terms of native ceremonial and political arrangements. In looking at the straggling early settlements, wholly dependent on native aid for food and training, they concluded that these outposts could be useful as allies and suppliers of trade goods. The goods themselves were incorporated into native life and assigned traditional meanings. This impulse was in many ways the mirror image of the English assumption that the Indians would naturally want to become civilized as Europeans understood civility. Powhatan's attempt to install Captain John Smith as a werowance under him through his adoption matched the Virginia Company's command that Powhatan be crowned as a vassal of King James. Incorporation was the first and obvious way to deal with the other. Before the three days of ritual that Smith experienced, his conversation was with Opechancanough, the Powhatans' war or outside chief. Only after he was ready for adoption, according to one reconstruction, was he brought into Powhatan's presence, and from then on he dealt directly with the inside chief. The rituals adopted the entire English colony through Smith, Jamestown's outside chief. The Powhatans assumed that the English system paralleled their own and that Captain Christopher Newport, the Virginia Company's admiral who was supreme in the colony when he was there, was the inside chief.[1]

Ethnohistorians argue that the newcomers were accepted precisely because the trade goods they brought replicated familiar items that had great spiritual meaning in native life—including a putative origin in the spirit world. This replication provided a basis for attempts at assimilation. English sources reported the esteem in which their goods were held without understanding the reasons.[2]

These analyses shed light on one of the most intriguing incidents in the early Jamestown record. After Smith's adoption, Powhatan expressed a desire to meet Smith's "father," Captain Newport, and an expedition was arranged. Smith, who prided himself on driving a hard bargain in trade goods for the corn he constantly sought from the Indians, was forced to stand by while his superior was, as he saw it, duped by Powhatan. Powhatan addressed Newport flatteringly as a fellow inside and higher chief, saying, "Captaine Newport it is not agreeable to my greatnesse, in this pedling manner to trade for trifles; and I esteeme you also a great Werowance. Therefore lay me downe all your commodities together; what I like I will take, and in recompence give you what I thinke fitting their value." Smith warned Newport he would be cheated, but the latter thought he could "outbrave this Salvage in ostentation of greatnesse." The result was that Powhatan so overvalued his corn that, Smith wrote, "I thinke it better cheape in Spaine," and the English got only a few bushels.

Smith set out to repair the damage and to restore his status as a shrewd bargainer. He "glanced in the eyes of Powhatan many trifles," and the chief especially desired some blue beads. Smith refused to sell them "as being composed of a most rare substance of the coulour of the skyes, and not to be worne but by the greatest kings in the world. This made him halfe madde to be the owner of such strange Jewells." The result was that Smith got "2. or 300. Bushells of corne" for "a pound or two of blew beades." And they "parted good friends." Whereas Smith thought he had turned the tables by cheating Powhatan, the chief had obtained items of great spiritual significance and therefore high value. The best analogy in Europe might have been gold, a soft metal with little intrinsic value, yet commanding the highest prices because of its ornamental and symbolic role.[3]

Americans sought to incorporate the newcomers into their universe of spiritual meanings. Native attempts to discipline the colonists and attempt to keep them in a client position were conducted in terms of the American ceremonial round and the Europeans' assigned place in it. Both the Roanoke and Jamestown colonists reported that conspiracies against them were planned to coincide with great gatherings to commemorate the deaths of fallen leaders. The Roanoke colonists were alarmed when Ensenore, an elder whom they considered their greatest friend, died. They learned he was to be honored in a "certaine kind of moneths minde which they do use to solemnise in their Savage maner for any great personage dead." Governor Ralph Lane heard rumors that from this assembly a mighty force was to attack the colony, kill him and all his captains (whom the Indians called werowances), and then burn the village and destroy the crops and fish weirs that natives had prepared for the settlers. Lane's response was a preemptive attack on the Roanokes, which may have saved his life but made it impossible for his settlers to remain on Roanoke Island. Lane's signal to begin the attack—"Christ our victory"—situated the English offensive within a European cosmology, much as the Indians' plan had drawn on their religion.[4] Similarly, the great attack of 1622 in Virginia, which aimed to assault all the plantations at once and extirpate the colonists, was planned for a time when large numbers would assemble to solemnize the final placement of Powhatan's bones, the chief having been dead four years.[5]

The specter of Indian conjuration stalked the fearful English, and the Americans played on these fears to great effect. In Jamestown's early days, George Percy reported a "very remarkable" instance of "the Salvages Sorceries and Charmes": "Some of the better sorte sitteinge in An Indyans howse A fantasy possessed them thatt they imagined the Salvages were sett upon them eache man Takeinge one another for an Indyan[.] And so did fall pell mell one upon An other beateinge one another downe and breakeinge one of Anothers heades." Fortunately the Christian God intervened, broke the "fantasy," and restored the English to reality. Reverend Alexander Whitaker sent a different report, which may have been of a second incident. Sir Thomas Dale, leader of the company in both stories, proposed to travel with a small contingent to the falls of the James River, but Powhatan "forbidd him" and demanded he return two Indians the English held prisoner. If they were not returned within six or seven days, "the Kinge of the Indians" threatened to "make us drunke and then kill us." Dale was "very merry" at this threat and went ahead on his expedition without returning the prisoners. One night the company heard "hup hup" and "Oho Oho" repeated hypnotically outside their quarters, and found themselves "confusedly amased." The English again fell on each other, picking up their weapons by the wrong end; they could say nothing but "Oho Oho." Once again the hallucination passed quickly, but Whitaker earnestly requested interpretations of this incident from learned men in London. In both cases the writers were convinced the English had been the victims of American sorcery.[6]

Americans placed the newcomers within their cosmology in other ways. Many early encounters led venturers to believe, as John Smith wrote of his meeting with the Susquehannocks, that only with "much adoe" were they "restrained from adoring us as Gods," and the notion that the Europeans were seen as gods gained wide circulation. The reality, however, was more subtle.[7] With their notion of Manitou, the divine force that could exist in any thing or person, the Americans could detect spiritual power in colonists and their technology, just as they would in things and persons native to America. As Roger Williams explained, native exclamations of wonder at English technology stemmed from their "naturall" conviction that all excellency is from God.[8] While the English speculated on whether the Indians might be descended from the Ten Lost Tribes or Madoc's Welsh venturers, and thus fit into old-world stories, the Indians were also concerned to determine the Europeans' origins in a spiritual as well as a physical sense. The name the Narragansetts applied to the English meant, as Williams wrote, "These strangers." "Tassantasse" was the label in the Chesapeake, and when the Chickahomonies agreed to become "King JAMES his subjects," they said they were "no longer Naturalls of that place, but Tossantessars." The Wabanaki name initially for all Europeans was "wenooch," derived from the word for "who is that?"[9]

Answering the question "Who is that?" required understanding where the Europeans came from. Captain John Smith asked Amoroleck, a Manahoac captive from the Virginia piedmont, why his people were hostile to the English. "He answered, they heard we were a people come from under the world, to take their world from them."[10] A ship appearing on the horizon might seem to come from under the world, and Amoroleck's statement has been interpreted in this way. But in fact many natives indicated that they thought the English had literally come from the underworld, that, as Ralph Lane reported from Roanoke, "wee be dead men returned into the world againe." Many reports of native religion, as we have seen, asserted that the dead went to live in another world from which, after they had led full lives there, they would reemerge in this world.[11]

The belief that the newcomers were from the underworld allowed the Indians to explain otherwise inexplicable phenomena, such as English resistance to the diseases that so devastated native populations. Thomas Harriot formed a sympathetic relationship with his Roanoke informants, and he had "special familiarity with some of their priestes." The Roanoke leaders learned that when the English had been at any place, strange diseases broke out, the like of which, according to "the oldest men in the countrey never happened before, time out of minde." Because the English were not affected, and because they had no women in their company and, according to Harriot, were not interested in Indian women, the Roanokes decided that the English had been dead, "men of an old generation many yeeres past" who had risen and taken on human form. Moreover, the air around them was filled with others who had not yet assumed physical shape and were still invisible; these spirits, the Indians thought, were shooting "invisible bullets" into them and making them sick. A similar interpretation of English powers and origins may have underlain the response of a party of Niantics that challenged a mixed force of Connecticut men under Captain John Mason and Mohegans led by Uncas shortly after the Pequots' surrender in 1637. They said they would not fight with the English "for they were Spirits, but would fight with ONKOS."[12]

The English, like the Indians, struggled to explain novel vulnerability and invulnerability within their own cosmology. Harriot was certain that the diseases only struck villages where some harm had been planned against the English, but he and his fellow colonists were also disturbed by these extraordinary happenings. Although some were prepared to assume God was killing Indians "for our sakes," others thought the epidemics must be related to other recent potent and dangerous manifestations of divine power—a comet and an eclipse.

Roanoke religious beliefs gave them a framework for understanding extraordinary events, and leaders sought to incorporate the power they witnessed. Thinking that "wee by him [God] might kil and slaie whom wee would without weapons and not come neere them," the colonists' Indian friends asked them to arrange the deaths of other people who had offended both the English and Wingina, the Roanoke leader, pointing out that it would greatly enhance the "credite and profite" of both. The English refused, saying the request was "ungodlie." But a fatal disease soon broke out among the target groups, so the Indians believed they had been accommodated and rendered thanks.[13]

The elder Narragansett sachem Canonicus, on being approached by Roger Williams about Massachusetts Bay's plans to make war on the Pequots, was "very sour." Williams discovered that Canonicus believed the English had deliberately sent the recent plague among his people. In reply Williams told him that God alone controlled the plague and all disease, and that he sent it to the English for their sins as well as to the Indians. In fact God, angry with the English "for lying, stealing, idleness and uncleanness, (the natives' epidemical sins,) smote many thousands of us ourselves with general and late mortalities." Williams referred to the great epidemics of plague, sometimes compounded with fevers, smallpox, and typhus, that swept through England in the middle years of the 1620s and the later 1630s, leading to crisis levels of mortality in 1624 and 1638. One-fifth of London's population was swept away in the 1625 plague. Williams was not alone in applying the same interpretation to misfortunes befalling the English as to those affecting Americans.

Colonists in America were keenly aware of the epidemics raging in England; in January 1637 the churches in Massachusetts Bay held a fast for, among other problems, "the plague raging exceedingly."[14] English men and women, imbued with the belief that God's providence could be read in events, scrutinized all events for their revelation of the divine will, and they interpreted adversity as evidence of God's disapproval of their actions.

God's justice was not commanded by human beings, however godly, but those who could read providence could align themselves with God's purposes. Thomas Harriot expressed horror that the Roanokes believed God would kill on order, but he and individuals in all the early English colonies worked to encourage the notion that they brought powerful new cosmological forces, and they did this self-consciously within native frames of reference. These men studied native culture intensively, particularly the conjuring and healing roles of shamans. They presented themselves to the Indians, at least in part, in forms that mirrored those roles.

Several accounts of early encounters centered on English demonstrations of scientific instruments and on the American impression that they represented a superior kind of magic. In each case the Englishman enthusiastically played the role of a conjurer, presenting his wonders with a dramatic flourish. Captain George Waymouth, in New England in 1605, after several days of trading and visiting and when his Indian guests had become "verie merrie and bold," put on such a demonstration at night. He magnetized his sword by touching it with the ship's "Loadstone" and demonstrated its power to draw a knife and make it turn, and to pick up the knife and a needle, "whereat they much marvelled. This we did to cause them to imagine some great power in us: and for that to love and feare us."[15]

Thomas Harriot in Roanoke, one of the few who had the scientific background actually to understand the operation of his instruments, wrote of a similar response—his early report may have inspired some of the other attempts to overawe the Americans. He wrote: "Most things they sawe with us, as Mathematicall instruments, sea compasses, the vertue of the loadstone in drawing yron, a perspective glasse whereby was shewed manie strange sightes, burning glasses, wildefire woorkes, gunnes, bookes, writing and reading, spring clocks that seeme to goe of themselves and manie other thinges that wee had, were so straunge unto them, and so farre exceeded their capacities to comprehend the reason and means how they should be made and done, that they thought they were rather the works of gods then of men. or at the leastwise they had bin given and taught us of the gods." Captain John Smith read Harriot's

Briefe and True Report and learned its lessons. When he was taken into Opechancanough's presence as a captive, the first thing he did was give the chief "a round Ivory double compass Dyall." He was gratified by the response: "Much they marvailed at the playing of the Fly and Needle, which they could see so plainely, and yet not touch it, because of the glasse that covered them." Smith went on to explain the positions of the earth, stars, and planets, and the world's continents using the compass and his audience was "amazed with admiration." Smith believed the compass, which Opechancanough held up before his vengeful men, had saved his life.[16]

These dramatic flourishes, often staged by military leaders, impressed their audiences. Smith also revived an Indian man who was thought dead. The man was held in "the dungeon" at Jamestown as hostage for a stolen pistol. Smith sent him food and charcoal to build a fire and when his brother returned with the pistol the prisoner was found unconscious, overcome by smoke and "pittiously burnt." The brother "broke forth in . . . bitter agonies," and Smith said, on the promise of their future good behavior, he would "make him alive againe," although he had no idea whether he could actually accomplish it. Smith administered some brandy and vinegar and the victim regained consciousness, but was so disoriented that he "seemed Lunaticke." After a good sleep, he was restored to his senses. Each man was given a piece of copper and they spread the word "among all the Salvages for a miracle, that Captaine Smith could make a man alive that was dead." The result, he wrote, was that everything that had been stolen was returned, and the Indians desired peace with the English.[17]

A small group of educated English men, often principal advisors to colony governors, brought European medicine to the Americans in ways that fit closely into native patterns. Men such as Harriot, Edward Winslow in Plymouth, Roger Williams in Narragansett country, and Father Andrew White in Maryland became emissaries to the neighboring Indians and carried important aspects of European civility while adopting native roles. Like shamans, who were close advisors to chiefs and healers to their people, these men acted as healers. They did so in response to native requests; Indians may have reasoned that Europeans would know more about healing the new diseases. They may also have found the newcomers' magic impressive and sought its benefits.

Because they had studied Indian religion and healing and the close connection between them, these emissaries were able to fit naturally into the village's expectations, particularly the involvement of the entire community in treatment. Winslow was particularly attentive to his patients' expectations, especially when the Pilgrims received word that

Massasoit, the Pokanoket chief who was their friend and closest neighbor, was "like to die." Winslow, acknowledging the "commendable manner of the Indians, when any, especially of note, are dangerously sick, for all that profess friendship to them to visit them in their extremity," accepted governor Bradford's commission and "cordials" and set off for the sickbed several days' journey away with an English and an Indian companion. On the journey the party received various bits of news; some told them Massasoit was already dead and buried. When they finally arrived, they found the house crammed full of people. The Americans were "in the midst of their charms for him, making such a hellish noise, as it distempered us that were well, and therefore unlike to ease him that was sick." Women chafed the chief's arms and legs.

Someone told Massasoit, who could not see, that Winslow had come. Winslow took his hand, and recorded their exchange, explaining that Indians found the letter L unpronounceable: Massasoit said "twice, though very inwardly, *Keen Winsnow?* which is to say, 'Art thou Winslow' I answered, *Ahhe*, that is Yes. Then he doubled these words; *Matta neen wonckanet namen, Winsnow!* that is to say, 'O Winslow, I shall never see thee again.'" At this, Winslow, carefully specifying that he came on the orders of Governor Bradford, offered his "confection of many comfortable conserves." After receiving permission, he forced a small amount through the chief's clenched teeth on the point of his knife, which Massasoit swallowed. The witnessing throng "much rejoiced," because he had swallowed nothing for two days. Winslow, examining Massasoit, found his difficulty in swallowing came from his mouth being "furred" and his tongue swollen, so Winslow washed and scraped out his mouth, "and got abundance of corruption out of the same." Massasoit then was able to take more and more of the "confection," and within half an hour his condition began visibly to alter; soon his sight began to return.

Winslow offered to send to Plymouth for other medicines (one bottle had broken on the journey) and for chickens to make broth. Massasoit's recovery was rapid, and Winslow was pressed to create medicines and nourishing food to keep up with his needs; he resorted to improvising with the herbs he could gather. Massasoit asked him to go around the village, washing out the mouths of the sick and giving them medicines, because they were "good folk. This pains I took with willingess, though it were much offensive to me, not being accustomed with such poisonous savours." Meanwhile Massasoit recovered so fast that he ate too richly after his long fast and became sick again, vomiting so violently that he bled profusely from the nose. His people now expected his death, "which we much feared also." Bleeding from the nose was considered "a symptom of death" among the Indians. The bleeding finally stopped, however, and Massasoit then slept for a long time, waking refreshed. When the medicines and chickens arrived from Plymouth, Massasoit felt so well that he decided not to kill the chickens, but "kept them for breed."

While Massasoit was sick, Indians had come from all the surrounding countryside, some from a hundred miles away. One chief, who was there before Winslow's party arrived, had told Massasoit "now he might see how hollow-hearted the English were, saying if we had been such friends in deed, as we were in show, we would have visited him in this his sickness." Now all was changed; Winslow said that everyone who came heard the saga of how the chief had been near death until the English had arrived and "suddenly they recovered him to this strength they saw." Winslow concluded his account, saying he feared he had been "too tedious"; he had spent more pages on this incident than any other. Clearly, his shamanlike success was very important.[18] Roger Williams mentioned that the English were often asked for "physicke"; he believed he had saved many natives and, like Winslow, had been pushed "beyond my powers" in improvising cures.[19]

Father Andrew White reported a successful cure with momentous consequences. Shortly after he had come to live with the Tayac or emperor at Pascataway, where he had been welcomed because his coming had been foretold in a dream, the Tayac fell dangerously ill. Only after forty conjurers had tried and failed to cure him did Father White undertake treatment. With the Tayac's permission, he administered "a certain powder of known efficacy mixed with holy water." On the second day, he bled the Tayac from a vein in his leg, after which the patient began to regain his strength day by day. When he was recovered the Tayac resolved that he and his family would all become Christians.[20]

Because the Roanokes associated the devastating diseases that struck them directly with the English settlers and their vengeful deity, they sought relief not in English medicines but in intercession. Harriot wrote that Wingina, the Roanoke chief, and his people often came to pray and sing psalms with the colonists as they moved around the countryside. Twice when Wingina was "so grievously sicke that he was like to die, and . . . doubting of anie helpe by his owne priestes," he sent for "some of us to praie and bee a meanes to our God" either for his recovery or for him to "dwell with him in blisse" if he died. Harriot scornfully wrote that the priests "to excuse their ignorance" encouraged the idea that invisible bullets were causing the diseases, and claimed to find evidence in the bodies of their patients. In Roanoke as elsewhere in these early accounts English intervention won out where native shamans failed, and many others made requests for prayers. In the event, Wingina died not by English diseases but by their weapons in Governor Lane's preemptive strike.[21]

However much they may have believed in their ability to inspire awe, English colonists never let down their guard. On their way home from curing Massasoit, Winslow's party spent the night with the Nemasket sachem Corbitant, a rival of Massasoit's, who wondered whether Bradford would send Winslow with "*maskiet*, that is, physic" if he were "dangerously sick." Winslow's affirmative answer elicited "many joyful thanks." Corbitant then asked why Winslow was not afraid to travel with only one other Englishman and an Indian "so far into the country." Winslow answered, "where there was true love, there was no fear." At this Corbitant rejoined with the question that all native friends asked all English colonists: If you love us, why do you stand with your weapons pointed at us when we come to your village? Winslow replied that this was a traditional and honorable English greeting for "our best respected friends," but no one was convinced. Powhatan asked Captain John Smith the same question and received the same answer.[22]

Winslow and Harriot both concluded, as James Rosier had of Waymouth's demonstration of magnetism, that through display of English medicine and scientific lore, the Indians would be brought to stand in awe of them. Both men used variations of Rosier's formula: the Americans, according to Harriot, would come to "honour, obey, feare and love" the English.[23] This claim involved a large share of bravado, and the English were keenly aware of their vulnerability. Not only did they fear native attacks, they were also dependent on neighboring Indians for food and knowledge about the environment and agriculture. Their physical weakness may have led to great claims for their medical and supernatural control, but they were always aware that these claims opened them to scorn if they experienced failure. When Roanoke governor Ralph Lane's exploring party, shunned by the tribes through whose land they traveled and desperate for food, made a mad dash back to the colony, they found that news of their plight had preceded them. The Roanokes "began to blaspheme, and flatly to say, that our Lord God was not God, since hee suffered us to sustaine much hunger, and also to be killed. . . ." Later Virginia's governor and council appealed against a royal proclamation prohibiting the importation of tobacco into England. They pointed to the straitened circumstances in which they lived, and asked the king either to revoke the proclamation or to call the settlers home. The only other alternative was "to suffer the Heathen to triumph over us and to saye Where is now their God?"[24]

When the Powhatans and their allies struck plantations all along the James River on the morning of March 22, 1622, with devastating results, the planters agreed that this had happened because they had let down their guard. But in the famine and illness that followed, many voices, aware that the surrounding natives would draw the same conclusion, pointed to God's judgment as the cause of their misery. George Sandys, son of an archbishop of York, wrote from Virginia to his friends and patrons of "the heavie hand of God" and called himself and the other colonists "we whom the hand of heaven hath humbled." Although the settlers now defiantly vowed unbridled vengeance, no one on either side could fail to realize, as planter Edward Hill wrote to his brother, "we lyve in the fearefullest age that ever christians lyved in." In reply the Virginia Company advised the settlers to "labor to apease the wrath of God, that burneth so fiercely."[25] At least one colonist pinpointed the causes of that wrath. John Penreis wrote that whereas the Indians had formerly called the English gods because of their justice and virtuous government, now they were considered "worse than Divels" for the "treacherous & inhumaine Cruelty" of private traders who seized Indians' goods and persons without restraint. In recompense "(I feare me) Gods punishment is & wilbe uppon us."[26] Efforts by English individuals to take on the roles of powwows and enact the power of European science and the Christian God were thus restrained by their own limitations and greed and by their inability to command God's aid. They were always aware that they played a dangerous game in deploying their skills because of the danger of failure.

The English were not the only ones who tried such boundary-crossing enterprises. Their accounts also reveal that some native practitioners crossed over into English life and attempted to bring their own natural and supernatural powers to bear on the project of controlling the newcomers.

Many years after Edward Winslow's dramatic cure of Massasoit, John Winthrop reported a strange twist in the relationship reminiscent of that early rush to the bedside of the rumored dying or dead chief. Winslow, returning from a trip to Connecticut in 1634, wanted to go overland from Narragansett Bay to Plymouth. He asked "Osamekin the Sagamore his olde Allye" to conduct him home; Osamekin was another name for Massasoit. The chief agreed, but sent a runner ahead to tell those at Plymouth that Winslow was dead, "and directed him to shewe how & where he was killed: whereupon there was muche feare & sorrow at Plim." When asked on their arrival the next day why he had done that, "he answeared, that it was their maner to doe so, that they might be more wellcome when they came home." John Winthrop recorded this as a "pleasant passage," but it is tempting to wonder what this manipulation of English consciousness meant to Massasoit.[27]

Other leaders entered directly into English life in the earliest colonies in order to control the colonists' perceptions of American events, and these boundary crossers construed their roles in spiritual terms. They conveyed the solemnity of their missions in the names they chose. In March 1621, just a few months after Plymouth was founded in Massachusetts, the Pilgrims were approached by an Indian man named Samoset. His first word, "Welcome," indicated his grasp of the English language, learned from fishermen in Maine; the name he gave to the Pilgrims was probably "Somerset," given him by the fishermen. Samoset soon returned with Squanto who, as "the only native of Patuxat, where we now inhabite," indicated his intention to stay with the Pilgrims. Squanto, also called Tisquantum by the Pilgrims, had lived in Spain and in England after his kidnapping by Thomas Hunt; he was a very experienced man of the world. On his return to America he found his village deserted after the plague that had swept through the region in 1616. When he decided to live at Plymouth, he was returning home. Governor William Bradford recorded that he "was a special instrument sent of God for their good beyond their expectation."[28]

During the Pilgrims' first summer, according to governor Bradford's account, "there was another Indian called Hobomok come to live amongst them, a proper lusty man, and a man of account for his valour and parts amongst the Indians and continued very faithful and constant to the English till he died." Squanto died early in Plymouth's history, in September 1622, but Hobbomock, who came with his wife, continued his association with the colony for twenty years, serving as translator and guide.[29]

The presence of men named Squanto and Hobbomock among these extreme puritans was remarkable because of the highly provocative names they bore. Squanto and Hobbomock were the deities most closely involved in native daily life; they appeared to priests and gave them knowledge and powers, including the ability to foretell the future. Pilgrim leader Winslow was one of those who said that Hobbomock "is the devil," and Francis Higginson said that "their evill God whom they feare will doe them hurt, they call Squantum."[30] Thus it is quite striking that the pious Pilgrims welcomed Squanto and Hobbomock among them.

Squanto and Hobbomock and many other Indian leaders adopted the names of gods as they took up English association to indicate that they were entering a liminal state with all the power and danger that that entailed. As we have seen, American priests gained their power and the respect of their communities precisely because of their ability to cross over into the spirit world and to command the presence of spirits in this world. Americans who chose to become agents advertised their project by adopting the names of the deity who crossed over.

Names had power in Algonquian cultures, and there is evidence that, just as they created pidgins to protect their languages, Americans tried to keep the English intruders from knowing the most central or intimate names of the people they dealt with. After Pocahontas was baptized Rebecca, the English found out that Pocahontas had never been more than a nickname, and they were told various versions of her authentic name. Uttamatomakkin told Samuel Purchas in England that her real name was Matoaka, which they had kept hidden "in a superstitious feare of hurte by the English if her name were knowne." William Strachey reported that Pocahontas's name had been Amonute.[31] Roger Williams may have witnessed a similar phenomenon. He reported that some Narragansetts, when asked their names, simply replied: "I have forgot my Name." Williams concluded that "Obscure and meane persons amongst them have no Names," but a plausible explanation is that his informants did not want him to have the power over them that knowing their names would give.[32] Those who dealt directly with the English did give their names, but these "names" were often actually titles. Wahunsonacock, for example, was known to the Virginia colonists by one of his titles, Powhatan, and he was known to have other names and titles. The Pilgrims knew their Pokanoket ally as both Massasoit and Osamekin.[33]

Americans took new names at key points in their lives. Edward Winslow of Plymouth wrote, "All their names are significant and variable; for when they come to the state of men and women, they alter them according to their deeds or dispositions," and this was later confirmed by Samson Occum. William Strachey wrote similarly of the Chesapeake, comparing the practice of bestowing new names in honor of great deeds to ancient Roman custom.[34] Name changes could also advertise intentions. Wingina, chief of the Roanokes, signaled his purpose to form a coalition to resist the English by changing his name to Pemisapan, just as Opechancanough became Mangopeesomon and Itoyatan became Sasawpen just before the Powhatans attacked the Virginia plantations in 1622.[35] When Mosco, thought to be "some French mans sonne, because he had a thicke blacke bush beard," joined the Jamestown expedition exploring Chesapeake Bay under John Smith, he changed his name to Uttasantasough. The English thought the name meant "stranger," because it was also applied to the English.[36] This was the same name as the Tassantasse assumed by the Chickahominies when they became English allies. *New England's First Fruits* of 1643, advertising early cross-cultural successes, described one man who, having decided to live with the English, said "he would be called no more by his Indian name, but would be named William."[37]

Other kinds of intentions were signaled by name changes. Americans who took up boundary-crossing roles, far from being selected by accidental kidnapping, may actually have chosen to approach the English and go with them in order to become mediators between worlds, and the names they assumed at that point in their lives indicated the spiritual dimension of their choice. As they prepared to enter the English world, they very likely thought they were entering a spiritually dangerous zone. If, as the Roanokes told Thomas Harriot, the Indians believed the English were risen dead, then close association with them, while it could confer great power, would be dangerous. Thomas Morton wrote that the dead were buried "ceremoniously" and then the place of burial was abandoned. New England reports held that natives avoided even the names of the dead, and apparently powwaws there took no part in burials and avoided the threshold where the soul entered the underworld.[38]

When Uttamatomakkin or Tomocomo, a priest, accompanied the newly married Pocahontas to London, he traveled as Powhatan's personal emissary; Smith wrote that he was a member of Powhatan's council, "being amongst them held an understanding fellow." One part of his commission was to find and talk with Smith. The colonists had repeatedly told Powhatan that Smith, who had been eased out of Jamestown years earlier, was dead; but Powhatan wanted to know for certain, because, as Pocahontas said, "your Countriemen will lie much." He wanted Smith "to shew him our God, the King, Queene, and Prince, I so much had told them of." Smith "told him the best he could" about God and reminded Uttamatomakkin that he had already seen King James I. Uttamatomakkin denied that he had seen the king until Smith convinced him he had, at which Powhatan's emissary became thoughtful. Just as the English had tests of royal carriage and deportment by which they judged Indian leaders, so Uttamatomakkin had found James's behavior unkingly. When Smith "by circumstances" convinced Uttamatomakkin he had been in the royal presence, "Then he replyed very sadly, You gave Powhatan a white Dog, which Powhatan fed as himselfe, but your King gave me nothing, and I am better than your white Dog." Both English and Indians found meanness a fatal defect in the great. As we have seen, Uttamatomakkin held extensive discussions with the Reverend Samuel Purchas in London, describing his own religion, and resisting attempts to convince him of the superiority of Christianity. His expectation of what would happen on his return to Tsenacommacah indicates that he had crossed a line that was not easily recrossed; he told

Purchas that he would not enter the temple where he acted as priest "till Okeeus shall call him."[39]

Thomas Harriot wrote that the divine force among the coastal Carolina Algonquians was Montóac; the man from that region who went to England twice and who was baptized as the friend of the Roanoke colonists was named Manteo. Like Hobbomock, Manteo was described as a "lustie" man, which meant vigorous and healthy. Manteo repeatedly moved between English and Algonquian villages, interpreting each culture to the other. The English never doubted his loyalty to them; he had become, in their view, "a most faithfull English man." He was often placed in the middle of hostilities, and twice was forced to confront the fact that rash, hasty attacks by the English with whom he lived had resulted in deaths and maiming among his own people who had been mistaken for enemies. The second occurred after the Croatoans, the tribe led by Manteo's mother, had pleaded for badges that would clearly show them to be friends. Both attacks took place at night and, as John White governor of the 1587 colony explained, in the dark they could not distinguish men from women, much less enemies from friends.

Although these deaths "somewhat grieved Manteo," he reportedly acknowledged the governor's rationale for them, and accepted incorporation into the English system. Three significant events were placed in a series in White's report. His account of the attack on the Croatoans and its aftermath was followed by description of Manteo's baptism (still as Manteo) and creation as lord of Roanoke. Next in White's journal was the birth of Virginia Dare, Governor White's granddaughter. Shortly the colonists and Manteo were left together on Roanoke Island, and White and the ships sailed home to organize the next shipment of supplies and colonists. Circumstances prevented the sailing of the supply ships and when an English ship once again called at Roanoke the settlement was deserted. We do not know what part Manteo took in events after the abandonment of these lost colonists, but the colonists left an indication that at least some of them had gone to Croatoan, where Manteo's people lived.[40]

"Montóac" was one variant of the more common "Manitou." Several Indians who stepped into English life or who attempted to manipulate the relationship between Indians and English adopted versions of this name as Manteo did. Pocahontas's name Amonute suggests a self-presentation as Manitou when she crossed over into English life.[41] One of her father's names or titles, "Mamanotowick," which "signifyes great Kinge" according to William Strachey, had Manito embedded in it. Frederic Gleach points out that another of his names, Powhatan, contained the priestly title powwaw.[42] Mannedo was the name of an

Abenaki "Gentleman" from Maine who was taken to England with four others by Captain George Waymouth in 1605. His name was also written Manida, Maniddo, Manedy, and even Maneduck.[43] Also in Maine, on the Kennebec River in 1605, Champlain met a chief named Manthoumermer, who said "he desired an alliance with us, and through our mediation to make peace with their enemies."[44] John Winthrop mentioned an Indian youngster living in his house who may have done the same thing via an English name: he called himself "Knowe-God."[45]

One of the most compelling figures who assumed a Manitou identity was Munetute or Nemattanew; he created a role between Powhatan and English cultures. As George Percy reported, the Jamestown colonists called this charismatic leader among the Powhatans "Jack of the Feathers. By reason that he used to come into the field all covered over with feathers and Swans' wings fastened unto his shoulders as though he meant to fly."[46] He first entered the records resisting the extension of settlements up the James River and orchestrated the episode in which the soldiers were bewitched, but he also proposed the cooperative English-Powhatan punitive venture against a tribe beyond the falls that the Virginia Council discussed in 1619. Munetute was regarded as supremely fitted for the role of mediator between worlds: "for his courage and policy" he was "accounted amongst the Salvages their chiefe Captaine, and immortall from any hurt could bee done him by the English," especially because he had "so long escaped so many dangers without any hurt." The Indians regarded him as "supernatural." George Wyatt thought his claims of an "Ointment that could secuere them from our Shot" were believed because English guns were so notoriously inaccurate that most shots missed and "few in proofe were found mortal." When he was eventually shot by two servants in very doubtful circumstances, they claimed that "Jack finding the pangs of death upon him, desired of the Boyes two things; the one was, that they would not make it knowne hee was slaine with a bullet; the other, to bury him amongst the English." At his death Opechancanough, according to Smith, "much grieved and repined, with great threats of revenge." The English thought they had overawed Opechancanough with their own threats, but within a few days the settlements faced the great Indian uprising of 1622 that came close to destroying the Virginia colony.[47]

Pnieses among New England's Algonquians, "men of great courage and wisdom," occupied roles similar to Munetute's among the Powhatans; the spirit Hobbomock appeared to them "more familiarly than to others," and their remarkable courage stemmed from the belief that they were invulnerable to wounds.[48] William Bradford's description of the man known as Hobbomock, who claimed that Massasoit would not act without "his privity," gave him the attributes of a pniese, and Edward Winslow acknowledged that the Pilgrims actively sustained him in that role.[49]

Never in all their voluminous writings did the Pilgrims ever confront the odd fact that their resident intermediaries bore the name of the devil. The conclusion that the Pilgrims welcomed not only these men but also their names precisely because they understood the powers the names implied and they wished to associate that power with their own cause seems inescapable. Early on, Robert Cushman had written that with Squanto living among them, the Pilgrims "can know what is done or intended towards us among the savages; also we can acquaint them with our courses and purposes, both human and religious."[50] Moreover, they did not seek to extinguish the power of those names. Squanto was baptized as Squanto; like Manteo and unlike most Indian converts, he was not asked to take a new baptismal name. There is no record of Hobbomock's baptism. He was allocated land within Plymouth in the prime area where the original Mayflower migrants lived.[51]

Incorporating Squanto and Hobbomock's powers may have made sense to the vulnerable Pilgrims, but they were often uncomfortable with the men and their roles, especially as they came to believe that Squanto was using his English base for his own purposes. When an injured relative of Squanto's came running with a report that Massasoit was assembling a force to attack Plymouth, Hobbomock assured the nervous colonists that not only did Massasoit continue to be their friend but the Pokanoket chief would never undertake such an action without consulting him. Hobbomock was asking the Pilgrims to believe not only in Massasoit's good will but also that he, Hobbomock, continued to be the chief's principal advisor while living at Plymouth. The colonists were convinced only after Hobbomock's wife went privately "(pretending other occasions)" to "Puckanokick," Massasoit's principal residence, and found "all things quiet." On other occasions they expressed reservations about Hobbomock's advice.

Both the Pilgrims and Massasoit, according to Winslow and Bradford, increasingly distrusted Squanto. The English learned that he presented himself to the Indians as a pniese whose position as advisor to the Plymouth leaders was the same as that claimed by Hobbomock with Massasoit. He persuaded his native clients that "he could lead us to peace or war at his pleasure." His technique was to warn Plymouth's neighbors that the English intended to kill them and to offer to dissuade them from attacking. He was so persuasive that many "had him in greater esteem than many of their sachims." Winslow believed that he had arranged the alarm about an impending attack on Plymouth to try to entice the Pilgrims to end the state of peace with the Pokanokets, thereby enhancing his own power to manipulate relationships. Despite Squanto's reported misbehavior and Massasoit's demands that he be executed, however, "yet was he so necessary and profitable an instrument, as at that time we could not miss him." Pilgrim leaders acknowledged the Indians' claim: "if he were dead, the English had lost their tongue."

The English leaders were particularly outraged to learn that Squanto, "to possess his countrymen with the greater fear of us, and so consequently of himself," had claimed the settlers manipulated the plague, recalling the devastation that had swept through the region on the eve of Plymouth's settlement. He told his clients that the plague was buried under the storehouse, "which at our pleasure, we could send forth to what place or people we would and destroy them therewith, though we stirred not from home." In fact it was their powder that was buried in the storehouse, evoking echoes of the Roanoke reports associating European bullets and the imported diseases. When Hobbomock asked one of the English whether it was true that they could command the plague, the response claimed superior power without responsibility. The answer was "No; but the God of the English had it in store, and could sent it at his pleasure to the destruction of his and our enemies." Bradford boasted that he and Captain Miles Standish devised a method for controlling Squanto and Hobbomock: "the Governor seemed to countenance the one, and the Captain the other, by which they had better intelligence, and made them both more diligent."[52]

There may have been other men who assumed a deity's identity. William Wood wrote of an Indian named Abamoch in early Massachusetts who set a trap for his unfaithful wife; there is no way to tell if this is the Hobbomock who lived with the Pilgrims. Thomas Morton told a story involving a powwow named Tantoquineo. And, as we have seen, one of the leaders opposing the English in King Philip's War was named Squando.[53]

The Pequots were believed to have extremely powerful individuals among them, which contributed to their lack of fear when confronting the colonists before the Pequot War of 1636–37. Roger Williams warned John Winthrop that, in addition to their "store of guns," they had a "witch amongst them [who] will sinck the pinnaces by diving under water and making holes etc." In the early stages of the Pequot War, taunting Pequots said that they had one among them, probably their sachem Sassacus, who, if he killed just one more Englishman, would be equal to God: "and as the Englishman's God is, so would he be." Indians allied with the English were "stricken, and as it were amazed with Fear" when told of the English intention to attack Sassacus's fort, because the sachem's "very Name was a Terrour" to them. Trembling Narragansetts told Captain John Mason that Sassacus was "all one a God, no Body could kill him." Kiswas, a Pequot brought to the English fort at Saybrook in Connecticut by the Mohegans who captured him, "braved the English, as though they durst not kill a Pequot" and was disabused in the most vicious way: "they tied one of his legs to a post, and 20 men with a rope tied to the other, pulled him in pieces" until Captain Underhill dispatched him with a bullet. Pequot boasting of the superiority of their gods was incorporated as an important part of the story. Edward Johnson, in his history of New England published in 1653, wrote that in the war's early stages when the English had seemed tentative, the Pequots were reported to have claimed "Englishmans God was all one Flye, and that English man was all one Sqawe, and themselves all one Moor-hawks."[54]

Some English people may have undertaken, voluntarily or involuntarily, similar crossings into fear-inspiring spiritual realms. Before the final attack on the Pequots, twenty-two year old Thomas Stanton, "a Man well acquainted with Indian Language and Manners," offered to go into the swamp where they had taken refuge to bring out the women, children, and old men. Captain John Mason recorded that the military leaders were "somewhat backward" to this notion because of the hazard Stanton would undergo, but he insisted and soon returned with two hundred Pequots. Stanton's venture was hazardous because he went among the enemy, but it may have seemed particularly dangerous because, as among the ancient Germans, swamps were especially sacred places, thresholds between worlds, where Indians conjured and met with Hobbomock. When Plymouth was founded, for example, before neighboring chiefs approached the recently arrived English, all their priests met for three days of "conjurations, which assembly and service they held in a dark and dismal swamp."[55]

John Rolfe feared that his projected marriage to Pocahontas might involve a spiritually dangerous crossing of lines, and that what he thought of as his Christian impulse to bring her into the fold of the saved might in fact be "wicked instigations, hatched by him who seeketh and delighteth in mans destruction." The Reverend William Symonds had preached to the Virginia Company and the "Planters for Virginia," whose number included John Rolfe, as they set out to renew the colony in a great fleet in 1609. In his sermon he reminded his hearers that Abraham's descendants were enjoined to "keepe them to themselves. They may not marry nor give in marriage to the heathen, that are uncircumcised." The point was emphasized in a marginal note: "Marrie not with Infidels." Symonds warned that breaking this rule risked destroying the entire venture. Five years later, as he contemplated marriage, Rolfe remembered "the heavie displeasure which almightie God conceived against the sonnes of Levie and Israel for marrying strange wives." He was keenly aware that not only were Pocahontas's education and manner "rude" and "barbarous" but, more importantly, "her generation accursed"—that is, she was conceived and born in sin.

As Rolfe struggled to resolve the "mightie warre" within him, he insisted that his motives were pure, but his feelings for Pocahontas were entangled in "so intricate a laborinth" that until God took him by the hand he could not "discerne the safe paths wherein to treade." God insisted that Rolfe take up the challenge, even waking him in the night as we have seen. So finally Rolfe believed that his desire to marry was sent by God and that he placed himself in spiritual danger by resisting rather than by accepting it.[56]

Opinion remained divided in England about intermarriage. In 1624 two promoters of colonization in the far north offered opposing thoughts. William Alexander, earl of Stirling, traced the beginning of success in Virginia to Pocahontas's marriage and praised it as a precedent because it calmed the Indians' natural and realistic fears of being overrun, which they would inevitably resist "(libertie being valued above life)." If the Americans became Christians, amalgamation "were in some sort tolerable" because the "promiscuous offspring" of those marriages, "extinguishing the distinction of persons," would create a new mixed American reality. Richard Eburne, on the other hand, recommended Newfoundland for settlement, and one of his reasons was the relatively small population, so colonists need not fear strong enemies or "corruption of language or blood." One of his reasons for recommending that young men not be sent to the colonies was that they would have no marriage partners except for native women, "which haply will be nor handsome nor wholesome for them." Interethnic mixing was a subject on which no consensus existed in England, but even those who favored it insisted that the partners must be integrated into English Christian life.[57]

When influence pulled in the other direction, every effort was made to blunt its effects. Some people may have been too contaminated by their entanglement with native life to be acceptable in English settlements. Twenty-year-old Anne Jackson went to Virginia in 1621 with her brother John Jackson, a substantial colonist who had gone home and now returned to the settlement of Martin's Hundred. Anne's father came to the ship to see her off; the records specify that she went with his consent. When Martin's Hundred was destroyed in the great attack of March 1622, John's child was killed and Anne was taken prisoner. In April 1626 John Jackson and Robert Linsey "went . . . with certaine Indians unto

Pamunkey"; Jackson was given "leave to come away home," but Linsey was "detained there." In 1628 without explanation Anne was back with the English in Jamestown. But she may have been a reluctant repatriate; shortly after her return, the General Court ordered "that Anne Jackson which Came from the Indians shall bee sent for England with the first oportunity of Shipping and that her brother John Jackson shall give security for her passage and keepe her safe till shee bee shipped aboard." The clear implication is that if she were free to come and go, Anne Jackson would have endeavored to return to her Indian family. Therefore she had to be sent back to England.[58] One man, Robert Marcum, did apparently leave Jamestown for a permanent Indian identity as Moutapass; Linsey's fate is not known. Other men, including William White, Thomas Graves, and Henry Fleet, did return to English life after years of captivity with Chesapeake Bay area natives.[59]

Cases of boundary crossing were also reported from New England. Governor William Bradford of Plymouth was outraged to learn that the colony's business agents had arranged to bring back Edward Ashley to run a new trading venture in the Penobscot region. Although he had "wit and ability," the Pilgrims considered him "a very profane young man"; he had lived with the Indians "as a savage and went naked amongst them and used their manners, in which time he got their language." Not only did the Pilgrims believe he had cheated them, but they also accused him of trading guns to the Indians and committing "uncleanness" with native women; they seized him and sent him back to England, and Bradford was gratified to hear that he had been lost at sea on another venture— "by the hand of God taken away."[60]

Roger Williams wrote to John Winthrop about William Baker of Plymouth, who lived with the Mohegans and "is turned Indian in nakednes and cutting of haire, and after many whoredomes, is there maried." Williams reported that Baker "can speake much Indian," and he predicted great treachery from him. Baker was returned to the English, but escaped back to his Indian community, where he was held in great affection. When he was recaptured, he was brought to Hartford and subjected to two whippings. William Coddington wrote Winthrop of another renegade, a thief and "lude Felowe" named Thomas Saverye, who had a child by one Indian woman and attempted relationships with others. Coddington lamented "that those that professe them selvs to be Christians, should be more barberous and wyld then Indeans, to the proproch of our nation, and the dishoner of God."[61]

If the Pilgrims sought to make use of the powers or of the Indians' belief in the powers of the deity who most readily crossed between the spirit

and human realms, we might wonder what a man like Hobbomock—
"their Indian," as Bradford called him—made of his long life between
the Pilgrims and the Pokanokets and their neighbors as he "continued
very faithful and constant to the English till he died." How would he
have identified himself? The stress of life in the intersection of English
and native cultures must have been crushing, and the sources give us occasional glimpses of that experience.

Hobbomock, as he appears in the early sources, clearly continued to
think of himself as Massasoit's man. When he and Winslow, rushing to
the ailing sachem's bedside, were told that Massasoit had died,
Hobbomock was deeply troubled and cried out, "Neen womasu sagimus,
neen womasu sagimus, &c. 'My loving sachim, my loving sachim! Many
have I known, but never any like thee.'" He told of Massasoit's virtues
at great length and with "unfeigned sorrow." On their return when
Winslow and Hobbomock visited Corbitant, who elicited Winslow's tortured answer to the question of why the English approached their friends
with their guns pointed, Winslow called Hobbomock to verify that this
was a traditional greeting. "But shaking the head, he answered, that he
liked not such salutations."[62]

Those who were baptized or who were incorporated into English life
felt their identity stretched. *New England's First Fruits* reported that
children who had been brought up in English houses could not bear to
return to the Indians even for visits. In most cases we can only guess at
the cost of the choices converts made. Three accounts written in 1612
of Kemps, a Powhatan man captured with another by Captain John
Smith, give a sense of the difficulties and the range of relationships they
faced while acting in two cultures. Smith called the two captives" the
two most exact villaines in all the Country," but he described them as
valuable assets. They taught the colonists "how to order and plant our
fields." When food was scarce, the two were set free, and they continued to aid the colony. When desperate colonists ran to the Indians for
food, Kemps made sure they were returned, after first making them
work for the Indians as Smith made the colonists work in Jamestown.
Later, after Smith had left Jamestown, George Percy led a punitive expedition against Powhatan's people and forced Kemps to act as guide.
Percy had him handcuffed to the provost marshal; when they discovered that "This Subtell Salvage" was leading the troops in the wrong direction, Percy beat him and threatened to cut off his head until he took
them the right way. Percy and his men carried out a bloody and devastating attack that day. The third picture was by William Strachey, who
mentioned that Kemps had died the previous year of scurvy. Kemps, according to Strachey, had lived in Jamestown almost a year and was

"much made of by our Lord Generall." He spoke "a pretty deale of English" and was a faithful churchgoer, both for daily prayers and Sunday services. Strachey learned much about Indian society from his conversations with Kemps—and also with Machumps, who had spent time in England and was now a frequent visitor to Jamestown, where he dined at the governor's table. Machumps also gave Strachey hope that the colonists might find the most important English boundary crossers, Roanoke's lost colonists.[63]

The English found two Indian heroes in the story of the concerted Powhatan attack on the English settlements in 1622, but only one of their names is recorded. One was Chauco, a Pamunkey man who returned to his own people after giving warning of the impending attack. We know the other only as "an Indian belonging to one Perry" who lived with Richard Pace, "that used him as a Sonne." This man's brother came and urged him to kill Pace at the time appointed for the attack next morning. Instead "Perries Indian rose out of his bed" and revealed everything to Pace, thus allowing Jamestown to be forewarned and saved. The unnamed man and his anguish then disappear from the records, but Chauco reappeared in Jamestown early in 1623 with a message from the "great Kinge" asking for an end to the bloodshed. Although the colonists professed themselves ready for peace and the most prominent person among the Powhatans' prisoners, Mrs. Boyce, was returned, negotiations came to nothing and a decade of intermittent war ensued.[64]

We know much more about the choices faced by Pocahontas, who had acted in both her own and English settlements from childhood. When Pocahontas was still a child, Smith said that "for wit and spirit" she was "the only Nonpariel of [Powhatan's] Country." She repeatedly came to Jamestown as an emissary for her father even as a child, and Smith believed that she had defied Powhatan and risked his wrath to warn the English of danger and to supply them with food.[65] As she matured, and in the continuing warfare after Smith left the colony, Pocahontas no longer came to Jamestown. When, in 1613, an expedition from Jamestown headed by Captain Samuel Argall discovered Pocahontas in a village along the Potomac River, the English took advantage of her pleasure at renewing her acquaintance with them to take her prisoner. Argall's rationale was that she could be exchanged for English men and weapons in Powhatan's possession. But instead she and leading colonists grew entangled in ties of affection and her conversion became top priority in the colony. Both governor Sir Thomas Dale and the Reverend Alexander Whitaker testified that Dale "had laboured along time" to bring her to the point where she "renounced publickly her countrey Idolatry" and "openly confessed her Christian faith."[66]

The choice of baptismal name for her, Rebecca, was intensely meaningful, evoking the Genesis account of the origins of the people of Israel.
The aged Abraham did not want his son Isaac to marry a Canaanite
woman, so he sent his senior servant to his own birthplace to find a suitable woman and the servant returned with Rebecca, who was Abraham's
grandniece. Abraham's servant set a test by stopping near a well outside
the city where he asked for water as women came out to the well.
Rebecca passed the test by giving water not only to him but to his
camels, and offering hospitality. Pocahontas, with her "compassionate,
pittiful heart," had been the first of her people to befriend the Jamestown
colonists, and had brought them food. Rebecca, like Pocahontas, was
born in paganism because her people had not followed Abraham when
he was called by God. Most important, Rebecca's family blessed her as
she left them to join Abraham's family and predicted her progeny would
"growe into thousand thousandes." When Rebecca was pregnant with
twins, God told her that she carried two nations and "two maner of people." Moreover, "the one people shalbe mightier then the other, and the
elder shal serve the yonger." The union of Rebecca and Isaac both
brought Rebecca into God's way and, through their son Jacob who was
given the name Israel by the angel with whom he wrestled, began the
twelve tribes of Israel. The English hoped the marriage of Pocahontas
and John Rolfe would ensure her salvation and the couple would be the
progenitors of a new Christian American people.[67] Richard Crakanthorpe, in a major sermon at the inauguration of James I as king, had
looked forward to such a new united identity when he predicted "so
happy a worke, not only to see a new BRITTAINE in another world, but
to heare also those, as yet Heathen, Barbarous, and Brutish people, together with our English, to learne the speech and language of Canaan:"
Both peoples would learn this new way of speaking.[68]

Powhatan consented to Pocahontas's marriage; two of her brothers had
visited her and "much rejoyced" to see that she was treated so well, and
her father decided that his people should play a role in the proceedings.
Powhatan sent "an olde uncle of hirs, named Opachisco, to give her as
his deputy in the Church, and two of his sonnes to see the mariage sol-
emnized." No one mentioned Pocahontas's earlier marriage or betrothal
to a man named Kocoum.[69]

Governor Dale sent Ralph Hamor, accompanied by Thomas Savage,
on a mission to Powhatan shortly after the wedding. Powhatan received
them in state, despite Dale's careless failure to supply Hamor with the
chain of pearls Powhatan had given him for official ambassadors to wear.
After they had smoked a pipe of tobacco together, Powhatan asked
Hamor about Pocahontas and "his unknowne sonne, and how they liked,

lived and loved together." Hamor assured him that they were both well
and Pocahontas was "content . . . whereat he laughed heartily, and said
he was very glad of it." Then Powhatan told Hamor to explain the cause
of his coming, which Hamor said he would do only in private.

Hamor's mission was delicate indeed; he was charged to ask Powhatan
for another daughter, "the bruite of the exquisite perfection of your
yongest daughter" having come to the governor's ears, Dale wished to
make her "his neerest companion, wife and bedfellow." As with
Kocoum, Dale's English wife was not mentioned. When Powhatan said
his daughter was promised, that he had "sould" her a few days earlier to

The de Bry workshop created this engraving to illustrate Ralph Hamor's account of his
embassy to Powhatan. The foreground shows Powhatan checking Hamor's neck for the
special rope of pearls that official ambassadors were supposed to wear to show that they
spoke for the governor in Jamestown. Thomas Savage stands next to Hamor. In the background are two scenes in which an Englishman speaks to a group of Pamunkeys. In the
interior scene, Hamor asks Powhatan for a second daughter; the scene at the left may
show Hamor attempting to secure the release of William Parker. The John Carter Brown
Library at Brown University.

another werowance, Hamor replied that one of his greatness could call his daughter home again if he wished—especially since the intended bride was not yet twelve years old and therefore not of marriageable age. Powhatan then replied that this daughter was so dear to him that he could not live without being able to see her often. And he went on, "I holde it not a brotherly part of your King, to desire to bereave me of two of my children at once." Nor was there any need of living pledges of the peace between the Powhatans and the English, "for I am now olde, and would gladly end my daies in peace."

Peaceful intentions were soon tested. While he was with Powhatan, Hamor encountered William Parker, who had been a captive for three years and was now indistinguishable from his Indian hosts; Hamor identified him as English only by his speech. Parker begged Hamor to secure his release, and Hamor was indignant because, when they had inquired after him, the English had been told that Parker was dead. When Hamor insisted on taking Parker with him, Powhatan grew indignant in turn: "You have one of my daughters with you, and I am therewith well content, but you can no sooner see or know of any English mans being with me, but you must have him away, or else breake peace and friendship." He let Parker go nonetheless, and did grudgingly furnish the party with a guide and food. But he insisted on receiving a variety of tools from Jamestown in recompense, and several times quizzed Hamor to see if he remembered everything. It was on this occasion that Powhatan brought out his notebook to induce Hamor to make a note of his requirements.[70]

John Rolfe, the Lady Rebecca, and their infant son Thomas went to England in 1616, where they were enthusiastically received; John Smith was pleased to see that she had "become very formall and civill after our English manner." The Virginia Company gave them an allowance and they were lodged at the Belle Sauvage Inn. A portrait of Pocahontas lavishly and expensively dressed was rushed into print, and the Rolfes attended fashionable events all over London. Just as Pocahontas and her attendants had performed "A Virginia Maske" for John Smith, so she and Uttamatomakkin attended the masque "The Vision of Delight," created by Ben Jonson and Inigo Jones, at the royal court on Twelfth Night. Masques were lavish and expensive entertainments in which the audience was drawn into the dance. The successive scenes, as in all masques, proceeded from disorder to the order that radiated over the land from the court, and the early scenes of this masque were replete with lewd references to lechery and gluttony and the mad scramble after novelty in fashion; in its conclusion, order was restored by the godlike king. "The Vision of Delight" was performed to celebrate the elevation of the king's favorite, James Villiers, as earl of Buckingham and he was the central dancer. We know that queen Anne danced with Villiers that night and that the American visitors were "well placed" to see the entertainment.[71] Uttamatomakkin's scorn for his mean treatment by the king may have grown partly out of seeing the lavishness of this production.

Toward the end of their seven-month stay the Virginia Company appropriated the very large sum of £100 to be given to the Rolfes for missionary activities among the Powhatans. As they waited for a favorable wind to carry them west, Pocahontas sickened and died; she was buried at Gravesend. Rolfe returned to America alone; sickly baby Thomas was left with relatives in England. Several of Pocahontas's attendants also remained in London, and three were baptized. One, who lived with Virginia Company leader George Thorpe, was baptized with the name George Thorpe and was buried just two weeks later in 1619. Two women who accompanied her were still in London four years after Pocahontas's death, and the Virginia Company decided to send them back to America in 1621. They sent them to Bermuda, not Virginia, and each woman had two servant boys to accompany her, indicating their high rank as the daughters of "Viceroyes" in Virginia. One died at sea, but the other was married in the governor's house to "as fitt and agreeable an husband as the place would afford" and with lavish feasting. The company intended that after some stay in Bermuda, the couple would go to Virginia and work to convert the Indians, as Pocahontas had been expected to do. Bermuda governor Nathaniel Butler said the bride was the sister of Powhatan's successor. Meanwhile Rolfe wrote from Virginia that the colony was doing well. "The Indyans very loving, and willing to parte with their childeren. My wives death is much lamented; my childe much desyred . . ."[72]

Many opinions have been offered, but no one knows what caused Pocahontas's death. One observer, John Chamberlain, who was critical of everything that had to do with the Virginia enterprise, and who was one of the few who found the Rolfes ridiculous rather than impressive, sent his correspondent her picture saying she was "no fayre Lady." He wrote of the Rolfes' preparation for their return to America "(though sore against her will)," and some have said she died of a broken heart. It is tempting to wonder how that £100 bequest sat on her conscience. As long as she stayed wholly in Jamestown or in England she could be an English lady, but living in and between two cultures was impossible. Clearly she did not think of herself as utterly transformed. She said to Smith, "*your* Countriemen will lie much." The prospect of going among her own people as an English agent and attempting to subvert their beliefs, to convert them to Christianity, must have been unbearable. The Virginia Company document recording the grant says that it was Rolfe

VIRGINIÆ · MATOAKA ALS REBECCA FILIA POTENTISS · PRINC : POWHATANI IMP : VIRGINIÆ ·

Ætatis suæ 22. A.
1616.

Matoaks als Rebecka daughter to the mighty Prince
Powhatan Emperour of Attanoughskomouck als virginia
converted and baptized in the Christian faith, and
wife to the wor.ll M.r Joh Rolff.

This engraving of Pocahontas in London in 1616 demonstrates the English understanding that her true name had been Matoaka; the name Pocahontas does not appear on it. She is identified as the daughter of the "mighty Prince" and "Emperour" Powhatan. Her hat of expensive white felt, and the braid and lace on the tapestry fabric of her dress, show that the Virginia Company spent lavishly in preparing her to meet the public. The John Carter Brown Library at Brown University.

A visitor to London made a watercolor sketch of this Virginia Algonquian, Eiakintomino, in St. James's Park in 1615 or 1616. This engraving from the sketch was used to decorate a Virginia Company broadside for the great lottery that helped to finance the colony. Society of Antiquaries of London.

who promised "in behalfe of him selfe and the said Ladye, his wife," to use all "good meanes of perswasions and inducemts" to win the Virginians to the "embraceing of true religion." The paper's endorsement, however, describes it as a warrant for £100 "for the Ladie Rebecca . . . for sacred use in Virginia." As they prepared for their homeward voyage, both Uttamatomakkin and Pocahontas must have pondered the shape their lives would take in Virginia. Uttamatomakkin knew that he could not reenter the temple in which he served as priest until called by Okee after having been among the English. The prospect for the young Pocahontas, charged with responsibility for actively working to oust Okee and the worldview associated with him, was infinitely more distressing. Whatever disease attacked her, the intolerable stress created by this assignment must have made her vulnerable.[73]

Other Indians faced with similar prospects of divided identity and inner conflict solved the problem by abandoning the Europeans altogether. Don Luís de Velasco was a Powhatan, the son of a chief, who agreed to go with a Spanish venture that visited Chesapeake Bay in 1561. He lived in Spain, Havana, and Mexico City with the Dominicans and was always accorded treatment due an aristocrat. In Spain he was maintained at royal expense, and the viceroy of Mexico stood as sponsor when he was baptized. He returned to Chesapeake Bay in the company of a Jesuit mission in September 1570, and the Spanish expected him to be the bridge between themselves and the natives; he had confirmed his desire to bring Christianity to his people. So secure did the priests feel in Don Luís's attachment to Christianity that they founded their mission without any soldiers to protect them. Much to their amazement, he began to pull away from them as soon as they landed in Chesapeake Bay. The land was in the grip of a devastating six-year drought, and the Powhatans believed he had returned from the dead; Don Luís took steps to cross back into the world of his people and resume his membership. Five days after their arrival, Don Luís abandoned the missionaries. In February three priests went to find him; they asked for corn for the mission and especially that Don Luís return and begin the planned conversion campaign. The three priests were followed and killed, and five days later the entire mission was exterminated, except for a boy, Alonso de Olmos, who represented no threat to the Powhatans' religious life; Don Luís led both attacks. Pocahontas could have known Don Luís. The evidence suggests that he was fifteen or sixteen in 1561, so he would have been in his early fifties when Pocahontas was born. His stories of Mexico and Spain and his ultimate rejection of Christianity and the Spanish presence must have been in her mind as she pictured herself leading the English Christian mission to the Powhatans.[74]

Wanchese was another man who crossed the Atlantic but severed his European ties on his return. He had gone to England with the first Roanoke party and Manteo in 1584, but broke all contact with the English as soon as he was back on the Outer Banks the next year. He made only two further appearances in the records, both times as a foe of the English.[75] Others who left English life took up roles as intermediaries like Henry Spelman and other English boys who had spent part of their youth with the Indians. An embassy from Indians on the Connecticut River to the recently founded Massachusetts Bay colony included "Jacke Strawe (an Indian which had lived in England, & had served Sir Walter Earle, & was now turned Indian againe)."[76]

Manteo, like all Indians who chose to remain with the English, endured constant taunts and challenges from the natives among whom he moved. Roanoke colony governor Ralph Lane and his men, traveling up the Chowan and Roanoke Rivers in search of the gold they had been told of and helpless without Indian food aid, were delighted when they heard natives call to Manteo from the bank, "hoping for some friendly conference with them." Manteo answered them and the Indians "presently began a song." At that Manteo picked up his gun and told Lane that an attack was intended. A similar provocation was intended when Block Island natives challenged the native interpreter, possibly Sassamon, who accompanied Captain John Underhill, with "what are you an Indian or an English-man." Underhill reported the taunt's fatal consequences: "come hither, saith he, and I will tell you; hee pulls up his cocke and let fly at one of them, and without question was the death of him."[77]

New Englands First Fruits wrote of an "Indian of good quality" who lived with the Pilgrims and was probably Hobbomock, although his name was not given. This man had been amazed at a demonstration of the power of the English God and therefore had decided "to forsake the Indians, and cleave to the English." He labored constantly to learn more about God, according to the pamphlet, and he endured much abuse from his compatriots: "and (though he was much tempted by inticements, scoffes and scornes from the Indians) yet, could he never be gotten from the English." He died among them "leaving some good hopes in their hearts, that his soule went to rest." Squanto, much earlier, expressed a similar wish; he died asking Governor Bradford to pray for him "that he might go to the Englishman's God in Heaven."

Conviction of conversion was difficult for all puritans to attain, and the cautious way the Pilgrim leaders wrote of Hobbomock's and Squanto's state at their deaths indicates uncertainty. The pamphlet *New Englands First Fruits* was rushed into print in 1643 to proclaim the news of Wequash's conversion and death as a Christian. Wequash was a Pequot who had been living for some time with the Niantics and had aided the English at the siege and destruction of the Pequot fort at Mystic. His divided heart continued to cause him trouble as he wrestled with Christianity. The authors of *New Englands First Fruits* wrote that although he had formerly claimed disdain for the Christian God, saying he was "but a Musketto God, or a God like unto a flye" and thought his worshippers "weake men," he had "had his mind wonderfully struck with great apprehensions about the glory of the Englishmans God" when he saw the slaying of so many Pequots "in an houre." Wequash then avidly searched for knowledge of the Christian God, engaging the English in long dialogues. Without irony the authors wrote that he repudiated his two major sins, lust and revenge, and achieved "an eminent degree of meeknesse and patience." That vengeful English acts had first awakened his thirst for knowledge of God caused no logical problem in their rendition. The main thing was that he had come to a state of self-loathing, and preached repentance to his people. "With prodigious Patience" Wequash "bore a Thousand Injuries from the other *Indians* for his Holy Profession." So disturbing was Wequash's behavior that some Indians, inspired by the devil, poisoned him. But, according to "Mr Sh[epard] a godly Minister in the Bay," he had been a Christian for a year and a half and died a martyr, asking for his child to be brought up among the English; Wequash was "certainly in Heaven."

The authors of *New Englands First Fruits* apparently knew Wequash's story by relation; he lived in Connecticut. Roger Williams published his firsthand account of his visit to the dying sachem also in 1643, and his account demonstrated the dividedness and uncertainty Wequash felt up to the very end. Williams wrote that, as "some of my Worthy Countrymen" had written about Wequash, he would "relate mine owne Hopes of Him (though I dare not be so confident as others." Williams "closed with him concerning his Soule," and Wequash reminded him of their conversations years earlier, in which Williams had acquainted him with the condition of all humankind and the need to turn to the Christian God. Wequash said these teachings "were never out of my heart." But, despite his efforts to pray, the dying man said he did not feel its effects: "Me so big naughty Heart, me heart all one stone!" Wequash died two days later, and "this was the summe of our last parting."[78]

Hiacoomes, the first convert by Thomas Mayhew on Martha's Vineyard, was an insignificant man, but the sachems and powwows were "much alarmed" when they learned that he was conversing with the minister, and tried with "all their might" to dissuade him. When he entered an Indian's house, his neighbors "laughed and scoffed at him, saying *Here comes the English man.*" A sachem asked him how he would cope if his children got sick. But, Mayhew was glad to report, the Christian Indians had much less sickness than others; and the powwows' attempts to use witchcraft against Hiacoomes were unsuccessful. Ultimately the scoffing sachem, too, became a convert.[79]

All natives who were attracted to English life found themselves subject to the scorn of their compatriots, and some were not able to shrug it off. As early as 1632 Massachusetts Bay colonists wrote home hopefully of the projected conversion of Sagamore John "to be civilized and a Christian"; it was this prospect that caused Edward Howes to suggest scarlet coats be given to Indian leaders as a mark of respect. Sagamore John loved the English and emulated their behavior and wanted to forsake Indian life, according to *New Englands First Fruits* more than a decade later, "but yet kept downe by the feare of the scoffes of the Indians, had not power to make good his purpose." At his death he lamented that God was angry with him; "I was affraid of the scoffes of these wicked Indians."[80]

The English boys who were left with Indian leaders around the Chesapeake in Jamestown's early days developed affectionate ties with and endured scoffs from both sides; they became truly interstitial / liminal people, needed by both and trusted by neither.[81] Like Don Luís, Pocahontas, and Hobbomock, they may have found their sense of self stretched unbearably. Thomas Savage arrived in Virginia in January 1608, and in February the thirteen-year-old boy was given to Powhatan by Smith and Captain Christopher Newport during their great embassy; Newport told Powhatan that Savage was his son, so he was known among the Indians as Thomas Newport. Powhatan sent Namontacke "his trusty servant" to live with the English. Smith's marginal note played up the significance: "The exchange of a Christian for a Salvage." Like Henry Spelman, Thomas Savage found strong ties of affection in the Indian villages, as well as anger over his divided loyalties. Once, early on, an irritated Powhatan sent Savage back to Jamestown but immediately sent Pocahontas, "a child of tenne yeares old," after him to beg "that the Boy might come againe, which he loved exceedingly."[82]

Spelman arrived in 1609 and he was also loved by his American host Iopassus, a Patawomeck subchief. On one occasion when Iopassus was away, Spelman was left with two of the werowance's wives. One of the women wanted to visit her father a day's journey away and asked Spelman to accompany her and carry her child. He refused, whereat she hit him; when he hit her back, both wives began to beat him so hard he "thought they had lamd me." When Iopassus returned, Spelman told him of these events and without a word the werowance picked up a tool and struck one of the women unconscious. Spelman ran away to a neighbor's house, where Iopassus sent his youngest child, presumably stirred up by the turmoil, because Spelman could quiet the child when no one else could. Iopassus sent for Spelman, but fear kept the boy in hiding until the next morning when the werowance came to the house where he was and kindly asked whether he had run away because he was afraid. When Spelman inquired after Iopassus's wife, the werowance said "all was well" and asked the boy to return with him, "telling me he loved me, and none should hurt me." Smith recorded that later "Pokahontas the Kings daughter saved a boy called Henry Spilman" in the period of disorder following Smith's departure from the colony.[83] Spelman and Savage lived extremely complicated and difficult lives among and between the colonists and the Americans during the next several years, which saw constant skirmishing, a period that ended in 1614 with the marriage of Pocahontas to John Rolfe.

During the period of hostilities, after Savage had returned to live in Jamestown, he endured the scorn of his Indian friends just as Hobbomock did, and he was wounded in one skirmish. William Strachey recorded a song that circulated after the capture of an English fort at the falls of the James River and the taking of some prisoners:

1. Mattanerew shashashewaw crawango pechecoma
   Whe Tassantassa inoshashaw yehockan pocosack
   Whe, whe, yah, ha, ha, ne, he, wittowa, wittowa

2. Mattanerew shashashewaw, erawango pechecoma
   Capt. Newport inoshashaw neir in hoc nantion matassan
   Whe whe, yah, ha, ha, etc.

3. Mattanerew shashashewaw erowango pechecoma
   Thom. Newport inoshashaw neir in hoc nantion monocock
   Whe whe etc.

4. Mattanerew shashashewaw, erawango pechecoma
   Pockin Simon moshasha mingon nantian Tamahuck.
   Whe whe, etc.

Strachey explained that the song told of how they killed the English for "all our Poccasacks, that is our Guns" even though Captain Newport brought them copper. And they could hurt Thomas Newport [Savage] "for all his Monnacock that is his bright Sword" and could capture Simon "for all his Tamahauke, that is his Hatchett." Simon may have been another boundary-crossing Englishman; Governor Dale said "Simons" had "thrice plaied the runnagate." The refrain "Whe whe" was the crying of the English as they were killed, "which they mock't us for and cryed agayne to us Yah, ha ha, Tewittaw, Tewittawa, Tewittawa." Nonetheless, when peace was concluded with Pocahontas's marriage and Savage accompanied Hamor's mission to Powhatan, the chief's first words were to "the Boy" as his adopted son, saying "my childe you are welcome, you have bin a straunger to me these foure yeeres. . . ."[84]

The English also treated divided loyalties unsympathetically. Their capture of Pocahontas was made possible by the intercession of Iopassus, whom Captain Samuel Argall considered "an old friend, and adopted brother." "Powhatans delight and darling" was living with "the great king Patowomeke," Iopassus's brother and superior chief, and Argall, learning her whereabouts on a trading expedition up the Potomac River, told Iopassus that he must "betray Pokahuntis unto my hands" or no longer be considered a friend. Iopassus, with the consent of his brother and the Patawomeck council, acquiesced and brought his wife into the plot "(which sex have ever bin most powerfull in beguiling intice-ments)." The plan was soon put into operation: the two brought Pocahontas to the river bank to see Argall's ship, and the wife began to plead with her husband to go aboard. His role was to seem to be angry, and to point out that she could not enter the ship without accompany-ing women. At which she began to weep "(as who knows not that women can command teares)" and then her husband, apparently moved by "those counterfeit teares" allowed her to board the ship if Pocahontas would go with her. After great persuasion, Pocahontas agreed; "and thus they betraied the poore innocent Pocahontas aboord." She realized her mistake when Iopassus and his wife left the ship and she was detained, at which she was "exceeding pensive and discontent." Iopassus kept up his role and complained as bitterly as she, but he had already been se-cretly rewarded; throughout their time aboard, he and his wife constantly nudged Argall as if to indicate "tis done, she is your own."

Ralph Hamor was as contemptuous of Iopassus as of his wife's femi-nine wiles; Argall gave a copper kettle and some other less valuable "toies" and Hamor remarked that Iopassus would have betrayed his own father for them. Smith, in retelling the story, fastened on Iopassus's feigned distress when Pocahontas was not allowed to leave. He wrote that "the old Jew and his wife began to howle and crie as fast as Pocahontas," but as soon as their part was played and the reward given, they "went merrily on shore."[85]

Captain Argall noted in passing that Iopassus brought Ensign Swift to their initial meeting, and went on to say that he had left Swift behind as a pledge of mutual friendship on his previous voyage. Many boys and young men were put in such positions. Smith, for example, mentioned that he had left "Samuell Collier his page to learne the language" at

The artist who created this engraving of Pocahontas being inveigled aboard Samuel Argall's ship captured the drama of the situation. Iopassus urges a hesitant Pocahontas, her face and posture full of doubt and fear, to go on the ship while his wife stands by. Iopassus and his wife already carry the loot they had gained for their treachery. Iopassus's small beard, combined with the tail of the skin he wears and the hornlike feathers in his hair, give him a devilish appearance. The John Carter Brown Library at Brown University.

Weraskoyack.[86] Those boys who grew up in both cultures were viewed with the same kind of mistrust and scorn as Iopassus; they had steadfast loyalty to neither side and yet were absolutely essential. The Reverend Jonas Stockham arrived in 1620 and was scornful of the entire Virginia project, especially of the hope of peaceful relations with the natives, and he wrote "We have sent boies amongst them to learne their Language, but they returne worse than they went." When these young men served the English they were taunted by their Indian friends, but the English also viewed them with suspicion. Henry Spelman was tried before the first meeting of the Virginia Assembly in 1619 on treason charges. Another interpreter, Robert Poole, accused him of having spoken "very unreverently and maliciously against the present Governor" to Opechancanough, thereby bringing the colony and its government "into contempte." Spelman hotly denied the charges, although he did admit that he had told Opechancanough "that within a yeare there would come a Governor greatter then this that nowe is in place."

It was true that the colony anticipated the arrival of Sir Francis Wyatt as governor, but the council decided that Spelman was guilty of having placed the settlements in danger from the Indians' "slippery designes." He could have been subjected to the horrifying death of a traitor, but his skills were clearly too valuable for that outcome. Instead he was sentenced to degradation from his rank of captain and to serve the colony for seven years as an interpreter. Thus the colony, like Plymouth with Squanto, placed the crucial control of Indian relations in the hands of one they no longer trusted. And Spelman was not properly grateful for their clemency. Rather, "as one that had in him more of the Savage then of the Christian," he muttered under his breath in anger. Secretary John Pory, who wrote the official report of the assembly, hoped that he might redeem himself in the future "(God's grace not wholly abandoning him)."[87]

Robert Poole was, if anything, more suspected than Spelman despite the assembly's reliance on his testimony. John Rolfe wrote that he dealt dishonestly both with the Indians and the English, and was "even turned heathen." But at the same time John Pory wrote that it was not "convenient" to call Poole to account; because of his close relationship with Opechancanough he was "a publique, and as it were a neutral person," a man between sides. Accounts of events after the great attack of 1622 demonstrate that, even in those fraught and tangled circumstances, Poole was regarded with respect by Indian leaders, and was essential to the colony's plans.[88]

Thomas Savage was also regarded with mistrust. He had gathered warnings from friends on the Eastern Shore that Opechancanough was planning an attack on the settlements in advance of March 1622, but governor Wyatt, convinced that his league of friendship with Opechancanough was solid, allowed the colony to fall into a false sense of security. Smith wrote indignantly in London that Savage had served the colony "with much honestie and good successe . . . without any publike recompence."[89] Henry Spelman, who, according to Smith, had "done much good service, though but badly rewarded" and had been "one of the best Interpreters in the Land," was killed in an ambush in March 1623 in the continuing fighting following the great attack; he was

28 years old. Some colonists thought he had been killed by Patawomecks, the tribe which had befriended and adopted him, after hot-headed soldiers had killed some Patawomecks and seized their chief. Peter Arundel wrote home in sorrow: "Wee our selves have taught them how to bee trecherous by our false dealinge with the poore kinge of Patomeche that had alwayes beene faythfull to the English. . . . Spilmans death is a just revenge." But that death was "a great loss to us for that Cap. was the best linguist of the Indian Tongue of this Country." Ironically, Robert Poole had conveyed the rumors that led to the attack on the Patawomecks. Samuel Collier was also killed following the 1622 attack, but accidentally by a sentinel's gun. [90]

It was not only children with consciousness still in formation who could be suspect. The learned theologian Roger Williams, who contin-ued to correspond warmly with Massachusetts Bay leaders even after he had been expelled for his religious opinions, was seen as susceptible to liminality as he became increasingly interested in Narragansett culture. Accused by John Winthrop in 1638 of credulously believing and trans-mitting Miantonomi's lies, Williams hotly replied that his English iden-tity was intact: "Sir, let this barbarian be proud and angry and covetous and filthy, hating and hateful, (as we ourselves have been till kindness from heaven pitied us, etc.) yet let me humbly beg belief, that for my-self, I am not yet turned Indian, to believe all barbarians tell me. . . ."[91]

The dilemma of stretched identities in individuals, American and English, who lived within and between cultures in the early colonies brings to mind the plight of Tom Stoppard's Cold War double agent, Rupert Purvis: "That's what I can't remember. I've forgotten who is my primary employer and who my secondary. For years I've been feeding stuff in both directions, following my instructions from either side, hav-ing been instructed to do so by the other, and since each side wanted the other side to believe that I was working for *it*, both sides were often giv-ing me genuine stuff to pass on to the other side . . . so the side I was ac-tually working for became . . . well, a matter of opinion really . . . it got lost."[92]

7 Resisting the Other

It is the property of mans nature to hate those, whom they have hurtt.
—Thomas Gainsford*

Individuals crossed lines and moved between English and American identities; some may have crossed permanently, but most entered a state of liminality. Grounded in one identity, individuals sometimes possessed the capability of seeing events and beliefs from the other side's point of view. When English and Indians behaved in groups, however, the definitions became harder, although they were not necessarily drawn on the ethnic lines that we might see as the most relevant ones. Rivalries and partnerships that grew out of the new trades and the changed political relationships sometimes led to unexpected alignments.

While American Indians and English colonists were scrutinizing each other and trying to formulate their impressions, realities on the ground were also changing. By the middle of the seventeenth century all participants lived in circumstances they had only dimly foreseen. Native communities had been ravaged by imported diseases and their attendant high death rates. One result had been intensified pressure toward political consolidation under stronger chiefs—the emergence of the tribes the Europeans had expected to find. Enhanced territoriality and emphasis on powerful lineages led to greater social and gender differentiation within native life. At the same time the enlarged trade in which Americans engaged—the native trade in wampum that enriched coastal people and the

---

* The epigraph is from Thomas Gainsford, "Observations of State, and millitary affaires for the most parte collected out of Cornelius Tacitus," 1612, MS Huntington Lib. EL 6857, 36.

furs and other goods traded with Europeans—also contributed to increased power for sachems, who increasingly functioned as "managers" of trade and production. Leaders of tribes located near European settlements who could handle trade and other relationships with the newcomers were especially powerful in the short run, particularly during the early period of greatest colonial dependence on native aid. Tools imported from Europe made native artisans more efficient and further enhanced production and trade, but this enhancement led to economic specialization that had not been part of earlier life. The Narragansetts, for example, became the "Mint-masters" of New England. Roger Williams wrote that Narragansett-produced wampum was traded to the Dutch, French, and English as well as other Americans in a system that ranged over six hundred miles.[1] The English were largely unaware of wampum's spiritual significance and thought of it purely as money.

William Strachey offered a telling example of consolidation in the face of new challenges and opportunities. He wrote that "Powhatan had manie enemies, especially in the westerly Countryes, before we made our Forts and habitacions so neere the Falls, but now the generall Cause hath united them." Strachey advised efforts to divide western people such as the Monacans and their tributary tribes from the Powhatans and bind them to the English. Powhatan had worked to keep the western tribes and English apart to their mutual detriment. By doing so, he had been able to "monopolize all the Copper brought into Virginia by the English," cheating the colonists by keeping the price of corn high and the western Indians by selling them copper "for 100. tymes the value." According to Strachey, Powhatan kept most of the copper for securing allies.[2]

Strachey's account points to the most fundamental fact about the English colonies: they were first and foremost business ventures, and trade with the American natives was the best way of getting them established and making them profitable. The joint-stock companies that backed them were interested in advancing the interests of the English nation in the world, but they invested in American ventures because they expected to make a profit. Pouring money into a drain did nothing for England, and few would continue it for long.

Recent literature has focused so heavily on rhetorical and performative power that we have forgotten the economic power that exerted such a powerful force on every life, and this has led to a fundamental error. Much scholarly writing argues that the English wished to sweep the Indians out of the way and did so without qualms. This line of thinking is belied by a glance at the economic realities. Creating a colony was inconceivably expensive, and the expense lasted over many years. No group of investors had resources to meet such commitments; nor would they have put their money into full-scale colonization unless there was some reasonable hope of success, and the poor record of the early plantations offered little hope. Difficult though it is to erase our knowledge of the eventual course of colonization, we must try to view the situation as those involved did ca. 1612 or 1618 or 1620 and see the tentativeness and insecurity they all felt. In those circumstances, the colonists needed the Indians. The Indians were the principal, almost the only, food source for the Roanoke, Jamestown, and early Plymouth colonies; trade in corn and other foodstuffs was the first crucial trade relationship. Native neighbors trained the English in coping with the American environment. And American hunters brought in the beaver pelts, deerskins, and other commodities with which colonists repaid their investors and paid for new supplies in the early years. Only madmen would have dreamed of extirpating the Indians.

This is not to say that the relationship was a sweet one, nor that the English were enlightened. They were fearful and paranoid, constantly on the lookout for treachery, which they expected at every turn. They reacted to even the slightest challenge with horrifying vengeance, and they did so in a spirit of self-righteousness. These responses proceeded from weakness, not from strength, and, accompanied as they were by the colonists' poor record of self-discipline and economic endeavor, they earned scornful responses from England. No one would have predicted a glorious future for English empire in America in these early years.

American leaders, certain of their own control in the face of English weakness, offered incorporation into relationships of interdependence and reciprocity through trade. The English wanted to conceptualize these as simple economic exchanges, but they also understood deference and reciprocity; the system of patron-client relationships on which England ran involved just such ties. Thomas Morton told a story of an Indian trader who had been hired to act as a factor in the beaver trade and found himself caught between two powerful patrons. His English contractor gave him a parcel of goods, containing one particularly fine coat, to trade throughout the country for pelts. The factor returned with some pelts, but not equal to the value of the trade goods; and the contractor learned that the factor had given the special coat as a present to his powwow Tantoquineo. The English man was enraged, and his employee was equally furious, saying, "what you speake; you are not a very good man, wil you not give Tantoq. a coat? whats this? as if he had offered Tantoquineo, the greatest indignity that could be devised."[3] Lack of generosity in relationships was despicable. Uttamatomakkin's indignation that King James gave him, Powhatan's emissary, nothing when Powhatan had lavished care even on the white dog given him by Captain Newport issued from his belief in balanced relationships.

Members of the first reconnoitering expedition to Roanoke in 1584 were given a clear demonstration of the principles of reciprocity: goods should be given freely rather than exchanged through hard bargaining. The first Indian they saw came to a point of land nearest the ship and stood waiting for them to come to him. When the English leaders rowed ashore he addressed them, speaking "of many thinges not understoode by us." He came willingly aboard the ship and the English gave him "a shirt, a hatte, and some other things, and made him taste of our wine, and our meate, which he liked very well." As soon as he left the ship, he took out his canoe and began fishing, filling the canoe with fish in half an hour, and then returned to the point of land and divided the fish into two piles, indicating by sign language that one pile was for each of the two boats. In so doing Arthur Barlowe acknowledged he had "(as much as he might) requited the former benefits receaved."[4]

When Powhatan told Captain Newport that they should not bargain, but each should give the other what he thought proper, he was operating within the system of reciprocity. Gifts entailed responsibilities for the recipient, and everyone alternately played the role of giver and recipient.[5] Many of the reports of stealing by natives in the early days may actually have been attempts to force reciprocity on the English. Roger Williams reported that the Indians he knew believed they were often cheated. The Narragansetts were indignant when the value of their wampum dropped because the price of beaver had fallen in England. From their point of view, they delivered the same goods, and yet the English gave them less in return—a failure of reciprocity.[6]

John Winthrop reported another instance when Narragansetts, through their leader Miantonomi, tried to get the English to acknowledge the principles of reciprocity, in justice as well as trade. When they agreed to alliance with the colonists against the Pequots in 1636, the Narragansetts stipulated "That if any of theirs should kill our cattle, that we would not kill them, but cause them to make satisfaction." They concluded that they considered their treaty firm, "and two months hence they would send us a present." Other New England Indians, including the Pequots, repeatedly tried to get the English to accept the principle of payment rather than vengeance when violations were reported.[7]

In the earliest colonies the chief trade was for food, and English dependence gave American leaders great power. Powhatan reminded John Smith of this in the "subtill discourse" that Smith labeled "Powhatans discourse of peace and warre":

> What will it availe you to take that by force you may quickly have by love,
> or to destroy them that provide you food. What can you get by warre, when
> we can hide our provisions and fly to the woods? whereby you must fam-
> ish by wronging us your friends. . . . Thinke you I am so simple, not to
> know it is better to eate good meate, lye well, and sleepe quietly with my
> women and children, laugh and be merry with you, have copper, hatch-
> ets, or what I want being your friend: then be forced to flie from all, to lie
> cold in the woods, feede upon Acornes, rootes, and such trash, and be so
> hunted by you, that I can neither rest, eate, nor sleepe. . . .[8]

Powhatan and his people faced an uncomfortable life in war, but the
English faced starvation.

When the English pressure for corn from the Americans' drought-
depleted supplies became too burdensome, the Indians warned them off.
The Croatoans, approached by their kinsman Manteo and a group from
the newly arrived final Roanoke colony in 1587, embraced the English as
friends. But they asked the colonists "not to gather or spill any of their
corne, for that they had but little." In the winter of 1609–10 when the
Jamestown colonists were living through their notorious "starving time,"
they found "Lieftenantt Sicklemore" and some of his men dead at their
fort on the coast with "their mowthes stopped full of Breade beinge donn
as it seamethe in Contempte and skorne thatt others mighte expecte the
Lyke when they shold come to seeke for breade and reliefe amongste
them." The episode reminded George Percy of the story of "Baldivia A
Spanish Generall" in Chile who was forced to drink molten gold,
"Baldivia haveinge there sowghte for gowlde as Sicklemore did here for
foode."[9]

Percy wrote at a time when out-of-control colonists represented a massive problem to him and other leaders. As he did, we need to put early
relationships in context. Sicklemore and his party were vulnerable partly
because most of his men, looking for an easier life, had deserted; those
men were also found dead. Stories of comparable carelessness and lawlessness were repeated countless times. The impossibility of controlling
English colonists in America was at least as serious a challenge as developing a secure relationship with the Indians. In Jamestown the men
were routinely referred to as the "very scumme of the Land," and they
became famous at home as "loose, leaud, licentious, riotous, and disordered" people. Moreover, some said that "no English men are able to endure" the "hard and miserable conditions" there. John Smith summed
up the problem: "Much they blamed us for not converting the Savages,
when those they sent us were little better, if not worse."[10]

Every colony reported problems with settlers, particularly young men.
Massachusetts Bay governor John Winthrop wrote to his wife: "I think

here are some persons who never shewed so much wickedness in England as they have done here." The situation grew worse rather than better; after five years of settlement Reverend Nathaniel Ward complained of the "multitudes of idle and profane young men, servants and others" in Massachusetts and concluded "we have made an ill change, even from the snare to the pit."[11]

The "snare" lay in England, and many commentators thought problems in America mirrored those of England. Plymouth's Robert Cushman warned off prospective colonists "of dissolute and profane life" and said that, despite England's long exposure to the Gospel, he saw there "such vices as the heathen would shame to speak of." Crashaw preached that Jamestown's difficulties simply revealed the "pusillanimitie, the basenesse, the tendernesse and effeminatenesse of our English people: into which our nation is now degenerate."[12] Civility, especially among the lower orders, was fragile, hard won, and shallow rooted; as the poet Edmund Spenser remarked, "yt is but even the other daye, since England grewe Civill."

Spenser, like many commentators, was concerned about what he saw as the powerful effects of environment on civility, a concern exemplified by England's first colony, that in Ireland. The Anglo-Irish, the descendants of English settlers who had emigrated in the reign of Henry II, were described as degenerate. Civilized people were supposed to lift the level of the men and women among whom they lived, but many feared that the influence had gone the other way in Ireland, and they found confirmation when Anglo-Irish participated in the Irish uprising of 1641. As Spenser put it, "So much can libertie and ill example doe."[13]

As promoters and officers looked at the behavior of their colonists in America, they feared that regression could happen there. Their primitive environmentalism led them to see powerful shaping forces that would free people, and all living things, from their thin veneer of cultivation. Early accounts from America strove to counter such fears, as when Cushman reassured his readers that the Plymouth colonists remained true Christians "though we be in a heathen country." Such assertions occurred in many contexts. When colonists wrote that they did not tyrannize over their wives "and keepe them in servile subjection" as they claimed the Indians did, or when they explained, as Captain John Underhill did in his account of the Pequot War, that the multiplication of officers in the militia did not proceed from indiscipline or leveling, but was rather a response to the American way of fighting in small groups, they were all replying to accusations from home.[14]

When venturers wrote that the Indians could be brought to fear and love the English, they were not advocating repression of a racial other so much as simply applying the commonsense political theory of the times. In America as in England, fear was required to bring the lower orders into line. Although William Crashaw was disgusted by the degeneracy and disorder he saw both in England and in reports from Jamestown, he also argued that the basest men, given good government, could be good citizens. The ministers in Massachusetts delivered the opinion that "stricte Discipline bothe in Criminall offences & in martiall affaires was more needfull in plantations then in a setled state."[15] Virginia's situation required a more concrete statement; in 1610, having lived through the harrowing winter, Sir Thomas Gates instituted a system of martial law in the colony that dictated a life of complete regimentation and terrible punishments for even small infractions. Everyone was to rise together, march to meals by drumbeat, go to work in a body, and retire at the same time. Anyone who left work before the signal to quit was to lie all night with his back arched, with his heels tied and drawn up toward his head. The second offense merited a whipping, and the third meant service in the galleys for a year. Running away to the Indians was punished by death, as was stealing food from gardens or fields. Much fear and little love was the order of the day for unmanageable English colonists, and George Percy's account of this period made clear that the punishments were actually carried out in the most cruel manner: "Some he appointed to be hanged Some burned Some to be broken upon wheles, others to be staked and some to be shott to death." Some men who stole from the food stores were tied to trees and slowly starved to death.[16]

The swaggering great, especially military men, were as dangerous as the unruly lower orders and also required control. Edward Winslow, in his list of three main factors that brought plantations to ruin, put "Ambition in their governors and commanders, seeking only to make themselves great, and slaves of all that are under them" ahead of poor-quality colonists. John Rolfe, while he and Pocahontas were in London in 1616, wrote *A True Relation of the state of Virginia*, in which he traced the colony's well-known problems in its early years to the fact that it was originally governed "Aristocratycallie" by a council that chose its own president, who was effectively the governor. The councillors displayed "such envie, dissentions, and jarrs . . . that they *choaked* the *seedes* and *blasted* the *fruits* of all mens labors. . . . All would be Keisars, none inferior to other." Now, however, the colony was improving daily under its "more absolute goverment . . . *Monarchally*. A few years later he was less sure the situation was better, and again laid the blame on leading men among the colonists. He warned Virginia Company leader Sir Edwin Sandys that vengeful letters were being sent home against the acting governor, Samuel Argall, and went on, citing his eleven years' experience: "I never amongst so few, have seene so many falseharted, envious and malicious people (yea amongst some who march in the better ranck)."[17] Strict control was necessary for all levels within the nation. Except for the very few public-spirited leaders, no one was expected to have internalized the controls essential to society's operation.[18] Fear made government and settled life possible. When planners presumed that the Indians would come to love and fear the English, what they meant was that they expected to incorporate them into the system by which English men and women were governed.

The earliest reports from every region rang with hope that the Americans, with their developed political and religious systems, would see the superiority of European civility and Christianity and would quickly and easily come to emulate the English. Despite reports from Ireland about the powerful effect of wild environments, promoters continued to believe that civility and Christianity would be irresistible to the Indians, and they cited the counterexample of the Romans bringing both to their own savage ancestors. Though the Romans had imposed their system by force, the English had seen its benefits. The intelligent and aspiring Indians, accustomed to manipulating their self-presentation, would naturally seek to transform themselves into Europeans. Early writers willfully misled themselves and their audiences on both the American desire for that transformation and the ease of realizing it. Roger Williams, for example, wrote that the Indians, hearing that the English had once been deprived of books, letters, and the knowledge of God like them, "are greatly affected with a secret hope concerning themselves."[19]

But even while they recounted friendly meetings and emphasized the Indians' curiosity about everything English, every person on the ground constantly expected treachery. The clearest statement of their assumptions came, without conscious irony, from Captain Gabriel Archer just after the arrival of the first Jamestown colonists: "They are naturally given to trechery, howbeit we could not finde it in our travell up the river, but rather a most kind and loving people." English expectation of American treachery was a direct result of their own vulnerability, and their assumption that fear is what holds society together. As long as they were dependent on the Indians for food and knowledge, and outnumbered by highly skilled marksmen, they expected treachery in America as they would have done in Europe.[20]

Treachery in an opponent was not only expected but even in some ways admired. A treacherous foe or rival was capable, one to be taken seriously and not easily dismissed. Roger Williams twice wrote the story of Sassawwaw, a Pequot who joined the Narragansetts. He pretended to return to the Pequots and "drew them out to battel" against the

Narragansetts. But at the moment of attack, he turned and killed the chief Pequot captain, "in a trice fetcht off his head, and returned immediatly to his own againe." Wequash, who had also left the Pequots, tried to kill Sassawwaw, Miantonomi's "special darling and a kind of Generall of his forces." In recounting Sassawwaw's story shortly after the event in the midst of war, Williams wrote that "their treacheries exceede Machiavills etc." When he wrote of Sassawwaw's act in his *Key into the Language of America* six years later, he made it a single pretended defection rather than the double defection in the original letter, and concluded that "his act was false and trecherous, yet herein appeares policie, stoutnesse and activitie etc."[21]

Both the Americans and the English were always aware that, however friendly their relationships, enmity lay just over the horizon. The Virginia Company's instructions directed that the fort should be situated so that no Indian villages lay between it and the coast, "for you Cannot Carry Your Selves so towards them but they will Grow Discontented with Your habitation." In composing their colony, promoters had actually violated one of the principal tenets of early modern competition by sending inexperienced men, thereby contributing to the venture's vulnerability. The company's instructions sought to rectify this weakness by warning that the Indians should only be allowed to see experienced marksmen shoot their guns, "for if they See Your Learners miss what they aim at they will think the Weapon not so terrible." That such a warning was necessary reflected badly on the preparedness of both the company and the leadership in Virginia.[22]

Two basic guiding principles were at work for the English both in Europe and America. The first was that if challenged—and what constituted a challenge could be interpreted very broadly—then one had to be on the winning side at all costs. The sentiment of the times held that any show of weakness invited further attack and, ultimately, destruction. Massive retaliation, making an example, was kinder in the long run, because it forestalled escalating violence. Once war was begun, victory was everything, and the rules were very broad. There was no action taken against "savages" that was not also taken against Christian Europeans.[23]

Plans for Jamestown were made in light of the experience of Ralegh's Roanoke experiment; though the colony was gone, the documents from it had been published and were studied by promoters. Roanoke relationships had begun in a spirit of friendliness. Arthur Barlowe's account of the initial reconnoitering voyage reported "a more kinde and loving people, there can not be found in the world, as farre as we have hitherto had triall." Yet Barlowe and the men were constantly on their guard.[24]

When the first contingent of colonists arrived the next year, bringing back Manteo and Wanchese, they were keenly aware of their both their vulnerability and their reliance on their native neighbors. Their flagship ran aground as they approached their landing site at the Carolina Outer Banks and almost all their food supplies were soaked and ruined by seawater. It was far too late in the summer for them to plant crops if they had been prepared to do that, so their very survival depended on the Indians; no resupply from England could be expected before spring. While the men built their fort the commander of the fleet, Sir Richard Grenville, conducted an exploring mission around the sound in which Roanoke Island sits. Someone kept a terse diary of the stops they made at various villages, which suddenly exploded into prose when the admiral sent a boat to Aquascococke, where they had been two days previously to retrieve a stolen silver cup, "and not receiving it according to his promise, we burnt, and spoyled their corne, and Towne, all the people beeing fledde." Grenville exemplified the psychology that made men of his class so dangerous—massive retaliation for every perceived challenge was the only way to keep the Indians in line. He soon sailed back to England, and the colonists faced the approaching winter.[25]

During that winter, John White and Thomas Harriot conducted the researches that resulted in their unparalleled combined report on the natives and environment of America, and they were able to do that because of their friendship with the Americans. Harriot reported how their prayers had cured Wingina when he had been attacked by the new diseases. Other friendly relationships were forged. But the expectation and fear of treachery was never absent because the colonists never forgot their vulnerability. Lane's hungry expedition up the Roanoke River—when the Indians along the way abandoned the riverbanks and the men were reduced to eating their mastiff dogs stewed with sassafras leaves—was one warning that the Indians also understood the situation. In this context Lane, like Grenville, believed that only those who struck first and inspired fear would survive. When he heard rumors that Wingina (now Pemisapan) had called together men from miles around (ostensibly to mourn their great man Ensenore but, Lane believed, actually to attack the colony), he struck first. Wingina's severed head was left as a warning of what happened to those who challenged the English. But Lane and his colonists abandoned the settlement and returned to England at the first opportunity because their life there had become untenable. It was the final group of colonists the next year who were asked to leave the Croatoans' corn alone. Without support from England, that colony disappeared; presumably the fortunate among them became Indians.[26]

In Jamestown colonists saw treachery everywhere—both from Indians and English—and wreaked vengeance again and again. Captain John Smith, when he was president, sent George Percy and Captain John Martin downriver to Nansemond, where the English sent messengers to the chief to ask for rights to an island nearby. The messengers did not return, and Percy and the others were told they had been "sacrificed." The English then "Beate the Salvages outt of the Island burned their howses Ransaked their Temples Tooke down the Corpes of their deade kings from of their Toambes And caryed away their pearles Copper and braceletts, wherewith they doe decore their kings funeralles."

Captain Francis West with another group had been sent upriver to the falls of the James, where they lost several men, and here Percy found multiple sources of treachery. Percy, son and brother of earls of Northumberland, was a rival of Captain John Smith, son of a yeoman farmer; West was the brother of Lord de la Warr, future governor of Virginia, and Martin was the son and brother of leading figures in government in London. None of these men liked taking orders from the upstart Smith, and Percy even accused him of conspiring with the Indians against his own colonists at the falls. Smith was soon involved in a serious accident and was forced to return to England; Percy took over as acting governor.

The colony now faced the starving winter of 1609–10. The English had just found the warning left in the bodies of Lieutenant Sicklemore and his men, but Percy set about to try to find food, first sending Captain John Ratcliffe to approach "the subtell owlde foxe" Powhatan. Powhatan at first seemed amenable but soon seized on Ratcliffe's lack of caution and killed many of his men. Ratcliffe was taken alive and tortured to death by Powhatan women, according to Percy, who wrote that his fate stemmed from his "want of circumspection." Those who let down their guard deserved what they got.

Meanwhile Captain West did gain a shipload of corn, although Percy regretted he "used some harshe and Crewell dealinge." More treachery followed, however, as West's men mutinied, "hoysed upp Sayles and shaped their course directly for England and lefte us in thatt extreme misery and wante." Jamestown became "A Worlde of miseries," and the colonists were reduced to eating whatever they could find; those who ventured out in the woods foraging were "slayne by the Salvages." Men who stole from the common store were executed, and one who was suspected of killing and eating his wife was tortured until he confessed. Many ran away to the Indians "whome we never heard of after." Percy found out later that the men living near the coast had plenty of food, which they had treacherously concealed from Jamestown.

When reinforcements arrived, the desperate colonists were actually abandoning Jamestown. Now revived, they embarked on a campaign of vengeance for their treatment over the winter. Percy led the party attacking Paspahegh and forced an unwilling Kemps to guide them. Several natives were killed in the attack and many fled; "the Quene and her Children" and another Indian were taken prisoner. The Indian man was immediately executed while Percy's men burned the village and took the corn. But his men were angry that the other prisoners yet lived. A council decided the children should die, "the which was effected by Throweinge them overboard and shoteinge owtt their Braynes in the water yett for all this Crewellty the Sowldiers weare not well pleased."

After burning other villages and taking corn, the force returned to Jamestown, where newly arrived governor de la Warr was reported (falsely, Percy thought) to be angry that the queen was still alive. Some of the officers wanted to burn her to death, but Percy replied that "haveinge seene so mutche Bloodshedd thatt day now in my Cowldbloode I desyred to see noe more," and he argued that it was not "fittinge" to kill her in that way. European rules of war made strict distinctions between acts done in hot and cold blood. Captain James Davis took her into the woods and killed her with his sword. Indian warfare spared women and children; the English could have committed no more heinous acts in American eyes.

Other forces went out in similar campaigns and many skirmishes and attacks ensued during these months in 1610. When Indians came to Jamestown they were treated as spies. In one instance the governor directed that the hands of one of them should be cut off as a warning. Later, when some natives came with gifts of food, another governor had some of them executed "for A Terrour to the Reste to cawse them to desiste from their subtell practyses." William Strachey, who was in Jamestown at this time, agreed that "audatious" Indians came into the fort "crying all freindes" and were kept from doing "mischief" only by fear. When some "greedy fooles" let down their guards and accepted an invitation to a feast they got what they deserved.[27] Intermittent warfare, which was accompanied by the harsh martial law regime in Jamestown, continued for four years until the marriage of John Rolfe and Pocahontas offered an occasion for a truce. Certainly the Americans would have been as convinced of the treacherous nature of the English as the English were of theirs. Both sides believed they were acting only in retaliation, and both believed they had been attacked without reason.

On April 18, 1622, Patrick Copland preached a sermon before the Virginia Company in London thanking God for the past year's "Happie successe." Neither Copland nor the company members yet knew that the Powhatans under the leadership of Opechancanough had made a massive attack on the English plantations in Virginia less than a month before, and that a significant percentage of the colonists had been killed and the rest were in distress. The great attack set in motion the investigation that would end in the revocation of the Virginia Company's charter. Copland had helped to raise money to create a college in Virginia for the conversion of the Indians, and George Thorpe had gone to Virginia to oversee its building. Thorpe, according to Copland, had recorded a conversation with Opechancanough in which the emperor had shown "more motions of religion in him, then could be imagined in so great a blindnesse, since he willingly acknowledged that theirs was not the right way." Thorpe had also reported that, not only did Opechancanough seek instruction in Christianity, he even acknowledged "that God loved us more then them." According to Thorpe, Opechancanough thought God was angry with his people because of "their custome of making their children Blacke-boyes, or consecrating them to Sathan." When the attack came, Opechancanough's apparent duplicity made it all the worse. Given the general assumption that those who let down their guard invited attack, many agreed with Captain John Smith, who wrote that "the greatest cause of their destructions" was "careless neglect of their owne safeties."[28]

Thorpe himself was killed in the attack, and reports said that his body had been mutilated. He became an emblematic figure for the English. Company propaganda presented him as the prime exhibit of the innate and irredeemable treachery of the American character, but colonists saw him as the Virginia Company representative in forcing the kind of complacency that made them vulnerable. The Virginia Council hotly answered charges from the company at home "as yf we alone were guiltie," and they went on:

> You may be pleased to Consider what instructions you have formerly given us, to wynn the Indyans to us by A kinde entertayninge them in our howses, and yf it were possible to Cohabitt with us, and how ympossible it is for any watch and warde to secure us against secrett Enemies that live promiscouslie amongst us, and are harbored in our bosomes, all Histories and your owne Discourse may Sufficyently informe you.

The council assured the company that they had set "uppon the Indyans in all places" and had killed more that year than in the entire period since the colony's founding.[29]

As they read accounts of the great attack and the next decade of warfare, observers in England might have compared the Powhatans to their own British ancestors. The popular recently published translation of

This de Bry workshop engraving of the concerted attack against the Virginia colony in 1622 shows the attack as an episode of unparalleled violence and savagery in which peaceful unsuspecting English were set upon by hordes of bloodthirsty natives, and this picture, which accompanied an account of the events, acted powerfully to affect attitudes in England. The John Carter Brown Library at Brown University.

Tacitus's *Agricola* celebrated the Britons' defiant stance toward the invading Romans. Tacitus's Britons had risen up against the oppressing Romans because they, like the Powhatans, realized that humble submission only created contempt. Tacitus placed his comment on imperial schemes and their civilizing mission in the mouth of the ancient British leader Galgacus: "To take away by maine force, to kill and to spoile, falsely they terme Empire and government: when all is waste as a wildernesse, that they call peace." When they attacked the Roman colony, "no kinde of crueltie was omitted" by the wronged Britons.[30]

Sir Francis Wyatt, who arrived as governor five months before the attack, had the high rank the colony demanded, but lacked experience. He

was the "greatter" governor that Henry Spelman had told Opechancanough was coming to take over the colony.[31] Wyatt's father wrote
him a letter of advice on how to proceed in the difficult circumstances
he faced, and he cautioned against underestimating the Indians: "I doe
not with contempt reccon of them as cowards, as our common opinions
esteemes." And he pointed out their attack did not lack "politie or cor-
age," and as to their running away afterward, "it is the manner of their
fight." He commended the planning and the intelligence gathering on
which the attack was based, and suggested the English should be equally
assiduous in studying the enemy and planning their campaigns. He concluded by recommending various stratagems, techniques of treachery,
saying that "Art of Strategems is a politie of war by wils of wit rather
then force to make benefit of an Enimise Error." Stratagems were taught
by nature: "The most Savage knows and can teache them, as you have
felt." The Virginia natives were formidable enemies, demanding all the
sophistication the English possessed.[32] The colonists had already embarked on ten years of fighting, conducted primarily at harvest season
when the Indians were most vulnerable.

The puritan Pilgrims who settled Plymouth in New England in 1620,
just as matters in Virginia were approaching a breaking point, established
friendly relations with the neighboring Pokanokets and their chief
Massasoit, but they also assumed that treachery was always just beneath
the surface. In the beginning when the colony was weak and the Indians
"might easily have swallowed us up," according to Edward Winslow, God
prevented an attack. Plymouth's leaders chose a region for settlement
that placed the colonists amidst complex relationships; they attempted
to manipulate these, but were also subject to manipulation. The
Narragansetts, the largest group to the south, were well situated between
the Dutch at the mouth of the Hudson River and the English to the north;
they thought of the Pokanokets as clients of theirs and saw the Pilgrims
as meddling in that relationship when they formed a friendship with
Massasoit's tribe. The Pilgrims believed that the Narragansetts sought an
opportunity to attack them from the beginning. Then in January 1622 a
messenger came from Canonicus, the superior Narragansett chief, bringing a rattlesnake skin wrapped around "a bundle of new arrows." When
questioned, the messenger said that Canonicus intended war, and particularly mentioned the offensive meanness of the things governor
Bradford had sent him in comparison to what he had formerly sent to the
colony's leaders. When Squanto saw the snakeskin, he interpreted it as a
challenge, and Bradford sent the skin back stuffed with gunpowder and
shot. Canonicus, terrified according to the Plymouth reports, refused the
skin and sent it back to Plymouth. The colonists, believing that the

Narragansetts' hostile intentions were now clear, then set to work to build a pale around their village. Anthropologist Paul Robinson postulates that Canonicus may have sent the snakeskin as a gift, intending to create a mutual relationship of gift giving and interdependence despite the unsatisfactory quality of earlier gift exchanges. When the Pilgrims refused his gift and he in turn refused their responding presentation, both sides were rejecting such a relationship.[33]

They also had tense relationships on their other flank. After Winslow cured Massasoit, the chief told Hobbomock that the Massachusetts were conspiring against a small independent colony at Wessagusset and ultimately against Plymouth, and the English decided to strike a preemptive blow in March 1623. Following much deliberation, Captain Miles Standish went with a troop of men who pretended to be traders. They found the Wessagusset English in bad straits, and portrayed the Massachusetts lording it over them. A Massachusett pniese, Pecksuot, told Hobbomock that he knew the English had come to kill the Indians there, but they had no fear. Pecksuot mocked Standish's small stature, and he and Wituwamat sharpened their knives in front of the English with bragging speeches. Wituwamat's knife had a picture of a woman's face on the handle. He said he had another at home with a man's face and that with that knife he had killed both French and English, "and by and by these two must marry." Pointing to the knife he had with him he said, "By and by it should see, and by and by it should eat, but not speak."

During the early fighting "Hobbamock stood by all this time as a spectator, and meddled not." Pecksuot and Wituwamat, the Massachusett pnieses, were killed; according to Edward Winslow, "it is incredible how many wounds these two pineses received before they died, not making any fearful noise, but catching at their weapons and striving to the last." Hobbomock told Standish that though he was a "little man" he was big enough to bring these enemies down. When Massachusett reinforcements renewed the fighting and directed their arrows at Miles Standish and Hobbomock, Hobbomock "cast off his coat, and being a known pinese, (theirs being now killed) chased them so fast as our people were not able to hold way with him."[34]

William Bradford wrote to John Robinson, who had been pastor to the Pilgrims in Leiden before they went to America, and described the attack. Wituwamat's head was impaled "on our forte for a terror unto others." Robinson was horrified by Bradford's account: "It is also a thing more glorious in men's eyes than pleasing in God's or convenient for Christians, to be a terror to poor barbarous people, and, indeed, I am afraid lest, by these occasions, others should be drawn to affect a kind of

ruffling course in the world," and concluded, "oh! how happy a thing
had it been if you had converted some before you had killed any!"[35] Two
centuries later Pequot William Apess voiced similar horror about the puritans' record in New England: "How they could go to work to enslave
a free people and call it religion is beyond the power of my imagination
and outstrips the revelation of God's word."[36]

In New England, as in Virginia, English planters accused each other of
treacherously creating dangerous situations. Thomas Morton, who preferred to live in a small mixed community of English and Indians, alleged that Plymouth's true purpose in attacking the Massachusetts had
been to make the small Wessagusset colony, their rivals in the fur trade,
untenable. The "new creede of Canaan" held that the "Salvages are a
dangerous people, subtill, secreat, and mischeivous, and that it is dangerous to live separated." He said the Indians were enraged by Plymouth
men's desecration of sachems' family graves. Henceforth the Massachusett word for Englishman was "Wotawquenange, which in their
language signifieth stabbers or Cutthroates." Morton concluded, "I have
found the Massachussets Indian more ful of humanity, then the
Christians." Governor Bradford blamed Morton for making New
England much less safe. The Pilgrims alleged that he not only sold guns,
powder, and shot to the Indians, but also taught them how to shoot, to
make bullets, and even to make gunpowder. "O, the horribleness of this
villainy!"[37]

Roger Williams wrote that the Narragansetts often asked him, "Why
come the Englishmen hither?"[38] The answer to this question began to
change through the 1620s and perceptibly as the 1630s opened; the emphasis moved from obtaining commodities from America for consumption at home to exporting large numbers of people who would create
their own commodities and life. The trickle of immigration in the
Chesapeake and New England turned into a flood into both regions. The
colony of Massachusetts Bay, beginning with a thousand colonists in its
first year, 1630, swamped the tiny Plymouth colony just entering its second decade. Large numbers also migrated into the Chesapeake; Virginia
began to grow dramatically and Maryland was founded in 1635 as a
Roman Catholic refuge.[39] Thomas Savage and Robert Poole lived on to
become wealthy planters. Savage settled on the Eastern Shore and facilitated its opening to English planters, but his friendly relations with
Indian neighbors continued to be viewed with suspicion until he died in
1635. Thomas Rolfe came home to Virginia in 1635; he was about the
same age as his mother had been when she died.[40] Virginia's first great
war between Americans and settlers, begun by the attack of 1622 and
continued intermittently for a decade, ended in the early 1630s as the

plantations spread over the land. The Pequot War in New England erupted in the middle of the 1630s as colonists spread west to the Connecticut River and south to Connecticut and Rhode Island.

In southern New England the wampum trade enhanced powerful sachemships among the Narragansetts and the Pequots, and these tribes formed differing relationships with the English who flooded into their territory after 1630. Before and during the English war against the Pequots, Roger Williams, who had just been expelled from Massachusetts Bay for his uncompromising religious position and his refusal to be silenced, became that colony's liaison with the Pequots' main rivals, the Narragansetts. His self-identification was firmly English, yet over the years he would become one of the most sympathetic recorders of American life. He recorded a "solemne Oration" of Canonicus, "the old high Sachim of the Nariganset Bay (a wise and peaceable Prince)." Canonicus said "I have never suffered any wrong to be offered to the English since they landed; nor never will." If the English are equally faithful, he said, then we will live peaceably together. Williams answered that he knew from long experience that the English did not break their word. At which Canonicus took a stick and broke it into ten pieces, "and related ten instances (laying downe a sticke to every instance) which gave him cause thus to feare and say." Williams answered some of the charges, but took the rest to the English leaders, and hoped they would not give cause for the Indians to question their word.[41]

Others also came to realize that from the Americans' point of view it was the English who seemed to be innately treacherous. William Eyre, who returned to England to fight in the Civil War, found perfidy among the leaders there and contrasted the actions of Christians with the Indians he had known: "I have lived among heathens, who have nothing but the light of nature to be their Rule, yet they abhor men that break their Engagements, or commit any dishonest action."[42]

As open conflict with the Pequots neared, the middle ground disappeared and all groups were forced to choose sides; Uncas, according to Mohegan oral tradition, was a Pequot sachem who led a splinter group that revived the "old clan name of 'Mohegan'" and allied with the English.[43] The Narragansetts also cast their lot with the English side.

As war approached, Indians on all sides were concerned about European modes of warfare, particularly targeting noncombatants. A group of Pequots approached the English contingent under Lion Gardiner at Saybrook in Connecticut and asked first if the English were through fighting. Given a noncommittal answer, they then asked "if we did use to kill women and children?" The reply was that the Pequots would find out "hereafter." At this the Pequots fell silent for a while, after which they replied with bravado, saying they had killed Englishmen and would kill women and children. Even the English allies were concerned. Roger Williams sent a series of letters to Massachusetts Bay leaders relaying the suggestions of the Narragansetts for bringing down the Pequots. In a letter sent days before the English attack on the Pequots' fort in Mystic, Williams mentioned that "it would be pleasing to all natives, that women and children be spared, etc."[44] The American allies understood the unforgiving relentlessness of European war and hoped that, as allies, they might be able to gain a hearing for Indian notions of limited war. At Mystic the allies saw just the kind of consequences they had feared, as everyone in the fort of whatever age or sex was burned or put to the sword.

Following the war the colonists decreed the extinction of the tribe and its name (or so they thought). Pequots were distributed among allied tribes, and male leaders were sent to slavery in the West Indies. The lessons first learned by Indians of the Chesapeake Bay area were now brought home in the north; native allies responded with horror to the climactic burning of the Pequot fort and slaughter of all inside. Underhill reported that although they "rejoiced at our victory, and greatly admired the manner of Englishmen's fight," the allies "cried Mach it, mach it; that is, It is naught, it is naught, because it is too furious, and slaies too many men." In seventeenth-century usage, "naught" conveyed pure evil or viciousness.[45]

An unbridgeable gap separated English and Indian notions of correct behavior, and the Americans might be forgiven for thinking that civilized Christian behavior was savage. Captain John Underhill acknowledged that some in England questioned the brutality of this war, saying, "should not Christians have more mercy and compassion?" Such questioners he referred to the Bible, to the account of King David's war, and concluded: "We had sufficient light from the word of God for our proceedings."[46] Reverend William Hooke congratulated New England on the peace in which it lived in 1640, after "God . . . subdued the proud Pequats."[47]

The dichotomy we see between the words and the actions of the English in America would not have been apparent to their contemporaries. The rules of warfare, and the laws of self-preservation, sanctioned behavior that is, to our eyes, wholly unacceptable. The Thirty Years' War raged in Europe during much of the period under study here and the Dutch fought to free themselves of Spanish domination. The English set forth many campaigns to bring Ireland under their control, and English men and women suffered at the hands of their compatriots in the English Civil War of the 1640s.

John Underhill, one of the commanders in the Pequot War of 1636–37, published his account of the war under the title *Newes from America.* This engraving of the English attack on the Pequots' fort at Mystic shows a ring of English soldiers and an outer ring of Indians shooting the inhabitants as they flee the burning fort. Recent archaeological work has uncovered the foundations of a fort that may be the one pictured here. The John Carter Brown Library at Brown University.

Besieged cities in Ireland, in England during the Civil War, and in Germany in the Thirty Years' War were called on to surrender and cut short the danger and hardship of the siege for the soldiers and themselves. If they resisted, as Henry V warned the French town of Harfleur in Shakespeare's *Henry V,* written in 1599 as the earl of Essex prepared an expedition to put down Tyrone's rebellion in Ireland, "The gates of mercy shall be all shut up." If the town's governors did not surrender, Henry warned, they should "look to see the blind and bloody soldier with foul hand defile the locks of your shrill-shrieking daughters; your fathers taken by the silver beards, and their most reverend heads dashed to the walls; your naked infants spitted upon pikes."[48] Although the play was set in the fifteenth century, Shakespeare's contemporaries would have understood this as a description of the costs of war in their time. War was fought according to generally accepted rules, "a kind of contractual etiquette of belligerence," so the impression of forces simply running amuck is false, yet the kinds of vengeance the rules allowed in certain circumstances seem astonishingly harsh, and of course the soldiers could not always be controlled.[49]

The enemy—people who were permanently on ideological or religious grounds or temporarily for strategic reasons outsiders—was treated as the other. Captain John Smith, when he was very young, fought in the religious wars in Europe; then, seeking further experience, he joined the armies fighting to push back the Turkish invasion in the East, "both lamenting and repenting to have seene so many Christians slaughter one another." The Turks were a foe he felt more comfortable fighting than European Catholics, but most of his countrymen were not so scrupulous.[50]

Service in war was often a rite of passage for young men, many of whom were later involved in American colonization. Walter Ralegh, beginning as a teenager, served in France and in Ireland fighting against Roman Catholic forces.[51] In Ireland he was at the siege of Smerwick where, after the defenders surrendered on what they thought was a promise that they would be allowed to leave peacefully, Ralegh and another captain were given the task of overseeing the executions of the garrison of six hundred, Italian and Spanish volunteers as well as Irish, in a single day. Most were put to the sword, but some of the men and the women, including several pregnant women, were hanged. After several days of interrogation, according to the official report, an English man found in the garrison and an Irish priest were killed: "theire armes and Legges were Broken and hanged uppon a Gallowes upon the Wall of the fforte." When the stripped bodies were all laid out, the commander who had ordered the executions, Lord Grey of Wilton, is reported to have said the slaughtered garrison were "as gallant goodly personages as ever were beheld." Queen Elizabeth wrote to him that "this late enterprise" was "greatly to our lyking."[52]

A decade earlier Ralegh's half-brother Sir Humphrey Gilbert had waged a campaign of terror in Munster; he was said to have left no living creature in the wake of his army. If a garrison did not surrender when he first demanded it, he would accept nothing less than unconditional surrender followed by the execution of all within. Gilbert, who later died at sea in one of the earliest English attempts to found an American colony, became famous for lining the path to his tent with the heads of the slaughtered Irish, so those who came to see him, recognizing dead friends and kinsmen, were made aware of his vengeance as they approached.[53]

Such behavior continued in the seventeenth century as repeated expeditions set out to subdue Irish antagonists, and every action was proclaimed to show the will of God. Where Catholic forces were victorious in the 1640s, they dug up the corpses of Protestants and used them to make gunpowder.[54] When the armies of parliament invaded Ireland in 1649 they set out on a course of exemplary vengeance. As Drogheda fell, two thousand defenders were "put to the sword." About one hundred fled into three towers, and, in actions that echo the New Englanders' treatment of the Pequots, Cromwell ordered one tower burned with all the people inside. The men in the other two were sent to Barbados. Cromwell wrote that these actions "will tend to prevent the effusion of blood for the future." A thousand of the dead were executed in St. Peter's church, which he said was just punishment for their "insolent" observance of a "public mass" in that Protestant church. Three months later the army laid siege to Wexford where, during the surrender negotiations, the soldiers suddenly stormed the town and killed, according to Cromwell, "not less than two-thousand." He wrote that he had intended "better to this place than so great a ruin . . . yet God would not have it so." He went on, "The soldiers got a very good booty in this place."[55] Every war in Europe provided similar examples, and each army believed that God endorsed, even directed, its actions.[56]

It was not only against Roman Catholic foreigners that English people could erect such mental barriers of alterity. All were aware of the fragility of peace as other countries were devastated by conflict, and war was interpreted as God's punishment for a nation's sins, so no nation was safe. Accounts of the sufferings of Germany in the Thirty Years' War (1618–1648), some illustrated by graphic woodcuts, circulated widely to an avid readership.[57] Philip Vincent connected events in the savage German wars with New England's Pequot War; he published a compilation of reports from Germany a year after he published his account of the Pequot War, in which he had participated as chaplain. Chapter 3 of Vincent's book on Germany, "On Tortures," had page after page of horrific descriptions accompanied by illustrations, "the more to affect the Reader," and he alleged instances of cannibalism. Vincent included one atrocity in his book on New England's Pequot War: the captive pulled apart before being dispatched with a pistol shot. Like Cromwell in Ireland, he justified the burning of the Pequot fort on the grounds that it would prevent future bloodshed by terrifying the settlers' native neighbors. The colonists willfully submerged their natural pity: "Mercy marres all somtimes, severe Iustice must now and then take place."[58]

In the preface to *The Lamentations of Germany* Vincent told his readers that, although England had suffered like the Germans in the past, the

English were now free to sit under their own vine and fig tree in peace.
But this was not to last. During the 1640s, civil war brought the horrors
of war home to England. Even before its outbreak William Hooke, in the
same sermon that congratulated New England on God's destruction of
the Pequots, called on his congregation to contemplate the dangers faced
by "many a dear friend and countryman and kinsman" in England as
conflict loomed: "there are many times robberies without warre, and
murthering of passengers, ravishing of matrons, deflouring of virgins,
cruelties and torments, and sometimes barbarous and inhumane practices without warre but warre goes seldome or never without them."
God would visit this devastation upon England, Hooke warned, as a punishment for the nation's sins: "the Lord is gone forth this day to call that
Land to an account."[59] When war came, cities, merchants, and farmers
were plundered and lands laid waste to prevent them from being useful
to the other side. Many towns were put to the torch, and epidemics
spread over parts of the country visited by the armies.[60] As news of atrocities spread, propagandists feared that England had embarked on the horrors of a "German war."[61]

"Nature, heavens daughter," made all mankind "fierce, injurious, re-
vengefull, and ingenious in the device of meanes for the offence of those
we take to be our enemies," and all was grounded in the right of self-
defense.[62] The first principle of any kind of encounter was the absolute
necessity of assuming the dominant position in every relationship. The
lesson of history and contemporary society was that all connections were
unequal; if you did not dominate, then the other side would.

The other guiding principle in all confrontations was that rank or social standing mattered. What happened to the bulk of the people, whose
role was to serve, seemed to matter little. What happened to the "better
sort" was important. This division of human beings into two status
groups was far more important than race or even ethnicity. A modern
person who reads the literature of exploration and colonization is constantly struck by the cavalier way in which ordinary English men and
women were treated as expendable. If ships were deemed overcrowded,
passengers or mariners were dropped off on a handy coast to fend for
themselves—or not. Children were left with Indians as hostages for peace
and so that they could be useful in the future; some were reclaimed and
some were not. The famous Lost Colonists of Roanoke were just one
among many groups that were simply abandoned because it was considered impossible to go back for them.

The corollary is that Americans of the "better sort" were regarded with
the same mixture of respect, fear, and suspicion as their equivalents in
Europe. Status distinctions were immensely powerful for these people

and they were innate unlike mutable ethnic and cultural categories. John Smith cared deeply that Pocahontas carried herself as a king's daughter while she was in London. The great were naturally suited to leadership, and their carriage exemplified their status. But they also had the capacity to do powerful damage, and channeling of their energies was crucial, both in England and America. The constant use of the words "subtle" and "proud" to describe American leaders in these early sources is testimony to their greatness and the difficulty of controlling them. Colonial leaders hoped to win some of them as allies by offering European technology and aid against their enemies. Chiefs in all early colonial regions did see the utility of such alliances, but they never submitted to English control, although the colonists sometimes thought they had. Those who did offer partnership became rich and powerful in the short run, but ultimately the erratic behavior of English venturers shattered those arrangements. In the early years fear and their own assumptions about human nature fostered the English pattern of lashing out against friends and enemies alike; the settlers' assumption that the natives would overwhelm them if they did not retaliate against every challenge meant that they would inevitably wound friends as much as foes. As English colonialism turned to massive export of population to America, settlers spread over the land, disrupting native political and economic foundations. Competition for land increasingly became the underlying cause of conflict, and undermined the ability of Indian governors to maintain their own ways.

The Narragansetts and their sachem Miantonomi exemplify these developments. Many sources describe how they became rich and powerful because of their proximity to Long Island Sound shell beds as the wampum trade exploded in the early years of colonization. William Wood wrote that the "Pequants" jeered at the Narragansetts, calling them "Women-like men" because they did not go to war, but they "seeke rather to grow rich by industrie, than famous by deeds of Chevalry." Although Plymouth felt threatened by them, the Narragansetts cooperated with Massachusetts Bay against their Pequot rivals through their sympathetic link, Roger Williams. Following the war, a new rivalry grew up between Miantonomi and the Mohegan chief Uncas, who had also been an English ally in the war, and leaders in Boston attempted to manipulate this rivalry.[63]

After their demonstration of power colonial officials expected New England natives, and particularly those who had been allied to them, to operate as dependents within the English system. Disputes arose over the distribution of Pequot captives following the conflict, and Boston repeatedly demanded that the Narragansetts give up Pequots who were thought to be living among them. Miantonomi refused, or said that the English information was wrong; absorption of captives was a long-standing tradition which no native saw reason to break. Miantonomi, seeking to incorporate colonial leaders in his system, made gifts of land to Roger Williams and John Winthrop in the expectation of reciprocal care for his interests in the captives and promised goods and was disappointed when the Massachusetts Bay governor failed in his responsibilities. Miantonomi said of Winthrop's behavior, "Chenock eiuse wetompatimucks? that is, Did ever friends deal so with friends?"[64]

The Mohegans absorbed many of the defeated Pequots, and Uncas consolidated his position through joining important lineages to his own. He was reported to have married—or sought as wives—at least seven Pequot high-ranking women, including the sister and stepmother of the dead sachem Sassacus. Christian leaders who preached to the Indians found they insistently resisted the commandment that they must have only one wife. The evidence suggests that the prohibition of multiple wives struck at the foundations of political organization.[65]

As Uncas was increasingly favored by the English leaders, Miantonomi's position both with the English and with native client tribes eroded. Roger Williams had settled in Narragansett country after he was expelled from Massachusetts, and other religious migrants whose views were unacceptable in the Bay Colony found their way to Rhode Island. While Williams had facilitated Narragansett cooperation in the Pequot War, Boston officials were irked that their outspoken opponents had found a refuge so close by from which to comment on affairs in Massachusetts. Their censure was much less terrifying when protection was so handy. Miantonomi came in for his share of blame for selling lands to these settlers.[66] Just after the Pequot War, Miantonomi had told the English that the large and powerful Narragansetts were "as a great tree" and the Mohegans were "but as a twig." But now Uncas was building a powerful and numerous Mohegan confederation by absorbing former Pequots and others.[67]

Ultimately Miantonomi attempted to deal with his people's isolation as Wingina, Opechancanough, and the Pequots had: he tried to build a coalition to oppose the English. On the eve of the Pequot War, according to Bradford, the Pequots had approached the Narragansetts and offered an alliance. They warned that the English were overspreading the country and would eventually deprive them all. Moreover, if the Pequots were defeated, it was only a matter of time before the Narragansetts, too, would be targets. Rather than confront the English in battle, the Pequots proposed to "fire their houses, kill their cattle, and lie in ambush for them as they went abroad upon their occasions." If they stuck to this plan, the newcomers would be starved out and forced to leave. In the event the Narragansetts chose the English side and the Pequots were forced into massed battle.[68]

After a few years rumors began to circulate among the New Englanders of a new coalition. Perhaps to reassure natives about the colonists' intentions, the colonies of Connecticut, New Haven, and Aquiday jointly sent a letter to Massachusetts Bay expressing their dislike of "such as would have the Indians rooted out, as being of the cursed race of Ham," suggesting instead a policy of "seeking to gain them by justice and kindness," but also asking for help if danger erupted. In their reply, the Massachusetts authorities again demonstrated that their vengeance against erring English was as great as against the Indians. Although they wrote Connecticut and New Haven agreeing with their propositions, the Massachusetts leaders refused to have anything to do with Aquiday where Anne Hutchinson and her closest followers had settled.[69]

Reports circulated that Miantonomi was appealing for a united front to extirpate the colonists. Bradford wrote Winthrop that Miantonomi had sent wampum to the Mohawks and "it was accepted," a clear demonstration that the English knew the meaning of accepting a gift. Connecticut colony also forwarded rumors of Narragansett activities. Winthrop sent emissaries to the Narragansett sachems to summon them to Boston. Miantonomi said he would come if Roger Williams accompanied him as interpreter, but that request was refused. Despite the close working relationship between him and Winthrop, Williams had been expelled from Massachusetts Bay on pain of death for expressing his religious opinions and could not return. Miantonomi did come in October 1640 and was offended when he found the interpreter was to be a Pequot woman. He was forced to speak through her, however, and left angry. Both sides were dissatisfied with the interview.[70]

Then in August 1641 Lion Gardiner, a leader in the Pequot War, heard of Miantonomi's speech to Long Island leaders at Montauk. Miantonomi gave the assembled leaders gifts and addressed them as "brethren and friends":

> for so are we all Indians as the English are, and say brother to one another; so must we be one as they are, otherwise we shall be all gone shortly, for you know our fathers had plenty of deer and skins, our plains were full of deer, as also our woods, and of turkies, and our coves full of fish and fowl. But these English having gotten our land, they with scythes cut down the grass, and with axes fell the trees; their cows and horses eat the grass, and their hogs spoil our clam banks, and we shall

all be starved; therefore it is best for you to do as we, for we are all the Sachems from east to west, both Moquakues and Mohauks joining with us, and we are all resolved to fall upon them all, at one appointed day; and therefore I am come to you privately first. . . . when you see the three fires that will be made forty days hence, in a clear night, then do as we, and the next day fall on and kill men, women, and children, but no cows, for they will serve to eat till our deer be increased again.[71]

Miantonomi left Long Island more isolated than when he arrived, as his pleas fell on deaf ears and were even reported by the Montauks. Connecticut leaders were alarmed and appealed for aid; once again Miantonomi was summoned to Boston, and he was systematically humiliated by being denied the marks of leadership Massachusetts officials had formerly accorded him.[72]

Miantonomi, drawn into fighting between the Mohegans and one of his client tribes, was captured; according to Mohegan oral tradition it was the famous runner Tantaquidgeon who leaped across the falls of the Yantic River "to lay hands on" the Narragansett leader who was delivered to the authorities at Hartford. The colonies of Connecticut, New Haven, Massachusetts Bay, and Plymouth came together in 1643 to form a league, the New England Confederation, to look after their common interests and mutual defense; Roger Williams's Rhode Island was excluded. Deciding Miantonomi's fate was the commissioners' first task. They wanted Miantonomi dead but did not want to carry out the execution, so they returned him to Uncas, telling the Mohegan that he should kill his rival as soon as he was out of their territory; and they sent two English to watch as Uncas's brother Wawequa "clave his head with an hatchet."[73]

Cotton Mather, writing at the very end of the seventeenth century when local English vulnerability was a distant memory and native people's autonomy was severely reduced, wrote extravagantly of Miantonomi's campaign:

> When these Ammonites perceived that they had made themselves to stink before the New-English Israel, they tried by all the Enchanting Insinuations that they could think upon, to reconcile themselves unto the other Nations of Indians, with whom they had been heretofore at Variance: Demonstrating to them how easie 'twould be for them, if they were United, quickly to extirpate the English, who if they were Divided, would from thence take their Advantage to Devour them one after Another. But although no Machiavel or Achitophel could have insinuated this Matter with more of Plausibility, yet the prospect of a Sweet Revenge, which the other Nations of the Indians did now hope to have by the help of the English upon these their Old Enemies, prevailed with them to renounce all Proposals of accommodation.[74]

As the English colonies grew and forced the native communities into smaller portions of their lands or pushed them west or north, the remarks of some colonists became similarly distanced and triumphant. The immediacy of trying to understand a very different culture with which they were trying to live, and on which they depended, gave way in some accounts to harsh and lifeless stereotyping. But there was never a time when the distanced stance became the sole viewpoint. Although it was increasingly possible for English settlers to live without intimate contact with Americans, many still sought out or were driven into close relationships with Indians and some of the most thoughtful accounts were written after these periods of warfare. Roger Williams's enormously sympathetic *Key into the Language of America* was published in 1643, the year of his friend Miantonomi's death. At no time was there a single hegemonic voice in the Euramerican population.

Nor did the American Indians see the future in a single way. The great powwow-sachem Pissaconaway, whose abilities had so impressed William Wood and Thomas Morton in the early years of settlement, addressed a huge gathering in 1660. Now that he was at the end of his life, he said, "I will now leave this Word of Counsel with you, that you take heed how you quarrell with the English for though you may do them much mischief, yet assuredly you will all be destroyed, and rooted off the Earth if you do." He went on to say that he had been as great an enemy of the newcomers as anyone when they first came, but found no way to destroy or expell them.[75] Many other leaders disagreed and joined Metacom in 1676 in a war to extirpate or push back English settlement to the coast.[76]

And the Indians remained. Only in very recent times have scholars begun to acknowledge that, contrary to popular belief, the American natives did not disappear. They withdrew into enclaves and became invisible to those who did not want to see them. They learned to manipulate the English system and developed mutually beneficial relationships with substantial men who could speak for their common interests in colonial government. Autonomy was no longer theirs and they were marginalized economically and socially, but they retained a degree of leverage. Family names might or might not indicate their lineage, but Indians kept their traditions and identity alive and remained a daily presence for most Euramericans.[77] In 1686, for example, William Byrd wrote to his friend John Clayton that he had, as requested, got an "Indian habitt for your boy." It consisted of "a flap or belly clout 1 pair stockings & 1 pair mocosins or Indian shoes allso some shells to put about his necke & a cap of wampum. I could not gett any dyed hair, which would have been better & cheaper. These things are put up in an Indian baskett, directed as you desired, there are a bow & arrows tyed to itt." Byrd obtained this outfit from "our neighbour Indians," and incidentally offered valuable evidence on the persistence of native life.[78]

Native people, such as the Chickahominy community visited by Theodore Stern in the mid-twentieth century, stubbornly resisted erasure. As Mercy Ann Nonesuch Mathews, a Nehantic, commented, "They may declare me extinct, that does not make me extinct." Moreover these traditions were specific: Fidelia Fielding wrote in her Mohegan-language diary for May 23, 1904: "I am from Mohegan! I am not Pequot! Anyone saying I am Pequot he is a continual liar, that is so. White man think [they] know all things. Half [the things they are] saying not are so." [79]

In the late twentieth century groups such as the Mohegans of Connecticut have won United States recognition of their continuous status as tribes by demonstrating conclusively through accumulation of thousands of records that, even when their neighbors were certain that no Indians existed in the region, they continued to maintain their traditional links and functions. Indians along the entire east coast, like their Euramerican counterparts, have developed and changed over time, but they have not disappeared.[80]

Notes

Introduction

1. For comprehensive evidence on this point see Karen Ordahl Kupperman, *Settling With the Indians: The Meeting of English and Indian Cultures in America, 1580–1640* (Totowa, N.J., 1980).

2. John Easton, "A Relacion of the Indyan Warre," 1675, in *Narratives of the Indian Wars, 1675–1699*, ed. Charles H. Lincoln (New York, 1913), 10.

3. See Robert Brenner, *Merchants and Revolution: Commercial Change, Political Conflict, and London's Overseas Traders, 1550–1653* (Princeton, 1993), pt. 1.

4. Roger Williams, *A Key into the Language of America* (London, 1643), A3v–A4.

5. Parkhurst to Richard Hakluyt the elder, in *The Original Writings and Correspondence of the Two Richard Hakluyts*, ed. E. G. R. Taylor (London, 1935), 1:131.

6. On this process of identity definition, see Philip J. Deloria, *Playing Indian* (New Haven, 1998), esp. chap. 1.

7. Samuel Purchas, *Purchas His Pilgrimage*, 3d ed. (London, 1617), 954–55; Thomas Commuck, *Indian Melodies* (New York, 1845), 63; Mabel Knight, "Wampanoag Indian Tales," *Journal of American Folklore* 38 (1925): 137. William Simmons, *The Spirit of the New England Tribes: Indian History and Folklore, 1620–1984* (Hanover, N.H., 1986) reprints Tantaquidgeon's record as well as other traditions of such foreknowledge; pp. 68–72. For a 1950s version of the music heard in the air before the coming of Europeans, see Bernd C. Peyer, *The Tutor'd Mind: Indian Missionary-Writers in Antebellum America* (Amherst, 1997), 96 and n. 114.

8. William Wood, *New Englands Prospect* (London, 1634), 77; Simmons, *Spirit of the New England Tribes*, 65–66.

9. Gabriel Archer, *The Relation of Captaine Gosnols Voyage to the North part of Virginia*, in *The English New England Voyages, 1602–1608*, ed. David B. Quinn and Alison M. Quinn (London, 1983), 114–38; and John Brereton, *A Briefe and true Relation of the Discoverie of the North part of Virginia*, in ibid., 143–65.

10. Edward Augustus Kendall, *Travels through the Northern Parts of the United States in the Years 1807 and 1808* (New York, 1809), 2:230. For other examples of this kind of oral tradition of early encounters, see Melissa Jayne Fawcett, *The Lasting of the Mohegans: The Story of the Wolf People* (Uncasville, Conn., 1995), 10–11; Nanepashemet, "Wampanoag Cultural Survival: The Dynamics of a Living Culture,"

in *Connecticut History* (special issue, *Reshaping Traditions: Native Americans and Europeans in Southern New England*) 35 (1994), 46–49; Simmons, *Spirit of the New England Tribes*, 68–71.

11. Smith, *The Generall Historie of Virginia, New-England and the Summer Isles, 1624*, in *The Complete Works of Captain John Smith*, ed. Philip L. Barbour, 3 vols. (Chapel Hill, 1986), 2:196.

12. On this point see the introduction by Neil L. Whitehead to his edition of Sir Walter Ralegh's *The Discoverie of the Large, Rich and Bewtiful Empyre of Guiana, 1596* (Norman, Okla., 1997).

Chapter 1. Mirror Images

1. John Donne, *A Sermon Preached to the Honourable Company of the Virginian Plantation*, in his *Five Sermons Upon Special Occasions* (London, 1626), 44.

2. John Lyly, *Midas* (London, 1592), in *The Complete Works of John Lyly*, ed. R. Warwick Bond, 3 vols. (Oxford, 1902), 3:115. On this point see Steven Mullaney, *The Place of the Stage: License, Play, and Power in Renaissance England* (Chicago, 1988), chap. 1.

3. Richard Brathwait, in his *The English Gentlewoman, drawne out to the full Body* (London, 1631), constantly returned to the dangers posed by importation of "Phantasticke habits or forraine fashions," A4, B3v, 10, 14–15, 23, 25.

4. Aileen Ribeiro, *Dress and Morality* (New York: Holmes and Meier, 1986), chaps. 4–5, quotes pp. 72–73. I thank John Styles for calling this source to my attention. Arjun Appadurai characterizes England during this period as "a society of sumptuary law slowly changing into a society of fashion." *Modernity at Large: Cultural Dimensions of Globalization* (Minneapolis, 1996), 71–72.

5. On the contemporary obsession with honor and anxiety over eroding gender distinctions and cross-dressing, see Anthony Fletcher, *Gender, Sex and Subordination in England, 1500–1800* (New Haven, 1995), 23–24, 28, 121, 126–53.

6. Michael Drayton, *Works*, ed. W. J. Hebel (Oxford, 1961), 3:206–8.

7. On contemporary perceptions of the dangers of wealth and acquisition of new territories to the commonwealth, see Quentin Skinner, *The Foundations of Modern Political Thought*, vol. 1, *The Renaissance* (Cambridge, 1978), chap. 6, esp. 149–50, 162–65.

8. Lorraine Daston and Katharine Park, *Wonders and the Order of Nature, 1150–1750* (New York, 1998), and "Unnatural Conceptions: The Study of Monsters in France and England," *Past and Present* 92 (1981): 20–54; Malcolm Smuts, "Cultural Diversity and Cultural Change at the Court of James I," in *The Mental World of the Jacobean Court*, ed. Linda Levy Peck (Cambridge, 1991), 99–112; Caroline Walker Bynum, "Wonder," *American Historical Review* 102 (1997): 1–26.

9. Robert Burton, *The Anatomy of Melancholy*, ed. Thomas C. Faulkner, Nicolas K. Kiessling, and Rhonda L. Blair, 3 vols. (Oxford, 1989–94), 2:85, 87. The reference to Fratres à Bry is to the work published by Theodor de Bry.

10. Richard Hakluyt, "To the favourable Reader," in *The Principall Navigations, Voiages, Traffiques, and Discoveries of the English Nation, 1589*, in *The Original Writings and Correspondence of the Two Richard Hakluyts*, ed. E. G. R. Taylor (London, 1935), 2:408. I thank Peter Mancall for this reference.

11. Christian Feest, "The Collecting of American Indian Artifacts in Europe, 1493–1750," in *America in European Consciousness, 1493–1750*, ed. Karen Ordahl Kupperman (Chapel Hill, 1995), 324–60.

12. Clare William, trans. and ed., *Thomas Platter's Travels in England, 1599* (London, 1937), 171–73; David B. Quinn, "'Virginians' on the Thames in 1603," in *England and the Discovery of America* (New York, 1974), 419–31.

13. John Tradescant, *Musaeum Tradescantium: or, a Collection of Rarities, preserved at South-Lambeth neer London* (London, 1656); Peter Mundy, *The Travels of Peter Mundy, in Europe and Asia, 1608–1667*, ed. R. C. Temple, 3 vols. (London, 1919), vol. 3, pt. 1, 1–3; Arthur MacGregor, "The Cabinet of Curiosities in Seventeenth-Century Britain," in *The Origins of Museums: The Cabinet of Curiosities in Sixteenth and Seventeenth-Century Europe*, ed. Oliver Impey and Arthur MacGregor (Oxford, 1985), 147–58; and John Dixon Hunt, "*Curiosities* to adorn *Cabinets* and *Gardens*," in ibid., 193–203. On the growth in the number of known plants, see Henry Lowood, "The New World and the European Catalog of Nature," in Kupperman, *America in European Consciousness*, 295–323; on American items in Tradescant's collection see Feest, "Collecting of American Indian Artifacts," 333. Captain John Smith left some of his books to John Tradescant; Smith's will is printed in Philip L. Barbour, ed., *The Complete Works of Captain John Smith* (Chapel Hill, 1986), 3:382–83.

14. Mullaney, *Place of the Stage*, chap. 3. On the way in which news of foreign lands entered the popular consciousness see Charles Frey, "*The Tempest* and the New World," *Shakespeare Quarterly* 30 (1979): 29–41.

15. Shakespeare, *Macbeth* 1.3. For the identification of the *Tiger* see Edward Alleyn Loomis, "Master of the Tiger," *Shakespeare Quarterly* 7 (1956): 457; and Garry Wills, *Witches and Jesuits: Shakespeare's Macbeth* (New York, 1995), app. 1. Andrew Fitzmaurice demonstrates that vivid descriptions were a part of the persuasive repertory of classical rhetoric in "Classical Rhetoric in the Literature of Discovery, 1570–1630" (Ph.D. diss., Cambridge University, 1995), 110–14.

16. Shakespeare, *Twelfth Night*, ed. Elizabeth Story Donno (Cambridge, 1985), 3.2; and p. 105 n. See David B. Quinn, "Sailors and the Sea in Elizabethan England," in *England and the Discovery of America*, 199–226, esp. 211.

17. Henry Farley, *St. Paules-Church. Her Bill for the Parliament* (London, 1621), E4-E4v. I thank Thomas Cogswell for bringing this source to my attention.

18. *The Tempest* 2.2.

19. Farley, *St. Paules-Church*, E4v.

20. Harriot, "Notes" to woodcuts of John White's paintings published by Theodor de Bry and printed in David Beers Quinn, ed., *The Roanoke Voyages, 1584–1590*, 2 vols. (London, 1955), 1:430, 438. On Ben Jonson's use of the masque form to urge restraint in ostentation, as well as in eating and drinking , see Martin Butler, "Ben Jonson and the Limits of Courtly Panegyric," in *Culture and Politics in Early Stuart England*, ed. Kevin Sharpe and Peter Lake (Stanford, 1993), 91–115.

21. Thomas Morton, *New English Canaan*, 1637, in *Tracts and Other Papers, Relating Principally to the Origin, Settlement, and Progress of the Colonies in North America*, comp. Peter Force, 4 vols. (1844; reprint, Washington, D.C., 1963), 2:39.

22. Richard Hakluyt, "To the Right Honourable Sir Robert Cecil Knight," 1599 dedication to vol. 2 of *The Principal Navigations, Voyages, Traffiques, and Discoveries of the English Nation*, in Taylor, *Original Writings and Correspondence*, 2:457.

23. William Crashaw, *A Sermon Preached in London before the right honourable the Lord Lawarre* (London, 1610), Cv–C2, D2.

24. Worden, "Ben Jonson among the Historians," in Sharpe and Lake, *Culture and Politics in Early Stuart England*, 69. On the tie between colonial projects and study of Roman history see Lisa Jardine, "Mastering the Uncouth: Gabriel Harvey, Edmund Spenser and the English Experience in Ireland," in *New Perspectives on Renaissance Thought: Essays in the History of Science, Education, and Philosophy in Memory of Charles B. Schmitt*, ed. John Henry and Sarah Hutton (London, 1990), 68–82.

25. John Speed, *The History of Great Britaine* (London, 1611), 179.

26. Donald R. Kelley, "*Tacitus Noster:* The *Germania* in the Renaissance and Reformation," in *Tacitus and the Tacitean Tradition*, ed. T. J. Luce and A. J. Woodman

(Princeton, 1993), 152–67, quote p. 153; J. H. M. Salmon, "Seneca and Tacitus in Jacobean England," in Peck, *Mental World of the Jacobean Court*, 169–88.

27. On the way in which men on the public stage studied the classics, particularly Livy and Tacitus, as guides to action, see Peter Burke, "A Survey of the Popularity of Ancient Historians, 1450–1700," *History and Theory* 5 (1966): 135–52, quote p. 151; and "Tacitism, Scepticism, and Reason of State," in *The Cambridge History of Political Thought, 1450–1700*, ed. J. H. Burns (Cambridge, 1991), 484–90; Anthony Grafton and Lisa Jardine, "Studied for Action: How Gabriel Harvey Read His Livy," *Past and Present* 129 (1990): 30–78; and Alan T. Bradford, "Stuart Absolutism and the 'Utility' of Tacitus," *Huntington Library Quarterly* 46 (1983), 127–55. On concern about the dangers of luxury and flattery see Worden, "Ben Jonson among the Historians," in Sharpe and Lake, *Culture and Politics in Early Stuart England*, 71, 85–87, quote p. 85; and Malcolm Smuts, "Court-Centred Politics and the Uses of Roman Historians, c. 1590–1630," in ibid., 34–37. On the great hunger for news in England see R. P. Cust, "News and Politics in Early Seventeenth-Century England," *Past and Present* 111 (1986): 60–90; and Thomas Cogswell, *The Blessed Revolution: English Politics and the Coming of War, 1621–1624* (Cambridge, 1989), 21–24.

28. David Armitage, "John Milton: Poet against Empire," in *Milton and Republicanism*, ed. David Armitage, Armand Himy, and Quentin Skinner (Cambridge, 1995), 206–25.

29. Cornelius Tacitus, *The Description of Germanie: and Customes of the People*, trans. Richard Grenewey, and *Life of Julius Agricola*, trans. Henry Savile (London, 1598).

30. For the argument for Saxon origins, and for the description of the ancient German polity, see William Camden, *Britaine, Or A Chorographicall Description of the most flourishing Kingdomes, England, Scotland, and Ireland*, trans. Philemon Holland (1586; London, 1610), 127–41; Richard Verstegan, *A Restitution of Decayed Intelligence: In antiquities. Concerning the most noble and renowned English nation* (Antwerp, 1605), 2 and passim; John Speed, *The History of Great Britaine Under the Conquests of the Romans, Saxons, Danes and Normans* (London, 1614), 287–89; Robert C. Johnson et al., eds., *Proceedings in Parliament 1628*, 6 vols. (New Haven, 1977–83), *Commons Debates 1628*, II, 330, 333–34; *Lords Proceedings 1628*, V, 162, 172–73, 180. Verstegan's book was dedicated to James I and was distributed in England by the king's publishers, as he announced on his title page. I thank Mary Floyd-Wilson for bringing Verstegan to my attention, and Thomas Cogswell for discussion of its printing history. For modern treatments of the issues see Hugh A. MacDougall, *Racial Myth in English History: Trojans, Teutons, and Anglo-Saxons* (Hanover, N.H., 1982); Christopher Hill, "The Norman Yoke," in *Puritanism and Revolution: Studies in Interpretation of the English Revolution of the Seventeenth Century* (London, 1958); D. R. Woolf, *The Idea of History in Early Stuart England: Erudition, Ideology, and "The Light of Truth" from the Accession of James I to the Civil War* (Toronto, 1990); Kevin Sharpe, "The Foundation of the Chairs of History at Oxford and Cambridge: An Episode in Jacobean Politics," in *Politics and Ideas in Early Stuart England: Essays and Studies* (London, 1989); Blair Worden, *The Sound of Virtue: Philip Sidney's "Arcadia" and Elizabethan Politics* (New Haven, 1996); and Arthur Ferguson, *Utter Antiquity: Perceptions of Prehistory in Renaissance England* (Durham, 1993), chap. 5. On the sources and meaning of the Trojan myth of English origins, see Sidney Anglo, "The *British History* in Early Tudor Propaganda," *Bulletin of the John Rylands Library* 44 (1961): 17–48. Gordon Sayre demonstrates that French writers on America discussed American natives in terms of their own ancestors, the Gauls; Gordon M. Sayre, *Les Sauvages Américains: Representations of Native Americans in French and English Colonial Literature* (Chapel Hill, 1997), 159–60.

31. Nathanael Carpenter, *Geography Delineated* (London, 1625), 281–82; Stuart Piggott, *Ancient Britons and the Antiquarian Imagination: Ideas from the Renaissance to the Regency* (London, 1989), chap. 3.

32. For a full development of these points, see Kelley, "*Tacitus Noster*," 152–67, and Chapter 7 below.

33. William Strachey, *The Historie of Travell into Virginia Britania*, 1612, ed. Louis B. Wright and Virginia Freund (London, 1953), 24–25.

34. Burton, *Anatomy of Melancholy*, 1:74.

35. For examples, see Captain John Smith, *The Generall Historie of Virginia, New-England and the Summer Isles*, 1624, in Barbour, *Works*, 2:163; George Percy, "Observations Gathered out of a Discourse of the Plantation of the Southerne Colonie in Virginia by the English," in *The Jamestown Voyages under the First Charter, 1606–1609*, ed. Philip L. Barbour, 2 vols. (Cambridge, 1969), 1:137.

36. On Baconian engagement see Richard Tuck, *Philosophy and Government, 1572–1651* (Cambridge, 1993), 80–82, 112–13; Fitzmaurice, "Classical Rhetoric."

37. Robert Cushman, *A Sermon Preached in Plimmoth in New-England* (London, 1622), A2v.

38. Edmund Garrard, *The Countrie Gentleman Moderator* (London, 1624), 54–55.

39. Donne, *Sermon Before the Virginia Company*, in *Five Sermons*, 22; Alexander Whitaker, "To my verie deere and loving Cosen M. G. Minister of the B. F. in London," published in Ralph Hamor, *A True Discourse of the Present Estate of Virginia* (London, 1615), 60.

40. Neil L. Whitehead's introduction to his edition of Sir Walter Ralegh's *The Discoverie of the Large, Rich and Bewtiful Empyre of Guiana*, 1596 (Norman, Okla., 1997). See also James Axtell, "The Exploration of Norumbega: Native Perspectives," in *American Beginnings: Exploration, Culture, and Cartography in the Land of Norumbega*, ed. Emerson W. Baker et al. (Lincoln, Neb. 1994), 149–65, on reading evidence for native views.

41. Harriot, *A Briefe and True Report of the new found land of Virginia*, 1588, 1590, in Quinn, *Roanoke Voyages*, 1:374–75.

42. John Smith, *A True Relation of such occurrences and accidents of noate as hath hapned in Virginia*, 1608, in Barbour, *Works*, 1:59. The imputed error was Smith's denial that Indians believed in an afterlife. The *True Relation* was published while Smith was still in Virginia, without his knowledge or consent, and in a garbled form. On false reports see Samuel Purchas, *Purchas His Pilgrimage*, 3d ed. (London, 1617), 952–55.

43. Morton, *New English Canaan*, 66.

44. Winslow's correction is in his *Good Newes from New England* (London, 1624), 52. His earlier letter was printed in William Bradford and Edward Winslow, *A Relation or Journall of the English Plantation setled at Plimoth in New England* (London, 1622), known as *Mourt's Relation*, 61.

45. William Apess, *Eulogy on King Philip, as Pronounced at the Odeon, in Federal Street, Boston*, 1836, in *A Son of the Forest and Other Writings by William Apess, a Pequot*, ed. Barry O'Connell (Amherst, 1997), 103–38; Gladys Tantaquidgeon, "Notes on the Gay Head Indians of Massachusetts," *Indian Notes* 7 (1930): 1–26; Nanepashemet (Wampanoag), "It Smells Fishy to Me: An Argument Supporting the Use of Fish Fertilizer by the Native People of Southern New England," in *Algonkians of New England: Past and Present*, ed. Peter Benes (Boston, 1993), 42–50. See also Melissa Fawcett, "The Role of Gladys Tantaquidgeon," in *Papers of the Fifteenth Algonquian Conference*, ed. William Cowan, 135–45.

46. Edward Augustus Kendall, *Travels through the Northern Parts of the United States in the Years 1807 and 1808* (New York, 1809), 2:220. These themes are further developed in Chapter 3.

47. Deeds, wills, and other documents incorporating the oral tradition can be seen in Ives Goddard and Kathleen Bragdon, eds., *Native Writings in Massachusett*, 2 vols. (Philadelphia, 1988); and Elizabeth A. Little, ed., *Nantucket Indian Studies*, nos. 3 and 7 (Nantucket, 1981). Similar oral tradition of relationships and land also appear in "Zaccheus Macy's Account of the Indians of Nantucket, Three Versions," ed. Marie Sussek, *Nantucket Indian Studies*, no. 7, 1–19. Tantaquidgeon's comments are in "Notes on the Gay Head Indians," 17–18. Commuck's record is in his "Sketch of the Brothertown Indians," *Collections of the State Historical Society of Wisconsin* 4 (1859): 291–98, esp. 297.

48. On the partnership between the Mashantucket Pequot Tribal Nation and the archaeological team led by Kevin McBride see Laurence M. Hauptman and James D. Wherry, eds., *The Pequots in Southern New England: The Fall and Rise of an American Indian Nation* (Norman Okla., 1990), esp. Kevin A. McBride, "The Historical Archaeology of the Mashantucket Pequots, 1637–1900: A Preliminary Analysis," 96–116; and McBride, "The Mashantucket Pequot Ethnohistory Project," in *Rooted Like the Ash Trees: New England Indians and the Land*, ed. Richard G. Carlson, rev. ed. (Naugatuck, Conn., 1987), 18–21.

49. For the Mohegan oral tradition and Martha Uncas see Melissa Jayne Fawcett, *The Lasting of the Mohegans: The Story of the Wolf People* (Uncasville, Conn., 1995), 7–10, 23 (the quote is from p. 10); and J. D. Prince, "Tribute to Memory of Fidelia Fielding," *Narragansett Dawn*, July 1936, 54–55. See the website of the Mashantucket Pequot Tribal Nation (www.MPTN.org) for their tribal history. For the archaeological evidence see Bert Salwen, "Indians of Southern New England and Long Island: Early Period," in *Handbook of North American Indians*, ed. William C. Sturtevant, vol. 15, *Northeast*, ed. Bruce G. Trigger (Washington, D.C., 1978), 172. On interpreting conflict between various types of sources, see Paul A. Robinson, "A Narragansett History from 1000 B.P. to the Present," in *Enduring Traditions: The Native Peoples of New England*, ed. Laurie Weinstein (Westport, Conn., 1994), 79–90.

50. "Baske-shallop" is from Brereton, *Briefe and true Relation of the Discoverie of the North part of Virginia*, in *The English New England Voyages, 1602–1608*, ed. David B. Quinn and Alison M. Quinn (London, 1983), 145; Arthur Barlowe, *The First Voyage Made to the Coastes of America, 1584*, in Quinn, *Roanoke Voyages*, 1:104, 111. Samoset's greeting is in Bradford and Winslow, *Mourt's Relation*, 32. Samoset had learned English from fishermen in Maine. For contemporary dissemination of Brereton's description see Strachey, *Historie of Travell*, 152. The phenomenon of Americans picking up and using European clothes and tools can be seen from the earliest period. James Axtell points out that in 1501, less than a decade after Columbus's first voyage, Gaspar Corte-Real kidnapped Indians from the Maine coast who possessed Venetian earrings and a piece of an Italian-made sword; James Axtell, "The Exploration of Norumbega: Native Perspectives," in Baker et al., *American Beginnings*, 154; see also Bruce J. Bourque and Ruth H. Whitehead, "Trade and Alliances in the Contact Period," in ibid., 131–47. Norse voyages first came to Newfoundland in about 1000, and occasional ships touched northern coasts in the ensuing centuries; see William W. Fitzhugh, "Early Contacts North of Newfoundland before A.D. 1600: A Review," in *Cultures in Contact: the Impact of European Contacts on Native American Cultural Institutions, A.D. 1000–1800*, ed. William Fitzhugh (Washington, D.C., 1985), 23–43.

51. Thomas Dermer to Samuel Purchas, December 27, 1619, in Samuel Purchas, *Hakluytus Posthumus or Purchas His Pilgrimes, 1625*, 20 vols. (Glasgow, 1906), 19:129; Cushman, *Sermon Preached in Plimmoth*, A3; Morton, *New English Canaan*, 19. Alfred W. Crosby, *Ecological Imperialism: The Biological Expansion of Europe, 900–1900* (Cambridge, 1986). On estimating the pre-Columbian population see John D. Daniels, "The Indian Population of North America in 1492," *William and Mary Quarterly*, 3d ser., 49 (1992): 298–320.

52. Thomas Shepard, *The Clear Sun-shine of the Gospel Breaking Forth upon the Indians in New-England*, 1648, in *Collections of the Massachusetts Historical Society*, 3d ser., 4 (1834): 44.

53. William Bradford, *Of Plymouth Plantation, 1620–1647*, ed. Samuel Eliot Morison (New York, 1952), 270–71.

54. On the drought see David W. Stahle et al., "The Lost Colony and Jamestown Droughts," *Science* 280 (1998): 564–67. On Little Ice Age conditions in America, see Karen Ordahl Kupperman, "The Puzzle of the American Climate in the Early Colonial Period," *American Historical Review* 87 (1982): 1262–89, and "Climate and Mastery of the Wilderness in Seventeenth-Century New England," in *Seventeenth-Century New England*, ed. David G. Allen and David D. Hall (Charlottesville, 1985), 3–37. For examples of drought-induced dearth in the colonial records see Harriot, *Briefe and True Report*, 377; John White, "The Fourth Voyage Made to Virginia," 1587, in Quinn, *Roanoke Voyages*, 2:526; Smith, *The Proceedings of the English Colony in Virginia, 1612*, in Barbour, *Works*, 1:239, 255, 264, 274.

55. Pory, "Observations," in Smith, *Generall Historie*, 2:289–90.

56. For discussions of this process in the Southeast see Helen C. Rountree, *Pocahontas's People: The Powhatan Indians of Virginia through Four Centuries* (Norman, Okla., 1990), 10–14; and Christian F. Feest, "Virginia Algonquians" and "North Carolina Algonquians" in Trigger, *Handbook of North American Indians*, 15:253–70, 271–81. For New England, see Peter A. Thomas, "Cultural Change on the Southern New England Frontier, 1630–1665," in Fitzhugh, *Cultures in Contact*, 131–61, esp. 138–39, 156–57; Neal Salisbury, *Manitou and Providence: Indians, Europeans, and the Making of New England, 1500–1643* (Oxford, 1982); Bert Salwen, "Indians of Southern New England and Long Island: Early Period," in Trigger, *Handbook of North American Indians*, 15:160–76; and Dean Snow, "Eastern Abenaki," in ibid., 137–47.

57. McBride, "Historical Archaeology of the Mashantucket Pequots," 96–116, esp. 97–106; William F. Starna, "The Pequots in the Seventeenth Century," in Hauptman and Wherry, *Pequots in Southern New England*, 33–47; Robert S. Grumet, *Historic Contact: Indian People and Colonists in Today's Northeastern United States in the Sixteenth through Eighteenth Centuries* (Norman, Okla., 1995), 56–58; Harald E. L. Prins, "Children of Gluskap: Wabanaki Indians on the Eve of the European Invasion," in Baker et al., *American Beginnings*, 95–117.

58. On precontact native life and indigenous versus introduced change see Neal Salisbury, "The Indians' Old World: Native Americans the Coming of Europeans," *William and Mary Quarterly*, 3d ser., 53 (1996): 435–58. On the timing of the emergence of tribes with "hereditary authority structures" in the Chesapeake region see Helen C. Rountree and Thomas E. Davidson, *Eastern Shore Indians of Virginia and Maryland* (Charlottesville, 1997), chap. 1 (the quote is from p. 26).

59. Karen Ordahl Kupperman, "Scandinavian Colonists Confront the New World," in *New Sweden in America*, ed. Carol E. Hoffecker et al. (Newark, Del., 1995), 89–111.

60. On the timing and impetus for the growth of political consolidation in the Chesapeake, see Stephen R. Potter, *Commoners, Tribute, and Chiefs: The Development of Algonquian Culture in the Potomac Valley* (Charlottesville, 1993), chap. 4; E. Randolph Turner, "Native American Protohistoric Interactions in the Powhatan Core Area," in *Powhatan Foreign Relations, 1500–1722*, ed. Helen C. Rountree (Charlottesville, 1993), 76–93; Rountree, "Summary and Implications," in ibid., 206–28; and Frederic W. Gleach, *Powhatan's World and Colonial Virginia: A Conflict of Cultures* (Lincoln, Neb., 1997), chap. 1. On the great king see Ralph Lane, *An Account of the Particularities of the imployments of the English men left in Virginia, 1586*, in Quinn, *Roanoke Voyages*, 1:259–61. For presentations of differing viewpoints on the sources of development, see Turner, "Socio-Political Organization within the Powhatan

Chiefdom and the Effects of European Contact, A.D. 1607–1646," in Fitzhugh, *Cultures in Contact*, 193–224; and J. Frederick Fausz, "Patterns of Anglo-Indian Aggression and Accommodation along the Mid-Atlantic Coast, 1584–1634," in ibid., 225–68, and commentary by Fitzhugh, 187–92.

61. Kathleen J. Bragdon, *Native People of Southern New England, 1500–1650* (Norman, Okla., 1996), esp. "Introduction," chaps. 1, 2, and "Conclusion"; Lynn Ceci, "Radiocarbon Dating 'Village' Sites in Coastal New York: Settlement Pattern Change in the Middle to Late Woodland," *Man in the Northeast* 39 (1990): 1–28; Bruce J. Bourque and Ruth Holmes Whitehead, "Tarrentines and the Introduction of European Trade Goods in the Gulf of Maine," *Ethnohistory* 32 (1985): 327–41, and "Trade and Alliances in the Contact Period," in Baker et al., *American Beginnings*, 131–47.

62. Trudie Lamb Richmond, "A Native Perspective of History: The Schaghticoke Nation, Resistance, and Survival," in Weinstein, *Enduring Traditions*, 103–12, esp. 107. See the very interesting internal dialogue in the article coauthored by Helen C. Rountree and E. Randolph Turner III, "On the Fringe of the Southeast: The Powhatan Paramount Chiefdom in Virginia," in *The Forgotten Centuries: Indians and Europeans in the American South, 1521–1704*, ed. Charles Hudson and Carmen Chaves Tesser (Athens, Ga., 1994); and T. J. Brasser, "Early Indian-European Contacts," in Trigger, *Handbook of North American Indians*, 15:78–88.

Chapter 2. Reading Indian Bodies

1. After Queen Elizabeth granted Ralegh the right to call his American lands Virginia in her honor, the name was applied to the entire east coast of North America between Florida and Newfoundland. Early voyages to New England were said to be to the "North part of Virginia." Ralegh's actual colony was on Roanoke Island within the North Carolina Outer Banks.

2. Since Harriot and White never completed the great work on Virginia for which their research was intended, de Bry's edition is the fullest record we have of what they found. The White watercolors and de Bry engravings are best compared in Paul Hulton and D. B. Quinn, eds., *The American Drawings of John White, 1577–1590* (London and Chapel Hill, 1964), which also includes the best scholarly discussion of both. Both are also in Paul Hulton, *America in 1585* (Chapel Hill, 1985). Dover Books has published a facsimile of the 1590 edition with the woodcuts. On the de Bry workshop and the *Great Voyages* project, see Bernadette Bucher, *Icon and Conquest: A Structural Analysis of the Illustrations of de Bry's "Great Voyages,"* trans. Basia Miller Gulati (Chicago, 1981).

3. John Peacock, "The Politics of Portraiture," in *Culture and Politics in Early Stuart England*, ed. Kevin Sharpe and Peter Lake (Stanford, 1993), 99–128.

4. On this point see Keith Thomas, introduction to *A Cultural History of Gesture*, ed. Jan Bremmer and Herman Roodenburg (Ithaca, N.Y., 1991), 1–14.

5. Karen Ordahl Kupperman, "Fear of Hot Climates in the Anglo-American Colonial Experience," *William and Mary Quarterly*, 3d ser., 41 (1984): 213–40.

6. Virginia Company, "Instructions Given by way of Advice," 1606, in *The Jamestown Voyages under the First Charter, 1606–1609*, ed. Philip L. Barbour, 2 vols. (Cambridge, 1969), 52–53. See the similar advice from Edward Howes to John Winthrop, Jr., *Winthrop Papers*, 3:292.

7. "Instructions to be observed by Thomas Bavin," in *New American World: A Documentary History of North America to 1612*, ed. David B. Quinn, 5 vols. (New York, 1979), 3:242–44.

8. William Strachey, *The Historie of Travell into Virginia Britania*, 1612, ed. Louis B. Wright and Virginia Freund (London, 1953), 64–65.

9. On increasing concern with the presentation and control of the body see Norbert Elias, *The Civilising Process: The History of Manners*, trans. Edmund Jephcott (Oxford, 1978), chap. 2; and Anna Bryson, "The Rhetoric of Status: Gesture, Demeanour and the Image of the Gentleman in Sixteenth- and Seventeenth-Century England," in *Renaissance Bodies: The Human Figure in English Culture c. 1540–1660*, ed. Lucy Gent and Nigel Llewellyn (London, 1990), 136–53. On the sources of aristocratic honor see Mervyn James, *English Politics and the Concept of Honour, 1485–1642, Past and Present Supplement 3* (Oxford, 1978); William Hunt, "Civic Chivalry and the English Civil War," in *The Transmission of Culture in Early Modern Europe*, ed. Anthony Grafton and Ann Blair (Philadelphia, 1990), 204–37; A. J. Fletcher, "Honour, Reputation and Local Officeholding in Elizabethan and Stuart England," in *Order and Disorder in Early Modern England*, ed. Anthony Fletcher and John Stevenson (Cambridge, 1985), 92–115; and Frank Whigham, *Ambition and Privilege: The Social Tropes of Elizabethan Courtesy Theory* (Berkeley, 1984), chap. 2.

10. John Brereton, *A Briefe and true Relation of the Discoverie of the North part of Virginia*, 1602, in *The English New England Voyages, 1602–1608*, ed. David B. Quinn and Alison M. Quinn (London, 1983), 157–59; William Wood, *New Englands Prospect* (London, 1634), 63.

11. John Underhill, *Newes from America* (London, 1638), 5; Thomas Morton, *New English Canaan*, 1637, in *Tracts and Other Papers, Relating Principally to the Origin, Settlement, and Progress of the Colonies in North America*, comp. Peter Force, 4 vols. (1844; Washington, D.C., 1963), 2:24; John Smith, *A Map of Virginia*, 1612, in *The Complete Works of Captain John Smith*, ed. Philip L. Barbour, 3 vols. (Chapel Hill, 1986), 1:150. On the relatively healthier bodies of Americans see Douglas H. Ubelaker, "Human Biology of Virginia Indians," in *Powhatan Foreign Relations, 1500–1722*, ed. Helen C. Rountree (Charlottesville, 1993), 53–75; and Helen C. Rountree and Thomas E. Davidson, *Eastern Shore Indians of Virginia and Maryland* (Charlottesville, 1997), 38–39.

12. On the tradition of ancient and medieval travel writing see James S. Romm, *The Edges of the Earth in Ancient Thought: Geography, Exploration, and Fiction* (Princeton, 1992); Mary B. Campbell, *The Witness and the Other World: Exotic European Travel Writing, 400–1600* (Ithaca, N.Y., 1988); and Joy Kenseth, ed., *The Age of the Marvelous* (Hanover, N.H., 1991). Sir Walter Ralegh did weave reports of Amazons, acephali, and other fabulous peoples into his *Discoverie of the Large, Rich and Bewtiful Empyre of Guiana* (1596); Neil L. Whitehead argues that he drew on indigenous oral tradition rather than classical lore, and his report rested on decades of Spanish experience of native culture. See his edition of Ralegh's *Discoverie* (Norman, Okla. 1997).

13. Ingram, *The Relation of David Ingram of Barking*, in Richard Hakluyt, *The Principall Navigations, Voiages, Traffiques, and Discoveries of the English Nation* (London,1589), 558; George Peckham, *A True Reporte of the Newfound Landes*, 1583, in *Voyages and Colonising Enterprises of Sir Humphrey Gilbert*, ed. David B. Quinn, 2 vols. (London, 1940), 2:452; Purchas, *Purchas His Pilgrimage*, 2d ed. (London, 1614), 756. On cannibalism, see Peter Hulme, *Colonial Encounters: Europe and the Native Caribbean, 1492–1797* (London, 1986), chap. 1.

14. Philip Vincent, *A True Relation of the Late Battel fought in New England, between the English, and the Salvages* (London, 1637), 16–17; Wood, *New Englands Prospect*, 57–60.

15. Samuel Purchas, *Hakluytus Posthumus or Purchas His Pilgrimes*, 1625, 20 vols. (Glasgow, 1906), 16:112; Purchas, *Purchas His Pilgrimage*, 2d ed., 756; Wood, *New Englands Prospect*, 62.

16. Roger Williams, *A Key into the Language of America* (London, 1643), 13, 16, 45, 49.

17. On Indian nakedness see Richard White, "Discovering Nature in North America," *Journal of American History* 79 (1992): 874–91, esp. 878–80. When John Williams of Deerfield was roused from sleep and captured by Indians in 1704, he wrote that they "bound me naked, as I was in my shirt." Williams, *The Redeemed Captive Returning to Zion*, 1707, ed. Edward W. Clark (Amherst, 1976), 45.

18. John Speed, *The History of Great Britaine under the Conquests of the Romans, Saxons, Danes and Normans* (London, 1614), 179–80. On Speed's history see D. R. Woolf, *The Idea of History in Early Stuart England: Erudition, Ideology, and "The Light of Truth" from the Accession of James I to the Civil War* (Toronto, 1990), 64–72.

19. William Bradford and Edward Winslow, *A Relation or Journall of the English Plantation setled at Plimoth in New England* (London, 1622), known as *Mourt's Relation*, 32, 34, 62; George Percy, "Observations Gathered out of a Discourse of the Plantation of the Southerne Colonie in Virginia by the English," 1606, in Barbour, *Jamestown Voyages*, 1:136.

20. Wood, *New Englands Prospect*, 96; Williams, *Key into the Language of America*, 118–19 [misnumbered 110²–11²]; Morton, *New English Canaan*, 22–23; Bradford and Winslow, *Mourt's Relation*, 59. Norbert Elias argues that modesty was linked to internalization of a sense of shame; *Civilizing Process*, chap. 2, pt. 9, esp. 181. Richard Brathwait, in his *The English Gentlewoman, drawne out to the full Body* (London, 1631), wrote that modesty is the highest virtue in women, 180.

21. Williams, *Key into the Language of America*, 118–21 [misnumbered 110²–13²].

22. James Rosier, *A True Relation of the most prosperous voyage . . . in the Discovery of the land of Virginia*, 1605, in Quinn and Quinn, *English New England Voyages*, 276; Purchas, *Pilgrimes*, 18:343.

23. Richard Whitbourne, *A Discourse and Discovery of Newfoundland* (London, 1620), 55; George Best, *Experiences and reasons of the Sphere, to proove all partes of the worlde habitable*, 1578, in Richard Hakluyt, *The Principal Navigations, Voyages, Traffiques, and Discoveries of the English Nation*, 1598–1600, 12 vols. (Glasgow, 1903–5), 7:260–61.

24. Richard Hakluyt, *A Particuler Discourse concerninge the Greate Necessitie and Manifolde Commodyties that are like to growe to this Realme of Englande by the Westerne Discoveries Lately Attempted, written in the yere 1584*, ed. David B. Quinn and Alison M. Quinn (London, 1993), known as *The Discourse of Western Planting*, 67; see also 29–31, 115. See Edward Hayes, *A Treatise, conteining important inducements for the planting in these parts*, in Brereton, *Discoverie of the North part of Virginia*, in Quinn and Quinn, eds., *The English New England Voyages*, 172; and Ralph Lane, "An extract of Master Lanes letter, to Master Richard Hakluyt Esquire, and another gentleman of the middle Temple, from Virginia," 1585, in *The Roanoke Voyages, 1584–1590*, ed. David Beers Quinn, 2 vols. (London, 1955), 1:209.

25. Richard Eden, "To the Reader" in his translation of Peter Martyr, *The Decades of the New World or West India*, 1555, in *The First Three English Books on America*, ed. Edward Arber (Birmingham, 1885), 57; Peckham, *True Reporte of the Newfound Landes*, 471; Hayes, *A Treatise*, 175. See also Anon., "For Master Rauleys Viage," in Quinn, *Roanoke Voyages*, 1:130; and Richard Hakluyt, "Epistle Dedicatorie" to Sir Walter Ralegh, 1587, in *The Original Writings and Correspondence of the Two Richard Hakluyts*, ed. E. G. R. Taylor (London, 1935), 2:377.

26. These are the words of the Geneva Bible of 1560; see also Elaine Pagels, *Adam, Eve, and the Serpent* (London, 1988), chap. 1; Brathwait portrayed Adam as clothed in purity though naked in Eden (*English Gentlewoman*, 2).

27. Gen. 3:19 Geneva Bible; Barlowe, *First Voyage Made to the Coastes of America*, in Richard Hakluyt, *The Principall Navigations, Voiages, Traffiques, and Discoveries of the English Nation*, 1589, ed. David B. Quinn and Raleigh A. Skelton, 2 vols.

(Cambridge, 1965), 2:731; and Hakluyt, *Principal Navigations*, 1598–1600, 8:305; Harriot to Kepler, July 13, 1608, quoted in Edward Rosen, "Harriot's Science: The Intellectual Background," in *Thomas Harriot: Renaissance Scientist*, ed. John W. Shirley (Oxford, 1974), 4. The original is in the National Library in Vienna. Barlowe may have been familiar with Richard Eden's translation of Peter Martyr's *The Decades of the newe worlde or west India*, 1555, which describes the people discovered by Columbus as living "simplye and innocentlye without enforcement of lawes" as in "that goulden worlde of the whiche owlde wryters speake so much." But Martyr wrote that even in that time ambition and war had entered human life; Edward Arber, ed., *The First Three English Books on America* (Birmingham, 1885). I thank David Harris Sacks for pointing this passage out to me. On the charges against Ralegh see Ernest A. Strathmann, *Sir Walter Ralegh: A Study in Elizabethan Skepticism* (New York, 1951), 40–52; Robert Lacey, *Sir Walter Ralegh* (New York, 1974), 194–98; and M. C. Bradbrook, *The School of Night: A Study in the Literary Relationships of Sir Walter Ralegh* (Cambridge, 1936). On suspicion directed at Harriot, see Stephen Greenblatt, "Invisible Bullets," in *Shakespearean Negotiations: The Circulation of Social Energy in Renaissance England* (Berkeley, 1988), 21–65, esp. 21–39. The Garden of Eden and the Golden Age had become conflated in this period; see Peter Lindenbaum, *Changing Landscapes: Anti-Pastoral Sentiment in the English Renaissance* (Athens, Ga., 1986), 14–16. The first edition of the *Principall Navigations* had been published by the queen's own printer under the patronage of Sir Francis Walsingham, chief minister to Queen Elizabeth, and therefore had not been subject to the scrutiny of the licensing authorities. A second edition, even if greatly expanded as this was, did not need relicensing, but Hakluyt's caution may have been directed at its reception. I thank Cyndia Clegg for explaining the intricacies of censorship and licensing to me.

28. Alexander Whitaker, *Good Newes from Virginia* (London, 1613), 1, 24; Crashaw, "Epistle Dedicatorie," in ibid., A2v–A3v.

29. On this point see Susi Colin, "The Wild Man and the Indian in Early 16th Century Book Illustration," in *Indians and Europe: An Interdisciplinary Collection of Essays*, ed. Christian F. Feest (Aachen, 1987), 23–26.

30. Robert Cushman, *A Sermon Preached in Plimmoth in New-England* (London, 1622), A4; Robert Beverley, *The History and Present State of Virginia*, ed. Louis B. Wright (Chapel Hill, 1947), 9.

31. Morton, *New English Canaan*, 23, 39; Wood, *New Englands Prospect*, 63, 65.

32. On this point see Lois Green Carr, Russell R. Menard, and Lorena S. Walsh, *Robert Cole's World: Agriculture and Society in Early Maryland* (Chapel Hill, 1991), 71; and Laurel Thatcher Ulrich, *Good Wives: Image and Reality in the Lives of Women in Northern New England, 1650–1750* (New York, 1982), 28.

33. Barlowe, *First Voyage Made to the Coastes of America*, in Quinn, *Roanoke Voyages*, 1:98–99; Sir Walter Ralegh, *The History of the World* (London, 1614), bk. 1, chap. 8, 175–76.

34. Williams, *Key into the Language of America*, A4, 52, 59; 145, 151, 204 [misnumbered 137, 143, 196].

35. Bradford and Winslow, *Mourt's Relation*, 34; Gabriel Archer, *The Relation of Captaine Gosnols Voyage to the North part of Virginia*, 1602, in Quinn and Quinn, *English New England Voyages*, 117; Edward Winslow, *Good Newes from New England* (London, 1624), 60; Wood, *New Englands Prospect*, 65; Morton, *New English Canaan*, 22; Strachey, *Historie of Travell*, 73.

36. Smith, *Map of Virginia*, 161; Strachey, *Historie of Travell*, 73; Wood, *New Englands Prospect*, 65; Martin Pringe, *A Voyage Set Out from the Citie of Bristoll*, 1603, in Quinn and Quinn, *English New England Voyages*, 222. On the colonization of Ireland as a model for American ventures see James Muldoon, "The Indian as Irishman," *Essex*

Institute Historical Collections 111 (1975): 267–89; Nicholas Canny, "The Ideology of English Colonization: From Ireland to America," *William and Mary Quarterly*, 3d ser., 30 (1973): 575–98; and H. C. Porter, *The Inconstant Savage: England and the North American Indian, 1500–1660* (London, 1979), 202–3. Alden Vaughan argues that the Irish example was only incidental in English descriptions of the American Indians; "Early English Paradigms for New World Natives," *Proceedings of the American Antiquarian Society* 102 (1992): 46–50. For discussion of the issues involved in Irish and American colonies, see Nicholas Canny, *Kingdom and Colony: Ireland in the Atlantic World, 1560–1800* (Baltimore, 1988), esp. chap. 1.

37. Jesuit Letter, 1639, in *Narratives of Early Maryland, 1633–1684*, ed. Clayton Colman Hall (New York, 1910), 125.

38. H. R. McIlwaine, ed., *Minutes of the Council and General Court of Colonial Virginia, 1622–1632, 1670–1676* (Richmond, 1924), 194–95. On the lines of authority in interpretation of Hall's case see Kathleen Brown, "'Changed . . . into the fashion of man': The Politics of Sexual Difference in a Seventeenth-Century Anglo-American Settlement," *Journal of the History of Sexuality* 6 (1995): 171–93; and Mary Beth Norton, *Founding Mothers and Fathers: Gendered Power and the Forming of American Society* (New York, 1996), pt. 2, "Prologue." For similar cases in the early modern period, see Stephen Greenblatt, "Fiction and Friction," in *Shakespearean Negotiations: The Circulation of Social Energy in Renaissance England* (Berkeley, 1988), 73–80.

39. During the 1640s parliamentarian pamphleteers ridiculed the long hair affected by the "cavaliers"; see Tamsyn Williams, "'Magnetic Figures': Polemical Prints of the English Revolution," in Gent and Llewellyn, *Renaissance Bodies*, 93–94.

40. On Ireland, see Ann Rosalind Jones and Peter Stallybrass, "Dismantling Irena: The Sexualizing of Ireland in Early Modern England," in *Nationalisms and Sexualities*, ed. Andrew Parker et al. (London, 1992), 157–71. Jones and Stallybrass argue that English analysts saw Irish life as deficient in order because the mantle was worn by all classes and both genders (165–66).

41. Strachey, *Historie of Travell*, 73–74; Brereton, *Discoverie of the North part of Virginia*, 157–58; Wood, *New Englands Prospect*, 63; Henry Spelman, "Relation of Virginea," c. 1613, in *Travels and Works of Captain John Smith*, ed. E. Arber and A. G. Bradley, 2 vols. (Edinburgh, 1910), cxiii; Purchas, *Purchas His Pilgrimage*, 3d ed., 954; Francis Higginson, *New-Englands Plantation*, 1630, in Force, *Tracts*, 2:12; Brathwait, *English Gentlewoman*, 24.

42. Theodore Stern, "Chickahominy: The Changing Culture of a Virginia Indian Community," *Proceedings of the American Philosophical Society* 96 (1952): 200.

43. Williams, *Key into the Language of America*, 29; Morton, *New English Canaan*, 23; Strachey, *Historie of Travell*, 114; Winslow, *Good Newes from New England*, 59; Percy, "Observations Gathered out of a Discourse," 142. On this point see Kathleen J. Bragdon, *Native People of Southern New England, 1500–1650* (Norman, Okla., 1996), 171–72.

44. Roger Williams to John Winthrop, June 7, 1638, in *The Correspondence of Roger Williams*, ed. Glenn W. LaFantasie, 2 vols. (Hanover, N.H., 1988), 1:161. Winslow, *Good Newes from New England*, 58. William Prynne, *The Unlovelinesse, of Love-Locks* (London, 1628), argued that in ancient times English people had cut their hair in sign of grief, and suggested they should do so in the 1620s because of the grievous situation into which England had fallen (61).

45. John Smith, *The Generall Historie of Virginia, New-England and the Summer Isles*, 1624, in Barbour, *Works*, 2:173; Wood, *New Englands Prospect*, 64.

46. Brereton, *Discoverie of the North part of Virginia*, 158.

47. Barlowe, *First Voyage Made to the Coastes of Virginia*, in Quinn, *Roanoke Voyages*, 1:102.

48. Bradford and Winslow, *Mourt's Relation*, 11–12.

49. Barlowe, *First Voyage Made to the Coastes of Virginia*, in Quinn, *Roanoke Voyages*, 1:111–12. For oral traditions of prophecies of the coming of Europeans, see William Simmons, *The Spirit of the New England Tribes: Indian History and Folklore, 1620–1984* (Hanover, N.H., 1986), 67–72; and Colin Calloway, ed., *The World Turned Upside Down: Indian Voices from Early America* (Boston, 1994), 32–42. I thank the members of the McNeil Center seminar for raising this issue and especially Kathleen Brown and Bruce Dorsey for their suggestions.

50. Pringe, *Voyage Set Out from Bristoll*, 221; Brereton, *Discoverie of the North part of Virginia*, 157; Strachey, *Historie of Travell*, 70. "Sodden" meant stewed.

51. Strachey, *Historie of Travell*, 70; Smith, *Map of Virginia*, 160; Gabriel Archer, *A Breif discription of the People*, 1607, in Barbour, *Jamestown Voyages*, 1:103; Wood, *New Englands Prospect*, 62–63. Strachey cited John Smith as his source. On the introduction of "red" to describe the Americans see Wesley Frank Craven, *White, Red, and Black: The Seventeenth-Century Virginian* (Charlottesville, 1971), 39–42; Alden T. Vaughan, "From White Man to Redskin: Changing Anglo-American Perceptions of the American Indian," *American Historical Review* 87 (1982): 917–53. Nancy Shoemaker argues that Indians themselves adopted the label red in the early eighteenth century; "How the Indians Got to be Red," *American Historical Review* 102 (1997): 625–44.

52. Ralph Hamor, *A True Discourse of the Present Estate of Virginia* (London, 1615), 44.

53. Wood, *New Englands Prospect*, 62–63; Pringe, *Voyage Set Out from Bristoll*, 221; Strachey, *Historie of Travell*, 70.

54. Speed, *History of Great Britaine*, 180–82.

55. Bradford and Winslow, *Mourt's Relation*, 33; Crashaw, "Epistle Dedicatorie," A2v–A3v; Fr. Andrew White, *A Briefe Relation of the Voyage unto Maryland*, 1634, in Hall, *Narratives of Early Maryland*, 42. See also color as persuasiveness in David Norbrook, "Rhetoric, Ideology and the Elizabethan World Picture," in *Renaissance Rhetoric*, ed. Peter Mack (London, 1994), 140–64, esp. 149.

56. White, *Briefe Relation of the Voyage unto Maryland*, 42; Strachey, *Historie of Travell*, 71.

57. Williams, *Key into the Language of America*, 43, 52, 165, 192 [misnumbered 157, 184].

58. Strachey, *Historie of Travell*, 70–71. On control and creativity in the face-painting debate see Frances E. Dolan, "Taking the Pencil Out of God's Hand: Art, Nature, and the Face-Painting Debate in Early Modern England," *PMLA* 108 (1993): 224–39. Many English authors wrote against the use of cosmetics by English women; see Lucy Gent, *Picture and Poetry, 1560–1620: Relations between Literature and the Visual Arts in the English Renaissance* (Leamington Spa, England, 1981), 7–8. One notable example occurs in Prynne, *Unlovelinesse, of Love-Locks*, who argued that the "Meretricious, Execrable, and Odious Art of Face-painting" was insulting to God, as implying that he was a bungling or unskilfull workman (2).

59. J. Canne, *The Discoverer* (London, 1649), 32. I owe this source to Paul Hardacre.

60. Percy, "Observations Gathered out of a Discourse," 136–37, 142. Similar reports came from New England; see, for example, the description of the "Antick" designs painted on the faces of Massasoit's train in Bradford and Winslow, *Mourt's Relation*, 38.

61. Ellen Chirelstein, "Lady Elizabeth Pope: The Heraldic Body," in Gent and Llewellyn, *Renaissance Bodies*, 36–59.

62. Joaneath Spicer, "The Renaissance Elbow," in *A Cultural History of Gesture*, ed. Jan Bremmer and Herman Roodenburg (Ithaca, N.Y. 1991), 84–128. The queen was virtually alone among women in being painted in this posture.

63. John Bulwer, *Chirologia: or the Naturall Language of the Hand . . . Whereunto is added Chironomia: or the Art of Manuall Rhetoricke*, 2 vols. (London, 1644), "The Apochrypha of Action," sec. 9, 219.

64. Endecott to John Winthrop, April 12, 1631, *Winthrop Papers*, 3:25.

65. Francis Bacon, *The Advancement of Learning*, bk. 6, chap. 1, in *The Works of Francis Bacon*, ed. J. Spedding, R. L. Ellis, and D. D. Heath, 14 vols. (London, 1857–74), 3:400, 4:440.

66. On this convention see Chirelstein, "Lady Elizabeth Pope" (the quote is from p. 38). See Brathwait, *English Gentlewoman*, 42: "Chastity is an inclosed Garden."

67. Harriot notes in Quinn, *Roanoke Voyages*, 1:438–39; Smith, *Map of Virginia*, 150; Smith, *Generall Historie*, 106–7, 261. On the reception of Pocahontas, see Karen Robertson, "Pocahontas at the Masque," *Signs* 21 (1996): 551–83.

68. The list of the pictures with Harriot's notes are in Quinn, *Roanoke Voyages*, 1:390–462 (the quotes are from pp. 441, 443). On marks of status in New England, see Bragdon, *Native People of Southern New England*, 170–75.

69. Arthur Barlowe, *First Voyage Made to the Coastes of America*, in Quinn, *Roanoke Voyages*, 1:103.

70. Harriot notes in Quinn, *Roanoke Voyages*, 1:438–39.

71. Williams, *Key into the Language of America*, 157 [misnumbered 149].

72. Smith, *Map of Virginia*, 161. Rats had been introduced inadvertently by the colonists.

73. Wood, *New Englands Prospect*, 66.

74. Archer, *Breif discription of the People*, 91–92.

75. On this point see Robertson, "Pocahontas at the Masque," 568–73.

76. Robert Fabian, "Chronicle," in Richard Hakluyt, *Principal Navigations*, 7:155. In Ben Jonson's *Irish Masque at Court* (1613), New English leaders are restored to civility just by doffing their Irish cloaks; see Lisa Jardine, "Mastering the Uncouth: Gabriel Harvey, Edmund Spenser and the English Experience in Ireland," in *New Perspectives on Renaissance Thought: Essays in the History of Science, Education, and Philosophy in Memory of Charles B. Schmitt*, ed. John Henry and Sarah Hutton (London, 1990), 68–69.

77. Smith, *Generall Historie*, 237. For William Parker, see note 52 above.

78. Williams, *Key into the Language of America*, A4v.

79. Edward Howes to John Winthrop, Jr., March 1632, in *Winthrop Papers*, 3:74; The English Province of the Society of Jesus, Annual Letter from Maryland, 1639, in Hall, *Narratives of Early Maryland*, 127; White, *Briefe Relation of the Voyage unto Maryland*, 44.

80. See also the case of Captain John Underhill, who had been expelled from Massachusetts Bay for his challenges to the religious order. To signal his newfound humility when he sought readmission he "came in his worst clothes (being accustomed to take great pride in his bravery and neatness) without a band, in a foul linen cap pulled close to his eyes." John Winthrop, *The Journal of John Winthrop, 1630–1649*, ed. Richard S. Dunn, James Savage, and Laetitia Yeandle (Cambridge, Mass., 1996), 334–35; Cushman, *Sermon Preached in Plimmoth*, A4.

81. Williams, *Key into the Language of America*, 121 [misnumbered 113²].

82. Hamor, *True Discourse of the Present Estate of Virginia*, 11–15; Sir Thomas Dale, "To the R. and my most esteemed friend, M. D. M. Smith," 1614, in Purchas, *Pilgrimes*, 19:106–7; Smith, *Map of Virginia*, 146; Strachey, *Historie of Travell*, 69. For Chickahominy history and modern situation, see Stern, "Chickahominy," 157–225.

83. Virginia Council to Virginia Company, April 4, 1623, in *Records of the Virginia Company of London*, ed. Susan Myra Kingsbury, 4 vols. (Washington, D.C., 1906–35), 4:98; Bradford and Winslow, *Mourt's Relation*, 32–36, 50–53. Inga Clendinnen cites similar gestures by Moctezuma in the earlier Spanish-Mexican confrontation: see "Cortés, Signs and the Conquest of Mexico: Models of the Conquest," in Grafton and Blair, *Transmission of Culture*, 94–95.

84. Williams, *Key into the Language of America*, 166 [misnumbered 158].

85. Barlowe, *First Voyage Made to the Coastes of America*, in Quinn, *Roanoke Voyages*, 1:101.

86. Spelman, "Relation of Virginea," cv, cxii; Helen C. Rountree, *The Powhatan Indians of Virginia: Their Traditional Culture* (Norman, Okla., 1989), 109–12.

87. George Chapman, *Masque of the Middle Temple and Lincoln's Inn*, 1613, in *The Plays and Poems of George Chapman*, ed. Thomas Marc Parrott (London, 1914), 2:435–60, 823–29; Gent and Llewellyn, *Renaissance Bodies*, 36–59.

88. Higginson, *New-Englands Plantation*, 12; Purchas, *Purchas His Pilgrimage*, 3d ed., 954; Williams, "'Magnetic Figures,'" 93–94. On Essex see Aileen Ribeiro, *Dress and Morality* (New York, 1986), 78. For Southampton see the frontispiece portrait in G. P. V. Akrigg, *Shakespeare and the Earl of Southampton* (Cambridge, Mass., 1968); and Rowland Whyte to Sir Robert Sydney, January 21, 1598, in Historical Manuscripts Commission, Report on the Manuscripts of Lord de L'Isle and Dudley, ser. 77 (London, 1934), 2:311–12. I thank Katherine Duncan-Jones for pointing out the Southampton incident to me. Margaret Holmes Williamson argues that the assymetrical hair of Powhatan men was meant to indicate a nature that combined male and female elements; "Powhatan Hair," *Man*, n.s., 14 (1979): 392–413. I thank Cynthia Van Zandt for bringing this source to my attention.

89. Brathwait, *English Gentlewoman*, 24.

90. Prynne, *Unlovelinesse, of Love-Locks*, "To the Christian Reader," 4–8, 25, 32; Williams, *Key into the Language of America*, 49, 193 [misnumbered 185].

91. Vincent, *True Relation*, sig. B.

92. Williams, *Key into the Language of America*, 53.

93. William Crashaw, *A Sermon Preached in London before the right honourable the Lord Lawarre* (London, 1610), 35.

94. On these early years in Jamestown see Martin H. Quitt, "Trade and Acculturation at Jamestown, 1607–1609: The Limits of Understanding," *William and Mary Quarterly* 3d ser., 52 (1995): 227–58.

Chapter 3. Indian Polities

1. Henry Spelman, "Relation of Virginea," c. 1613, in *Travels and Works of Captain John Smith*, ed. E. Arber and A. G. Bradley, 2 vols. (Edinburgh, 1910), ci–cxiv (the quote is from pp. cx–cxi). For Spelman's background see Captain John Smith, *The Generall Historie of Virginia, New-England and the Summer Isles*, 1624, in *The Complete Works of Captain John Smith*, ed. Philip L. Barbour, 3 vols. (Chapel Hill, 1986), 2:236; J. Frederick Fausz, "Middlemen in Peace and War: Virginia's Earliest Indian Interpreters, 1608–1632," *Virginia Magazine of History and Biography* 95 (1987): 41–64. For Spelman's great-uncle's will disinheriting him in 1613, see Lothrop Withington, "Virginia Gleanings in England," *Virginia Magazine of History and Biography* 15 (1907–1908): 305.

2. On the Wild Man theme, see Richard Bernheimer, *Wild Men in the Middle Ages: A Study in Art, Sentiment, and Demonology* (Cambridge, Mass., 1952); Hayden White, "The Forms of Wildness: Archaeology of an Idea," in *The Wild Man Within: An Image in Western Thought from the Renaissance to Romanticism*, ed. Edward Dudley and Maximillian E. Novak (Pittsburgh, 1972), 3–38; Alden Vaughan, "Early English Paradigms for New World Natives," *Proceedings of the American Antiquarian Society* 102 (1992): 34–40.

3. Robert Johnson, *Nova Brittania*, 1609, in *Tracts and Other Papers, Relating Principally to the Origin, Settlement, and Progress of the Colonies in North America*, comp. Peter Force, 4 vols. (1844; Washington, D.C., 1963), 1:11.

4. Early illustrators used stock wild-folk images in depictions of the Americans, but these were subtly adapted as reports multiplied. See Susi Colin, "The Wild Man and the Indian in Early 16th Century Book Illustration," in *Indians and Europe: An Interdisciplinary Collection of Essays*, ed. Christian F. Feest (Aachen, 1987), 5–36.

5. Wilson, preface to *The Arte of Rhetorique* (London, 1553), 9–12; Henry Peacham, *The Garden of Eloquence*, rev. ed. (London, 1593), sig. AB, iii r–v. On the centrality of language in human society, see Quentin Skinner, *Reason and Rhetoric in the Philosophy of Hobbes* (Cambridge, 1996), Peacham reference on 94; Anthony Pagden, *The Fall of Natural Man: The American Indian and the Origins of Comparative Ethnology* (Cambridge, 1982), 15–26; Jonathan Bate, "The Humanist Tempest," in *Shakespeare: La Tempête, Etudes Critiques, Actes du Colloque de Besançon* (1993); and Stephen Greenblatt, "Learning to Curse: Aspects of Linguistic Colonialism in the Sixteenth Century," in *Learning To Curse: Essays in Early Modern Culture* (New York, 1990), 16–39, esp. 18–20. On the role of rhetoric in shaping the colonization literature, see Andrew Fitzmaurice, "Classical Rhetoric in the Literature of Discovery, 1570–1630" (Ph.D. diss., Cambridge University, 1995).

6. Harriot, *A Briefe and True Report of the new found land of Virginia,* in *Roanoke Voyages, 1584–1590,* ed. David Beers Quinn, 2 vols. (London, 1955), 1:317–87.

7. Roger Williams, *Key into the Language of America* (London, 1643), 84; Gordon Brotherston, "A Controversial Guide to the Language of America, 1643," in *1642: Literature and Power in the Seventeenth Century,* ed. Francis Barker et al. (Colchester, Essex, 1981), 84–100.

8. Genesis 11.1–9 and marginal commentary in the Geneva Bible (1560).

9. On the impact of American flora and fauna on European natural history categories, see Henry Lowood, "The New World and the European Catalog of Nature," in *America in European Consciousness, 1493–1750,* ed. Karen Ordahl Kupperman (Chapel Hill, 1995), 295–323; on interest in the nature of language after Babel, see Paul Cornelius, *Languages in Seventeenth- and Early Eighteenth-Century Imaginary Voyages* (Geneva, 1965), chap. 1; and Jane Donawerth, *Shakespeare and the Sixteenth-Century Study of Language* (Urbana, 1984), chap. 1.

10. Williams, "Directions for the use of the Language," in *Key into the Language of America,* n.p.

11. Vivian Salmon, "Thomas Harriot (1560–1621) and the English Origins of Algonkian Linguistics," *Historiographia Linguistica* 19 (1992): 25–56, quotes 26, 33. Salmon describes the twentieth-century rediscovery of Harriot's manuscripts and the process through which their true significance became recognized. See also Vivian Salmon, *Thomas Harriot and the English Origins of Algonkian Linguistics,* The Durham Thomas Harriot Seminar, Occasional Paper No. 8 (1993). On Harriot and his scientific work more generally, see John W. Shirley, *Thomas Harriott: A Biography* (Oxford, 1983); and John W. Shirley, ed., *Thomas Harriott: Renaissance Scientist* (Oxford, 1974). Shirley discusses Harriot's system for recording speech in *Harriott: A Biography,* pp. 107–12.

12. Edward Howes to John Winthrop, Jr., April 1632, in *Winthrop Papers,* 3:77; Samuel Hartlib, *Ephemerides,* 1635, part 4, c, October 1635, *Hartlib Papers* CD-ROM (Ann Arbor, 1994), folio 29 / 3 / 40B; Andrew Clark, ed., *"Brief Lives," chiefly of Contemporaries, set down by John Aubrey,* 2 vols. (Oxford, 1898), 1:285. On Harriot and Warner see Shirley, *Harriott: A Biography,* 4–7, chap. 9; on financial arrangements see Mark Nicholls, "'As Happy a Fortune as I Desire': The Pursuit of Financial Security by the Younger Brothers of Henry Percy, 9th Earl of Northumberland," *Historical Research* 65 (1992): 296–314. I thank Walter Woodward and Scott Mandelbrote for their help on these points.

13. *New Englands First Fruits* (London, 1643), 4; Comenius, *Porta Linguarum, The Gate of Tongues Unlocked and Opened* (London, 1631, 1637); Beck, *The Universal* CHARACTER (London, 1657), "To the Reader," prefatory verse. See Murray Cohen, *Sensible Words: Linguistic Practice in England, 1640–1785* (Baltimore, 1977), chap. 1; and Jean-Antoine Caravolas, "Comenius (Komensky) and the Theory of Language Teaching," *Acta Comeniana* 10 (1993): 141–62.

14. On the search for a philosophical universal language, which would represent fundamental knowledge authentically, see Robert Markley, "'*Babel* Revers'd': Real Characters, Philosophical Languages, and Idealizations of Order," chap. 2 of *Fallen Languages: Crises of Representation in Newtonian England, 1660–1740* (Ithaca, N.Y., 1993), 63–94; Umberto Eco, *The Search for the Perfect Language*, trans. James Fentress (Oxford, 1995), esp. chaps. 1, 8, 10; M. M. Slaughter, *Universal Languages and Scientific Taxonomy in the Seventeenth Century* (Cambridge, 1982); Gerard F. Strasser, "Closed and Open Languages: Samuel Hartlib's Involvement with Cryptology and Universal Languages," in *Samuel Hartlib and Universal Reformation: Studies in Intellectual Communication*, ed. Mark Greengrass, Michael Leslie, and Timothy Raylor (Cambridge, 1994), 151–61; Jana Prívratská and Vladimír Prívratsky, "Language as the Product and Mediator of Knowledge: The Concept of J. A. Comenius," in ibid., 162–73; James Knowlson, *Universal Language Schemes in England and France, 1600–1800* (Toronto, 1975); and Cornelius, *Languages in Imaginary Voyages*, chap. 6. On mathematics as a universal language see also Dilwyn Knox, "Ideas on Gesture and Universal Languages, c. 1550–1650," in *New Perspectives on Renaissance Thought: Essays in the History of Science, Education, and Philosophy in Memory of Charles B. Schmitt*, John Henry and Sarah Hutton (London, 1990), 128–29. Cave Beck proposed forming words with arabic numerals so that names for a thing would be written in the same way in all languages.

15. Dilwyn Knox, "Ideas on Gesture and Universal Languages, c. 1550–1650," in Henry and Hutton, *New Perspectives on Renaissance Thought*, 101–36; see also Stephen Greenblatt, *Marvelous Possessions: The Wonder of the New World* (Chicago, 1991), 92–94.

16. James Rosier, *A True Relation of the most prosperous voyage . . . in the Discovery of the land of Virginia*, in *The English New England Voyages, 1602–1608*, ed. David B. Quinn and Alison M. Quinn (London, 1983), 270, 273.

17. Bulwer, *Chirologia: Or the Naturall Language of the Hand . . . Whereunto is added Chironomia: Or, the Art of Manuall Rhetorique*, 1644, ed. James W. Cleary (Carbondale, 1974), 12. Jo. Harmarus may have been related to Ambrose Harmer and Charles Harmer, both burgesses in Virginia during the early period.

18. Williams, *Key into the Language of America*, 1–2.

19. Samuel Purchas, *Purchas His Pilgrimage*, 3d ed. (London, 1617), 1002.

20. Ben Jonson, *Timber: Or, Discoveries; Made upon Men and Matter: As they have flow'd out of his daily Readings; or had their refluxe to his peculiar Notion of the times*, 1640, reprinted in *Ben Jonson*, ed. C. H. Herford, Percy Simpson, and Evelyn Simpson, 11 vols. (Oxford, 1925–52), 8:625. Jonson drew on *De Ratione Discendi* by Juan Luis Vives (1555) in this passage, 11:270. Books on the criminal underworld included wordlists of their slang as a way to understanding that culture, just as Prince Hal studied the language of ordinary people in Shakespeare's *Henry IV*, part 1; see Stephen Greenblatt, "Invisible Bullets," in *Shakespearean Negotiations: The Circulation of Social Energy in Renaissance England* (Berkeley: University of California Press, 1988), 48–50.

21. Peter Wynne to Sir John Egerton, November 26, 1608, in *The Jamestown Voyages under the First Charter, 1606–1609*, ed. Philip L. Barbour, 2 vols. (Cambridge, 1969), 1:245–46. William Strachey, citing the research of William Camden, argued that Madoc's venture gave the British a claim to America under European law; Strachey, *The Historie of Travell into Virginia Britania*, 1612, ed. Louis B. Wright and Virginia Freund (London, 1953), 11–12.

22. Harriot, *Briefe and True Report*, 370. The phrase "confused tongues" comes from the non-eyewitness Robert Johnson in his *The New Life of Virginea: Declaring the former successe and present estate of that plantation*, 1612, in Force, *Tracts*, 1:8.

23. Christopher Levett, *A Voyage unto New England* (London, 1624), 22; William Wood, *New Englands Prospect* (London, 1634), 92.

24. Robert Cushman, *A Sermon Preached in Plimmoth in New-England* (London, 1622), 18; William Bradford, *Of Plymouth Plantation, 1620–1647,* ed. Samuel Eliot Morison (New York, 1952), 16.

25. Nebrija's comment is in Lewis Hanke, *Aristotle and the American Indians: A Study of Race Prejudice in the Modern World* (London, 1959), 8, 127 n. 31. On the consolidation of standard languages in Europe at this time see Benedict Anderson, *Imagined Communities: Reflections on the Origin and Spread of Nationalism,* rev. ed. (London, 1991), chap. 3.

26. William Harrison, *The Description of England,* ed. Georges Edelen (Ithaca, N.Y., 1968), 411–18; Richard Verstegan, *A Restitution of Decayed Intelligence: In antiquities. Concerning the most noble and renowned English nation* (Antwerp, 1605), 204. I thank Edward Gray for bringing Harrison to my attention. On concern about the status of English see Steven Mullaney, *The Place of the Stage: License, Play, and Power in Renaissance England* (Chicago, 1988), 76–80; and R. F. Jones, *The Triumph of the English Language* (Stanford, 1966), chap 1.

27. Richard Eburne, *A Plain Pathway to Plantations,* 1624, ed. Louis B. Wright (Ithaca, N.Y., 1962), 137.

28. John Smith, *A Map of Virginia,* 1612, in Barbour, *Works,* 1:150.

29. Ives Goddard, "The Use of Pidgins and Jargons on the East Coast of North America," in *The Language Encounter in the Americas,* ed. Edward Gray and Norman Fiering (Berghahn Books, forthcoming). See also T. J. Brasser, "Early Indian-European Contacts," in *Handbook of North American Indians,* ed. William C. Sturtevant, vol. 15, *Northeast,* ed. Bruce G. Trigger (Washington, D.C., 1978), 86. On the development and dissemination of a "lingua franca" in the St. Lawrence region and down into Maine, see Bruce J. Bourque and Ruth H. Whitehead, "Trade and Alliances in the Contact Period," in *American Beginnings: Exploration, Culture, and Cartography in the Land of Norumbega,* ed. Emerson W. Baker et al. (Lincoln, Neb. 1994), 137–39.

30. Michaëlius, "Letter of Reverend Jonas Michaëlius," 1628, in *Narratives of New Netherland, 1609–1664,* ed. J. Franklin Jameson (New York, 1909), 128.

31. Edward Winslow, *Good Newes from New England* (London, 1624), 61. See also Thomas Morton, *New English Canaan,* 1637, in Force, *Tracts,* 2:16–17.

32. Harrison, *Description of England,* 416; John Brereton, *A Briefe and true Relation of the Discoverie of the North part of Virginia,* in Quinn and Quinn, *English New England Voyages,* 158; Wood, *New Englands Prospect,* 91; Winslow, *Good Newes from New England,* 28. Michaëlius also wrote of the extreme difficulty of pronunciation; "Letter," 128.

33. On the search for terms for universal concepts see Slaughter, *Universal Languages and Scientific Taxonomy,* "Introduction."

34. Smith, *Map of Virginia,* 136–39. Wordlists were also included in William Wood's, *New Englands Prospect,* O2–O4, and as an appendix to Rosier's *True Relation,* 310–11.

35. Levett, *Voyage unto New England,* 22; Wood, *New Englands Prospect,* 92. On evidence for a pidgin English see Goddard, "Use of Pidgins and Jargons." Michael A. Gomez demonstrates that African slaves created a version of English for themselves; *Exchanging our Country Marks: The Transformation of African Identities in the Colonial and Antebellum South* (Chapel Hill, 1998), 170–81.

36. Williams, "Directions for the use of the Language," n.p., and 130 [misnumbered 122]. Ives Goddard has assessed Williams's progress in learning the complexities of Narragansett in "Use of Pidgins and Jargons." Christopher L. Miller and George R. Hamell point out that Frank Speck, researching among the Montagnais-Naskapis in the early twentieth century, found that their word for mirror resembled Williams's findings:

"see-soul-metal"; Speck, *Naskapi: The Savage Hunters of the Labrador Peninsula* (1935; reprint, Norman, Okla., 1977), 33; Miller and Hamell, "A New Perspective on Indian-White Contact: Cultural Symbols and Colonial Trade," *Journal of American History* 73 (1986): 317.

37. Williams, *Key into the Language of America*, "Directions for the Use of the Language," 2; 54–61; 131–34 [misnumbered 123–26]; Wood, *New Englands Prospect*, 92; Ives Goddard and Kathleen Bragdon, eds., *Native Writings in Massachusett*, 2 vols. (Philadelphia, 1988); and Elizabeth A. Little, ed., *Nantucket Indian Studies*, nos. 3 and 7 (Nantucket, 1981). Richard W. Cogley identifies Williams as the preacher whose language competence Wood praised in 1634; Cogley, *John Eliot's Mission to the Indians before King Philip's War* (Cambridge, Mass., 1999), 8.

38. Smith, *Generall Historie*, 148–49, 250; Ralph Hamor, *A True Discourse of the Present Estate of Virginia* (London, 1615), 45. For recent discussions of whether the power of writing contributed to the notion that Europeans had magical powers, see James Axtell, *The Invasion Within: The Contest of Cultures in Colonial North America* (Oxford, 1985), and "The Power of Print in the Eastern Woodlands," in *After Columbus: Essays in the Ethnohisory of Colonial North America*, ed. James Axtell (Oxford, 1988), 86–99; Peter Wogan, "Perceptions of European Literacy in Early Contact Situations," *Ethnohistory* 41 (1994): 407–30.

39. George Percy, "Observations Gathered out of a Discourse of the Plantation of the Southerne Colonie in Virginia by the English," in Barbour, *Jamestown Voyages*, 1:94.

40. Williams, *Key into the Language of America*, 22–26, 34, 62–67; 80, 178 [misnumbered 86, 170]; William Morrell, *New England* (London, 1625), 23; Winslow, *Good Newes from New England*, 60; Rosier, *True Relation*, 302; Council in Virginia to Virginia Company of London, January 1622, in *Records of the Virginia Company of London*, ed. Susan Myra Kingsbury, 4 vols. (Washington, D.C., 1906–35), 3:584. In the twentieth century Frank G. Speck recorded a Penobscot legend about the Great Bear constellation (the big dipper) and its relation to the little dipper; "Penobscot Tales and Religious Beliefs," *Journal of American Folklore* 48 (1935): 19–20.

41. John Pory, "Observations," in Smith, *Generall Historie*, 291; Purchas, "Occurrents in Virginia, 1613–1619," in *Hakluytus Posthumus or Purchas His Pilgrimes*, 1625, 20 vols. (Glasgow, 1906), 19:118–19. Mohegans Gladys Tantaquidgeon and Jayne Fawcett analyze the message of a beaded belt whose ownership is recorded back to Martha Uncas in 1770 in "Symbolic Motifs on Painted Baskets of the Mohegan-Pequot," in *Rooted Like the Ash Trees: New England Indians and the Land*, ed. Richard G. Carlson, rev. ed. (Naugatuck, Conn., 1987), 50–51.

42. Cornelius Tacitus, *The Description of Germanie: and Customes of the People*, trans. Richard Grenewey (London, 1598), 258. On discussion among contemporary scholars see *The New Science of Giambattista Vico*, trans. Thomas Goddard Bergin and Max Harold Fisch (Ithaca, N.Y., 1968), paras. 470, 841; J. H. M. Salmon, "Seneca and Tacitus in Jacobean England," in *The Mental World of the Jacobean Court*, ed. Linda Levy Peck (Cambridge, 1991), 169–88; and Donald R. Kelley, "*Tacitus Noster*: The *Germania* in the Renaissance and Reformation," in *Tacitus and the Tacitean Tradition*, ed. T. J. Luce and A. J. Woodman (Princeton, 1993), 165–66.

43. Harriot, *Briefe and True Report*, 373; John Lederer, *The Discoveries of John Lederer* (London, 1672), 3–5; John Lawson, *A New Voyage to Carolina*, ed. Hugh Talmage Lefler (Chapel Hill, 1967), 45; Melissa Jayne Fawcett, *The Lasting of the Mohegans: The Story of the Wolf People* (Uncasville, Conn., 1995), 23; Margo Lukens, "'I am from Mohegan! I am not Pequot': Cultural persistence in the Diary of Fidelia Fielding," Darcy McNickle Center for the History of the American Indian, *Occasional Papers in Curriculum*, no. 20 (Chicago, 1996), 243–57. I thank Susan Danforth for pointing out the similarity of the annual peregrination to Indian structures. On memory systems see Frances A. Yates, *The*

Art of Memory (Chicago, 1966); Jonathan D. Spence, *The Memory Palace of Matteo Ricci* (New York, 1984), 1–23; and Mullaney, *The Place of the Stage,* 16–17.

44. Verstegan, *A Restitution of Decayed Intelligence,* 211; John Ferne, *The Blazon of the Gentrie* (London, 1586), 25–26. I owe this reference to Richard Cust.

45. Edward Bland, *The Discovery of New Brittaine* (London, 1651), 8–9. Bland's party later encountered great piles of bones that commemorated the dead from Opechancanough's attack; ibid., 12. I owe this reference to Nancy Shoemaker.

46. Winslow, *Good Newes from New England,* 61.

47. Anon., "A Description of Mashpee in the County of Barnstaple. September 16th, 1802," in *Collections of the Massachusetts Historical Society* 2d ser., 3 (1815): 7–8; Edward Augustus Kendall, *Travels through the Northern Parts of the United States in the Years 1807 and 1808* (New York, 1809), 2:48–52; Earl Mills (Mashpee Wampanoag Chief Flying Eagle) testimony 1977 in "Identity in Mashpee," chap. 12 of James Clifford, *The Predicament of Culture: Twentieth-Century Ethnography, Literature, and Art* (Cambridge, Mass., 1988), 281; Kathleen J. Bragdon, "'Emphaticall Speech and Great Action': An Analysis of Seventeenth-Century Native Speech Events Described in Early Sources," *Man in the Northeast* 33 (1987): 108; Constance A. Crosby, "The Algonkian Spiritual Landscape," in *Algonkians of New England: Past and Present,* ed. Peter Benes (Boston, 1993), 35–41.

48. Lawson, *New Voyage to Carolina,* 29, 50; William Simmons, *Spirit of the New England Tribes: Indian History and Folklore, 1620–1984* (Hanover, N.H., 1986), 23; Lederer, *Discoveries of John Lederer,* 4, 9. On the erection of memorial pyramids, see also Robert Beverley, *The History and Present State of Virginia,* ed. Louis B. Wright (Chapel Hill, 1947), 213–14; and James H. Merrell, *The Indians' New World: Catawbas and Their Neighbors from European Contact through the Era of Removal* (Chapel Hill, 1989), 26.

49. Paul Connerton, *How Societies Remember* (Cambridge, 1989), chap. 2 (the quotes are from pp. 45, 50). For a modern example of natives remembering their history through associations with landscape, see Keith H. Basso, *Wisdom Sits in Places: Landscape and Language among the Western Apache* (Albuquerque, 1996).

50. On these reports see Karen Ordahl Kupperman, "Apathy and Death in Early Jamestown," *Journal of American History* 66 (1979): 24–40; and Edmund S. Morgan, *American Slavery, American Freedom: The Ordeal of Colonial Virginia* (New York, 1975), esp. chaps. 3–4.

51. Williams, *Key into the Language of America,* 128 [misnumbered 120].

52. Virginia Company prohibitions on compounding with Indian chiefs as kings are in Kingsbury, *Records of the Virginia Company,* 2:41, 94–95. For colonists calling Powhatan and other chiefs kings, see ibid., 2:115, 482, 3:438, 4:89, 98, 102.

53. Malcolm Smuts, "Cultural Diversity and Cultural Change at the Court of James I," in Peck, *Mental World of the Jacobean Court,* 99–112; Steven Mullaney, "Brothers and Others, or the Art of Alienation," in *Cannibals, Witches, and Divorce: Estranging the Renaissance,* ed. Marjorie Garber (Baltimore, 1987), 67–89. On the theatricality of power see also Roy Strong, *Art and Power: Renaissance Festivals, 1450–1650* (Woodbridge, Suffolk: Boydell, 1984), esp. chap. 5, "Illusions of Absolutism: Charles I and the Stuart Court Masque"; and Greenblatt, "Invisible Bullets," 64–65.

54. Strachey, *Historie of Travell,* 60–61, John Smith, *A True Relation of such occurrences and accidents of noate as hath hapned in Virginia,* 1608, in Barbour, *Works,* 1:53.

55. See Frank Whigham's discussion of the "enfranchising audience," *Ambition and Privilege: The Social Tropes of Elizabethan Courtesy Theory* (Berkeley: University of California Press, 1984), chap. 2 (the quote is from p. 45).

56. Smith, *True Relation,* 65.

57. Smith, *Generall Historie,* 182–83.

58. Cleland, *Propaideia, or The Institution of a Young Noble Man* (Oxford, 1607), 179. On changing concepts of honor, see Mervyn James, *English Politics and the*

Concept of Honour, 1485–1642, Past and Present Supplement 3 (Oxford, 1978); and Richard Cust, "Honour and Politics in Early Stuart England: The Case of Beaumont v. Hastings," *Past and Present* 149 (1995): 57–94.

59. Thomas Gainsford, "Observations of State, and millitary affaires for the most parte collected out of Cornelius Tacitus," 1612, MS Huntington Lib. EL 6857, 13–15.

60. John Winthrop, *The Journal of John Winthrop, 1630–1649*, ed. Richard S. Dunn, James Savage, and Laetitia Yeandle (Cambridge, Mass., 1996), 183.

61. William Bradford and Edward Winslow, *A Relation or Journall of the English Plantation setled at Plimoth in New England* (London, 1622), known as *Mourt's Relation*, 37, 50.

62. Wood, *New Englands Prospect*, 69–74.

63. Morrell, *New England*, 18–22.

64. Andrew White, *A Briefe Relation of the Voyage unto Maryland*, 1634, in *Narratives of Early Maryland, 1633–1684*, ed. Clayton Colman Hall (New York, 1910), 44.

65. Barlowe, *The First Voyage Made to the Coastes of America*, 1584, in Quinn, *Roanoke Voyages*, 1:98–99.

66. Gabriel Archer, *A Breif discription of the People*, 1607, in Barbour, *Jamestown Voyages*, 1:92; Tacitus, *Life of Julius Agricola*, trans. Savile, 190.

67. Strachey, *Historie of Travell*, 64–65. Helen Rountree demonstrates that gathering the purple feathers necessary to make this cloak from the species present in the Chesapeake would have taken several years of work; "Powhatan Indian Women," *Ethnohistory* 45 (1998): 18–19.

68. Purchas, *Pilgrimes*, 19:118.

69. Smith, *Generall Historie*, 261.

70. J. S. A. Adamson, "The Architecture and Politics of the London Aristocratic Town House, 1590–1660," paper presented to the Huntington Early Modern British History Seminar, San Marino, Calif., October 14, 1995.

71. The English Province of the Society of Jesus, Annual Letter from Maryland, 1639, in Hall, *Narratives of Early Maryland*, 124.

72. William Powell to Sir Edwin Sandys, April 12, 1621, in Kingsbury, *Records of the Virginia Company*, 3:438; see also ibid., 174.

73. Quentin Skinner, *Foundations of Modern Political Thought* (Cambridge, 1978), 2:85–89; Roger A. Mason, "Scotching the Brut: Politics, History and National Myth in Sixteenth-Century Britain," in *Scotland and England, 1286–1815*, ed. Mason (Edinburgh, 1987), 69–70; Steven J. Gunn, "State Development in England and the Burgundian Dominions, c. 1460–c. 1560," paper delivered to the Huntington Early Modern British History Seminar, February 24, 1996.

74. Wood, *New Englands Prospect*, 80. On Erasmus, see Bate, "Humanist Tempest."

75. Williams, *Key into the Language of America*, 141, 185 [misnumbered 132, 177]. On the journey see Williams to Winthrop, September 1638, in *The Correspondence of Roger Williams*, ed. Glenn W. LaFantasie, 2 vols. (Hanover, N.H., 1988), 1:182–83.

76. Gainsford, "Observations of State . . . collected out of Cornelius Tacitus," 18; Levett, *Voyage unto New England*, 20; Hamor, *True Discourse of the Present Estate of Virginia*, 53.

77. John Smith, *The Proceedings of the English Colony in Virginia*, 1612, in Barbour, *Works*, 1:236–37.

78. Morton, *New English Canaan*, 28–29.

79. For examples see A. J. Fletcher, "Honour, Reputation and Local Officeholding in Elizabethan and Stuart England," in *Order and Disorder in Early Modern England*, ed. Anthony Fletcher and John Stevenson (Cambridge, 1985), 92–115; and Cust, "Honour and Politics," 57–94.

80. John Chamberlain, *The Letters of John Chamberlain*, ed. Norman Egbert McClure, 2 vols. (Philadelphia, 1939), 1:188.

81. The phrase "Savage Seignior" appears in Gabriel Archer, *The Relation of Captaine Gosnols Voyage to the North part of Virginia*, in *The English New England Voyages, 1602–1608*, ed. David B. Quinn and Alison M. Quinn (London, 1983), 134. Archer thought one Virginia chief tried so hard to be stately that "to our seeming he became foole." See *A relatyon of the Discovery of our River*, 1607, in Barbour, *Jamestown Voyages*, 1:92.

82. Barlowe, *First Voyage Made to the Coastes of America*, 98–103.

83. Smith, *Map of Virginia*, 174.

84. Wood, *New Englands Prospect*, 79.

85. Smith, *Map of Virginia*, 173–74; Strachey, *Historie of Travell*, 56; William W. Fitzhugh, "Commentary," in *Cultures in Contact: the Impact of European Contacts on Native American Cultural Institutions, A.D. 1000–1800*, ed. Fitzhugh (Washington, D.C., 1985), 188.

86. John Martin, "How Virginia May be Made a Royal Plantation," in Kingsbury, *Records of the Virginia Company*, 3:708. E. Randolph Turner III believes that Powhatan governed thirty-one "discrete territorial units or districts," and that he had inherited six to nine. Some of these would have been more fully integrated under Powhatan's control than others. "Native American Protohistoric Interactions in the Powhatan Core Area," in *Powhatan Foreign Relations, 1500–1722*, ed. Helen C. Rountree (Charlottesville, 1993), 76–93.

87. Smith, *Map of Virginia*, 173–74. On annual tribute, see also Strachey, *Historie of Travell*, 63, 87.

88. Spelman, "Relation of Virginea," cv, cxii; Helen C. Rountree, *The Powhatan Indians of Virginia: Their Traditional Culture* (Norman, Okla., 1989), 109–12. For a similar description of New England see Winslow, *Good Newes from New England*, 57.

89. Turner, "Protohistoric Interactions," in Rountree, *Powhatan Foreign Relations*, 76; see also Fitzhugh, "Commentary," 188–90; and Turner, "Socio-Political Organization within the Powhatan Chiefdom and the Effects of European Contact, A.D. 1607–1646," in Fitzhugh, *Cultures in Contact*, 193–224. For a full description of Powhatan government and its operation see Rountree, *Powhatan Indians*, chap. 7, epilogue; Stephen R. Potter, *Commoners, Tribute, and Chiefs: The Development of Algonquian Culture in the Potomac Valley* (Charlottesville, 1993), chaps. 1, 4; and Frederic W. Gleach, *Powhatan's World and Colonial Virginia: A Conflict of Cultures* (Lincoln, Neb., 1997), chap. 1.

90. Williams, *Key into the Language of America*, 95, 141, 176 [misnumbered 93, 133, 168].

91. Hamor, *True Discourse of the Present Estate of Virginia*, 6; Samuel Argall, "A Letter of Sir Samuell Argoll touching his voyage to Virginia," 1613, in Purchas, *Pilgrimes*, 19:93; Gorton, *Simplicities defence, against seven-headed Policy*, 1646, in Force, *Tracts*, 4:91. For deeds embodying orally transmitted memory, see Goddard and Bragdon, *Native Writings in Massachusett*; and Little, *Nantucket Indian Studies*, nos. 3 and 7. For an example of a petition revealing oral traditions of ownership, see Farmington Indians to the Connecticut General Assembly, May 13, 1672, reprinted in *Connecticut Speaks for Itself*, ed. David P. Shuldiner (Middletown, Conn., 1996), 27–28; and "State of the Indians in Mashpee," *Collections of the Massachusetts Historical Society*, 2d ser., 3 (1815): 17. See also Rountree, *Powhatan Indians*, 101.

92. Tacitus, *Description of Germanie*, 260–61; John Speed, *The History of Great Britaine* (London, 1611), 287–89. On the role of the orator, see Skinner, *Reason and Rhetoric*, chap. 2. On the German origin of English practices of sovereignty, see Paul Christianson, "Royal and Parliamentary Voices on the Ancient Constitution, c. 1604–1621," in Peck, *Mental World of the Jacobean Court*, 71–95, esp. 82–83. On Saye and the issues of the relation between parliament and monarch, see Richard Tuck, *Philosophy and Government, 1572–1651* (Cambridge, 1993), 74–75, chap. 6.

93. Williams, *Key into the Language of America*, 142 [misnumbered 134]; Trudie Lamb Richmond, "A Native Perspective of History: The Schaghticoke Nation, Resistance, and Survival," in *Enduring Traditions: The Native Peoples of New England*, ed. Laurie Weinstein (Westport, Conn., 1994), 107; and Paul A. Robinson, "A Narragansett History from 1000 B.P. to the Present," in ibid., 82–84. See also Christopher Hill, *Puritanism and Revolution: Studies in Interpretation of the English Revolution of the Seventeenth Century* (London, 1958), 63–67.

94. John Lawson, *A New Voyage to Carolina*, ed. Hugh Talmage Lefler (Chapel Hill, 1967), 204.

95. White, *Briefe Relation of the Voyage unto Maryland*, 44; Anon., *Relation of Maryland*, in Hall, *Narratives of Early Maryland*, 38–39; Wood, *New Englands Prospect*, 73; Aupaumut's description was published in Electa Jones, *Stockbridge Past and Present* (1854) and reprinted in *Native Heritage: Personal Accounts by American Indians, 1790 to the Present*, ed. Arlene Hirschfelder (New York, 1995), 92–94; Williams, *Key into the Language of America*, 48. On Aupaumut, see Alan Taylor, "Captain Hendrick Aupaumut: The Dilemmas of an Intercultural Broker," *Ethnohistory* 43 (1996): 431–57; and Jeanne Ronda and James P. Ronda, "'As they were faithful': Chief Hendrick Aupaumut and the Struggle for Stockbridge Survival, 1757–1830," *American Indian Culture and Research Journal* 33 (1979): 43–55. On the Stockbridge Mohicans, see Patrick Frazier, *The Mohicans of Stockbridge* (Lincoln, Neb., 1992).

96. Smith, *True Relation*, 61; *Map of Virginia*, 174.

97. For an overview of the issue of matrilineality, see Richard White, "What Chigabe Knew," *William and Mary Quarterly*, 3rd ser., 52 (1995): 151–56, esp. 153, and response by Carole Shammas, ibid., 163–64.

98. For Powhatan's sons and brothers as sub-werowances, see Strachey, *Historie of Travell*, 63–65, 67, 69.

99. Pory, "Observations," 290–91; Williams, *Key into the Language of America*, 140 [misnumbered 132]. The colonists believed that both Itoyatan and Opechancanough were brothers of Wahunsonacock, but some modern analysts believe the latter was a cousin. On dual chiefships see Kathleen J. Bragdon, *Native People of Southern New England, 1500–1650* (Norman, Okla., 1996), 140–42; and Gleach, *Powhatan's World and Colonial Virginia*, 3, 22–60, 140–47. On the relationship between Miantonomi and Canonicus see Paul A. Robinson, "Miantonomi and the English in Seventeenth-Century Narragansett Country," in *Northeastern Indian Lives*, ed. Robert S. Grumet (Amherst, 1996), 13–28, esp. 14.

100. For an example of a regency, see White, *Briefe Relation of the Voyage unto Maryland*, 41. On sharing power in Accomack, see Pory, "Observations," 290–91. Leonard Calvert's letter to Lord Baltimore, 1638, is in Hall, *Narratives of Early Maryland*, 150–59 (the quotes are from pp. 158–59). On the tiered system of governance in the Chesapeake, see Rountree, *Powhatan Indians*, 117–21; and Helen C. Rountree and E. Randolph Turner III, "On the Fringe of the Southeast: The Powhatan Paramount Chiefdom in Virginia," in *The Forgotten Centuries: Indians and Europeans in the American South, 1521–1704*, ed. Charles Hudson and Carmen Chaves Tesser (Athens, Ga., 1994), 364–65.

101. Digges, April 7 and 9, 1628, in *Proceedings in Parliament 1628*, ed. Robert C. Johnson et al., 6 vols. (New Haven, 1977–83), 2:330, 333–34, 5:162, 172–73, 180.

102. Levett, *Voyage unto New England*, 20; Smith, *Map of Virginia*, 174; Digges, April 7 and 9, 1628, in *Commons Debates 1628*, 2:330, 333–34, 5:162, 172–73, 180; Hamor, *True Discourse of the Present Estate of Virginia*, 11. On customary law see Donald R. Kelley, "'Second Nature': The Idea of Custom in European Law, Society, and Culture," in *The Transmission of Culture in Early Modern Europe*, ed. Anthony Grafton and Ann Blair (Philadelphia, 1990), 131–72; Christianson, "Royal and Parliamentary Voices on the Ancient Constitution," 71–95.

103. Kelley, "'Second Nature,'" 145–46.

104. Spelman, "Relation of Virginea," cx–cxi; Harriot, *Briefe and True Report*, 374–75. On what the writers witnessed, see Rountree, *Powhatan Indians*, 114.

105. Williams, *Key into the Language of America*, 144 [misnumbered 136]. Williams's friend Miantonomi would be executed in secret by his rival Uncas with the agreement of colonial leaders; see Chapter 7 below.

106. John Smith, *A Description of New England* (London, 1616), in Barbour, *Works*, 1:332.

107. Anon., *Relation of Maryland*, 32; Morrell, *New England*, 18, 22; Wood, *New Englands Prospect*, 80; Williams, *Key into the Language of America*, 76, 143 [misnumbered 135].

108. Tacitus, *Description of Germanie*, 263.

109. Felicity Heal, *Hospitality in Early Modern England* (Oxford, 1990); and Anthony Fletcher, *Gender, Sex and Subordination in England, 1500–1800* (New Haven, 1995), 136–43.

110. John Done, "To his Friend Captaine John Smith, and his Worke," in Smith, *Generall Historie*, 49; Alexander Whitaker, *Good Newes from Virginia* (London, 1613), 6–7, 11; Daniel Price, *Sauls Prohibition Staide* (London, 1609), sig. F. Richard Brathwait also drew the analogy between the self-indulgent rich and thieves; *The English Gentlewoman, drawne out to the full Body* (London, 1631), 15, 22. On cannibalism as the mark of the savage, see Peter Hulme, *Colonial Encounters: Europe and the Native Caribbean, 1492–1797* (London, 1986).

111. Williams, *Key into the Language of America*, 4, 29; Chamberlain to Sir Dudley Carleton, October 14, 1618, in Chamberlain, *Letters of John Chamberlain*, 2:170. On child vagrants sent to Virginia see Robert Hume, *Early Child Immigrants to Virginia, 1619–1642* (Baltimore, 1986); James Horn, *Adapting to a New World: English Society in the Seventeenth-Century Chesapeake* (Chapel Hill, 1994), 63–65; and Robert C. Johnson, "The Transportation of Vagrant Children from London to Virginia, 1618–1622," in *Early Stuart Studies*, ed. Howard F. Reinmuth (Minneapolis, 1970).

112. Tacitus, *Description of Germanie*, 264.

113. Williams, *Key into the Language of America*, 16.

114. Winslow, *Good Newes from New England*, 57.

115. Ibid.

116. Wood, *New Englands Prospect*, 69–72, 77–80; Aupaumut, "Teaching the Children," in Hirschfelder, *Native Heritage*, 93; Morton, *New English Canaan*, 39; Morrell, *New England*, 18–19.

117. Anon, *Relation of Maryland*, 33. See Helen C. Rountree, "Powhatans as Travelers," in *Powhatan Foreign Relations*, 39–42.

118. Barlowe, *First Voyage Made to the Coastes of America*, 107–10.

119. Barbara Donagan, "Codes and Conduct in the English Civil War," *Past and Present* 118 (1988): 74–76; Williams, *Key into the Language of America*, 76, 144 [misnumbered 136].

120. Kingsbury, *Records of the Virginia Company*, 3:228. There is no evidence to indicate whether this expedition took place. One incentive offered the Virginians was a share in the food and children that would be captured in the war; see Chapter 5 below.

121. Anon., *Relation of Maryland*, 41–43; Lawson, *New Voyage to Carolina*, 27.

122. Tacitus, *Description of Germanie*, 261, 264.

123. Francis Jennings dissects the dimensions of the savage war myth in *The Invasion of America: Indians, Colonialism, and the Cant of Conquest* (Chapel Hill, 1975), chap. 9.

124. Archer, *A Relatyon of the Discovery of our River*, 91.

125. Skinner, *Reason and Rhetoric*, 292; Smuts, "Cultural Diversity and Cultural Change," 110–11; and Malcolm Smuts, "Court-Centred Politics and the Uses of Roman

Historians," in *Culture and Politics in Early Stuart England*, ed. Kevin Sharpe and Peter Lake (Stanford, 1993), 37–38.

126. Tacitus, *Life of Julius Agricola*, 188.

127. John Mason, *A Brief History of the Pequot War*, ed. Thomas Prince (Boston, 1736), 19–20; Williams, *Key into the Language of America*, 180, 188–89 [misnumbered 180–81]; John Underhill, *Newes from America* (London, 1638), 40–43. On contrasting styles of war see Patrick M. Malone, *The Skulking Way of War: Technology and Tactics among the New England Indians* (Plimoth Plantation, 1991; Baltimore, 1993), esp. chap. 1, "The Aboriginal Military System"; and Adam J. Hirsch, "The Collision of Military Cultures in Seventeenth-Century New England," *Journal of American History* 74 (1988): 1187–1212.

128. Rountree, *Pocahontas's People*, 19–20; Spelman, "Relation of Virginea," cxiv; Williams, *Key into the Language of America*, 180, 188–89 [misnumbered 180–81].

129. Dale, "To the R. and my most esteemed friend, M. D. M. Smith," in Purchas, *Pilgrimes*, 19:103; Smith, *Map of Virginia*, 165; Winslow, *Good Newes from New England*, 58–59; Williams, *Key into the Language of America*, 72–73. On the conduct of warfare among the Powhatans see Rountree, *Powhatan Indians*, 121–24; and Gleach, *Powhatan's World and Colonial Virginia*, chap. 1.

130. Smith, *Map of Virginia*, 167; Strachey, *Historie of Travell*, 85–86.

131. Williams, *Key into the Language of America*, 186–87 [misnumbered 178–79].

132. Ibid., 179 [misnumbered 171]; Wood, *New Englands Prospect*, 73–74, 85–86; Tacitus, *Description of Germanie*, 264–65. See also Morton, *New English Canaan*, 20.

133. Strachey, *Historie of Travell*, 84; Spelman, "Relation of Virginea," cxiv.

134. For oral traditions of religious festivals see Trudie Lamb Richmond, "A Native Perspective of History," 105.

Chapter 4. The Names of God

1. *The Tempest* 1.2. The spelling is that of the first folio, 1623.

2. Owen Griffin's account was published twice, and this is a composite of the two. The first publication was in Rosier, *True Relation of the most prosperous voyage . . . in the Discovery of the land of Virginia*, in *The English New England Voyages, 1602–1608*, ed. David B. Quinn and Alison M. Quinn (London, 1983), 278, 282. When Rosier's account was reprinted in Samuel Purchas, *Hakluytus Posthumus or Purchas His Pilgrimes*, 1625, 20 vols. (Glasgow, 1906), 18:344–45, more details were added, including the description of the New Englanders' attempt to understand Griffin's worship.

3. Ralph Lane, "An extract of Master Lanes letter," in *The Roanoke Voyages, 1584–1590*, ed. David Beers Quinn, 2 vols. (London, 1955), 1:203; William Symonds, *Virginia. A Sermon Preached at White-Chappell, In the Presence of the Adventurers and Planters for Virginia* (London, 1609), A3v; Howes to Winthrop, Nov. 23 1632, in *Winthrop Papers*, 3:94.

4. John T. McNeill, ed., *John Calvin on the Christian Faith: Selections from the Institutes, Commentaries, and Tracts* (New York, 1957), 9; John Smith, *A Map of Virginia*, 1612, in *The Complete Works of Captain John Smith*, ed. Philip L. Barbour, 3 vols. (Chapel Hill, 1986), 1:168; Roger Williams, *A Key into the Language of America* (London, 1643), 67–68; William Morrell, *New England* (London, 1625), 22.

5. Richard Hakluyt, "Epistle Dedicatory to the Council of Virginia," in his translation of Hernan De Soto, *Virginia Richly Valued*, in *The Original Writings and Correspondence of the Two Richard Hakluyts*, ed. E. G. R. Taylor (London, 1935), 2:503; John Smith, *A True Relation of such occurrences and accidents of noate as hath hapned in Virginia*, 1608, in Barbour, *Works*, 1:59. The reader's marginal refutation is in the British Library copy.

6. Winslow's correction is in his *Good Newes from New England* (London, 1624), 52. His earlier letter was printed in William Bradford and Edward Winslow, *A Relation or Journall of the English Plantation setled at Plimoth in New England* (London, 1622), known as *Mourt's Relation*, 61.

7. Andrew White, *Briefe Relation of the Voyage unto Maryland*, 1634, in *Narratives of Early Maryland, 1633–1684*, ed. Clayton Colman Hall (New York, 1910), 44.

8. George Peckham, *A True Reporte of the Newfound Landes*, 1583, in *Voyages and Colonising Enterprises of Sir Humphrey Gilbert*, ed. David B. Quinn, 2 vols. (London, 1940), 2:468, 476: Robert Gordon of Lochinvar, *Encouragements to Under-takers* (Edinburgh, 1625), B3–B3v.

9. William Strachey, *The Historie of Travell into Virginia Britania*, 1612, ed. Louis B. Wright and Virginia Freund (London, 1953), 24, 90; Samuel Purchas, *Purchas His Pilgrimage*, 3d ed. (London, 1617), 987.

10. Purchas, *Purchas His Pilgrimage*, 2d ed., 766; Henry Spelman, "Relation of Virginea," c. 1613, in *Travels and Works of Captain John Smith*, ed. E. Arber and A. G. Bradley, 2 vols. (Edinburgh, 1910), 1:cv–cvi. For a modern analysis, see Helen C. Rountree, *The Powhatan Indians of Virginia: Their Traditional Culture* (Norman, Okla., 1989), 80–84.

11. Alexander Whitaker, *Good Newes from Virginia* (London, 1613), 24; Purchas, *Purchas His Pilgrimage*, 3d ed., 952–55.

12. Smith, *The Generall Historie of Virginia, New-England and the Summer Isles*, 1624, in Barbour, *Works*, 2:150–51, 260–61; see also the marginal note about Smith's adoption in Purchas, *Purchas His Pilgrimage*, 2d ed., 757. This interpretation was suggested by Philip L. Barbour in *Pocahontas and Her World* (Boston, 1969), 23–26.

13. Winslow, *Good Newes from New England*, 53–56.

14. Strachey, *Historie of Travell*, 101–3.

15. Harriot, *A Briefe and True Report of the new found land of Virginia*, 1588, 1590, in Quinn, *Roanoke Voyages*, 1:372–73.

16. Williams, *Key into the Language of America*, preface, 132–35.

17. Ibid., 54, 103 [misnumbered 105], 126 [misnumbered 118], 173 [misnumbered 165].

18. Kathleen J. Bragdon, *Native People of Southern New England, 1500–1650* (Norman, Okla., 1996), 184–85; "Letter of Reverend Jonas Michaëlius, 1628," in *Narratives of New Netherland, 1609–1664*, ed. J. Franklin Jameson (New York, 1909), 126.

19. Ives Goddard and Kathleen Bragdon, *Native Writings in Massachusett* (Philadelphia: American Philosophical Society, 1988); Williams, *Key into the Language of America*, 192 [misnumbered 184].

20. "The Diary of Mrs. Fielding," ed. Frank Speck, in *Forty-third Annual Report of the Bureau of American Ethnology, 1925–26* (Washington, D.C., 1928), 229–51.

21. Francis Higginson, *New-Englands Plantation*, 1630, in *Tracts and Other Papers, Relating Principally to the Origin, Settlement, and Progress of the Colonies in North America*, comp. Peter Force, 4 vols. (1844; Washington, D.C., 1963), 1:13; Christopher Levett, *A Voyage unto New England* (London, 1624), 19; William Wood, *New Englands Prospect* (London, 1634), 82–83; Winslow, *Good Newes from New England*, 34; Thomas Morton, *New English Canaan*, 1637, in Force, *Tracts*, 2:34–35; Williams, *Key into the Language of America*, 124 [misnumbered 116], 130 [misnumbered 122]; Samuel de Champlain, *Voyages and Discoveries Made in New France, from the Year 1615 to the End of the Year 1618*, repeated in *The Voyages to Western New France . . . from the year 1603 until the year 1629*, in *The Works of Samuel de Champlain*, ed. H. P. Biggar, 6 vols. (Toronto, 1922–36), 3:143–44; 4:319–20 (the Champlain quote is from vol. 4).

22. Higginson, *New-Englands Plantation*, 1: 13; Winslow, *Good Newes from New England*, 53.

23. Occum, "Account of the Montauk Indians," 1761, *Collections of the Massachusetts Historical Society*, 1st ser., 10 (1809): 106–11; Bragdon, *Native People of Southern New England*, 188–90. William Wood said that Abamacho ruled over "the infernal dwellings," *New Englands Prospect*, 93. On religious beliefs, see also William S. Simmons, "Narragansett," in *Handbook of North American Indians*, ed. William C. Sturtevant, vol. 15, *Northeast*, ed. Bruce G. Trigger (Washington, D.C., 1978), 191–92. On the way in which this religious framework shaped native views of Christianity see Charles L. Cohen, "Conversion among Puritans and Amerindians: A Theological and Cultural Perspective," in *Puritanism: Transatlantic Perspectives on a Seventeenth-Century Anglo-American Faith*, ed. Francis J. Bremer (Boston, 1993), 233–56.

24. Strachey, *Historie of Travell*, 88–89; Smith, *Map of Virginia*, 168–71; Harriot, *Briefe and True Report*, 373; Purchas, *Purchas His Pilgrimage*, 2d ed., 765; White, *Briefe Relation of the Voyage unto Maryland*, 45.

25. Williams, *Key into the Language of America*, 54, 103 [misnumbered 105], 124–26 [misnumbered 116–18], 173 [misnumbered 165]; Tantaquidgeon, interview, 1994, in *Connecticut Speaks for Itself*, ed. David P. Shuldiner (Middletown, Conn., 1996), 231.

26. Morton, *New English Canaan*, 21, 34–35.

27. William Apess, *A Son of the Forest and Other Writings by William Apess, a Pequot*, ed. Barry O'Connell (Amherst, 1997), 10, 34.

28. Whitaker, *Good Newes from Virginia*, 24, 27; White, *Briefe Relation of the Voyage unto Maryland*, 44–45; Council in Virginia to Virginia Company, January 1622, in *Records of the Virginia Company of London*, ed. Susan Myra Kingsbury, 4 vols. (Washington, D.C., 1906–35), 3:584.

29. John White, *The Planters Plea*, 1630, in Force, *Tracts*, 2:7–9; White, *Briefe Relation of the Voyage unto Maryland*, 44–45. See also Winslow, *Good Newes from New England*, 59. William Strachey argued that the Indians were descended from Cham, the son of Noah; *Historie of Travell*, 53–55. For discussion of similar issues with respect to natives of South America and Mexico, see Sabine MacCormack, "Limits of Understanding: Perceptions of Greco-Roman and Amerindian Paganism in Early Modern Europe," in *America in European Consciousness, 1493–1750*, ed. Karen Ordahl Kupperman (Chapel Hill, 1995), 79–129.

30. Williams, *Key into the Language of America*, A4v ff., 26, 128 [misnumbered 120], 130 [misnumbered 122]. Wetucks is identified by Kathleen Bragdon as one of a group of "giant culture heroes or tricksters," *Native People of Southern New England*, 195. Morton thought the Indians spoke a mixed language and that study of this language would provide clues to their origins; see *New English Canaan*, 16–18. William Strachey argued that the crosses reportedly found by Spaniards proved the presence of the Welsh prince Madoc and his followers several hundred years earlier; *Historie of Travell*, 11–12.

31. Harriot, *Briefe and True Report*, 372, 375.

32. For the argument that reduction implied use of force, see James Axtell, *The Invasion Within: The Contest of Cultures in Colonial North America* (New York, 1985), chap. 7. Axtell also reminds readers that colonization reduced the number of Indians dramatically; *The European and the Indian: Essays in the Ethnohistory of Colonial North America* (New York, 1981), 306–7. The issues are discussed in the introduction to Kupperman, *America in European Consciousness*, 10–11. I especially thank James Muldoon for pointing out the varied meanings of the term "reduce" to me.

33. Hakluyt, "Epistle Dedicatory to Cecil," 1599, in Taylor, *Original Writings and Correspondence*, 2:457; "Epistle Dedicatory to Sir Walter Ralegh," 1587 [Document 56], in ibid., 367–68. Emphasis added.

34. Vico, *The New Science of Giambattista Vico*, trans. Thomas Goddard Bergin and Max Harold Fisch (Ithaca, N.Y., 1968), paras. 375, 437, pp. 116–17, 143–44.

35. Smith, *Map of Virginia*, 168–69, and *Generall Historie*, 122; White, *Briefe Relation of the Voyage unto Maryland*, 44–45; Williams, *Key into the Language of America*, 54, 103 [misnumbered 105], 126 [misnumbered 118], 173 [misnumbered 165]. See also Gabriel Archer, *A Breif discription of the People*, 1607, in *The Jamestown Voyages under the First Charter, 1606–1609*, ed. Philip L. Barbour, 2 vols. (Cambridge, 1969), 1:104; and Purchas, "Virginian Affaires since the yeere 1620. till this present 1624," in *Pilgrimes*, 19:164. Fotherby's *Atheomastix* was published in 1622.

36. Levett, *Voyage unto New England*, 18–19; John Winthrop, *The Journal of John Winthrop, 1630–1649*, ed. Richard S. Dunn, James Savage, and Laetitia Yeandle (Cambridge, Mass., 1996), 286; Wood, *New Englands Prospect*, 76–77, 83. Someone wrote the word "Quere" in the margin of Winthrop's journal. Winthrop may have thought the devil was particularly active in Aquiday because dissident Anne Hutchinson, who had been expelled from Massachusetts for her religious opinions, was there with her core followers at that time.

37. Purchas, *Purchas His Pilgrimage*, in *The English New England Voyages, 1602–1608*, ed. David B. Quinn and Alison M. Quinn (London, 1983), 349–50. Half of the settlers elected to leave with the last ship home in December 1607; see Charles M. Andrews, *The Colonial Period of American History*, 4 vols. (1934–1938; New Haven, 1975), 1:92–93.

38. Winthrop, *Journal*, 246; Wood, *New Englands Prospect*, 76–77, 83.

39. Experience Mayhew, *Indian Converts* (London, 1727), 3; Constance A. Crosby, "The Algonkian Spiritual Landscape," in *Algonkians of New England: Past and Present*, ed. Peter Benes (Boston, 1993), 37.

40. Strachey, *Historie of Travell*, 89–90.

41. Wood, *New Englands Prospect*, 76–78.

42. Purchas, *Purchas His Pilgrimage*, 3d ed., 954–55; Purchas, "Occurrents in Virginia, 1613–1619," in *Pilgrimes*, 19:118; Morton, *New English Canaan*, 35. See the excellent discussion in Kenneth Morrison, "Montagnais Missionization in New France: The Syncretic Imperative," *American Indian Culture and Research Journal* 10 (1986): 1–23.

43. Anthony Parkhurst, "A letter written to M. Richard Hakluyt of the middle Temple, conteining a report of the true state and commodities of Newfoundland, 1578," in Taylor, *Original Writings and Correspondence of Hakluyts*, 128; Strachey, *Historie of Travell*, 89.

44. Arthur Barlowe, *The First Voyage Made to the Coastes of America*, 1584, in Quinn, ed., *Roanoke Voyages*, 1:109, 114; Smith, *Generall Historie*, 144–45. Christopher L. Miller and George R. Hamell demonstrate that the colors white, red, and black carried powerful symbolic import; "A New Perspective on Indian-White Contact: Cultural Symbols and Colonial Trade," *Journal of American History* 73 (1986): 311–28, esp. 323–25. See also Smith's reference to the deployment of these colors in the ceremonies performed around him in his captivity below.

45. Williams, *Key into the Language of America*, 178 [misnumbered 170]; Frank G. Speck, "Penobscot Tales and Religious Beliefs," *Journal of American Folklore* 48 (1935): 20.

46. Harriot, "Notes" to woodcuts of John White's paintings published by Theodor DeBry and printed in David Beers Quinn, ed., *The Roanoke Voyages, 1584–1590*, 2 vols. (London, 1955), 1:430–32, 442–43. A government spy reported that the playwright Christopher Marlowe had been overheard to say "That Moyses was but a Jugler, & that one Heriots being Sir W Raleighs man Can do more then he." For this report, along with other contemporary evidence for freethinking in Ralegh's circle, see John Bakeless, *The Tragicall History of Christopher Marlowe*, 2 vols. (Cambridge, Mass., 1942), 1:107–40 (the quote is from p. 111). See Stephen J. Greenblatt, "Invisible Bullets," *Shakespearean Negotiations: The Circulation of Social Energy in Renaissance England* (Berkeley, 1988), 21–40.

47. William Simmons, *Spirit of the New England Tribes: Indian History and Folklore, 1620–1984* (Hanover N.H., 1986), 38–45.

48. Smith, *Map of Virginia*, 168–69.

49. Purchas, *Purchas His Pilgrimage*, 3d ed., 954–55; Purchas, "Occurrents in Virginia, 1613–1619," 118.

50. Spelman, "Relation of Virginea," cv; Winslow, *Good Newes from New England*, 53–58. According to William S. Simmons the name Hobbomock "was related to the words for death, the deceased, and the cold northeast wind." See *Spirit of the New England Tribes*, 39. See also Bragdon, *Native People of Southern New England*, 189–90.

51. Whitaker, *Good Newes from Virginia*, 26. John Rolfe, in England with Pocahontas and Uttamatomakkin, informed Samuel Purchas that many aspects of Whitaker's information needed amending, and Purchas began to set the record straight in his revised *Pilgrimage:* "Mr. Rolph affirmes that these Priests live not solitarily, and in other things is of opinion, which perhaps our former Author at his first comming, might have by relation of others." In other words, Whitaker just passed on hearsay. See also Winslow, *Good Newes from New England*, 53.

52. Shepard, *Journal*, in Michael McGiffert, ed., *God's Plot: Puritan Sprituality in Thomas Shepard's Cambridge*, rev. ed. (Amherst, 1994), 103, see also 86, 118, 132; W. C. Ford, ed., *Diary of Cotton Mather, 1681–1724*, 2 vols. (Boston, 1911–12), 2:190–91, 200. I owe the Mather reference to Harry S. Stout.

53. Williams, *Key into the Language of America*, 19–20, 130 [misnumbered 122]; Joseph Johnson, Diary, in Laura J. Murray, ed., *To Do Good to My Indian Brethren: The Writings of Joseph Johnson, 1751–1776* (Amherst, Mass., 1998), 124–25; John Rolfe, "The coppie of the Gentle-mans letters to sir Thomas Dale, that after maried Powhatans daughter, containing the reasons moving him thereunto," in Ralph Hamor, *A True Discourse of the Present Estate of Virginia* (London, 1615), 65.

54. Jesuit Letter, 1639, in *Narratives of Early Maryland, 1633–1684*, ed. Clayton Colman Hall (New York, 1910), 124–27.

55. Levett, *Voyage unto New England*, 18–19.

56. Strachey, *Historie of Travell*, 104–5. On the fate of the Chesapeakes and their involvement with the Roanoke colony see Rountree, *Powhatan Indians*, 120–21, and *Pocahontas's People: The Powhatan Indians of Virginia through Four Centuries* (Norman, Okla., 1990), 20–28; and David Beers Quinn, *Set Fair for Roanoke: Voyages and Colonies 1584–1606* (Chapel Hill, 1985), chap. 19.

57. George Percy, "Observations Gathered out of a Discourse of the Plantation of the Southerne Colonie in Virginia by the English," in Barbour, *Jamestown Voyages*, 1:135–36, 143, 145–46.

58. Smith, *Generall Historie*, 149–50. Other versions appear in Smith's *True Relation* and his *Map of Virginia*, 59, 170–71; Smith's statement of the ceremony's purpose is on 170. Helen Rountree remarks that the answer produced by this ceremony was "the wrong one"; *Powhatan Indians*, 132.

59. Williams, *Key into the Language of America*, 126–29 [misnumbered 118–21]. On Williams's quarrel with Massachusetts Bay over worship with the unregenerate and the need to acknowledge the sin of having worshipped in England, see Edmund S. Morgan, *Roger Williams: The Church and the State* (New York, 1967), 29–40. Ephesians 5, in the Geneva Bible, urges believers to "have no fellowship with the unfruteful workes of darkenes," and verse 14 urges them to "stand up from the dead."

60. Winslow, *Good Newes from New England*, 55. Archaeological evidence bears out the observation that the Narragansetts intensified their religious practices in the face of the English presence: Paul A. Robinson, Marc A. Kelley, and Patricia E. Rubertone, "Preliminary Biocultural Interpretations from a Seventeenth-Century Narragansett Indian Cemetery in Rhode Island," in *Cultures in Contact: the Impact of European*

Contacts on Native American Cultural Institutions, A.D. 1000–1800, ed. William Fitzhugh (Washington, D.C., 1985), 107–30, esp. 110–11; Simmons, "Narragansett" in Trigger, *Handbook of North American Indians*, 15:191–92; Neal Salisbury, *Manitou and Providence: Indians, Europeans, and the Making of New England, 1500–1643* (Oxford, 1982), 106.

61. Harriot, *Briefe and True Report*, 345; and Harriot, Notes to White's pictures, in ibid., 421–23, 428–29.

62. Spelman, "Relation of Virginea," cxiii; Archer, *A Breif discription of the People*, 104.

63. Virginia Frances Voight, *Mohegan Chief: The Story of Harold Tantaquidgeon* (1965; Mohegan, Conn., 1983), 29–30.

64. Anon., *Relation of Maryland*, 1635, in Hall, *Narratives of Early Maryland*, 40.

65. Occum, "Account of the Montauk Indians," *Collections of the Massachusetts Historical Society*, 1st ser., 10 (1809): 109. For comparisons between powwows and English witches, see Whitaker, *Good Newes*, 24, 26; and Levett, *Voyage unto New England*, 19. Richard Godbeer writes, "Seventeenth-century New Englanders used magic to predict the future, to heal the sick, to destroy their enemies, and to defend themselves against occult attack"; *The Devil's Dominion: Magic and Religion in Early New England* (Cambridge, 1992), 7 and chaps. 1–2 generally. See also Keith Thomas, *Religion and the Decline of Magic: Studies in Popular Beliefs in Sixteenth and Seventeenth-Century England* (London, 1971), chaps. 7–9; Linda Pollock, *With Faith and Physic: The Life of a Tudor Gentlewoman, Lady Grace Mildmay, 1552–1620* (New York, 1993), chap. 5; Patricia A. Wilson, *The Angelical Conjunction: The Preacher-Physicians of Colonial New England* (Knoxville, 1991), chap. 1.

66. Williams to John Winthrop, February 28, 1638, in *The Correspondence of Roger Williams*, ed. Glenn W. LaFantasie, 2 vols. (Hanover, N.H., 1988), 1:145; Williams, *Key into the Language of America*, 127–28 [misnumbered 119–20], 169 [misnumbered 161], 198–99 [misnumbered 190–91]. The story of Simon Magus is rendered from the Geneva Bible, 1560, Acts of the Apostles 8.9–24. On Williams's objection to salaried ministers, see Morgan, *Roger Williams*, 74–76, 110–12. On the controversy over medical fees for ministers see Watson, *Angelical Conjunction*, chap. 2.

67. Wood, *New Englands Prospect*, 82–83. Pissacanawa, or Passaconaway, was a Pawtucket "powwow-sachem" located on the Merrimack River; see Simmons, *Spirit of the New England Tribes*, 61, 63.

68. Alexander Whitaker to Mr. Crashawe, August 9, 1611, in *The Genesis of the United States*, ed. Alexander Brown, 2 vols. (Boston, 1890), 1:498–99.

69. Winslow, *Good Newes from New England*, 54.

70. Spelman, "Relation of Virginea," cix–cx.

71. Morton, *New English Canaan*, 25–26.

72. Harriot, Notes to White's pictures, 425–27.

73. Smith, *Map of Virginia*, 169.

74. Morton, *New English Canaan*, 35–36.

75. Clare Gittings, *Death, Burial, and the Individual in Early Modern England* (London, 1984), chap. 5, esp. 102, 110–15; David Cressy, *Birth, Marriage, and Death: Ritual, Religion, and the Life-Cycle in Tudor and Stuart England* (Oxford, 1997), chaps. 17–20.

76. Morton, *New English Canaan*, 35–36.

77. Smith, *Map of Virginia*, 169; Wood, *New Englands Prospect*, 93.

78. Wood, *New Englands Prospect*, 93; Morton, *New English Canaan*, 34–35.

79. Occum, "Account of the Montauk Indians," 109–10; Elizabeth A. Little, ed., *Nantucket Indian Studies*, no. 3 (Nantucket, 1981), 2, docs. 2, 3A.

80. Williams, *Key into the Language of America*, 5, 43, 130 [misnumbered 122], 201–4 [misnumbered 193–96].

81. Strachey, *Historie of Travell*, 100, 103.
82. Harriot, *Briefe and True Report*, 374; Purchas, *Purchas His Pilgrimage*, 2d ed., 762–63.
83. Harriot, *Briefe and True Report*, 374–75; Strachey, *Historie of Travell*, 103;
84. Stockham's letter was printed by John Smith in his *Generall Historie*, 285–86.
85. The phrase "Ethnick darkness" is from Gordon of Lochinvar, *Encouragements to Under-takers*, D3; Rosier, *True Relation*, 297. On Rosier's biography see Quinn and Quinn, *English New England Voyages*, 62–64.
86. John Rolfe, *A True Relation of the state of Virginia lefte by Sir Thomas Dale Knight in May last 1616* (Charlottesville, 1951), 12.
87. Bernd Peyer, *The Tutor'd Mind: Indian Missionary-Writers in Antebellum America* (Amherst, Mass., 1997), chap. 3, esp. 82–88.
88. William Hubbard, *The History of the Indian Wars in New England*, ed. Samuel G. Drake, 2 vols. (Boston, 1865), 2:135, 153, 177.
89. Richard Treat's Memorial, 1737, in *The Talcott Papers*, 2 vols., *Collections of the Connecticut Historical Society* 4–5 (1892, 1896): 5:478–84. Samson Occum also wrote of holding a "great nightly dance" among the Montauks when it was time to "put off their mourning habit." See his "Account of the Montauk Indians," 110.
90. William Simmons and Cheryl L. Simmons, eds., *Old Light on Separate Ways: The Narragansett Diary of Joseph Fish, 1765–1776* (Hanover N.H., 1982), xxxi, 4–7, 93, and passim. Simmons argues that the Great Awakening allowed a new preaching style that was more attractive to Indian congregations; see his "Red Yankees: Narragansett Conversion in the Great Awakening," *American Ethnologist* 10 (1983): 253–71; and Robert Blair St. George, *Conversing by Signs: Poetics of Implication in Colonial New England* (Chapel Hill, 1998), 340–42. On conversion see Axtell, *Invasion Within*; William Simmons, "Conversion from Indian to Puritan," *New England Quarterly* 52 (1979): 197–218; James Ronda, "'We are Well as We Are': An Indian Critique of Seventeenth-Century Christian Missions," *William and Mary Quarterly*, 3d ser., 34 (1977): 66–82; Ronda, "Generations of Faith: The Christian Indians of Martha's Vineyard," *William and Mary Quarterly*, 3d ser., 38 (1981): 369–94.

Chapter 5. Village Life

1. John Smith, *The Proceedings of the English Colony in Virginia*, 1612, in *The Complete Works of Captain John Smith*, ed. Philip L. Barbour, 3 vols. (Chapel Hill, 1986), 1:256–57.
2. James Rosier, *A True Relation of the most prosperous voyage . . . in the Discovery of the land of Virginia*, 1605, in *The English New England Voyages, 1602–1608*, ed. David B. Quinn and Alison M. Quinn (London, 1983), 269–71, 297.
3. William Wood, *New Englands Prospect* (London, 1634), 81; Cornelius Tacitus, *The Description of Germanie: and Customes of the People*, trans. Richard Grenewey (London, 1598), 263; Roger Williams, *A Key into the Language of America* (London, 1643), 148 [misnumbered 140]; Samson Occum, "Account of the Montauk Indians," 1761, *Collections of the Massachusetts Historical Society*, 1st ser., 10 (1809): 106–8; Anon., *A Relation of Maryland*, in *Narratives of Early Maryland, 1633–1684*, ed. Clayton Colman Hall (New York, 1910), 35–36; Henry Spelman, "Relation of Virginea," c. 1613, in *Travels and Works of Captain John Smith*, ed. E. Arber and A. G. Bradley, 2 vols. (Edinburgh, 1910), 1:cvii. On customs in England see David Cressy, *Birth, Marriage, and Death: Ritual, Religion, and the Life-Cycle in Tudor and Stuart England* (Oxford, 1997), chaps. 10–11, 15–16.
4. "The observations of Master John Pory Secretarie of Virginia, in his travels," in John Smith, *The Generall Historie of Virginia, New-England and the Summer Isles*,

1624, in Barbour, *Works*, 2:291; Rosier, *True Relation*, 279; Williams, *Key into the Language of America*, 31–32, 41. English science and folklore held that menstruating women were powerful, and should be avoided or approached cautiously; see Patricia Crawford, "Attitudes to Menstruation in Seventeenth-Century England," *Past and Present* 91 (1981): 47–73.

5. Williams, *Key into the Language of America*, 146 [misnumbered 138]; Smith, *Generall Historie*, 128, 182–83; William Strachey, *The Historie of Travell into Virginia Britania*, 1612, ed. Louis B. Wright and Virginia Freund (London, 1953), 112–13, 116; Samuel Purchas, *Purchas His Pilgrimage*, 2d ed. (London, 1614), 768; Edward Winslow, *Good Newes from New England* (London, 1624), 59.

6. Gabriel Archer, *A Breif discription of the People*, 1607, in *The Jamestown Voyages under the First Charter, 1606–1609*, ed. Philip L. Barbour, 2 vols. (Cambridge, 1969), 1:104; Ralph Hamor, *A True Discourse of the Present Estate of Virginia* (London, 1615), 39; Andrew White, *A Briefe Relation of the Voyage unto Maryland*, 1634, in Hall, *Narratives of Early Maryland*, 44; Spelman, "Relation of Virginea," cvii–cviii; Anon., *Relation of Maryland*, 33–34; Tacitus, *Description of Germanie*, 262; Christopher Levett, *A Voyage unto New England* (London, 1624), 20.

7. Wood, *New Englands Prospect*, 81; William Morrell, *New England* (London, 1625), 19–20; Williams, *Key into the Language of America*, 147 [misnumbered 139]. Many English authorities advised against sexual relations while a woman nursed her baby. See Patricia Crawford, "'The Sucking Child,'" *Continuity and Change* 1 (1986): 30.

8. Levett, *Voyage unto New England*, 21; William Bradford and Edward Winslow, *A Relation or Journall of the English Plantation setled at Plimoth in New England* (London, 1622), known as *Mourt's Relation*, 45.

9. Tacitus, *Description of Germanie*, 263–64.

10. Williams, *Key into the Language of America*, 150–51 [misnumbered 142–43].

11. Archer, *Breif discription of the People*, 103; John Smith, *A Map of Virginia*, 1612, in Barbour, *Works*, 162.

12. Michael Roberts, "'Words They Are Women, and Deeds They Are Men': Images of Work and Gender in Early Modern England," in *Women and Work in Pre-Industrial England*, ed. Lindsey Charles and Lorna Duffin (London, 1985), 122–80.

13. Tacitus, *Description of Germanie*, 263.

14. Anon., *Relation of Maryland*, 33; Smith, *Generall Historie*, 151.

15. Williams, *Key into the Language of America*, 98–100, 156 [misnumbered 100–102, 148]; Anon. to A. Holmes, 1804, reprinted in *Connecticut Speaks for Itself*, ed. David P. Shuldiner (Middletown, Conn., 1996), 25–26; Spelman, "Relation of Virginea," cxi.

16. Wood, *New Englands Prospect*, 33, 68, 94–97.

17. On the proverbial wisdom that "England is a paradise for women," see Anthony Fletcher, *Gender, Sex and Subordination in England, 1500–1800* (New Haven, 1995), 3–4.

18. John Underhill, *Newes from America* (London, 1638), 5–6; Morrell, *New England*, 21.

19. Wood, *New Englands Prospect*, 96–97.

20. "Leift Lion Gardener his Relation of the Pequot Warres," *Collections of the Massachusetts Historical Society*, 3d ser., 3 (1833): 146.

21. Devon A. Mihesuah, "Commonalty of Difference: American Indian Women and History," in *Natives and Academics: Researching and Writing about American Indians*, ed. Mihesuah (Lincoln, Neb., 1998), 44–45; Helen C. Rountree, *The Powhatan Indians of Virginia: Their Traditional Culture* (Norman, Okla., 1989), chap. 5, esp. 88–89; and "Powhatan Indian Women: The People Captain John Smith Barely Saw," *Ethnohistory* 45 (1998): 1–29; Kathleen J. Bragdon, *Native People of Southern New England, 1500–1650* (Norman, Okla., 1996), 49–53, chaps. 3, 7. In "Powhatan Indian Women"

Rountree painstakingly reconstructs the roles of native women to counter the charge that they were "drudges." Bragdon argues that women's workload may have been increasing as a result of the changes native society had undergone over the preceding century (49–53, 179–82).

22. John Pory, "A Reporte of the Manner of Proceeding in the General Assembly Convened at James City," 1619, in *Records of the Virginia Company of London*, ed. Susan Myra Kingsbury, 4 vols. (Washington, D.C., 1906–35), 3:160.

23. Virginia Company, "A Coppie of the Subscription for Maydes," July 16 1621. The relevant paragraphs are excerpted in Kingsbury, *Records of the Virginia Company*, 3:493–94, and printed in full in David R. Ransome, "Wives for Virginia, 1621," *William and Mary Quarterly*, 3d ser., 48 (1991): 7–8.

24. On this point see Lois Green Carr and Lorena Walsh, "The Planter's Wife: The Experience of Women in Seventeenth-Century Maryland," *William and Mary Quarterly*, 3d ser., 34 (1977): 542–65; and Lois Green Carr, Russell R. Menard, and Lorena Walsh, *Robert Cole's World: Agriculture and Society in Early Maryland* (Chapel Hill, 1991), chaps. 2–3.

25. Wood, *New Englands Prospect*, 73. On the control of expression, especially the "endless discoursing of women," see Patricia Parker, "Motivated Rhetorics: Gender, Order, Rule," in *Literary Fat Ladies: Rhetoric, Gender, Property* (New York, 1987), 97–125. On ways of dealing with the threat represented by domineering women, see Elizabeth Foyster, "A Laughing Matter? Marital Discord and Gender Control in Seventeenth-Century England," *Rural History* 4 (1993): 5–21. On laudable female humility and the need to tame scolds, see Fletcher, *Gender, Sex and Subordination*, 14–19, 115.

26. Wood, *New Englands Prospect*, 90, 96. See also Gladys Tantaquidgeon and Jayne Fawcett, "Symbolic Motifs on Painted Baskets of the Mohegan-Pequot," in *Rooted Like the Ash Trees: New England Indians and the Land*, ed. Richard G. Carlson, rev. ed. (Naugatuck, Conn., 1987), 50–51.

27. William, *Key into the Language of America*, 37–38; 148–50 [misnumbered 140–42]. On the fear with which English women approached childbirth, see Linda A. Pollock, "Embarking on a Rough Passage: The Experience of Pregnancy in Early-Modern Society," in *Women as Mothers in Pre-Industrial England*, ed. Valerie Fildes (London, 1990), 47–49; see also Cressy, *Birth, Marriage, and Death*, chaps. 1–4, 9. Helen Rountree quotes physical anthropologist Donna Boyd, whose analysis of female Powhatan skeletons finds them "more robust" than most modern men's. On the other hand, both male and female skeletons show signs of arthritis by the age of thirty, "Powhatan Indian Women," 3, 27 n. 43.

28. Williams, *Key into the Language of America*, 31, 47, 73.

29. Tacitus, *Description of Germanie*, 263; Smith, *Map of Virginia*, 162; Wood, *New Englands Prospect*, 96; Rosier, *True Relation*, 276; Williams, *Key into the Language of America*, 29–30, 40; Levett, *Voyage unto New England*, 21. On contemporary English opinion, see Crawford, "'Sucking Child,'" 23–52.

30. On Job Kattenanit see Daniel Gookin, *An Historical Account of the Doings and Sufferings of the Christian Indians in New England*, 1677, in *Archaeologia Americana: Transactions and Collections of the American Antiquarian Society*, vol. 2 (1836), 480; Anon., *Relation of Maryland*, 34, 40; Thomas Morton, *New English Canaan*, 1637, in *Tracts and Other Papers, Relating Principally to the Origin, Settlement, and Progress of the Colonies in North America*, comp. Peter Force, 4 vols. (1844; reprint, Washington, D.C., 1963), 2:35.

31. Kingsbury, *Records of the Virginia Company*, 3:228.

32. Ralph Lane, *An Account of the Particularities of the imployments of the English men left in Virginia*, 1856, in *The Roanoke Voyages, 1584–1590*, ed. David Beers Quinn,

2 vols. (London, 1955), 1:262; Smith, *The Proceedings of the English Colony in Virginia,* 1612, in Barbour, *Works,* 1:228.

33. Bradford and Winslow, *Mourt's Relation,* 50.

34. Hamor, *True Discourse of the Present Estate of Virginia,* 4–6, 38–42; Smith, *Generall Historie,* in Barbour, ed., *Works,* II, 243–4; Argall, "A Letter of Sir Samuell Argoll touching his voyage to Virginia," in Purchas, *Pilgrimes,* XIX, 92–93; Smith, *Generall Historie,* in Barbour, ed., *Works,* II, 177. On the affectionate relationship of English boys and their adopted Indian hosts, see chapter 6 below.

35. Winslow, *Good Newes from New England,* 58; Williams, *Key into the Language of America,* 29; 123, 203–4 [misnumbered 115, 195–96].

36. Aupaumut, "Teaching the Children," in *Native Heritage: Personal Accounts by American Indians, 1790 to the Present,* ed. Arlene Hirschfelder (New York, 1995), 92–93; Morton, *New English Canaan,* 24–25. See also Anon., *Relation of Maryland,* 33; and Winslow, *Good Newes from New England,* 58.

37. Anon., *Relation of Maryland,* 36; Morton, *New English Canaan,* 20.

38. Strachey, *Historie of Travell,* 67; Lane, *Account of the Particularities,* 208.

39. Thomas Harriot, *A Briefe and True Report of the new found land of Virginia,* 1588, 1590, in Quinn, *Roanoke Voyages,* 1:370; White, *Briefe Relation of the Voyage unto Maryland,* 44; Francis Higginson, *New-Englands Plantation,* 1630, in Force, *Tracts,* 2:13; Anon., *Relation of Maryland,* 37; Strachey, *Historie of Travell,* 78–79. See the interview with Tantaquidgeon in Shuldiner, *Connecticut Speaks for Itself,* 231. Thomas Morton compared the structures to the houses of the "wild Irish," *New English Canaan,* 19.

40. Strachey, *Historie of Travell,* 78–79; Edward Waterhouse, *A Declaration of the State of the Colony and Affaires in Virginia* (London, 1622), 16; Purchas, *Pilgrimes,* 19:160; Smith, *Generall Historie,* 294–95.

41. Waterhouse, *Declaration of the State of the Colony,* 16; Williams, *Key into the Language of America,* 38–39.

42. Wood, *New Englands Prospect,* 94; Virginia Company, *A True Declaration of the estate of the Colonie in Virginia* in Force, *Tracts,* 3:20; William Strachey, *True Reportory,* in Purchas, *Pilgrimes,* 19:57. On the problem of explaining the extremes of the American climate, see Karen Ordahl Kupperman, "The Puzzle of the American Climate in the Early Colonial Period," *American Historical Review* 87 (1982): 1262–89.

43. Harriot, *Briefe and True Report,* 341–42; Williams, *Key into the Language of America,* 89–90; Samson Occum, "Report on the Montauk Indians," *Collections of the Massachusetts Historical Society,* 1st ser. (1810), 110; Frank Speck, "Penobscot Tales and Religious Beliefs," *Journal of American Folklore* 48 (1935): 25. On the method of growing corn and beans together, see also Virginia Company, *True Declaration of the estate of the Colonie in Virginia,* 12. Modern archaeological findings indicate that corn, beans, squash, and tobacco cultivation came to New England about a thousand years ago. See Dena F. Dincause, "A Capsule Prehistory of Southern New England," in *The Pequots in Southern New England: The Fall and Rise of an American Indian Nation,* ed. Laurence M. Hauptman and James D. Wherry (Norman, Okla., 1990), 29–32; and Robert S. Grumet, *Historic Contact: Indian People and Colonists in Today's Northeastern United States in the Sixteenth through Eighteenth Centuries* (Norman, Okla., 1995), 10.

44. On classical literature and improving agriculture, see Joan Thirsk, "Making a Fresh Start: Sixteenth-Century Agriculture and the Classical Inspiration," in *Culture and Cultivation in Early Modern England: Writing and the Land,* ed. Michael Leslie and Timothy Raylor (Leicester, 1992), 15–34; Andrew McRae, "Husbandry Manuals and the Language of Agrarian Improvement," in ibid., 35–62; and "'An Essay on Manures': Changing Attitudes to Fertilization in England, 1500–1800," in *English Rural Society, 1500–1800: Essays in Honour of Joan Thirsk,* ed. John Chartres and David Hey (Cambridge, 1990), 251–78.

45. Samuel Purchas, "Intelligence from Virginia," in *Pilgrimes*, 19:209–10; Gabriel Archer, *The Discription of the now discovered River and Country of Virginia*, in Barbour, *The Jamestown Voyages*, 1:100; Harriot, *Briefe and True Report*, 338, 342.

46. Anon., *Relation of Maryland*, 27; Smith, *Map of Virginia*, 157; Ralph Lane, "An extract of Master Lanes letter, to Master Richard Hakluyt Esquire, and another gentleman of the middle Temple, from Virginia," 1585, in Quinn, *Roanoke Voyages*, 1:207–8; Virginia Company, *True Declaration of the estate of the Colonie in Virginia*, 12.

47. Harriot, *Briefe and True Report*, 338; Bradford and Winslow, *Mourt's Relation*, 6; George Percy, "Observations gathered out of a Discourse of the Plantation of the Southerne Colonie in Virginia," in Barbour, *Jamestown Voyages*, 1:411.

48. Metacom in John Easton, "Relacion of the Indyan Warre," *Narratives of the Indian Wars, 1675–1699*, ed. Charles H. Lincoln (New York, 1913), 10; Wood, *New Englands Prospect*, 70; Williams, *Key into the Language of America*, 95–101 [misnumbered 97–103]; Winslow, *Good Newes from New England*, 63; William Bradford, *Of Plymouth Plantation, 1620–1647*, ed. Samuel Eliot Morison (New York, 1952), 85. For discussion of the source of Squanto's lore about setting corn with fish, see Lynn Ceci, "Fish Fertilizer: A Native North American Practice?" *Science* 188 (1975): 26–30; and Nanepashemet, "It Smells Fishy to Me: An Argument Supporting the Use of Fish Fertilizer by the Native People of Southern New England," in *Algonkians of New England: Past and Present*, ed. Peter Benes (Boston, 1993), 42–50.

49. Tacitus, *Description of Germanie*, 262; Wood, *New Englands Prospect*, 95; Strachey, *Historie of Travell*, 115. On the native tradition, see Trudie Lamb Richmond, "A Native Perspective of History: The Schaghticoke Nation, Resistance, and Survival," in *Enduring Traditions: The Native Peoples of New England*, ed. Laurie Weinstein (Westport, Conn., 1994), 105.

50. Smith, *Map of Virginia*, 156–59, 162–63; John Smith, *A True Relation of such occurrences and accidents of noate as hath hapned in Virginia*, 1608, in Barbour, *Works*, 1:59, 67; Smith, *Proceedings of the English Colony in Virginia*, 256–57; David W. Stahle et al., "Lost Colony and Jamestown Droughts," *Science* 280 (1998): 564–67; Helen C. Rountree and Thomas E. Davidson, point out the benefits of mixing wild and cultivated foods (*Eastern Shore Indians of Virginia and Maryland* [Charlottesville, 1997], 36–37).

51. Wood, *New Englands Prospect*, 67–68.

52. Morton, *New English Canaan*, 30. On the bee as model, see Karen Ordahl Kupperman, "The Beehive as a Model for Colonial Design," in *America in European Consciousness, 1493–1750*, ed. Karen Ordahl Kupperman (Chapel Hill, 1995), 272–92; and Timothy Raylor, "Samuel Hartlib and the Commonwealth of Bees," in Leslie and Raylor, *Culture and Cultivation in Early Modern England*, 91–129.

53. On Indian diet and subsistence strategies see Helen C. Rountree, ed., *Powhatan Foreign Relations, 1500–1722* (Charlottesville, 1993), 218–19; Stephen R. Potter, *Commoners, Tribute, and Chiefs: The Development of Algonquian Culture in the Potomac Valley* (Charlottesville, 1993), chap. 1; Bragdon, *Native People of Southern New England*, chaps. 2, 3; Peter A. Thomas, "Contrastive Subsistence Strategies and Land Use as Factors for Understanding Indian-White Relations in New England," *Ethnohistory* 23 (1976): 1–18, and "Cultural Change on the Southern New England Frontier," in *Cultures in Contact: the Impact of European Contacts on Native American Cultural Institutions, A.D. 1000–1800*, ed. William Fitzhugh (Washington, D.C., 1985), 136–37; and Neal Salisbury, *Manitou and Providence: Indians, Europeans, and the Making of New England, 1500–1643* (Oxford, 1982), 30–34. On increasing variety in the English diet, see Malcolm Thick, "Root Crops and the Feeding of London's Poor in the Late Sixteenth and Early Seventeenth Centuries," in Chartres and Hey, *English Rural Society*, 279–96. Bragdon argues that the English sources may have overemphasized the centrality of agriculture in American subsistence (*Native People*, 36–39).

54. Archer, *Breif discription of the People*, 103; Strachey, *Historie of Travell*, 84.

55. Rosier, *True Relation*, 275; Percy, "Observations gathered out of a Discourse," 135.

56. Norbert Elias, *The Civilising Process: The History of Manners*, trans. E. Jephcott (Oxford, 1978), chap. 2, parts 1–4; Anon., *Relation of Maryland*, 38; Spclman, "Relation of Virginea," cxiii. On the transition from semipublic to private dining, see Fletcher, *Gender, Sex, and Subordination*, 142–43.

57. White, *Briefe Relation of the Voyage unto Maryland*, 44; Thomas Harriot, "Notes" to woodcuts of John White's paintings published by Theodor DeBry, in Quinn, *Roanoke Voyages*, 1:430, 438; Wood, *New Englands Prospect*, 67–68; Williams, *Key into the Language of America*, 45, 143 [misnumbered 135].

58. Rosier, *True Relation*, 270; Virginia Company, *True Declaration of the estate of the Colonie in Virginia*, 15.

59. Gabriel Archer, *Relation of Captaine Gosnols Voyage to the North part of Virginia*, and John Brereton, *Discoverie of the North part of Virginia*, in Quinn and Quinn, *English New England Voyages*, 136, 156; Smith, *Map of Virginia*, 1612, 162; Strachey, *Historie of Travell*, 115. For other accounts, see Morton, *New English Canaan*, 22, 37, and Williams, *Key into the Language of America*, 73.

60. Wood, *New Englands Prospect*, 68; Bradford and Winslow, *Mourt's Relation*, 34; Williams, *Key into the Language of America*, 11, 50, 98 [misnumbered 100]. For modern use of nocake, see Theodore Stern, "Chickahominy: The Changing Culture of a Virginia Indian Community," *Proceedings of the American Philosophical Society* 96 (1952): 195; Virginia Frances Voight, *Mohegan Chief: The Story of Harold Tantaquidgeon* (1965; Mohegan, Conn., 1983), 29–30. 31–32; and Gladys Tantaquidgeon, "Notes on the Gay Head Indians," *Indian Notes* 7 (1930): 5–8. By the time of King Philip's War the English had adapted, and military expeditions carried nocake; see Patrick M. Malone, *The Skulking Way of War: Technology and Tactics among the New England Indians* (Plimoth Plantation, 1991; Baltimore, 1993), 124.

61. Richard Whitbourne, *A Discourse and Discovery of Newfoundland* (London, 1620), R3v–R4; Rosier, *True Relation*, 304; Harriot, *Briefe and True Report*, 330, 340; Morton, *New English Canaan*, 31. See also Robert Gordon of Lochinvar, *Encouragements to Under-takers* (Edinburgh, 1625), C4.

62. Thomas Harriot, "Note" to White's painting of "The Seething of their meate. in Pots of Earth," in Quinn, *Roanoke Voyages*, 1:437; Arthur Barlowe, *First Voyage Made to the Coastes of America*, 1584, in ibid., 1:109; Bradford and Winslow, *Mourt's Relation*, 12; Whitbourne, *Discourse and Discovery*, R3v–R4; Rosier, *True Relation*, 280.

63. Wood, *New Englands Prospect*, 61–62, 67; Morton, *New English Canaan*, 30; Winslow, *Good Newes from New England*, 29.

64. Williams, *Key into the Language of America*, 120; Kingsbury, *Records of the Virginia Company*, 3:228. William Wood, however, reported that the Narragansetts preferred English shoes; *New Englands Prospect*, 70–71.

65. Harriot, *Briefe and True Report*, 363–64, and Notes to John White's pictures, in Quinn, *Roanoke Voyages*, 432–33; Barlowe, *First Voyage Made to the Coastes of America*, 104–5; Smith, *Map of Virginia*, 163; Williams, *Key into the Language of America*, 106–7 [misnumbered 108–9]; Wood, *New Englands Prospect*, 43, 91.

66. John Winthrop, *The Journal of John Winthrop, 1630–1649*, ed. Richard S. Dunn, James Savage, and Laetitia Yeandle (Cambridge, Mass., 1996), 98; Martin Pringe, *A Voyage Set Out from the Citie of Bristoll*, 1603, in Quinn and Quinn, *English New England Voyages*, 222–23. William Wood described both kinds of canoes in *New Englands Prospect*, 91.

67. Stuart Piggott, *Ancient Britons and the Antiquarian Imagination: Ideas from the Renaissance to the Regency* (London, 1989), 62–64.

68. John Guy, "To Master John Slany Treasurer, and others of the Councell, and Company of the New-found-land Plantation, July 29 1612," in Purchas, *Pilgrimes*, 19:422–23; Smith, *Generall Historie*, 105, 188; Morton, *New English Canaan*, 45; Wood, *New Englands Prospect*, 91

69. Wood, *New Englands Prospect*, 91; Rosier, *True Relation*, 281–82; Williams, *Key into the Language of America*, 108–11 [misnumbered 110–13].

70. Harriot, Notes to John White's pictures, 434–35; Strachey, *Historie of Travell*, 75, 82; Lane, *Account of the Particularities*, 276, 282; Wood, *New Englands Prospect*, 89–90, 95; Smith, *Map of Virginia*, 163–64; Williams, *Key into the Language of America*, 112, 116 [misnumbered 114, 108²].

71. Smith, *Map of Virginia*, 164–65; Spelman, "Relation of Virginea," cvii; Wood, *New Englands Prospect*, 88–89; Williams, *Key into the Language of America*, 99, 171–75 [misnumbered 101, 163–67]. On the culture of hunting and manliness in England, see Fletcher, *Gender, Sex and Subordination*, 131–35.

72. Morton, *New English Canaan*, 33–34; Williams, *Key into the Language of America*, 71. J. B. Harley argues that Indian geographical knowledge contributed conceptual power as well as crucial information to European maps; "New England Cartography and the Native Americans," in *American Beginnings: Exploration, Culture, and Cartography in the Land of Norumbega*, ed. Emerson W. Baker et al. (Lincoln, Neb. 1994), 287–313.

73. John Mason, *A Brief History of the Pequot War*, ed. Thomas Prince (Boston, 1736), 21.

74. For an eloquently argued rendition of this position, see Kirkpatrick Sale, *The Conquest of Paradise: Christopher Columbus and the Columbian Legacy* (New York, 1990).

75. Virginia Company, *True Declaration of the estate of the Colonie in Virginia*, 15.

76. Brereton, *Discoverie of the North part of Virginia*, 152–53; George Wither, "To His Friend Captaine Smith, upon his description of New England," in John Smith, *Description of New England* (London, 1616), in Barbour, *Works*, 1:315; Smith, ibid., 332–33.

77. Hakewill, *An Apology or Declaration of the Power and Providence of God in the Government of the World* (Oxford, 1635), V, 156–57.

78. "Indians in the Land," a conversation between William Cronon and Richard White, *American Heritage* 37 (1986): 18–25, esp. 20–21.

79. For Indians' own reasoning about this practice, see Williams, *Key into the Language of America*, 73; 125–26 [misnumbered 117–18]. See Harald E. L. Prins, "Children of Gluskap: Wabanaki Indians on the Eve of the European Invasion," in Baker et al., eds., *American Beginnings*, 98.

80. Pringe, *A Voyage Set Out from the Citie of Bristoll*, 227–28; Wood, *New Englands Prospect*, 15; Smith, *Map of Virginia*, 145. On indigenous ecological practices and the impact of the coming of Europeans, see William Cronon, *Changes in the Land: Indians, Colonists, and the Ecology of New England* (New York, 1983); Colin Calloway, *New Worlds for All: Indians, Europeans, and the Remaking of Early America* (Baltimore, 1997); and Timothy Silver, *A New Face on the Countryside: Indians, Colonists, and Slaves in South Atlantic Forests, 1500–1800* (Cambridge, 1990).

81. Morton, *New English Canaan*, 37.

82. Hamor, *True Discourse of the Present Estate of Virginia*, 20; Harriot, *Briefe and True Report*, 331; Morton, *New English Canaan*, 51; Winslow, "A Letter Sent from New England," in *Mourt's Relation*, 60–61.

83. Smith, *Description of New England*, 351–52.

Chapter 6. Incorporating the Other

1. Frederic Gleach interprets the evidence in this way in *Powhatan's World and Colonial Virginia: A Conflict of Cultures* (Lincoln, Neb., 1997), 113–24.

2. Christopher L. Miller and George R. Hamell, "A New Perspective on Indian-White Contact: Cultural Symbols and Colonial Trade," *Journal of American History* 73 (1986): 311–28. See also Constance A. Crosby, "From Myth to History, or Why King Philip's Ghost Walks Abroad," in *The Recovery of Meaning: Historical Archaeology in the Eastern United States,* ed. Mark P. Leone and Parker B. Potter (Washington, D.C., 1988), 183–309; and Nancy O. Lurie, "Indian Cultural Adjustment to European Civilization," in *Seventeenth-Century America,* ed. J. M. Smith (Chapel Hill, 1959), 33–60.

3. John Smith, *The Generall Historie of Virginia, New-England and the Summer Isles,* 1624, in *The Complete Works of Captain John Smith,* ed. Philip L. Barbour, 3 vols. (Chapel Hill, 1986), 2:156. For a particularly insightful discussion of the developing relationship see Martin H. Quitt, "Trade and Acculturation at Jamestown, 1607–1609: The Limits of Understanding," *William and Mary Quarterly,* 3d ser., 52 (1995): 227–58. On disdain for merchants and their determination of value through bargaining see Jean-Christophe Agnew, *Worlds Apart: The Market and the Theater in Anglo-American Thought, 1550–1750* (New York, 1986); and Donna Merwick, "The Work of the Trickster in the Dutch Possession of New Netherland," in *Dangerous Liaisons: Essays in Honour of Greg Dening,* ed. Merwick (Melbourne, 1994), 115–34.

4. Ralph Lane, *An Account of the Particularities of the imployments of the English men left in Virginia,* 1586, in *The Roanoke Voyages, 1584–1590,* ed. David Beers Quinn, 2 vols. (London, 1955), 1:280–88.

5. Virginia Council to Virginia Company, January 20, 1623, in *Records of the Virginia Company of London,* ed. Susan Myra Kingsbury, 4 vols. (Washington, D.C., 1906–35), 4:9–11.

6. George Percy, "A Trew Relacyon of the Procedeinges and Ocurrentes of Momente . . . in anno Domini 1612," *Tyler's Quarterly Historical and Genealogical Magazine* 3 (1922): 277; Alexander Whitaker to Mr. Crashawe, August 9, 1911, in *The Genesis of the United States,* ed. Alexander Brown, 2 vols. (Boston, 1890), 1:497–99. Ivor Noël Hume posits that the men may have imbibed jimsonweed, which grew around Jamestown; *The Virginia Adventure* (New York, 1994), 301–3.

7. Smith, *Generall Historie,* 106. See William M. Hamlin, "Imagined Apotheoses: Drake, Harriot, Ralegh in the Americas," *Journal of the History of Ideas* 57 (1996): 405–28.

8. Roger Williams, *A Key into the Language of America* (London, 1643), 126 [misnumbered 118].

9. Williams, *Key into the Language of America,* 59; Ralph Hamor reported on the Chickahominies' adoption of the name Tassantasses; *A True Discourse of the Present Estate of Virginia* (London, 1615), 11–15. On the Wabanakis, see Harald E. L. Prins, "Children of Gluskap: Wabanaki Indians on the Eve of the European Invasion," in *American Beginnings: Exploration, Culture, and Cartography in the Land of Norumbega,* ed. Emerson W. Baker et al. (Lincoln, Neb. 1994), 114.

10. Smith, *Generall Historie,* 175. On the Mannahoacs, see Jeffrey L. Hantman, "Powhatan's Relations with the Piedmont Monacans," in *Powhatan Foreign Relations, 1500–1722,* ed. Helen C. Rountree (Charlottesville, 1993), 94–111.

11. See Chapter 4 above. On the "continuous flow" between the land of the living and the spirit world, see Crosby, "King Philip's Ghost," 189–92.

12. Lane, *Account of the Particularities,* 278; Thomas Harriot, *A Briefe and True Report of the new found land of Virginia,* 1588, 1590, in Quinn, *Roanoke Voyages,* 1:375, 378–81; John Mason, *Brief History of the Pequot War,* ed. Thomas Prince (Boston, 1736), 20. On the context of Harriot's report see Stephen Greenblatt, "Invisible Bullets," in *Shakespearean Negotiations: The Circulation of Social Energy in Renaissance England* (Berkeley, 1988), 21–40.

13. Harriot, *Briefe and True Report,* 378–81.

14. Williams to Sir Henry Vane and John Winthrop, May 13, 1637, in *Winthrop Papers*, 3:412–13; John Winthrop, *The Journal of John Winthrop, 1630–1649*, ed. Richard S. Dunn, James Savage, and Laetitia Yeandle (Cambridge, Mass., 1996), 207–8. On mortality in England see Paul Slack, *The Impact of Plague in Tudor and Stuart England* (Oxford, 1985), 53–64, 144–51; and Mary J. Dobson, *Contours of Death and Disease in Early Modern England* (Cambridge, 1997), 371–72.

15. James Rosier, *A True Relation of the most prosperous voyage . . . in the Discovery of the land of Virginia*, 1605, in *The English New England Voyages, 1602–1608*, ed. David B. Quinn and Alison M. Quinn (London, 1983), 273–74. The editors explain that every ship carried a loadstone to remagnetize the compass.

16. Harriot, *Briefe and True Report*, 375–76; Smith, *Generall Historie*, 147.

17. Smith, *Generall Historie*, 211. On coma and mental confusion induced by carbon monoxide poisoning see Jane Brody, "Watching for the Warning Signs of an Invisible Killer," *New York Times*, January 5, 1999, D6.

18. Edward Winslow, *Good Newes from New England* (London, 1624), 26–32. On bleeding from the nose, see William Bradford, *Of Plymouth Plantation, 1620–1647*, ed. Samuel Eliot Morison (New York, 1952), 114.

19. Williams, *Key into the Language of America*, preface, 194–95 [misnumbered 186–87].

20. The English Province of the Society of Jesus, Annual Letter from Maryland, 1639, in *Narratives of Early Maryland, 1633–1684*, ed. Clayton Colman Hall (New York, 1910), 126–27.

21. Harriot, *Briefe and True Report*, 377, 380.

22. Winslow, *Good Newes from New England*, 33; John Smith, *A True Relation of such occurrences and accidents of noate as hath hapned in Virginia*, 1608, in Barbour, *Works*, 1:69. On relationships in southern New England, see Neal Salisbury, *Manitou and Providence: Indians, Europeans, and the Making of New England, 1500–1643* (Oxford, 1982), esp. chaps. 4–5.

23. Harriot, *Briefe and True Report*, 381; William Bradford and Edward Winslow, *A Relation or Journall of the English Plantation setled at Plimoth in New England* (London, 1622), known as *Mourt's Relation*, 61.

24. Lane, *Account of the Particularities*, 277; Kingsbury, *Records of the Virginia Company*, 3:425.

25. Kingsbury, *Records of the Virginia Company*, 4:22, 65, 74, 228–39, 263 (the quote is from p. 234).

26. Ibid., 4:277.

27. Winthrop, *Journal*, 125; William Wood, *New Englands Prospect* (London, 1634), sig. O4. On Osamekin's identity, see Glenn LaFantasie, ed., *The Correspondence of Roger Williams* (Providence, 1988), 178–79.

28. William Bradford and Edward Winslow related Squanto's entry into Plymouth, and told the story of his kidnapping; see *Mourt's Relation*, 32–36, 41; Bradford, *Of Plymouth Plantation*, 80–81, 98–99. Smith, *Generall Historie*, 428, refers to the same man as Tanto. For the name Somerset see Christopher Levett, *A Voyage unto New England* (London, 1624), 9, 14, 16. On the careers of Squanto and Hobbomock in Plymouth, see Frank Shuffelton, "Indian Devils and Pilgrim Fathers: Squanto, Hobomok, and the English Conception of Indian Religion," *New England Quarterly* 49 (1976): 108–16; Neal Salisbury, *Manitou and Providence: Indian, Europeans, and the Making of New England, 1500–1643* (Oxford, 1982), esp. chap 4; and John H. Humins, "Squanto and Massasoit: A Struggle for Power," *New England Quarterly* 60 (1987): 54–70.

29. Bradford, *Of Plymouth Plantation*, 88–89, 114; On Hobbomock's long stay in Plymouth, see Kathleen J. Bragdon, *Native People of Southern New England, 1500–1650* (Norman, Okla., 1996), 29.

30. Francis Higginson, *New-Englands Plantation*, 1630, in *Tracts and Other Papers, Relating Principally to the Origin, Settlement, and Progress of the Colonies in North America*, comp. Peter Force, 4 vols. (1844; reprint, Washington, D.C., 1963), 1:13; Winslow, *Good Newes from New England*, 53.

31. Samuel Purchas, *Purchas His Pilgrimage*, 3d ed. (London, 1617), 943; Alexander Whitaker, "To my verie deere and loving Cosen M. G. Minister of the B. F. in London," in Ralph Hamor, *A True Discourse of the Present Estate of Virginia* (London, 1615), 59–60; William Strachey, *The Historie of Travell into Virginia Britania*, 1612, ed. Louis B. Wright and Virginia Freund (London, 1953), 113. On gaining power through names see Crosby, "King Philip's Ghost," 193.

32. Williams, *Key into the Language of America*, 5–6, 202 [misnumbered 194].

33. Strachey, *Historie of Travell*, 56.

34. Winslow, *Good Newes from New England*, 58–59; Occum, "Account of the Montauk Indians," *Collections of the Massachusetts Historical Society*, 1st ser., 10 (1809): 108; Strachey, *Historie of Travell*, 113–14. See the discussion of the accumulation of names by the valiant in Helen C. Rountree, *The Powhatan Indians of Virginia: Their Traditional Culture* (Norman, Okla., 1989), 80. On Powhatan's and his successors' names, see Gleach, *Powhatan's World and Colonial Virginia*, 3, 28, 32–33, 146.

35. Lane, *Account of the Particularities*, 265; Council in Virginia to the Virginia Company, January 1622, in Kingsbury, *Records of the Virginia Company*, 3:584.

36. Smith, *Generall Historie*, 173–78.

37. *New Englands First Fruits* (London, 1643), 9.

38. Thomas Morton, *New English Canaan*, 1637, in Force, *Tracts*, 2:19. On the significance of "metaphorical thresholds between this world and the other world," see George R. Hamell, "Mythical Realities and European Contact in the Northeast during the Sixteenth and Seventeenth Centuries," *Man in the Northeast* 33 (1987): 63–87; and Bragdon, *Native People of Southern New England*, 197–98.

39. Smith, *Generall Historie*, 261; Purchas, *Purchas His Pilgrimage*, 3d ed., 955. On Uttamatomakkin's return see Rountree, *Powhatan Indians*, 132.

40. Quinn, *Roanoke Voyages*, 1:116; Lane, *Account of the Particularities*, 287; John White, "The fourth voyage made to Virginia, 1587," in Quinn, *Roanoke Voyages*, 2:526–27, 531.

41. Strachey, *Historie of Travell*, 113.

42. Strachey, *Historie of Travell*, 56; Gleach, *Powhatan's World and Colonial Virginia*, 33.

43. Notes to Rosier, *True Relation*, in Quinn and Quinn, *English New England Voyages*, 309–10.

44. Champlain, *The Voyages of the Sieur de Champlain*, 1613, in *The Works of Samuel de Champlain*, ed. H. P. Biggar, 6 vols. (Toronto, 1922–36), 1:315–16.

45. Winthrop, *Journal*, 110.

46. Percy, "Trew Relacyon," 279–80; Kingsbury, *Records of the Virginia Company*, 3:228. John White's portrait of a conjurer is labeled "the flyer," and he has a flattened bird's body fastened to the side of his head; see Quinn, *Roanoke Voyages*, 1:442–43. Kathleen Bragdon argues that shamans are often linked symbolically to birds, who shift between the air and land; *Native People of Southern New England*, 204. On native oral traditions of the power of feathers see Laurie Weinstein, Delinda Passas, and Anabela Marques, eds., "The Use of Feathers in Native New England," in *Enduring Traditions: The Native Peoples of New England*, ed. Laurie Weinstein (Westport, Conn., 1994), 169–85.

47. Smith, *Generall Historie*, 293–305 (the quotes are from 293, 305); "Voyage of Anthony Chester to Virginia, made in the year 1620" (Leyden, 1707), reprinted as "Two Tragical Events," *William and Mary Quarterly* 9 (1901): 213; Council in Virginia, November 11, 1619, and January 20, 1623, in Kingsbury, *Records of the Virginia*

Company, 3:228, 4:11. George Wyatt wrote to advise his son Francis, governor of Virginia. Of Munetute's reported dying wish to be buried among the English so that his claimed invulnerability would not be disproven, he wrote that it "smels of a Jesuit"; J. Frederick Fausz and Jon Kukla, eds., "A Letter of Advice to the Governor of Virginia, 1624," *William and Mary Quarterly,* 3d ser., 34 (1977): 117. On the uprising and its context see J. Frederick Fausz, "George Thorpe, Nemattanew, and the Powhatan Uprising of 1622," *Virginia Cavalcade,* winter 1979, 111–17.

48. Winslow, *Good Newes from New England,* 55–56; Bragdon, *Native People of Southern New England,* 170, 189–90. For other claims of invulnerability, see William Simmons, *The Spirit of the New England Tribes: Indian History and Folklore, 1620–1984* (Hanover, N.H., 1986), 42–43.

49. Bradford, *Of Plymouth Plantation,* 98–99

50. Robert Cushman, *A Sermon Preached in Plimmoth in New-England* (London, 1622), A3.

51. David Pulsifer, ed., *Records of the Colony of New Plymouth, Deeds, etc. vol. 1, 1620–1651* (Boston, 1861), 4.

52. Winslow, *Good News from New England,* 5–11; Bradford, *Of Plymouth Plantation,* 98–99; Bradford and Winslow, *Mourt's Relation,* 53–59.

53. Wood, *New Englands Prospect,* 81; Morton, *New English Canaan,* 26; William Hubbard, *The History of the Indian Wars in New England,* ed. Samuel G. Drake, 2 vols. (Boston, 1865), 2:135, 153, 177.

54. Williams to Winthrop, August 1636, in LaFantasie, *Correspondence,* 1:54–55; John Underhill, *Newes from America* (London, 1638), 16; Cotton Mather, *Magnalia Christi Americana* (London, 1702), bk. 7, pp. 42–43; Philip Vincent, *A True Relation of the Late Battel fought in New England, between the English, and the Salvages* (London, 1637), B3v–B4; "Leift Lion Gardener his Relation of the Pequot Warres," *Collections of the Massachusetts Historical Society,* 3d ser., 3 (1833): 149; Hubbard, *History of the Indian Wars,* 2:23, 29; Johnson, *Wonder-Working Providence of Sion's Saviour,* ed. J. Franklin Jameson (New York, 1910), 164.

55. Mason, *Brief History,* 16–17; for another rendition of Stanton's role see John Winthrop to William Bradford, July 28, 1637, in *Winthrop Papers,* 3:457. On swamps as sacred places see Cornelius Tacitus, *The Description of Germanie: and Customes of the People,* trans. Richard Grenewey (London, 1598), 260; Bradford, *Of Plymouth Plantation,* 84. Roger Williams also reported that swamps were refuges in times of danger; *Key into the Language of America,* 46–47, 72–73. On the character of such places, see Bragdon, *Native People of Southern New England,* 192–93. In the negotiations about Pequot captives following the war, Miantonomi repeatedly told Roger Williams that he did not trust Thomas Stanton, and Williams also found Stanton's judgment untrustworthy; see Williams to Winthrop, September 9, 1637, and January 10, February 28, and May 27, 1638, in LaFantasie, *Correspondence,* 1:117, 140, 145, 157. But Stanton played an important role as Connecticut's interpreter; see Williams to Winthrop, August 1 and September 21, 1638, in ibid., 1:170, 184; see also 1:120, 242–43, 404–6.

56. Rolfe, "The coppie of the Gentle-mans letters to sir Thomas Dale, that after maried Powhatans daughter, containing the reasons moving him thereunto," in Hamor, *True Discourse,* 61–68; William Symonds, *Virginia. A Sermon Preached at White-Chappell, In the Presence of the Adventurers and Planters for Virginia* (London, 1609), 35. Paul Brown presents an analysis of Rolfe's letter in "'This thing of darkness I acknowledge mine': The Tempest and the Discourse of Colonialism," in *Political Shakespeare: New Essays in Cultural Materialism,* ed. Jonathan Dollimore and Alan Sinfield (Ithaca, N.Y., 1985), 49–51.

57. Alexander, *An Encouragement to Colonies* (London, 1624), 28; Eburne, *A Plaine Pathway to Plantations,* 1624, ed. Louis B. Wright (Ithaca, N.Y., 1962), 137, 143.

58. On John and Anne Jackson, see "The Catalogue of the names of the young woemen nowe sent in the Marmaduke," in *The Ferrar Papers, 1590–1790*, ed. David R. Ransome (Wakefield, Yorkshire, 1992), microfilm, 306; and "The names of the maydes sente in the Marmaduke bounde for Virginia 1621," in ibid., 309; H. R. McIlwaine, ed., *Minutes of the Council and General Court of Virginia*, 2d ed. (Richmond, 1979), 128, 181; David R. Ransome, "Wives for Virginia, 1621," *William and Mary Quarterly*, 3d ser., 48 (1991): 3–18.

59. For Moutapass and Graves, see "The Observations of Master John Pory," in Smith, *Generall Historie*, 289–90; on White see Purchas, *Purchas His Pilgrimage*, 2d ed., 766; Henry Fleet, "Henry Fleet of Fleet's Bay, Virginia, 1600–1660," *Northern Neck Historical Magazine* 12 (1962): 1068–76.

60. Bradford, *Of Plymouth Plantation*, 219–22, 226, 232–33, 237.

61. Williams to Winthrop, October 1637; January 10, 1638; February 28, 1638; May 22, 1638; May 27, 1638, in LaFantasie, *Correspondence*, 1:126, 140, 145, 155, 158; Coddington to Winthrop, May 22, 1640, in *Winthrop Papers*, 4:245–47.

62. Winslow, *Good Newes from New England*, 27, 33.

63. Smith, *Proceedings of the English Colony in Virginia*, in Barbour, *Works*, 1;261–65; Smith, *Generall Historie*, 210–14; Percy, "Trew Relacyon," 271; Strachey, *Historie of Travell*, 34, 61–62, 98. On native sources of scurvy-preventing vitamin C, see Helen C. Rountree and Thomas E. Davidson, *Eastern Shore Indians of Virginia and Maryland* (Charlottesville, 1997), 35.

64. Edward Waterhouse, *A Declaration of the State of the Colony and Affaires in Virginia* (London, 1622), 18, 20–21; "Two Tragical Events," *William and Mary Quarterly* 9 (1901): 212–13; Smith, *Generall Historie*, 297; Virginia Council to Virginia Company, April 4, 1623, in Kingsbury, *Records of the Virginia Company*, 4:98. On the identity of these two men see Rountree, "The Powhatans and the English," in Rountree, *Powhatan Foreign Relations*, 188–92.

65. Smith, *True Relation*, 93–95; Smith, *Proceedings of the English Colony in Virginia*, 274; Smith, *Generall Historie*, 152, 203–4.

66. Hamor, *True Discourse*, 4–7; Dale to "the R. and my most esteemed friend Mr. D. M.," in ibid., 55–56; Whitaker to "my verie deere and loving Cosen M. G.," in ibid., 59–60. On these points and the issues of this chapter generally, see Peter Hulme, *Colonial Encounters: Europe and the Native Caribbean, 1492–1797* (London, 1986), chap. 4.

67. The account of Rebecca and the beginnings of Israel is in Gen. 24–33. The quotes are from The Geneva Bible (Geneva, 1560), Gen. 24:60 and 25:23. On Pocahontas's compassion see Smith, *Generall Historie*, 258. Jill Lepore demonstrates how the colonists gave the Pokanoket chiefs Wamsutta and Metacom the names of the ancient Macedonian leaders Alexander and Philip, evoking the vision of Paul in Acts 16:9, in which a Macedonian appealed, "Come over into Macedonia, and help us." This vision was reproduced, with an Indian replacing the Macedonian, in the Massachusetts Bay Company seal; see Lepore, *The Name of War: King Philip's War and the Origins of American Identity* (New York, 1998), xvi.

68. Richard Crakanthorpe, *A Sermon at the Solemnizing of the Happie Inauguration . . . of King James* (London, 1609), D2v.

69. On the Pocahontas-Rolfe wedding see Hamor, *True Relation*, 10–11; Dale to D. M., in ibid., 54–55. William Strachey mentioned Pocahontas's previous marriage in *Historie of Travell*, 62.

70. Hamor, *True Relation*, 38–46.

71. I thank Ann Rosalind Jones and Peter Stallybrass and the Folger Library Seminar on Renaissance Fetishisms, October 1998, for discussion of Pocahontas's dress in the portrait. The text of "The Vision of Delight" is in *Ben Jonson: Selected Masques*, ed.

Stephen Orgel (New Haven, 1970), 149–59, and its presentation is discussed on pp. 21–22, 34–35. On the masque Pocahontas saw, in terms of the literature of colonization, see Karen Robertson, "Pocahontas at the Masque," *Signs* 21 (1996): 551–83. John Chamberlain discussed Pocahontas's placement and the queen's dancing in *The Letters of John Chamberlain*, ed. Norman Egbert McClure, 2 vols. (Philadelphia, 1939), 2:49–50.

72. Nathaniel Butler, *The Historye of the Bermudaes or Summer Islands*, ed. J. H. Lefroy (London, 1882), 271–72, 284; Rolfe to Sir Edwin Sandys, June 8, 1617, in Kingsbury, *Records of the Virginia Company*, 3:70–73 (the quote is from p. 71); David R. Ransome, "Pocahontas and the Mission to the Indians," *Virginia Magazine of History and Biography* 99 (1991): 81–94. There is no record of what happened to the couple married in Bermuda.

73. McClure, *Letters of John Chamberlain*, 2:50, 56–57; Smith, *Generall Historie*, 258–62; the text of the Virginia Company grant is in Ransome, "Pocahontas and the Mission to the Indians," 94. On Pocahontas's life see Philip L. Barbour, *Pocahontas and Her World* (Boston, 1969); on the causes of her death, see p. 181. Barbour demonstrates that the Belle Sauvage Inn had had that name for decades (159–60). On the continuing meaning of Pocahontas see Robert S. Tilton, *Pocahontas: The Evolution of an American Narrative* (Cambridge, 1994).

74. Charlotte Gradie, "The Powhatans in the Context of the Spanish Empire," in Rountree, *Powhatan Foreign Relations*, 154–72; Gradie, "Spanish Jesuits in Virginia: The Mission that Failed," *Virginia Magazine of History and Biography* 96 (1988): 131–56. Documents of the Spanish mission are published in Clifford M. Lewis, S. J., and Albert J. Loomie, S. J., *The Spanish Jesuit Mission in Virginia, 1570–1572* (Chapel Hill, 1953), see pp. 15–18 on Don Luís's age. Carl Bridenbaugh argued that Don Luís did indeed live to see Jamestown founded and that he was Opechancanough who led the two great attacks on the colony in 1622 and 1644; *Early Americans* (New York, 1981), chap. 1.

75. Lane, *Account of the Particularities*, 280; and White, "The fourth voyage made to Virginia," 2:527.

76. Winthrop, *Journal*, 47.

77. Lane, *Account of Particularities*, 270–71; Underhill, *Newes from America*, 7. Jill Lepore posits that the actor in this Pequot War incident was Sassamon, the man whose death would later trigger King Philip's War; Jill Lepore, "Dead Men Tell No Tales: John Sassamon and the Fatal Consequences of Literacy," *American Quarterly* 46 (1994): 479–512, esp. 487.

78. *New Englands First Fruits*, 4–11; Cotton Mather quoted extensively from Shepard's letter on Wequash in his *Magnalia Christi Americana*, bk. 7, p. 43. Williams, *Key into the Language of America*, "To the Reader." On Wequash's role in the Pequot War see Mason, *Brief History of the Pequot War*, 7, 13; Hubbard, *History of the Indian Wars*, 2: 20, 29; and Williams to Sir Henry Vane and John Winthrop, May 13 and 15, 1637, in *Winthrop Papers*, 3:410–14.

79. Experience Mayhew, *Indian Converts* (London, 1727), 1–4. See James Ronda, "Generations of Faith: The Christian Indians of Martha's Vineyard," *William and Mary Quarterly*, 3d ser., 38 (1981): 369–94.

80. Edward Howes to John Winthrop, Jr., March 1632, in *Winthrop Papers*, 3:74; *New Englands First Fruits*, 4–7; Bradford, *Of Plymouth Plantation*, 114. See Chapter 2 above.

81. French venturers also left boys, called *truchements*, with Indians they encountered; see Gordon Sayre, *Les Sauvages Américains: Representations of Native Americans in French and English Colonial Literature* (Chapel Hill, 1997), 7.

82. Smith, *True Relation*, 69, 91–93; Smith, *Proceedings of the English Colony in Virginia*, 216.

83. Henry Spelman, "Relation of Virginea," c. 1613, in *Travels and Works of Captain John Smith*, ed. E. Arber and A. G. Bradley, 2 vols. (Edinburgh, 1910), 1:cviii; Smith, *Generall Historie*, 232.

84. Strachey, *Historie of Travell,* 85–86; Hamor, *True Discourse,* 37–38; Dale to D. M., in ibid., 53–54.

85. "A Letter of Sir Samuell Argoll touching his Voyage to Virginia, and Actions there, 1613," in Samuel Purchas, *Hakluytus Posthumus or Purchas His Pilgrimes,* 1625, 20 vols. (Glasgow, 1906), 19:92–93; Hamor, *True Relation,* 4–6; Smith, *Generall Historie,* 243–44. Henry Spelman was in England at this time.

86. Smith, *Proceedings of the English Colony in Virginia,* 244–45.

87. Stockham, "Relation," in Smith, *Generall Historie,* 285–86; John Pory, "A Reporte of the manner of proceeding in the general Assembly convened at James City," July 30–August 4, 1619, in Kingsbury, *Records of the Virginia Company,* 3:174–75.

88. Rolfe to Sir Edwin Sandys, January 1620, in Kingsbury, *Records of the Virginia Company,* 3:244–45; Pory to Sandys, January 1620, in ibid., 3:253.

89. Smith, *Generall Historie,* 141–43; Edward Waterhouse, *A Declaration of the State of the Colony and Affaires in Virginia* (London, 1622), 21; Virginia Council to Virginia Company, January 1622 and January 1623, in Kingsbury, *Records of the Virginia Company,* 3:583–84, 4:10–11.

90. Smith, *Generall Historie,* 257, 312–15, 320–21; Arundel to William Caninge, April 1623, in Kingsbury, *Records of the Virginia Company,* 4:89. On the careers of these interpreters see J. Frederick Fausz, "Middlemen in Peace and War: Virginia's Earliest Indian Interpreters, 1608–1632," *Virginia Magazine of History and Biography* 95 (1987): 41–64.

91. Williams to Winthrop, June 1638, in LaFantasie, *Correspondence,* 1:163. The letter of Winthrop's that provoked this outburst has not been found.

92. Tom Stoppard, *The Dog It Was That Died,* in *Stoppard: The Plays for Radio, 1964–1983* (London, 1990), 181.

Chapter 7. Resisting the Other

1. William Wood, *New Englands Prospect* (London, 1634), 60–61; Roger Williams, *A Key into the Language of America* (London, 1643), 151–62 [misnumbered 145–54]; Kathleen J. Bragdon, "Conclusions," in *Native People of Southern New England, 1500–1650* (Norman, Okla., 1996), esp. 241–47; Robert S. Grumet, *Historic Contact: Indian People and Colonists in Today's Northeastern United States in the Sixteenth through Eighteenth Centuries* (Norman, Okla., 1995), 15.

2. William Strachey, *The Historie of Travell into Virginia Britania,* 1612, ed. Louis B. Wright and Virginia Freund (London, 1953), 105–7. On the shifting relationship between the Powhatans and the Monacans see Jeffrey L. Hantman, "Powhatan's Relations with the Piedmont Monacans," in *Powhatan Foreign Relations, 1500–1722,* ed. Helen C. Rountree (Charlottesville, 1993), 94–111.

3. Thomas Morton, *New English Canaan,* 1637, in *Tracts and Other Papers, Relating Principally to the Origin, Settlement, and Progress of the Colonies in North America,* comp. Peter Force, 4 vols. (1844; reprint, Washington, D.C., 1963), 2:26.

4. Arthur Barlowe, *The First Voyage Made to the Coastes of America,* 1584, in *The Roanoke Voyages, 1584–1590,* ed. David Beers Quinn, 2 vols. (London, 1955), 1:98.

5. Bragdon, *Native People of Southern New England,* 130–39.

6. Williams, *Key into the Language of America,* 153–55, 162–63, 165 [misnumbered 145–47, 154–55, 157].

7. John Winthrop, *The Journal of John Winthrop, 1630–1649,* ed. Richard S. Dunn, James Savage, and Laetitia Yeandle (Cambridge, Mass., 1996), 191; "Leift Lion Gardener his Relation of the Pequot Warres," *Collections of the Massachusetts Historical Society,* 3d ser., 3 (1833): 137–39.

8. Smith, *The Generall Historie of Virginia, New-England and the Summer Isles*, 1624, in *The Complete Works of Captain John Smith*, ed. Philip L. Barbour, 3 vols. (Chapel Hill, 1986), 2:196.

9. John White, "The Fourth Voyage Made to Virginia," 1587, in Quinn, *Roanoke Voyages*, 2:526; George Percy, "A Trew Relacyon of the Procedeinges and Ocurrentes of Momente . . . in anno Domini 1612," *Tyler's Quarterly Historical and Genealogical Magazine* 3 (1922): 264–65.

10. Patrick Copland, *Virginia's God Be Thanked* (London, 1622), 24; William Crashaw, *A Sermon Preached in London before the right honourable the Lord Lawarre* (London, 1610), E4v, F4; Smith, *Generall Historie*, 272.

11. Winthrop to Margaret Winthrop, July 23, 1630, in *Winthrop Papers*, 2:303; Ward to John Winthrop, Jr., December 24, 1635, in ibid., 3:215–17.

12. Cushman, *Reasons and Considerations touching the lawfulnesse of removing out of England into the parts of America*, in William Bradford and Edward Winslow, *A Relation or Journall of the English Plantation setled at Plimoth in New England* (London, 1622), known as *Mourt's Relation*, 72; Crashaw, *Sermon before the Lord Lawarre*, F4v.

13. Edmund Spenser, *A View of the Present State of Ireland*, ed. W. L. Renwick (Oxford, 1934), 82, 87; Gerard Boate, *Irelands Naturall History* (London, 1652), 7–8; Shuger, "Irishmen, Aristocrats, and Other White Barbarians," *Renaissance Quarterly* 50 (1997): 494–525; Nicholas Canny, *Kingdom and Colony: Ireland in the Atlantic World, 1560–1800* (Baltimore, 1988), esp. chap. 2.

14. Cushman, *A Sermon Preached in Plimmoth*, A4; John Underhill, *Newes from America* (London, 1638), 3–5; William Morrell, *New England* (London, 1625), 21; Wood, *New Englands Prospect*, 97–98. J. H. Elliott argues that the English were much more fearful than all other colonizing nations: "It is hard not to be struck by the almost obsessional fear among seventeenth-century English colonists of the dangers of cultural degeneration." *Britain and Spain in America: Colonists and Colonized* (Reading, U.K., 1994), quote p. 24.

15. Crashaw, *Sermon before the Lord Lawarre*, 40; Winthrop, *Journal*, 167.

16. William Strachey, *For the Colony in Virginea Britannia. Lawes Divine, Morall and Martiall, etc.* (London, 1612), reprinted in Force, *Tracts*, esp. 3:16–17; Percy, "Trew Relacyon," 280. Imposition of martial law on civilian populations was a subject of great concern in England; see Karen Ordahl Kupperman, *Providence Island, 1630–1641: The Other Puritan Colony* (Cambridge, 1993), 188–90; and Stephen Greenblatt, "Martial Law in the Land of Cokaigne," in *Shakespearean Negotiations: The Circulation of Social Energy in Renaissance England* (Berkeley, 1988), 129–63, esp. 148–55. Governor De la Warr, before whom Crashaw preached, approved the martial law regime when he arrived in June 1610; see Strachey, *Lawes*, 9.

17. Edward Winslow, *Good Newes from New England* (London, 1624), A3; John Rolfe, *True Relation*, 1616 (Charlottesville, 1951), 3–4; Rolfe to Sandys, January 1620, in *Records of the Virginia Company of London*, ed. Susan Myra Kingsbury, 4 vols. (Washington, D.C., 1906–35), 3:247. Spenser traced the degeneration of the English settlers in Ireland to dissension among their leaders; *View of the Present State of Ireland*, 82–83. Debora Shuger argues that the "primary objects of social discipline, regimentation, and repression" in sixteenth-century England were upper-class men; "Irishmen, Aristocrats, and Other White Barbarians," *Renaissance Quarterly* 50 (1997): 494–525 (the quote is from p. 494).

18. On this point see Michael Walzer, "Puritanism as a Revolutionary Ideology," *History and Theory* 3 (1964): 59–90.

19. Williams, *Key into the Language of America*, A4v.

20. Gabriel Archer, *A Breif discription of the People*, 1607, in *The Jamestown Voyages under the First Charter, 1606–1609*, ed. Philip L. Barbour, 2 vols. (Cambridge, 1969), 1:103–4. See Karen Ordahl Kupperman, "English Perceptions of Treachery, 1583–1640: The Case of the American 'Savages,'" *Historical Journal* 20 (1977): 163–87.

21. Williams to Winthrop, July 10, 1637, in *The Correspondence of Roger Williams*, ed. Glenn W. LaFantasie, 2 vols. (Hanover, N.H., 1988), 1:93–95; Williams, *Key into the Language of America*, 51; and Elisha R. Potter, Jr., *The Early History of Narragansett*, *Collections of the Rhode Island Historical Society* 3 (1835): 245–66. "Sassawwaw" was also written "Sosoa" or "Socho."

22. Virginia Company, "Instructions Given by way of Advice," in Barbour, *Jamestown Voyages*, 1:50–52.

23. On this point see James Axtell, "The Scholastic Philosophy of the Wilderness," in his *The European and the Indian: Essays in the Ethnohistory of Colonial North America* (New York, 1981), 131–67.

24. Barlowe, *First Voyage*, 91–116 (the quote is from p. 110).

25. Anon., "The voyage made by Sir Richard Greenvile, for Sir Walter Ralegh, to Virginia, in the yeere, 1585," in Quinn, *Roanoke Voyages*, 1:178–93, esp. 189, 191.

26. Lane's account of these events is in Quinn, *Roanoke Voyages*, 1:255–94. For fuller descriptions see David Beers Quinn, *Set Fair for Roanoke: Voyages and Colonies, 1584–1606* (Chapel Hill, 1985), and Karen Ordahl Kupperman, *Roanoke: The Abandoned Colony* (Totowa, N.J., 1984).

27. This account is from Percy, "Trew Relacyon," 259–82; Strachey, *Historie of Travell*, 74–75. On the rules of war see Barbara Donagan, "Atrocity, War Crime, and Treason in the English Civil War," *American Historial Review* 99 (1994): 1137–66, esp. 1144. Captain John Ratcliffe also went by the name of John Sicklemore; his possible relationship to Michael Sicklemore is not known.

28. Copland, *Virginia's God Be Thanked*, 28–29; Smith, *Generall Historie*, 297.

29. Council in Virginia to Virginia Company, January 20, 1623, in Kingsbury, *Records of the Virginia Company*, 4:9–11. On Thorpe see J. Frederick Fausz, "George Thorpe, Nemattanew, and the Powhatan Uprising of 1622," *Virginia Cavalcade*, winter 1979, 111–17.

30. Tacitus, *Life of Julius Agricola*, trans. Savile, 190, 195–96. Benedetto Fontana argues that this "brilliant epigram" may represent Tacitus's commentary on the consolidation of power within the Roman state itself; "Tacitus on Empire and Republic," *History of Political Thought* 14 (1993): 29. On redescription, see Quentin Skinner, *Reason and Rhetoric in the Philosophy of Hobbes* (Cambridge, 1996), 161–72, esp. 163 n. 148.

31. See Chapter 6 at note 87.

32. George Wyatt to Sir Francis Wyatt, June 1624, in "A Letter of Advice to the Governor of Virginia, 1624," ed. J. Frederick Fausz and Jon Kukla, *William and Mary Quarterly*, 3d ser., 34 (1977), 104–29.

33. Winslow, *Good Newes from New England*, 1–4; William Bradford, *Of Plymouth Plantation, 1620–1647*, ed. Samuel Eliot Morison (New York, 1952), 96; Paul A. Robinson, "Lost Opportunities: Miantonomi and the English in Seventeenth-Century Narragansett Country," in *Northeastern Indian Lives*, ed. Robert S. Grumet (Amherst, 1996), 18–19.

34. Winslow, *Good Newes from New England*, A2v, 40–45. See also Neal Salisbury, *Manitou and Providence: Indians, Europeans, and the Making of New England, 1500–1643* (Oxford, 1982), 127–33.

35. Bradford's letter of September 8, 1623, is excerpted and Robinson's reply of December 19, 1623, is printed in full in Walter H. Burgess, *John Robinson, Pastor of the Pilgrim Fathers: A Study of His Life and Times* (New York, 1920), 279–81. Robinson's letter is also printed in appendix 5 of Bradford, *Of Plymouth Plantation*, ed. Morison, 376–77.

36. William Apess, *Eulogy on King Philip, as Pronounced at the Odeon, in Federal Street, Boston, 1836*, in *A Son of the Forest and Other Writings by William Apess, a Pequot*, ed. Barry O'Connell (Amherst, 1997), 107.

37. Morton, *New English Canaan*, 71–79; Bradford, *Of Plymouth Plantation*, 206–7. See Karen Ordahl Kupperman, "Thomas Morton, Historian," *New England Quarterly* 50 (1977): 660–64.

38. Williams, *Key into the Language of America*, 59–60.

39. On the growth of the English colonies in the 1630s see Karen Ordahl Kupperman, "The Founding Years of Virginia—and the United States," *Virginia Magazine of History and Biography* 104 (1996): 103–12.

40. For Thomas Rolfe's career see Philip L. Barbour, *Pocahontas and Her World* (Boston, 1969), 214–15. On Savage see Helen C. Rountree and Thomas E. Davidson, *Eastern Shore Indians of Virginia and Maryland* (Charlottesville, 1997), 50–52.

41. Williams, *Key into the Language of America*, 57–58. This incident may have been in response to one in which Williams had tried to convince the Narragansetts that they had broken their league with the colonists "with breaking a straw in two or three places." Williams to Winthrop, August 20, 1637, in LaFantasie, *Correspondence*, 1:112.

42. *The Serious Representation of Col. William Eyre Prisoner in the Castle at Oxford; Tendred to the Consideration of the Parliament, Army, and Kingdom, For the clearing of his Innocency, and manifesting his Integrity toward the freedom of the Nation, and Establishment of the just Power of Parliaments equally representing the People* (n.p., 1649), 7.

43. Melissa Jayne Fawcett, *The Lasting of the Mohegans: The Story of the Wolf People* (Uncasville, Conn., 1995), 11–12.

44. "Gardener his Relation of the Pequot Warres," 145; Williams to Sir Henry Vane and John Winthrop, May 13 and 15, 1637, in *Winthrop Papers*, 3:410–14 (the quote is from p. 414).

45. Underhill, *Newes from America*, 42–43. For an excellent reconstruction of the events of the war see Alfred A. Cave, *The Pequot War* (Amherst, 1996). Cave's interpretation of English motivations differs from that presented here. For modern Pequots' tradition of these events see the Mashantucket Pequot Tribal Nation website: www.mashantucket.com.

46. Philip Vincent, *A True Relation of the Late Battel fought in New England, between the English, and the Salvages* (London, 1637), B4; Underhill, *Newes from America*, 39–40.

47. William Hooke, *New Englands Teares. For Old Englands Feares*, a sermon preached on July 23 1640 (London, 1641).

48. *Henry V* 3.3. In the introduction to his edition of *Henry V* (Oxford, 1982), Gary Taylor argues that the play was written in the spring of 1599 and that the Essex expedition was its self-conscious context.

49. Barbara Donagan, "Codes and Conduct in the English Civil War," *Past and Present* 118 (1988): 65–95. For a vivid description of the stages of cruelty that necessarily followed the fall of a besieged town, see Thomas Gainsford, "Observations of State, and millitary affaires for the most parte collected out of Cornelius Tacitus," 1612, Huntington Library MS EL 6857, 76. Gainsford had served in Ireland.

50. Smith, *The True Travels, Adventures, and Observations of Captaine John Smith*, in Barbour, *Works*, 3:157. Smith describes several sieges in eastern Europe and their bloody aftermaths; ibid., 163–86.

51. On military training and experience, see Barbara Donagan, "Halcyon Days and the Literature of War: England's Military Education before 1642," *Past and Present* 147 (1995): 65–100. On warfare and its codes as applied both in Europe and in America see Ronald Dale Karr, "'Why Should You Be So Furious?': The Violence of the Pequot War," *Journal of American History* 85 (1998): 876–909.

52. Sir John Pope Hennessy, *Sir Walter Ralegh in Ireland* (London, 1883), 10–18. The appendix prints both the official report of the action and the queen's reply, 207–14. David B. Quinn writes that if, as the English argued, Smerwick had surrendered unconditionally, the killings were allowed under "such laws of war as there were." *Ralegh and the British Empire* (London, 1947): 33–34.

53. David B. Quinn, ed., *The Voyages and Colonising Enterprises of Sir Humphrey Gilbert,* 2 vols. (London, 1940), 1:16–17.

54. Nicholas Canny, "Religion, Politics, and the Irish Rising of 1641," in *Religion and Rebellion, Historical Studies XX,* ed. Judith Devlin and Ronan Fanning (Dublin, 1997), 57–58.

55. Cromwell to William Lenthall, Speaker of the Parliament of England, September 17, 1649, and October 14, 1649, in *The Writings and Speeches of Oliver Cromwell,* ed. Wilbur Cortez Abbot, 4 vols. (Cambridge, Mass., 1937–47), 2:125–28, 140–43. See James Burke, "The New Model Army and the Problems of Siege Warfare, 1648–51," *Irish Historical Studies* 27 (1990): 1–29.

56. See J. R. Hale, *War and Society in Renaissance Europe, 1450–1620* (Baltimore, 1985), chap. 7, "The direct impact of war on civilians"; Geoffrey Parker, *The Dutch Revolt* (Ithaca, N.Y., 1977), 156–62.

57. See, for example, the volume in which are bound: [L. Brinckmair,] *The Warnings of Germany* (London, 1638); *Lacrymae Germaniae: Or the Tears of Germany* (London, 1638); *The Invasions of Germany* (London, 1638); *A True and Brief Relation of the Bloudy Battel* (London, 1638); and [P. Vincent,] *The Lamentations of Germany* (London, 1638).

58. Vincent, *Lamentations of Germany;* and Vincent, *True Relation of the Late Battel fought in New England,* B4–B4v, p. 20. Captain John Mason also argued that the English had been forced into burning the Pequot fort; Mason, *A Brief History of the Pequot War,* ed. Thomas Prince (Boston, 1736), 8–9. The *Dictionary of National Biography* says that the two Vincents are the same man. On the comparison of European and American wars see James Drake, "Severing the Ties that Bind Them: A Reconceptualization of King Philip's War" (Ph.D. diss., University of California at Los Angeles, 1996); Drake discusses Philip Vincent on pp. 205–8. Barbara Donagan ("Atrocity, War Crime, and Treason," 1144) demonstrates that cruelty in European wars was blamed on the victims who forced the armies into their actions.

59. Hooke, *New Englands Teares. For Old Englands Feares,* 12, 15, 20.

60. Ian Roy, "England Turned Germany? The Aftermath of the Civil War in its European Context," *Transactions of the Royal Historical Society,* 5th ser., 28 (1978): 127–44.

61. Donagan, "Atrocity, War Crime, and Treason," 1137–66. On Germany's experience see Geoffrey Parker, *The Thirty Years' War* (London, 1984), 125–30, and chap. 6.

62. Vincent, *True Relation of the Late Battel fought in New England,* B2. On "self-preservation as the fundamental natural right" in this period see Richard Tuck, *Philosophy and Government, 1572–1651* (Cambridge, 1993), quote p. xvi.

63. Wood, *New Englands Prospect,* 61–62.

64. Williams to Winthrop, July 10, 1637; August 20, 1637; and June 1638, in LaFantasie, *Correspondence,* 1:95–99, 112–14, 162–65; Robinson, "Lost Opportunities," 23–27.

65. Eric S. Johnson, "Uncas and the Politics of Contact," and Kevin A. McBride, "The Legacy of Robin Cassacinamon: Mashantucket Pequot Leadership in the Historic Period," in Grumet, *Northeastern Indian Lives,* 29–47, 74–92, esp. 76–78. Williams to Winthrop, September 9, 1637; February 28, June 7, and July 23, 1638; July 21, 1640, in LaFantasie, *Correspondence,* 1:119, 145–47, 161, 168–69, 202.

66. Winthrop, *Journal*, 458–62, 468; John A. Sainsbury, "Miantonomo's Death and New England Politics 1630–1645," *Rhode Island History* 30 (1971): 111–24. On the movement of religious radicals out of Massachusetts see Philip F. Gura, *A Glimpse of Sion's Glory: Puritan Radicalism in New England, 1620–1660* (Middletown Conn., 1984).

67. Williams to Winthrop, September 9, 1637, in LaFantasie, *Correspondence*, 1:119. On this period see Neil Salisbury, "Indians and Colonists in Southern New England after the Pequot War: An Uneasy Balance," in *The Pequots in Southern New England: The Fall and Rise of an American Indian Nation*, ed. Laurence M. Hauptman and James D. Wherry (Norman, Okla., 1990), 81–95.

68. Bradford, *Of Plymouth Plantation*, 294. In 1670, decades after the events, Roger Williams claimed that it was his negotiating that broke "to pieces the Pequts negociation and Designe"; Williams to Major John Mason and Gov. Thomas Prence, June 22, 1670, in LaFantasie, *Correspondence*, 2:611–12.

69. Winthrop, *Journal*, 341.

70. Ibid., 328–29, 336–37. Earlier, when he was seeking an alliance with the Narragansetts against the Pequots, Winthrop had acknowledged the importance of Williams's interpreting skills. He sent a copy of "the articles" to Williams, "who could best interpret them to them"; ibid., 191.

71. "Gardener his Relation of the Pequot Warres," 152–55. Roger Williams wrote that "of all the English Cattell, the Swine (as also because of their filthy disposition) are most hatefull to all Natives, and the call them filthy cut throats &c."; *Key into the Language of America*, 114–15 [misnumbered 106²–7²]. On the position of Miantonomi and other leaders in this period, see Bragdon, *Native People of Southern New England*, 244–17. Alfred Cave casts doubt on the authenticity of this speech, and on reports of Miantonomi's plotting against the English; *Pequot War*, 163–67.

72. "Relation of the Plott—Indian," *Collections of the Massachusetts Historical Society*, 3d ser., 3 (1833): 161–64; Winthrop, *Journal*, 408–12; Williams to Winthrop, July 21, 1640, in LaFantasie, *Correspondence*, 1:202–3. On the situation in Long Island see John A. Strong, "Wyandanch: Sachem of the Montauks," in Grumet, *Northeastern Indian Lives*, 48–73, esp. 53–56.

73. The Mohegan oral tradition of these events is in Fawcett, *Lasting of the Mohegans*, 14–15; for the English record see Winthrop, *Journal*, 471–73. On the formation and purpose of the New England Confederation see ibid., 432–40. On the course and context of New England relationships see Francis Jennings, *The Invasion of America: Indians, Colonialism, and the Cant of Conquest* (Chapel Hill, 1975) (for a particularly interesting treatment of the death of Miantonomi, see pp. 266–68); and Salisbury, *Manitou and Providence*.

74. *Magnalia Christi Americana*, bk. 7, p. 42.

75. William Hubbard, *A Narrative of the Troubles with the Indians in New-England*, 1677, in *The History of the Indian Wars in New England*, ed. Samuel Drake, 2 vols. (Roxbury Mass., 1865), 1:48–49. Pissaconaway was said to have been 120 years old the last time Daniel Gookin saw him; Gookin, *An Historical Account of the Doings and Sufferings of the Christian Indians in New England*, 1677, in *Archaeologia Americana: Transactions and Collections of the American Antiquarian Society*, vol. 2 (1836), 463. Wood knew him as Pissacannawa and Morton rendered his name as Papasiquineo. See Jill Lepore, *The Name of War: King Philip's War and the Origins of American Identity* (New York, 1998), 101.

76. On King Philip's War see Lepore, *Name of War*; Douglas Leach, *Flintlock and Tomahawk: New England in King Philip's War* (New York, 1958); Russell Bourne, *The Red King's Rebellion: Racial Politics in New England, 1675–1678* (New York, 1990); and Drake, "Severing the Ties that Bind Them."

77. On native persistence and strategies see Papers of Frances Manwaring Caulkins, Connecticut Historical Society; Jean O'Brien, *Dispossession by Degrees* (Cambridge, 1997); Daniel Mandell, *Behind the Frontier: Indians in Eighteenth-Century Massachusetts* (Lincoln, Neb., 1996).

78. Byrd to Clayton, May 25, 1686, in *The Correspondence of the Three William Byrds,* ed. Marion Tinling, 2 vols. (Charlottesville, 1977), 1:61.

79. Theodore Stern, "Chickahominy: Changing Culture of a Virginia Indian Community," *Proceedings of the American Philosophical Society* 96 (1952): 157–225; Jane T. Smith, *The Last of the Nehantics* (1894, 1916), ed. Carol Hallas and Mimi Amdur (East Lyme, Conn., n.d.), 26–30; "The Diary of Mrs. Fielding," ed. Frank Speck, in *Forty-third Annual Report of the Bureau of American Ethnology,* 1925–26 (Washington, D.C., 1928), 229–51 (the quote is from p. 217). Ella Wilcox Sekatau, Narragansett, and Ruth Wallis Herndon document both the practice of effacement by Rhode Island officials and the determined persistence of the Narragansetts through study of both the oral tradition and the documentary record in "The Right to a Name: The Narragansett People and Rhode Island Officials in the Revolutionary Era," *Ethnohistory* 44 (1997): 433–62.

80. See Fawcett, *Lasting of the Mohegans,* 31–34. For a vivid demonstration of the kind of reconstruction that can be developed using a wide variety of sources, see Donna Keith Baron, J. Edward Hood, and Holly V. Izard, "There Were Here All Along: The Native American Presence in Lower-Central New England in the Eighteenth and Nineteenth Centuries," *William and Mary Quarterly* 53 (1996): 561–86.

Index

Accomack, king of, 102
Adam and Eve, 51–52, 170
afterlife, beliefs, 137–39
age groups, roles, 55, 153–55
agriculture, 38, 143–61; ancient authors on, 158
Alexander, Sir William, 117–18, 193
Amoroleck, 177
Apess, William, 32, 118, 228
Appamatucks: queen, 69, 94; Pyancha, 90
Aquascococke, 221
Aquiday, 121, 237
Arahatec, 94
Archer, Gabriel: on New England, 5–11, 13–14, 34, 83, 162; on Virginia, 58, 69, 107, 132, 148, 158, 219
Argall, Captain Samuel, 115, 196, 208, 218
Arundel, Peter, 211
Ashley, Edward, 194
Aupaumut, Hendrick, 100, 105, 155
Aztecs, 113

Bacon, Sir Francis, 107
Baker, Emma Fielding, 33
Baker, William, 194
Barbados, 233
Barlowe, Arthur, 51, 53, 58, 69, 73, 96, 106, 215, 220–21
Bashabes, 37
Bavin, Thomas, 43

Beck, Cave, 82
Bermuda, 22; Pocahontas's attendant in, 200
Beverley, Robert, 52
Bible, 39, 51–52, 75, 80, 105–6, 112, 115, 118–19, 128, 131, 133, 170, 192–93, 196–97, 230, 237
Billington, John, 73
Bland, Edward, 90
body decoration, 62–72
Boudicca, 94
Boyce, Mrs., 72, 196
Bradford, William, 35–36, 49, 59, 84, 181, 183, 185, 189–92, 195, 204, 226–28, 236–37
Bragdon, Kathleen, 38
Brathwait, Richard, 74
Brereton, John, 5–11, 13–14, 34, 46, 56, 87, 162
Britons, ancient, 28–30, 48, 59, 94, 107, 113, 224–25
Brothertown, 140
Bulwer, John, 64, 83
burial practices, 135–41
Burton, Robert, 20, 30
Byrd, William, 239

Cabot, John, 71
Caesar, Julius, 48, 59
Calvert, Cecilius, Lord Baltimore, 102
Calvert, Leonard, 102, 129

Calvin, John, 112
Cambridge University, 29, 51
Camden, William, 28
Canne, John, 62
cannibalism, 47–48, 105, 113–14
Canonicus, 93, 102, 155, 178, 226–29
Cape Cod, 6
Carpenter, Nathaniel, 29
Chamberlain, John, 96, 105, 200
Champlain, Samuel de, 116, 189
Chapman, George, 73–74
Charles I, 20, 29, 69
Chauco, 196
Chesapeake Bay, 36, 38, 46, 86, 93, 160, 203, 206, 228, 230
Chesapeakes, 130
Chickahominies, 72, 103, 177, 186, 240
childbirth, parent–child relationships, 153–55
Cicero, 79, 112, 117
Clayton, John, 239
cleanliness, 53
Cleland, James, 93
climate, 36, 43, 49
clothing, as delineator, 63–74
Coddington, William, 194
Coke, Sir Edward, 29
Collier, Samuel, 208–9, 211
color, significance of, 56–62, 122–24, 130–31, 137–38
Columbus, Christopher, 85
Comenius, Jan, 82
commodities, 13
Commuck, Thomas, 5, 33
Connecticut, 13, 33, 35, 56, 178, 184, 192, 205, 229, 237, 240
Cope, Walter, 22
Copland, Patrick, 223–24
Corbitant, 183, 195
Cowyass, Tobe, 141
Crakanthorpe, Richard, 197
Crashaw, William, 27, 51, 59, 76, 217–18
creation accounts, 115–16
Croatoans, 188, 216, 221
Cromwell, Oliver, 233
Cronon, William, 171
Cummaquids, 73
curiosities, cabinets of, 20–22
Cushman, Robert, 31, 35, 51, 72, 84, 190, 217
Cuttyhunk Island, 6

Dale, Sir Thomas, 72, 74, 108, 176, 196–97, 207
Dare, Virginia, 188
Davis, James, 223
de Bry, Theodor, workshop of, 20, 41–45, 59, 64, 69–70, 143–46, 167
Dermer, Thomas, 34
Devereux, Robert, Earl of Essex, 74, 231
Dexter, goodman, 64
Digges, Sir Dudley, 29, 103
disease, impact of, 34–36, 177–83, 191, 195
Don Luís de Velasco, 203, 206
Donne, John, 17, 31
Dorislaus, Isaac, 29
Drayton, Michael, 19
Dutch, 226, 230

Eburne, Richard, 86, 193
Eden, Richard, 50
Eliot, John, 116
Elizabeth I, 11, 17, 20, 28, 53, 73, 85, 232
Endecott, John, 64
England: social change in, 16–18, 27–30, 55, 74–75, 104–5, 151–53, 161–62; Civil War in, 230–34
Ensenore, 175, 221
Epicurus, 138
Erasmus, 95
Eyre, William, 229

Farley, Henry, 23
Fielding, Fidelia, 34, 116, 140, 240
Fish, Rev. Joseph, 141
Fitzmaurice, Andrew, 31
Fleet, Henry, 194
food, 161–65
Fotherby, Martin, 121
Fowler, David, 140

Gainsford, Thomas, 93, 212
Galgacus, 225
games, gaming, 108–9
Gardiner, Lion, 151, 229, 237
Garrard, Edmund, 31
Gates, Sir Thomas, 159, 162, 218
Gay Head, 5, 33
gender roles: English, 18, 39, 74–75, 149–53; Indian, 49, 148–53
gentility, manuals for, 46

Germans: ancient, 28–30, 39, 85, 89–91, 98, 103–9, 120, 144–49, 153, 192; early modern, 107
Gilbert, Sir Humphrey, 232
Gleach, Frederic, 174, 188
Goddard, Ives, 86
Gomara, Francisco Lopez de, 84
Gorton, Samuel, 98
Gosnold, Bartholomew, 5–9, 13–14, 22, 162
government, Indian, 92–104; political consolidation of, 36–39, 212–13, 235
Granganimeo, 69, 73
Graves, Thomas, 194
Green Corn Festival, 109, 144
Greneway, Richard, 28–29
Grenville, Sir Richard, 221
Griffin, Owen, 110–11
Guy, John, 166

Hair, dressing, 55–58; lovelocks, 74–75
Hakewill, George, 171
Hakluyt, Richard, 15, 20, 41, 47–51, 71, 120
Hall, Thomasine/Thomas, 54–55
Hamor, Ralph, 58, 88–89, 95, 103, 172, 197–99, 208
Harmarus, Jo., 83
Harriot, Thomas, 23, 32, 41–45, 51, 59, 64, 69–70, 79, 84, 90, 103, 115–20, 125–27, 132, 135–39, 143–46, 155–59, 163–72, 177–84, 187–89, 221; system for recording languages, 80–83
Harrison, William, 85, 87
Hartlib, Samuel, 82
Hayes, Edward, 50
healing, 132–35
Henry VIII, 95, 156
Hiacoomes, 205–6
Higginson, Francis, 74, 156, 185
Hill, Edward, 184
Hobbomock, deity, 116–25, 128, 137, 185, 189, 192; person, 185, 188, 189–92, 204, 206–7, 227
Hooke, Rev. William, 230, 234
Hopewellians, 38
hospitality, 104–6
Howes, Edward, 71, 81–82, 111, 206
Hunt,Thomas, 154, 185
huskanaw, 113–14
Hutchinson, Anne, 237

Ingram, David, 47–48
Iopassus, 115, 206–9
Irish, 48, 54–55, 137, 162, 217–19, 231–33
Iroquois, 38
Israel, Lost Tribes of, 39, 92, 118–20, 139, 146, 177
Itoyatan, 102, 186
Iyanough, 73, 93

Jackson, Anne, 193–94
Jackson, John, 193–94
James I, 12, 17, 20, 29, 72–73, 92, 95–96, 148, 174, 177, 183, 187, 197, 199–200, 214
Jamestown, Virginia, 12–14, 27, 36–37, 56, 77, 84, 92–96, 106–7, 115, 124–25, 129, 147–48, 154, 157, 160–62, 174–77, 183–89, 193–203, 206, 214–28
Johnson, Edward, 192
Johnson, Joseph, 128, 140
Johnson, Robert, 78
Jones, Inigo, 73, 199
Jonson, Ben, 84, 107, 199

Kattenanit, Job, 153
Kecoughtan, 124, 130, 155
Kemps, 195–96, 223
Kendall, William, 33, 91
Kepler, Johannes, 51
Kiehtan, Cautantowit, Tanto, 116, 121–22, 128–29, 137–38, 157
King Philip. *See* Metacom
King Philip's War, 3, 140, 153, 239
Kiptopeke, 10
Kiswas, 192
Kocoum, 197

Lane, Ralph, 111, 154–55, 159, 168, 176–77, 183, 204, 221
language: changes in, 4–6; importance of, 71, 79–88; learning, 32,79; pidgins, 86–87
law, 102–4, 106
Lawson, John, 90–91, 100, 106
Lederer, John, 90
Levett, Christopher, 84–85, 87, 95, 102–3, 121, 129, 147, 153
Linsey, Robert, 193–94
Lyly, John, 17–18

Machumps, 196
Madoc, 84, 177
Madocawando, 140
Maine, 5, 12
Manahoacs, 177
Manitou, 116–20, 177, 188–90
Manteo, 79–81, 187–90, 204, 216, 221
Marcum, Robert (Moutapass), 194
marriage, 144–48
Martha's Vineyard, 6, 122, 205–6
Martin, John, 97, 222
Maryland, 13, 54, 61, 102, 104, 106, 149,
    155, 162, 228; Jesuits in, 71–72, 95, 104,
    129, 132, 153
Mashpee, 5, 91
Mason, John, 107, 170, 178, 192
masques, 92–93, 147
Massachusetts (tribe), 5, 35, 71, 88, 98,
    116, 128, 227
Massachusetts Bay, 13, 71, 82, 131, 137,
    179, 211, 216–18, 228–30, 235–39
Massasoit, Osamekin, 3, 7, 93, 172,
    181–84, 186, 190–91, 195, 226–28
Massawomecks, 108
Matachanna, 123
Matchipongo, 115
Mather, Cotton, 128, 238
Mathews, Mercy Ann Nonesuch, 240
Mayhew, Thomas, Jr., 91, 205–6
Menatonon, 154
Metacom, 3, 32–33, 159, 239
Miantonomi, 37, 102, 211, 215, 220,
    235–39
Michaëlius, Jonas, 86, 116
Micmacs, 5–6
Milton, John, 28
Mohawks, 47–48
Mohegans, 5, 33–34, 116–17, 128,
    132–33, 140–41, 156, 178, 194, 229,
    235–40
Monacans, 84, 213
Montauks, 117, 133, 140, 146–47,
    237–38
Morrell, William, 93, 104, 112, 147–48
Morton, Thomas, 32, 35, 46, 49, 52–53,
    56, 96, 106, 117–18, 124, 134–38,
    153–55, 160, 162, 170, 172, 187, 191,
    214, 228, 239
Mosco, 56, 186
Mundy, Peter, 22
Munetute, Nemattanew, "Jack of the
    Feathers," 189

Nahantics, Nehantics, Niantics, 141, 205,
    240
nakedness, meanings of, 49–53
Namenacus, 36
Namontacke, 71
Nanepashemet, 32
Narragansetts, 4, 33, 62, 71–72, 83, 88,
    93, 98, 108, 119–20, 131–33, 138, 141,
    148, 177, 186, 191–92, 211, 213–20,
    226–30, 235–39
Nausets, 59, 73
Navirans, 83, 89
Nebrija, Elio Antonio de, 85
Netherlands, 29
Newfoundland, 34, 86
New England Confederation, 238
New Haven, 237
New Netherland, 86
Newport, Captain Christopher, 58, 89, 92,
    174–77, 206, 215
Niles, Samuel, 141

Occum, Samson, 117, 133, 136, 140,
    146–47, 158, 186
Okee, Okeus, Kewas, 5, 56, 114, 116, 117,
    121–25, 136, 188, 203
Opechancanough, 83, 90, 92, 95–102, 106,
    108, 154, 156, 174–77, 180, 186–89,
    210–11, 224–26, 236
Opachisko, 197
oral tradition, Indian, 2–3, 5, 8, 32–33,
    90–91, 98, 109, 116–25, 133, 138, 140,
    149, 156, 158, 159, 164, 172–73
Osamekin. See Massasoit
Oxford University, 41
Oyeocker, 90

Pamunkeys, 194, 196–98
Papasiquineo, 96, 134–35
Parahunt, 77
Parker, William, 58, 71, 198–99
Parkhurst, Anthony, 4
Pascatoa, Pascataway, 95, 129, 182
Paspiha, Paspahegh, 114, 223; queen of,
    223
Patawomecks, 77, 108, 115–16, 206–11
Pawtuxets, 59, 185
Pawtuxents, 129
Peacham, Henry, 79
Peckham, Sir George, 47, 50, 113
Pecksuot, 227
Pell, John, 82

Penobscots, 124, 158
Penreis, John, 184
Pequots, 33, 56, 108, 118, 178, 191–92, 204, 215, 219–20, 229–39; Mystic fort, 230–31
Pequot War, 47, 56, 107–8, 170, 178, 191–92, 205, 217, 229–34
Percy, George, 49, 63, 69, 82–83, 89, 130, 176, 189, 195, 216–18, 222–23
Percy, Henry, earl of Northumberland, 82
Piscataways, 102
Pissacanawa, Pissaconaway, 134–35, 239
Plato, 106
Platter, Thomas, 21
Pliny, 78, 159
Plymouth, Pilgrims, 7, 13, 31, 34, 58, 72–73, 91, 93, 114, 117–18, 154, 159, 181–85, 190–95, 204, 214–17, 226–28, 235–39; Thanksgiving, 172
Pocahontas, 5, 31, 51, 64, 74, 77, 87, 89, 93–95, 114, 118, 123, 129, 147, 154, 186–88, 206–11, 218, 223, 235; marriage, 192–93; in London, 196–203
Pokanokets, 7, 122, 172, 181–84, 190–91, 194, 226, 235
Pomeiooc, 143–46
Poole, Robert, 210–11, 228
Pope, Elizabeth, 74
Porttobacco, 102
Pory, John, 102, 147, 151, 210
postures, meaning of, 63–68
Powhatan, 14, 26, 37, 58, 71–73, 77, 84, 88–89, 92–102, 108, 114, 123, 129–30, 154, 174–77, 183, 188, 196–203, 206–11, 213–16, 222
Powhatan chiefdom, 37, 72, 90, 97–100, 106, 108, 129–30, 147, 154, 156, 164, 174–77, 183–88, 195–203, 213; 1622 attack by, 72, 97, 108, 156, 176, 183–86, 189, 193, 196, 210, 223–28
Price, Daniel, 105
priests, powers of, 124–37
Pringe, Martin, 54, 58–59, 166
Prynne, William, 74–75
Purchas, Samuel, 15, 47–50, 56, 74, 84, 113–14, 117, 123–25, 139, 147, 186–88
Pym, John, 29
Pythagoras, 138

Ralegh, Sir Walter, 11–12, 28, 32, 41, 51, 53, 64–65, 120, 220, 232

Rapahannocks, 63, 69, 114, 154
Ratcliffe, John (alias John Sicklemore), 222
religious motivations, English, 31, 51, 120, 138–41; European conflict over, 111, 113, 117, 128–29, 131, 133, 139–40
Rhode Island, 13, 229, 236–39
Richmond, Trudie Lamb, 39, 98–100
Roanoke colony, 11–12, 28, 32, 34, 41–45, 51, 53, 74, 79, 96, 106, 111, 124, 130, 143–46, 154–55, 168, 175–77, 183, 188, 191, 204, 214–21, 234
Roanokes, 37, 79, 119–20, 132, 135–37, 143–46, 164–65, 175–78, 182–83, 188, 191
Robinson, John, 227–28
Robinson, Paul, 227
Rolfe, John, 74, 114, 129, 140, 192–93, 197–203, 207, 218–19, 223, 228
Rolfe, Thomas, 199–203, 228
Rome, ancient, 27–30, 78, 109, 113, 219, 225
Rosier, James, 50, 83, 88, 111, 139–40, 143, 147, 161–64, 179, 183
Rountree, Helen, 37

Sagadahoc colony, 47–48, 121
Sagamore, John, 71, 206
Salem, 119
Salmon, Vivian, 81
Samoset, 34, 185
Sandys, Edwin, 218
Sandys, George, 184
Sassacus, 191–92, 236
Sassamon, 204
Sassawwaw, 219–20
Savage, Thomas, 77, 197–98, 206–11, 228
Saverye, Thomas, 194
Savile, Sir Henry, 28
Saxons. *See* Germans
Saybrook, 229
Schaghticokes, 98
Scots, ancient, 113
Secoton, 143–46, 157
Shakespeare, William, 22; *The Tempest*, 22–23, 111; *Henry V*, 231–32
Shepard, Thomas, 35, 128, 205
Sicklemore, Michael, 216, 222
Simon, 207
Simmons, William, 5

Smith, Captain John, 13–14, 32, 46, 58, 62, 64, 69, 77, 84, 86–88, 92–100, 103, 108, 112–14, 121–25, 130–31, 135–38, 143, 146–49, 154, 156, 160–80, 183, 187, 189, 196–200, 206–9, 215–16, 222–24, 232, 235
Spain: as colonial rival, 12, 28–29, 50, 112–13, 143, 175, 185, 203, 230; Queen Isabella, 85
Speck, Frank, 158
Speed, John, 27, 48, 59
Spelman, Henry, 55, 73, 77–78, 97–98, 103, 108–9, 113–16, 132, 134, 138–39, 149, 162, 204, 206–11, 226
Spelman, Sir Henry, 77
Spenser, Edmund, 217
Squando, 140, 191
Squanto: deity, 116–20, 129, 190–91, 185; person, 59, 154, 185, 190–91, 204, 210, 226
Standish, Miles, 191, 227
Stanton, Thomas, 192
status differentiation, 69–75, 92–97, 147–49
Stern, Theodore, 240
Stockham, Rev. Jonas, 139, 209
Stoppard, Tom, 211
Strachey, William, 30, 54, 58–59, 62, 92, 95, 97, 108–9, 113, 122–24, 129–30, 138–39, 155–63, 186–88, 195–96, 207, 213, 223
Strawe, Jacke, 204
Susquehannocks, 37, 46, 176
Swift, Ensign, 208
Symonds, William, 111, 192–93

Tacitus, 27–30, 39, 89–91, 95, 98, 103–9, 120, 144–49, 159, 225
Tantaquidgeon (the famous runner), 238
Tantaquidgeon, Gladys, 5, 32–33, 117, 156
Tantaquidgeon, Harold, 132
Tantoquineo, 214
Tarrentines. *See* Wabanakis
Tartars, 168
technology, 162–70, 179–80
Thirty Years' War, 107, 111, 230–34
Thorpe, George, 200, 224
Tomocomo. *See* Uttamatomakkin
Tradescants, 22–26
Treat, Richard, 140–41
Trojans, 109

Tsenacommacah, 97, 185–89
Turks, 131, 137–38, 232

Uncas, 37, 178, 229, 235–39
Uncas, Martha, 33–34
Underhill, John, 46, 108, 192, 204, 217, 230–31
Uttamatomakkin, 5, 56, 74, 89, 122–25, 186–88, 197–203, 214

Verstegan, Richard, 28, 85–86
Vico, Giambattista, 120
Vincent, Philip, 47, 233–34
Virgil, 109
Virginia Company, 43, 71, 73–74, 78, 92, 95, 111, 151–52, 154, 156, 166, 170, 174, 183–84, 192–93, 200–203, 218–20, 223–26

Wabanakis, 47–48, 110–11, 177
Wampanoags. *See* Pokanokets
wampum, 38, 69, 106, 109, 131, 212–13, 229, 237
Wanchese, 79, 81, 204, 221
Warner, Walter, 82
warfare, 107–9
Ward, Nathaniel, 217
Waterhouse, Edward, 156
Watson, Thomas, 74
Wawequa, 238
Waymouth, George, 83, 161, 179, 183, 185
Wequash, 204–5, 220
Wessagusset, 227–28
West, Francis, 222
West, Thomas, Lord de la Warr, 222–23
Whitaker, Alexander, 31, 51–52, 59, 104–5, 114, 117–18, 128, 134, 176, 196–97
Whitbourne, Richard, 164
White, Father Andrew, 62, 72, 93, 95, 100, 113, 118–21, 129, 156, 180–82
White, John, painter and governor, 41–45, 49, 59, 64, 66–69, 124–27, 135–37, 143–46, 155–59, 163–70, 188, 221
White, Rev. John, 118–19
White, Richard, 171
White, William, 113–14
Whitehead, Neil, 32
Wild Man, tradition of, 78
Williams, Roger, 4, 32, 48–49, 53–54, 56, 62, 69, 71–75, 80–81, 83, 87–89, 92, 95, 98, 100–109, 112, 116–25, 128, 131–38,

146–58, 162–70, 177–82, 186, 191–94,
205, 211, 213, 219–20, 229–30, 235–39
Wilson, Thomas, 79
Wingfield, Edward Maria, 147
Wingina (Pemisapan), 37, 67, 69, 178,
182, 186, 221, 236
Winslow, Edward, 32, 49, 56, 59, 86–87,
89, 91, 105, 108, 113–16, 128, 131–38,
154–55, 180–88, 190–92, 195, 218,
226–29
Winthrop, John, 64, 93, 121–22, 166, 184,
189, 191, 194, 211, 215–17, 236–37
Winthrop, John, Jr., 71, 111
Withers, George, 171

Wituwamat, 227
Womanato, 36
Wood, William, 5, 46–49, 52–55,
58–59, 69, 84, 87, 93–96, 100,
104–9, 117–23, 134–38, 147–53,
157–70, 191, 235
Wright, Edward, 22
Wriothesley, Henry, earl of Southamp-
ton, 74
Wyatt, Sir Francis, 210, 225–26
Wyatt, George, 189, 226
Wynne, Peter, 84

Yeardley, George, 96